David Miles

# The Tale of the Axe

## How the Neolithic Revolution Transformed Britain

**Thames & Hudson**

*For Gwyn*

*Frontispiece*: Drawing of one of the Stonehenge trilithons by William Stukeley (1687–1765). Stukeley had the privilege of studying the prehistoric sites of Stonehenge and Avebury before the ancient earthworks were scoured away by the modern plough.

First published in the United Kingdom in 2016 by
Thames & Hudson Ltd, 181A High Holborn,
London WC1V 7QX

*The Tale of the Axe: How the Neolithic Revolution Transformed Britain* © 2016 Thames & Hudson Ltd, London

British Library Cataloguing-in-Publication Data
A catalogue record for this book is available from the British Library

ISBN 978-0-500-05186-3

Printed and bound in India by Replika Press Pvt. Ltd.

To find out about all our publications, please visit
**www.thamesandhudson.com**. There you can subscribe to our e-newsletter, browse or download our current catalogue, and buy any titles that are in print.

# The Tale of the Axe

# Contents

# Preface

*The human species requires not only a prodigious space of time, but likewise a happy concurrence of circumstances before they can raise themselves above animal life.*
VOLTAIRE, 1777[1]

This book is about how and why, from about 12,000 years ago, humans in Western Asia changed their way of life from foraging to farming, and how this transformation spread across Europe to the British Isles by about 4000 BC. Where did the new ideas, techniques, domesticated plants and animals come from? What difference did this transformation make to how people lived, to their population, their impact on the landscape and environment, their diet, social organization, beliefs and monuments, and attitudes to the living and the dead? And how has all this impacted upon us today?

Since our ancestors split from the chimpanzee line, seven million years ago, hominins developed from largely vegetarian forest dwellers to upright-walking inhabitants of the African savannah. By about one million years ago, human ancestors had evolved into large, fierce, omnivorous mammals near the top of the food chain, the only ones that did not depend upon big teeth and sharp claws for their survival. Instead, our ancestors developed increasingly big brains and subtle minds, an ability to cooperate, collaborate with, or even deliberately mislead their fellows through communication skills and speech, and ultimately language. Hominins made increasingly complex tools, controlled fire, cooked food and made protective clothing. Modern humans from about 100,000 years ago began to think symbolically, and created music, stories, art and religious beliefs.

Our ancestors lived in small-scale, but often interlinked, communities and had an ability to spread their kind and ideas across most of the planet, adapting to every environment except Antarctica. From their original homeland in Africa, hominins moved north and east at least 1.7 million years ago. After 60,000 years, *Homo sapiens* moved out of Africa and rapidly colonized the world. Humans learnt to cope with the cold and adapted genetically: a few of the new northerners even developed pale skin, blue eyes and fair or red hair.

It was just as well. Later hominins, especially Neanderthals and *Homo sapiens*, had to adapt to successive glacial periods and dramatic changes of climate.

Twelve thousand years ago, all human beings depended for food upon gathering wild plants and hunting or scavenging wild animals. Then the world warmed. The climate has stayed relatively stable ever since, although in 2013/14 the USA experienced one of its coldest winters on record and Britain, battered by gales, had its wettest winter since 1766. The waters of the flood were upon the Earth. This is part of a process of global warming and environmental change set in train by our ancestors. Nevertheless, farming developed in what is, by the alarming standards of the past, a period of benign climate.

Gradually, the relationship between humans and some plants and animals changed. Humans cultivated plants selectively and reared a narrow range of animals. The varying selection pressures encouraged domestication, which consisted of genetic and morphological changes to these plants and animals. They became entangled, increasingly dependent upon each other. Many humans like to think that they domesticated previously wild species for their own benefit – that they have dominion over them, in the words of Genesis. Alternatively, domestication could be seen as a two-way process: plants, such as wild grasses, and animals, notably sheep, cattle and pigs, hitched a ride with mobile and adaptable humans. As a result, many of the species involved – for example, dogs, cattle and cereals – were subject to genetic change. We humans also changed, to some extent genetically, but most of all culturally. The move to farming was, arguably, the most significant shift in human history, which launched the expansion of the human population, the surpluses of food that supported civilization, the growth of towns and a dramatic increase in material goods, particularly objects of symbolic importance. We became the dominant species in the world; the most creative, the most destructive and, for a big beast, incredibly numerous.

The process of domestication speeded up about ten millennia ago. Over the next few millennia most human beings adopted some form of agriculture or became herders. A species of hunter-gatherers, numbering perhaps seven million worldwide 11,000 years ago, was transformed into farmers and then, thanks to the success of farming, into city dwellers. In the early 21st century our numbers topped seven billion. Our impact on planet Earth is now so great that the Holocene, the 'wholly recent' epoch that began 12,000 years ago with the end of the Ice Age, has given way to the Anthropocene – 'the age of humans'.

Archaeologists in the 19th century recognized a shift in prehistoric stone technology, which produced ground or polished stone axes – they labelled this the 'Neolithic', or New Stone Age. For thousands of generations, hominins (who included the ancestors of *Homo sapiens*) had chipped suitable stone to form tools, including axes held in the hand. The distinctive new axes of the Neolithic were ground to give a smooth, polished surface. They could be hafted with wooden handles to make a proficient chopping tool, and sharpened more efficiently. These axes appeared at the same time as farming communities developed in the Near East and then later in Europe; the polished stone axe became an icon of what in the 20th century was termed the 'Neolithic Revolution': the appearance of farming. In the Neolithic, humans established settled communities, farmsteads, villages and towns, and began to store food, increasingly manufacture pottery and build monuments. The mid-20th-century prehistorian Vere Gordon Childe and his many successors have presented this as a landmark in human history, a revolution comparable with the Industrial Revolution of the 18th and 19th centuries. We now know that the story is more complex, but nevertheless this was a turning point for humanity from which there was no going back. If there was a Neolithic Revolution, it is still continuing.

Childe wrote in 1936: 'In the first place a long and wide view is essential; when short periods or confined regions alone are surveyed, the multiplicity of separate events is likely to obscure an underlying pattern.'[2] In spite of what he said, like most scholars of his generation (and earlier ones), Childe took limited interest in Old Stone Age hunter-gatherers. Their lives were seen as a nasty, brutish and short struggle for food. Nineteenth-century anthropological classifications still applied: hunter-gatherers were formally labelled as 'savages'. Like many archaeologists or prehistorians, Childe felt that humans became interesting when they adopted farming, developed hierarchies and specializations, and congregated in towns. In other words, became civilized. Some archaeologists have even argued that the modern mind only became fully developed when stimulated by the complexities of the Neolithic lifestyle.[3] Yet it is now apparent that no one in the past deliberately turned on a Neolithic switch. Human cognition, technology, social lives and relationships with plants and animals developed over many millennia. As I will explain, the mentalities and skills required to develop domestication go back into deep time.

The British Isles might be the end of the line for the Eurasian land mass – the outer limits of the prehistoric world – and a late adopter of agriculture;

the Australian poet, Les Murray, puts Great Britain in its place, when he says it is 'an archipelago off the north-west corner of Europe'.[4] It was, however, a place of enormous creativity and regional diversity; a group of islands whose communities interacted with the mainland of Europe, to varying degrees, to develop unique cultures. These can appear, to us, to be very strange, sharing a remarkable fondness for exotic and often huge stones, distributing the remains of their dead around impressive monuments, sky-watching, holding massive feasts and apparently avoiding the consumption of fish. The past is a foreign country wherever we come from, whether we are Asian, Australian, European or American. Our cultures, languages and religions constantly diversify, yet behind these surface differences lie basic, deep-seated similarities that we developed as hunter-gatherers, 100,000 years ago and beyond, on the African plains.

In 1955, W. G. Hoskins, an historian at Oxford University, wrote a marvellous book, *The Making of the English Landscape*.[5] At times he could be grumpy, conservative and donnish, but he brought the landscape to life and for many readers, including me, he transformed how we saw our historic environment. In the first edition of his book, Hoskins complained that historians of the landscape overemphasized the impact of 18th-century landscaping. 'Our countryside', he said, 'had been made by people, shaped over the past thousand to fifteen hundred years.' Later in life, Hoskins saw that the story went back much further.

Since the 1960s archaeological excavation, aerial survey, geophysics and new scientific techniques have illuminated the past and provided a precision to the dating of prehistory that would astonish previous generations of archaeologists. In Britain there have been spectacular results from multidisciplinary research projects: the structured investigation of the Stonehenge landscape and the monuments of Orkney, brilliant discoveries beneath the North Sea and new revelations from construction projects such as road building in Ireland, the Channel Tunnel Rail Link, Heathrow and Stansted airports and the Olympic rowing course at Dorney. There is a tsunami of genetic and isotopic data about humans, plants and animals. I would not argue that Britain is especially important in terms of world prehistory, but it is exceptionally well studied.

The idea of a Neolithic Revolution implies rapid change, yet the more we penetrate into the past, the deeper are our roots – and the more we appreciate that humans are part of nature, subject to the powerful pressures of evolution.

Two historians wrote: 'The history of food evidently needs a generous time frame if we are to understand it fully. Most of its stories started in deep time.'[6] In this book I will try to explain where we came from and current thinking about what makes us human. It takes us to Neolithic Britain by way of its geographical neighbours, and its ancient ancestors. Where we start any historical story is always a problem. Currently, there is a vociferous and acrimonious debate about the teaching of history in English schools. In a discussion on BBC Radio 4 in 2014 the participants were the Education Minister (since departed from the job) and academic historians, who were all, not surprisingly, specialists in the recent documentary history of the past few centuries. No schoolteachers or experts on our first million years were involved. Summing up the view of the historians, the chairman stated: 'Oh, so you would begin at the beginning, with the Anglo-Saxons!' W. G. Hoskins said the same in 1955, but a decade or so later he knew better.

Fortunately, there are many people who are interested in the deep past. There is also a vast literature about it and much of the recent research, excavation reports, surveys, scientific studies and academic syntheses, and more theoretical works have been published. Most of it does not make easy reading because it is either technical, complex, lengthy or written by specialist academics for each other. For many years I conducted classes in archaeology for adult audiences in the Bristol and Oxford areas and ran summer schools for the Smithsonian Institution, attended by inquisitive people from across the USA. My tolerant audiences included farmers' wives (and the odd farmer), an artificial inseminator of cows, schoolteachers and university professors, a future winner of the Booker Prize, estate agents, car factory workers, retired people from many walks of life and a gravedigger named Skellington (honestly!). I have tried to translate the work of the specialists for people like them, still curious enough to venture out on a winter's night, or even cross the Atlantic, to look at prehistoric sites at first hand. They are the taxpayers and volunteers without whom there would be no archaeological research. Those of us who are fortunate enough to spend our professional lives in archaeology should try to communicate what we are about. Then, perhaps, the story might be told to schoolchildren, and education ministers, that our history did not begin only a few centuries ago.

# A gift from the past

### An axe from the henge monument

It is not every day that someone brings you a five-thousand-year-old gift. It happened to me in the mid 1970s when we lived in Woodstock – the English Woodstock, near Oxford, which has Blenheim Park at the end of its high street. We were laying the table for dinner when there was a knock at the door. A man stood there, holding a sports bag. He introduced himself as Bob. 'I work in the gravel pit at Stanton Harcourt and a couple of years ago I noticed this thing on the conveyor belt. I heard that you were an archaeologist so I thought you might be interested.' He stuck his hand deep into the bag and pulled out a smooth greenish object. I recognized it with delight: a large, Neolithic polished stone axe head (see page 145). He passed it to me. To hold such a thing, a survivor from our ancient past, is always a thrill. There is a kind of magic in something that has time-travelled; a stone, itself millions of years old, yet crafted and transformed by another person thousands of years ago: heavy, smooth and solid.

Bob didn't seem so confident that his find was the real thing. 'Is it old?' he asked. 'I thought it looked unusual when I saw it lying there in the gravel on the conveyor belt.' 'It certainly is,' I replied. 'Probably about five or six thousand years old.'

I wanted to know, as accurately as possible, where Bob had found the axe. Context – the location and the object's relation to other things – is fundamental to archaeology. As long ago as 1865, William Greenwell, one of the founders of scientific excavation in Britain, emphasized that 'the urn, the dagger, and the arrow-head, possess a very trifling interest, and give us, comparatively, little information unless we know the circumstances of their deposition, and the objects with which they were associated'.[1] Obviously, as Bob had picked the axe off a conveyor belt, it had been ripped from the ground by a dragline – a kind of mechanical monster with huge jaws that gobbles gravel and vomits it onto a moving belt to be washed, sorted, crushed and turned into ballast and concrete for new roads and buildings (it was a miracle that our axe hadn't ended up in the foundations of the new M40 motorway extension, consigned to oblivion in the concrete, somewhere north of Oxford). Bob described where he was working: in the gravel pit at Stanton Harcourt, just to the south of the Devil's Quoits henge monument, one of the major prehistoric complexes in the upper Thames Valley.

I had spent a large part of my time in Woodstock mapping aerial photographs stored in the Oxfordshire County Museum. Some of the pioneers of aerial photography had flown the Thames Valley since the 1920s, revealing a new dimension to the British past. The face of the old country had been transformed by lines etched into its surface by its prehistoric, Roman and medieval inhabitants. From the air the pattern of settlements, burial sites, trackways and fields was visible as cropmarks. There were thousands of aerial photographs in the Woodstock archive – only by plotting out the cropmarks could we see the relationship between the masses of archaeological sites, or establish the extent of past and future damage from the extensive gravel quarries that operated in the Thames Valley.

Stanton Harcourt was an archaeological Mecca. A great, circular henge monument, contemporary with Stonehenge, once dominated the landscape and had a circle of standing stones inside it – hence the name of the village in Old English: 'Stanton' (the 'village of the stones'; Harcourt was the name of the Norman bully boys who took over the place after Duke William's victory in 1066). Unfortunately, the suspicious Christian villagers of medieval Stanton Harcourt did not appreciate their local prehistoric monument and had no idea how old it was. They assumed that it was ancient, the creation of pagans, so named the site the Devil's Quoits – 'the ring of the Devil'. They dug large pits into the ground and pushed the stones over, burying them in the furrows of their strip fields, erasing the work of the Devil and conveniently freeing the land for the plough. Farmers – and religious fanatics – make a habit of erasing the evidence of their predecessors.

Time takes its toll on archaeological sites, especially when later generations find new uses for the land. Only a couple of the standing stones survived the attention of the medieval farmers. These stones succumbed to the men from the British Ministry of Defence in 1940, who brought out a bulldozer (a rare sight in those days), flattened the stones and laid a wartime aerodrome on top. Fortunately, even in the trough of World War II, the Ministry employed an archaeologist who recorded the rough treatment of the Devil's Quoits. After the war the aerodrome was abandoned, then the post-war building boom demanded a regular supply of gravel. The great complex of prehistoric ritual monuments was out of sight and out of mind, and the quarries munched their way through their remains for the next thirty years. However, I am glad to say that the quarry owners agreed not to destroy the Neolithic circle of Devil's Quoits and it has been restored and its stones re-erected.[2]

At the time the Devil's Quoits axe arrived on my doorstep I was carrying out lots of what I used to call 'missionary work' – giving talks in schools, village halls and council offices in the Cotswolds and the Thames Valley in an attempt to excite local people about their history and raise awareness of the threat to archaeology posed by modern development. So this polished stone axe could be an appeal for help from the past; a kind of portal, and a vivid and tactile way into understanding our ancestors.

The reconstructed Devil's Quoits henge monument in Stanton Harcourt, Oxfordshire. The polished axe was unearthed in the adjacent quarry.

## Feeling the material of the past

I wanted people to be able to touch the axe: some of them would feel the shock of the old, experiencing its materiality, smoothness, the sharpness of the rim, its density and weight. A great Scottish writer, Nan Shepherd, captured the essence of touch: 'The hands have an infinity of pleasure in them.... The feel of things, surfaces, rough things like cones and bark, smooth things like stalks and feathers and pebbles rounded by water...nothing that I can touch or that touches me but has its own identity for the hand as much as for the eye.'[3] You can't get that through a glass case in a museum.

It is debatable whether objects like the axe can speak for themselves. People, however, are inquisitive and artefacts are a link to the past. Since it appeared on my doorstep, the axe has travelled around scores of schools, villages and towns, giving people the opportunity to experience the past in their own hands. Now, however, its final resting place is the Oxfordshire County Museum in Woodstock. Like every other archaeological object that has passed through my hands, the axe is safely curated in a museum.

John Aubrey, the quirky author of *Brief Lives* and father of English antiquarian studies, defined his aim: 'to make the stones give evidence for themselves'.[4] Aubrey admired the philosopher Francis Bacon, arguably the person who had launched the modern scientific method. For Bacon, the formulation and testing of hypotheses had to be grounded in observation, to overcome the tyranny of customary beliefs, whether they derived from Classical authorities, the Church or local superstitions.[5]

When the axe head is picked up, you feel its weight and density. It is heavier than expected, weighing 800 g (1¾ lb). The stone is remarkably smooth and dense, and highly polished. Someone has gone to a lot of trouble to create this beautiful object. The colour is olive green with some darker banding. It is trapezoidal in shape, with a symmetrical curving blade at the wide end, which shows no trace of wear. The blade is 70 mm (2¾ in.) across and the axe head 207 mm (8 in.) long, tapering to a narrow butt 32 mm (1¼ in.) wide. The butt end has some damage, but the marks do not appear to be deliberate flaking. Both faces of the axe are concave and the sides are ground to give flat edges. Halfway along the long axis the axe is very slightly waisted.

### How do we know it is an axe?

Up to now I have adopted the archaeological convention of referring to this object as an axe. Following strictly Baconian principles we should avoid any such terms, which jump to conclusions without arguing the case. As Ian Hodder, the British archaeologist based at Stanford University, has written: 'When an archaeologist digs an object out of the ground and says "this is an axe", how does he know?....The answer is, really, that he doesn't.'[6]

Well, I think we do in this instance, but we still have to make the case: by analogy with communities in Australia and New Guinea, for example, who used stone tools until recent times; by microscopic analysis of the artefact, which might show distinctive use-wear; from forensic evidence – for example, wood or bones may retain the distinctive impact of blows from such blades. In contexts that are exceptionally wet and airless, such as peatbogs, we might find a stone axe head with its wooden handle still attached. An experimental archaeologist could also replicate the object and see if it actually works as an axe. Analogy can be dangerous if it causes us to jump to convenient conclusions, but as we shall see later, there is plenty of evidence in the archaeological record that supports the axe interpretation and suggests we are not tumbling into an anachronistic trap.

### A bolt from the blue?

Not so long ago there were other interpretations. The Victorian polymath, Sir John Evans, put the study of stone implements on the academic map with his beautifully illustrated book *The Ancient Stone Implements, Weapons and Ornaments of Great Britain* (expanded second edition, 1893). He described local beliefs about stone axes like ours (he calls them 'celts'): 'Stone celts are held to preserve from lightning the house in which they are kept. They perspire when a storm is approaching; they are good for diseases of man and beast; they increase the milk of cows; they assist the birth of children; and powder scraped from them may be taken with some advantage for various childish disorders. It is usually nine days after their fall before they are found on the surface.'

The 'celts' were believed to be thunderbolts; apparently if you broke one it gave off a burning smell. They were often stored within the household fireplace, a form of magical insurance, and kept safely for generations as treasured possessions.[7] This, of course, is the kind of folk belief that Francis Bacon would have treated with extreme suspicion. Yet for country people who knew little of rational science, the stone axe was an exotic, mysterious object imbued with the miraculous powers of a protective amulet. Ironically, this might also have been part of its role for the people who lived five thousand or six thousand years ago.

When the axe was passed around, people often immediately asked: 'What was it for?' Functional explanations tend to come to mind first. Almost always, someone remarked, 'It would probably work pretty well as a weapon.' Native American tomahawks loom large in the Western imagination. Until recently, archaeologists tended to minimize the issue of aggression in prehistoric societies. However, recent detailed forensic work reveals that violence to human bodies is not uncommon, and from excavations there is clear evidence of attacks on Neolithic settlements. This green and pleasant land was not always at peace and sheep did not always safely graze.

When handling it, many people gripped the narrow end of the stone tool and thought it could be a handaxe. An archaeologist must always remember, however, that while some materials are durable, such as hard-fired pottery and stone, others fall victim to the corrosive forces of time: metals rust away or are recycled; wooden handles, basketry, hide, leather, or even human flesh, rapidly disintegrate in a damp, temperate climate like Britain's. Even the bones of animals and humans will disintegrate if they are buried in acidic soils. So we have to consider that our axe head could be part of a composite tool. The archaeological evidence confirms this, revealing a number of intact axes, complete with handles and bindings. Modern experimental exercises also demonstrate that the stone axes are effective tools for chopping down trees.

## The problem of time

Another question that was quickly posed was 'How old is it?' This is fundamental to the study of archaeology, and was until relatively recently one of the most difficult questions to answer. To make sense of the past we need to establish some sort of chronological order. In themselves stone tools do not tell us much about dates, and their study has not contributed a great deal to the chronology of prehistoric Britain. Of course, before there was science there was the Bible and theological certitude. Theologians and chronologists, like Archbishop Ussher of Armagh in the early 17th century, dissected the biblical text with surgical precision in order to calculate when God created the Earth. The fact that the Archbishop's conclusion – 23 October 4004 BC – was printed in the margin of the Book of Genesis in the King James Bible gave his date an almost divine authority. In the later 18th and 19th centuries, however, sacred authority was undermined by geologists, palaeontologists, natural historians and archaeologists. The 'young' Earth and its occupants began to age rapidly.

This did not mean that there was, suddenly, precision dating of either terrestrial rocks or human artefacts. As a Danish professor, Rasmus Nyerup, wrote in 1806 in a discussion of museum collections: 'Everything preceding, everything from the earliest heathen period hangs before us as if in a thick fog, in an unmeasurable period of time. We know it is older than Christendom, but if by a few years or a few hundred years – even maybe over a thousand years older, is sheer guesswork and at best only likely hypotheses.'[8]

When another Dane, Christian Thomsen, published the first guidebook to his National Museum in 1836, he ordered the prehistoric collections on the basis of the principal materials of which his artefacts were made: stone, bronze and iron. The Chinese and Greeks had similar notions of the past over two thousand years ago, but this was the first time a European rational-ist had specifically and coherently ordered prehistoric materials in this way. Not that the so-called Three Age System provided dates for anything. It simply gave a relative order for all this ancient stuff. And even this limited aim was contested. In 1867, the Archbishop of York, William Thomson, proclaimed: 'The theory of three periods…has been carried too far…people often forget that long after bronze and iron had been discovered, stone might continue to be used among the poorer and less civilized.'[9] He was right. Metals appeared in the Near East long before they were used in Britain, and even later in the Americas or Australia, where stone tools continued to be made to within living memory.

A key figure in explaining our axe, however, is Sir John Lubbock, friend and neighbour of Charles Darwin. Lubbock was another energetic and versatile Victorian – we can thank him for Bank Holidays, which were once known as Saint Lubbock Days, and he wrote a bestseller, *Prehistoric Times*, published in 1865. In it, Lubbock promoted the Three Age System to a wide audience, and divided the Stone Age into two: the Palaeolithic (Old Stone Age), characterized by chipped stone tools; and the Neolithic (New Stone Age), with its polished stone tools like our axe. As Professor Alasdair Whittle of Cardiff University has said: 'The study of the Neolithic began with a polished stone axe.'

In 1954 the late Stuart Piggott, an archaeologist I particularly admire, published what is still the only textbook on the Neolithic period in Britain, *The Neolithic Cultures of the British Isles*.[10] He more or less apologized for using the term 'Neolithic', which he said had 'a rather dubious validity'. However, his subtitle proved more of a hostage to fortune: *A Study of the Stone-using Agricultural Communities of Britain in the Second Millennium BC*. We now know that the Neolithic period was well and truly over by the second millennium BC. In the 1950s, Stuart Piggott and the rest of the community of prehistorians accepted a young 'Neolithic'. Sixty years later there has been a seismic shift in the chronology thanks to radiocarbon dating developed in post-war Chicago by Willard F. Libby and, subsequently, the appreciation that raw radiocarbon dates can be calibrated for greater accuracy. Colin Renfrew of Cambridge University wrote that Libby's Nobel Prize-winning breakthrough may be seen as 'the most significant advance in the study of prehistory since the establishment of the Antiquity of Man nearly a century earlier'.[11]

In the first decade of the 21st century there was another radiocarbon revolution, thanks to the manipulation of radiocarbon dates using Bayesian statistics and computing power. Much of the work took place in the next room to mine in English Heritage's offices at Bunhill Row, London. There, Dr Alex Bayliss and her colleagues applied the statistics developed by the Reverend Thomas Bayes (*c*. 1702–61) to radiocarbon dates from the Neolithic period.[12] I used to visit Reverend Bayes at lunchtime. He lies at peace, I hope, in the Bunhill Fields cemetery, which was just along the road from our offices close to the City of London, alongside other Nonconformists and dissenters, such as Daniel Defoe, the author of *Robinson Crusoe*, and John Bunyan, the author of *Pilgrim's Progress*. Thanks to the development of Bayes's statistical ideas, after a delay of over two centuries, we can date organic materials with a precision that would shock, awe and delight Sir John Lubbock and Stuart Piggott.

Prehistorians now confidently place the Neolithic period in Britain from just before 4000 BC to 2300 BC. There are still lots of questions about the precision dating of specific sites, monuments and artefacts including our axe head. The axe is not organic, so radiocarbon dating cannot help us date the object itself; neither are there any associated artefacts that might, themselves, fix the chronology. Neolithic stonework is relatively conservative in style, so the axe provides no typological precision either. We do know where the stone for our axe was quarried, however, and investigations at the site indicate that production probably began early in the fifth millennium BC.

In the following centuries, axes were exchanged into most of England and even reached Ireland. The axe may even have been several centuries old, an heirloom, when it was buried outside the Devil's Quoits henge, which was probably erected about 2500 BC.

## Location, location, location

On seeing the axe, people always asked, 'Where is the stone from?', and commented on its distinctive colour and density. If we were in southern England, they usually figured out that it was not local. It is not flint nor a soft sedimentary rock like chalk or limestone, and it is not a gritty sandstone. Its density suggests a rock of volcanic origin from western Britain – Cornwall, Wales and the Lake District were common suggestions. Not infrequently, someone asked, 'Could it be from a glacial erratic?' (a rock from elsewhere, carried and then dumped by a glacier in geologically foreign territory – there has been a long-running argument about erratics and the bluestones at Stonehenge, to which I will return in Chapter 17).

Fortunately, scholars have for many years pursued a programme of petrographic analysis of stone axes in Britain. This has identified the rocks used for Neolithic axe heads, and pinpointed the geological source of many of them. With new scientific techniques and exploratory fieldwork these sources are becoming increasingly precise, so we now know that Neolithic quarryworkers chipped the blank for our axe head out of the greenstone – or to be geologically more precise, the epidotized tuff deposits – of central Cumbria. The stone comes from one of the most spectacular parts of the Lake District: Great Langdale, dominated by Pike o' Stickle (possibly the actual stone source) and Scafell Pike, England's highest mountain at 978 m (3,208 ft).

Professor Richard Bradley of Reading University and a team of rugged fieldworkers investigated the Great Langdale complex of quarries in the late 1980s.[13] The main source of stone is perched high on the vertical face of the mountain, accessible with difficulty along a narrow ledge covered in loose stone debris. 'I suffer from vertigo,' Richard told me recently over lunch at Tate Britain. 'I had to go there by myself and try to get used to the place before the students turned up. And we didn't have health and safety in those days.' I told him that I was going to walk up Great Langdale in the next few weeks with my Himalayan-trekking son. 'I wouldn't try to get to the axe quarry,' he warned, 'we're both too old now.' He was right.

## Objects of desire?

The New Stone Age, or Neolithic, took its name from polished stone tools. So another obvious question is: 'Why did this new technology appear in Britain about six thousand years ago?' The usual answer given by archaeologists is that this was when the farming revolution reached the British Isles. The land, except for the highest areas, was covered in forest and farmers needed to clear space for domesticated plants and animals – the tool used to cut down trees, trim branches and make wooden tools was the polished stone axe. Certainly, polishing or grinding toughens the axe. It is more efficient and less wasteful of material to polish a worn blade than chip it, as was traditional with flint axes.

Flint was the material most prolifically used for axes in early Neolithic Britain. It is widely available in the chalklands of southern England and, as we shall see, prehistoric people went to great efforts to get it. The chalk downlands, a few hours walk to the south of Stanton Harcourt, are full of seams of flint. So why use greenstone from Great Langdale, 265 km (165 miles) away, when it was not notably more effective at chopping down trees than razor-sharp flint blades? It is obvious from the archaeological record that prehistoric people loved exotic materials. They quarried distinctively coloured igneous stone not only in Cumbria but also from sources all over the western and northern parts of the British Isles, from Shetland and Ireland to Wales and Cornwall. These objects travelled remarkably far. Spectacular and beautiful jade (technically, jadeitite) axes from the Italian Alps even turn up in Britain. Did these axes have some deeper purpose in Neolithic society? Perhaps they played a part in displaying the status and authority of individuals, or in the mythology, beliefs and memories of early farming communities. Their value seems to exceed the purely functional. Perhaps our axe, already antique, was deliberately buried outside a sacred site as an offering and a message to the gods.

These exotic materials indicate some sort of link between distant communities. If the axes travelled so far, by what mechanism did ours reach Stanton Harcourt? The French anthropologist Marcel Mauss wrote a book in 1950 entitled *Essai sur le Don* (*The Gift*).[14] From ethnographic studies of small-scale societies such as the Haida and Kwakiutl from the Pacific Northwest Coast he identified the importance of gift-giving as a major element in the exchange of goods. Giving valuables away might seem counter-intuitive to people like us, used to impersonal transactions with money and plastic cards. However, in pre-monetary societies, gift-giving through feasts, marriages and alliances was an important element in cementing social relations and the display of power and status. In the modern world, gift exchange still goes on, when presidents and royalty meet, when someone comes to your house for dinner or at the bar when you buy the drinks. The Roman poet Virgil warned us to 'Beware of Greeks bearing gifts', and even today we know that gifts often come with obligations. The undertaker in the film *The Godfather* knew that accepting a gift from Don Corleone would have future implications; the favour would have to be reciprocated. However, Marcel Mauss made us aware of the potential importance of this form of transaction in the Neolithic, kick-starting a perpetual cycle of exchange within and between communities.

If we peer into deep time we realize that the human obsession with exotic materials is far older than the Neolithic. The fascination with such stuff has bound people together for millennia, and these exchanges are part of what it is to be human. Our stone axe is more than a mere tool: it is an object that can take us on a voyage through space and time.

# PART ONE

## The emergence of humans

Upper Palaeolithic carving of a bison
from La Madeleine, Dordogne.

## CHAPTER ONE

# Discovering deep time

## Searching for handaxes

How far back in time does this story go? How deep is history? I will come to this later. However, the evidence of Neolithic communities is, literally, not always very deep in the ground. Aerial photographs of the Thames Valley cropmarks indicate remains that were surprisingly shallow. People who came to look at our excavations were often amazed that such old archaeological deposits were so close to the surface. Over the course of six thousand years, the soil over them had built up no more than the length of my arm, and this is because on the open, flat gravel terraces of the Thames Valley most of the work of burial has been done by earthworms.

It was Charles Darwin who first emphasized the importance of earthworms in burying ancient settlements and burial grounds. The Australian zoologist, Tim Flannery, summarized it beautifully: 'Darwin described how worms occur in great density over much of England, and how they emerge in their countless thousands in the darkest hours, their tails firmly hooked in their burrow entrances, to feel about for leaves, dead animals and other detritus which they drag into their burrows. Through their digging and recycling they enrich pastures and fields, and so enhance food production, thereby laying the foundations for English society. And in the process they slowly bury and preserve relics of an England long past.'[1]

Beneath the worm-turned plough-soil, and on the surface of the gravel terrace, we are still in the relatively recent past. A further time dimension lies below our feet. In the quarry, during the day the dragline gobbled through the gravel down to the geologically far more ancient claggy, grey Oxford clay that lies below. In the evenings, when the great draglines were silent, my two children and I would often search the floor of the quarry and the remaining cliff face of gravel. We often found fossils – ammonites and belemnites, creatures that inhabited the warm Jurassic seas in their millions. Occasionally, we hit upon something more exciting: great lumps like concrete concertinas. These were the teeth of extinct giants: straight-tusked elephants, or woolly mammoths.

Sometimes we met up with one of the great characters of the Oxfordshire gravel pits. A proper, upright, elderly figure, he was known to us rather formally as Mr McRae – I never did discover his first name. His profession was laying wooden parquet floors. His passion was searching for the oldest stone tools in Britain. Extracting these Stone Age artefacts from millions of tonnes of gravel required a kind of obsessional commitment, and Mr McRae saw objects that my eyes were simply not attuned to. As an amateur he put far more time into the quest than any professional archaeologist ever could.[2] He made important discoveries and worked closely with the Donald Baden-Powell Quaternary Research Centre in Oxford. On one occasion Mr McRae invited us to the laboratory. 'I've something special to show you,' he said. In a small room, a cloth lay on the table. Like a conjuror, Mr McRae took hold of the corner of the cloth and whipped it away: 'What about that!' There lay an enormous, teardrop-shaped handaxe made of flint – technically, what is known as an Acheulean biface, but much larger than usual at 269 mm (10½ in.) long.[3]

'Isn't that the biggest handaxe you have ever seen?' he asked. At Stanton Harcourt, near to where our polished greenstone axe head had been found, but from deep in the gravel, Mr McRae had turned up the third largest axe of its kind ever discovered in Britain. If the polished stone axe is an icon of the first farmers of six thousand years ago, this fantastic flaked handaxe symbolizes the earliest humans in Britain – the hominins who preceded us by several hundred thousand years. Here was an object fashioned between 250,000 and 100,000 years ago, by a skilled toolmaker, to a standard template.

Acheulean handaxes are sometimes compared to Swiss Army knives: all-purpose tools, for working wood, cutting through hides, slicing meat and splitting marrowbones – or perhaps rivals' heads in times of stress. The flint from which this axe was made had come from the Wallingford Fan gravels, 50 km (30 miles) downstream on the Thames. It suggests that the hominin who crafted it was capable of planning ahead, carrying the axe (in a hide bag perhaps?) to the hunting grounds at Stanton Harcourt. Yet the axe was massive by normal Acheulean standards, more like a showpiece to demonstrate the maker's skill, but still carefully tapered to reduce the weight and bulk. Some archaeologists have suggested that such objects indicate sexual competition among early hominin males, using artefacts like a peacock flourishes its feathers or a stag its antlers – male potency in stone.[4]

With our two axes, time itself has become deeper. We are seeing the work of skilled hands, and developing minds, a quarter of a million years into the past.

## 1859, *annus mirabilis*: breaking the barrier

It is remarkable to think that our understanding of the deep history of life on Earth is such a recent addition to human knowledge, one of the great advances of modern science. The year 1859 has been called 'one of the turning points in human thought, the year the time barrier was broken or unlocked'.[5] The key was another stone axe, found by another amateur obsessive. Jacques Boucher de Perthes was a French customs official who diligently searched the gravel terraces of the Somme, near Abbeville in northern France. He published his discoveries in 1847, challenging the 'Noah's flood' explanation for the association of extinct animals and tools made by humans. This is a classic example of not what you say, but who you are and who you know. Boucher de Perthes may have been an antiquary 'of indefatigable zeal and perseverance', but he was also a humble provincial, an outsider in French intellectual and scientific circles. Even the blessed Charles Darwin, who got most things right, thought his work was 'rubbish'.

Nevertheless, Boucher de Perthes's ideas chimed with a developing school of thought in England. As early as 1797, John Frere had reported to the Society of Antiquaries of London on some flint tools found at Hoxne in Suffolk. These were also located in beds of gravel along with the bones of extinct animals. Frere proposed that they were 'weapons of war' predating the use of metal and belonging 'to a very remote period indeed, even beyond that of the present world'. Frere was teetering on the edge of a major intellectual leap, but he was still restrained by the tethers of biblical authority.

The challenge was, however, gathering strength. James Hutton, the Scottish natural philosopher and a founding father of geological science, was a determined critic of biblical authority, and of the 'catastrophist' school that believed that Noah's flood had erased an earlier world and explained most geological phenomena. Hutton worked on the building of the Forth and Clyde Canal in the 1760s and 1770s and carefully observed this slice through the Scottish landscape. He noted the complex strata of rocks and the unceasing processes of natural erosion caused by wind, water and frost. To Hutton, geological formations could be explained by these slow transformations, observable in operation today, and by the forces unleashed from within the Earth, through volcanoes and earthquakes. This led him to believe that the world was far older than the received 4004 BC date. The Earth could be billions of years old.

The great American popularizer of science and evolutionary theorist, Stephen Jay Gould, said of Hutton: 'He burst the boundaries of time, thereby

The excavation at Saint-Acheul in 1859; the world's earliest photograph of an archaeological excavation. The figure on the right is pointing at the Palaeolithic handaxe embedded in the gravel deposits.

establishing geology's most distinctive and transforming contribution to human thought – deep time.'[6] Actually, the job was just beginning. Importantly, Hutton's belief in a 'dynamic yet ancient earth' had converted Charles Lyell, who set out the new ideas in his *Principles of Geology* (published between 1830 and 1833), which Charles Darwin packed into his trunk for the momentous voyage on *The Beagle* in 1831–36. Later, Darwin wrote to a friend in England that he had become a zealous disciple of Lyell's view. He saw evidence for himself on the voyage, when he observed the strata of an earlier beach at St Jago (modern-day Santiago), a volcanic island in the Cape Verde chain, which were raised 9 m (30 ft) above the existing sea level. Clearly, thought Darwin, Hutton and Lyell were correct. There were phenomena at work capable of raising the layers of the Earth.

So the younger cutting edge of the British scientific establishment was open to ideas that challenged the biblical dogma of a young Earth with humankind at the centre. In April 1859, two friends of Charles Lyell, the archaeologist John Evans and geologist Joseph Prestwich, crossed the channel to visit

Boucher de Perthes and test his claims. On 27 April, workmen in the gravel pit at Saint-Acheul brought the news that they had found a handaxe, still embedded with the gravel deposits below the surface, where polished axes and arrowheads of the Neolithic had previously been found. Evans and Prestwich boarded the train from Abbeville to see the in-situ evidence for themselves. A photograph was taken of the axe in the section (probably the first ever to illustrate prehistoric evidence). Evans drew the symmetrical axe and argued that it was a human tool. The local quarrymen were more circumspect, or poetic, naming the axes '*les langues de chats*' (cats' tongues). Being English, the quarrymen at Hoxne had called the axes found there, 'fighting stones'.

Evans went on to publish one of the great works of Victorian archaeology, *Ancient Stone Implements, Weapons and Ornaments of Great Britain* in 1872. He also appreciated the significance of Frere's discoveries at Hoxne, visiting the site and making further finds of stone tools and extinct fauna. At any rate, the English scientific grandees were convinced by Boucher de Perthes's claims. The antiquity of Man was becoming accepted. Archaeologists named the culture of the bifacial axe 'Acheulean' from Saint-Acheul, one of the many French site names that have subsequently been applied, somewhat confusingly, to Palaeolithic archaeology.

One hundred and fifty years later I attended a seminar in London to celebrate the anniversary of the discovery of the Acheulean handaxe. There on the desk at the front of the lecture room, under the stern gaze of a portrait of Queen Mary Tudor – one of England's more fundamentalist Christian monarchs – lay the original handaxe marked with a fading label: 'St Acheul, Amiens, April 27, 1859', and in Prestwich's handwriting, 'Present when found'. This was the stone that had shattered the time barrier.[7]

The year 1859 truly was a scientific *annus mirabilis*. A book entitled *On the Origin of Species by Means of Natural Selection, or the Preservation of Favoured Races in the Struggle for Life* by Charles Darwin was also published that year.

The Acheulean handaxe found in 1859. The stone that 'shattered the time barrier' now resides in London's Natural History Museum.

In the mid 19th century, the way was open to explore deep time. Nevertheless, beyond the shattered barrier there still lay a yawning void of chronological uncertainty. Sir John Lubbock, who, as we have seen, first launched the terms 'Palaeolithic' and 'Neolithic' into modern consciousness, also gave the word 'prehistory' popular currency with his bestselling *Prehistoric Times* of 1865 (the term was first used in English in 1851).

The opening words of *Prehistoric Times* announce: 'The first appearance of man in Europe dates from a period so remote that neither history nor tradition can throw any light on his origin or mode of life...some have supposed that the past is hidden from the present by a veil which will probably thicken, but never can remove....Some writers have assured us that, in the words of Palgrave, "We must give it up, that speechless past."' By the 'speechless past' he meant the time before written, documented history, or in the new terminology of the 19th century, 'prehistory'. Give it up! Lubbock had no intention of doing such a thing.

Nor did Sir John Evans, a man so devoted to the study of the past that he spent part of his honeymoon in the gravel pit at Saint-Acheul. History does not record what his wife thought of this. In 1882, Evans gave a lecture 'to the working classes' in Southampton. His theme was 'reading unwritten history', which he said could be 'the world from its first creation until the written annals of the historians begin'. However, he proposed to limit the term to the period 'during which the human race has dwelt on earth'.[8]

## To begin at the beginning

This brings us back to the question of beginnings – where does our tale begin? Our axe and the onset of farming in Britain can be dated to the fourth millennium BC, but to understand them requires a further step back in time and space. Biblical history had no problem – it all began once upon a time in the Garden of Eden, not so very long ago. The historical sciences have changed our perspective, particularly since the development of radiometric dating methods. These now provide a considerable degree of chronological precision to global prehistory, the origins of life and the Earth itself.

The formation of planet Earth is now put at about 4.5 billion years ago (or 45 million centuries to put it another way). After a mere half a billion years, life appeared as microscopic bacteria, within the waters that covered the globe, and probably assisted the formation of the continents by helping to break down the basaltic crust. Out of this brew, heated by volcanic energy from within the Earth, emerged the granite foundation on which we live, and which also produced the greenstone used to make our axe.

It was not until about 195 million years ago, in a Jurassic world dominated by dinosaurs, that mammals first appeared: small, furtive and nocturnal. Sixty-six million years ago, as my young dinosaur-loving daughter was so fond of telling us, a random accident changed the balance of life on Earth. If geological processes are usually slow, catastrophes can still happen. The asteroid that impacted in the Yucatán Peninsula of Mexico was catastrophic for the dinosaurs but created opportunities for the diminutive mammals. It provided vacant ecological niches that they could exploit and from which they could evolve. The tree of life might have been pruned, but new branches soon emerged.

## Once upon a time in Africa

The origins of the human story take us to Africa. My personal voyage began in 1993 when I met a Kenyan archaeology student named Gilbert Oteyo. At the time, I taught a class in archaeology for postgraduates at Oxford University. Gilbert was particularly impressive; tall and elegant, he stood up at the beginning of the first class to announce his name and that he was a member of the Luo people, from the shores of Lake Victoria. I later learnt from Gilbert that his father was a traditional tribal Luo with several wives, each of whom had her own round house within a circular compound. Among a crowd of siblings, Gilbert was the first not to have his central upper teeth removed – a Luo badge of identity – and the first to take only one wife.

Gilbert was an individual who encapsulated the change from the traditional to the modern world in his society. He went to university in Nairobi and fell foul of Kenya's dreadful dictator Daniel arap Moi. After getting out of one of arap Moi's jails Gilbert was barred from university, so worked as a merchant seaman on the Indian Ocean. During a visit to the port of Mombasa he came across an archaeological excavation. He had found his vocation and started to work for the British School in East Africa.

Thanks to Gilbert, I decided to go to Kenya. Gilbert picked me up at Nairobi airport in the British School's Land Rover and the next day we drove out of Nairobi for an hour, down into the almost solid heat of the Rift Valley. The cones of extinct volcanoes dotted the horizon. Troops of baboons hung about the roadside, the big males swaggering like streetwise gang bosses. Our destination was Olorgesailie, first excavated in 1942 by the pioneers of early hominin exploration in East Africa, Louis and Mary Leakey. A rudimentary wooden shelter covered the site of the excavation and from it led an elevated wooden walkway. I knew what to expect, but it was still an astonishing sight. The ground below us was covered with Acheulean handaxes, like pebbles on a beach, the largest in-situ collection in the world.

Shortly afterwards, in 2003, Rick Potts, director of the Smithsonian Institution's Human Origins Program, led a team re-excavating at Olorgesailie. He made the discovery of which every palaeoanthropologist dreams: a human fossil, the cranium of an adult *Homo erectus*, directly associated with the Acheulean industry.[9] New dating by the potassium-argon method placed this individual at about 900,000 years ago. For 100,000 years his kind had produced axes and butchered animals by the shifting shoreline of a lake now extinct – the bones of ancient forms of hippo, zebra, elephant, giraffe and baboon lay in clusters – then nearby volcanoes, Mount Suswa and Mount Longonot, spewed forth ash that blanketed the Olorgesailie site and preserved the old ground surface.

Acheulean handaxes litter the ground surface at Olorgesailie, Kenya.

The Acheulean axes at Olorgesailie take us back almost one million years, yet they are still not the beginning. Arguably, the story starts when our hominin ancestors separated from the great apes about seven million years ago. This approximate date is calculated from the slight genetic differences between ourselves and chimpanzees. Unfortunately, we do not, as yet, have any physical fossil evidence for this so-called Last Common Ancestor (LCA) and precious little data for the next couple of million years. Early hominins did, however, begin to walk upright, developing longer legs and shorter arms. We had come out of the forest into the potential of the versatile and dangerous savannah.

I still have on the shelf in front of me as I write a little book that I bought in 1967 (5th edition: price 5 shillings – 25 pence in modern British money). It is entitled *Man the Tool-Maker* and is by Kenneth Oakley of the Natural History Museum in London, who first published it in 1949. It begins: 'Man is a social animal, distinguished by "culture": by the ability to make tools and communicate ideas. Employment of tools appears to be his chief biological characteristic.' This was the idea of *Homo faber* – 'Man the Maker'. (I should emphasize that 'man' as a translation of *Homo* means humankind – it has no gender implications.) Dr Oakley qualified this statement. Apes, he admitted, can utilize simple tools when they have a visible reward as an incentive. 'Conceptual thinking…is generally regarded by comparative psychologists as distinctive of man. Systematic making of tools implies a marked capacity for conceptual thought.'[10] This simple statement has generated almost half a century of research into the big question, 'What makes us human?'

Our estimation of the toolmaking capabilities of chimps has risen since Dr Oakley wrote, thanks in part to such pioneers as Jane Goodall, who from the 1960s, encouraged by Louis Leakey, studied chimpanzees in the wild in order to throw light on the behaviour of human ancestors. Subsequently, Kathy Schick and Nick Toth have taught the chimpanzee Kanzi to knap stone tools.[11]

Mary Leakey analysed the then oldest-known stone tools in her classic study *Olduvai Gorge*, published in 1971.[12] At this now-famous site were basic stone chopping tools (now known as 'Oldowan') and sharp blades capable of slicing through animal carcasses. Mary Leakey's collaborators, her husband Louis and Phillip Tobias, identified an early hominin, *Homo habilis* ('handy-man'), as the maker of the Oldowan toolkit. Now we are not so sure. Earlier tools have since been dated to about 2.6 million years ago. It has been suggested that the makers may not have been of the genus *Homo*, and that australopithecines, or even another species, may have been the culprits. From about 2.4 million years ago, the remains of stone tools become increasingly common in the archaeological record. Not so the hominin bones; they remain elusive. What is clear is that in Africa this was a time of dramatic climatic and environmental change. The hominin species were in a state of flux. The origins of the genus *Homo* remain clouded because of the limitations of the fossil record between three million and two million years ago, especially in eastern Africa, although finds in 2013 from Ledi-Geraru, Afar, in Ethiopia, extend the fossil record back between 2.8 million and 2.75 million years ago.[13]

In terms of our 'tale of the axe', Mary Leakey drew our attention to an important clue. Many of the tools in Olduvai Bed I were made from local lava and quartzite. As the makers' skill increased, they sought out chert, a flint-like silicate, which they probably excavated from deposits along the local lake-shore. Next, they discovered and increasingly exploited a green, fine-grained lava (phonolite) that provided a fine cutting edge. It is not unlike the material from which our Langdale axe is made. This valuable material came from the volcano of Engelosen 17 km (12 miles) away. Early hominins were already geologists, searching for rocks with appropriate knapping properties, and somehow transporting or exchanging them across the African landscape.[14]

It is sometimes forgotten that Mary Leakey also identified some bone tools at Olduvai – then the oldest ever found. Fragments of horse, giraffe and elephant long bones, as well as the incisors of hippos, had been utilized if not deliberately shaped. Her discoveries may have influenced one of cinema's most impressive images: in Stanley Kubrick's film *2001: A Space Odyssey* (1968), the dominant 'ape-man' hurls his bone weapon into the air, and we see it spinning and morphing into a spacecraft, accompanied by the soaring bass and insistent percussion of Richard Strauss's *Also sprach Zarathustra*.

So, for at least 2.8 million years, the ancestors of human beings have been making tools of stone and other materials. In that time, the brains of hominins have increased in size enormously.

## The development of the hominin mind

Archaeologists and palaeoanthropologists have unearthed stones and bones, the remains of our family and other animals, from Africa and around the world. With physicists, geologists and mathematicians, they have developed chronologies of increasing precision. Animal behaviourists, cognitive archaeologists[15] and psychologists have also added a further dimension to the study of our early ancestors: they are asking questions about how hominins thought, communicated and organized their societies.

Thanks to Jane Goodall and her successors, we now appreciate that apes, particularly chimpanzees, are complex creatures. They are real individuals who cultivate friendships and alliances, and practise deception – attempting to deceive their fellows, particularly when sex and food are at stake. Researchers now talk of the 'social brain hypothesis': as groups become bigger, individuals need more brainpower to cope with the necessary social interactions. Without this social intelligence, larger groups fissure and divide. In fact, according to Robin Dunbar of Oxford University, brain size can be used to predict the approximate number of individuals in social groups of apes and monkeys. Strictly speaking, it is not the size of the brain that matters, but the volume of the neocortex. This makes up the larger part of the cerebral cortex, which covers the two cerebral hemispheres of the brain, and plays a vital part in our ability to learn and memorize. Dunbar calculated the social group size of different apes on the basis of neocortex volume: humans come out on top with a predicted group size of about 150. If this equation works it, should be possible to establish the group size and social complexity of our various ancestors.

There has to be a good reason to increase brain size; it is an expensive and demanding organ. The bigger the brain the more it demands good-quality fuel in the form of food. The question of how and why the brains of hominins grew and what this tells us about the evolution of the human mind was the subject of the British Academy's Centenary Research Project entitled 'From Lucy to Language: The Archaeology of the Social Brain', which ran between 2003 and 2010.[16] The team of researchers emphasized the dramatic growth of the brain size of hominins during the past three million years. Chimpanzees, and early hominins going back to the LCA (about seven million years ago), have brains whose volume is less than 400 cu. cm (cc). Dunbar's formula estimates their community size at 30–50 individuals. These creatures interact with their fellows by fingertip grooming, one to one, and this essential activity limits the size of the group, given that much of the day also has to be spent searching for and consuming food, avoiding predators and sleeping.

The physical changes that subsequently took place in hominins – notably the reduction in the massive ape canines (particularly for males who flashed them about for sexual display and used them as weapons), the reduction in gut size, shorter arms, hands capable of finer manipulation, feet made for walking rather than climbing and, of course, increasingly large brains – indicate these new apes were adaptable to evolutionary pressures. The changes suggest that these creatures were increasingly intelligent, manipulating tools and weapons, and exploiting a varied and rich diet. They also lived in larger groups.

There are many theories about why humans evolved big brains. As I pointed out above, big brains are a big and costly investment. The researchers in the Lucy project suggest that the need for security from predators promoted larger groups. The hominin response was to develop larger brains in order to maintain social interaction in a community containing more individuals. Laughter, speech, language, eating together, dancing, music, story-telling and common beliefs (religion) were forms of grooming and interaction that eventually bound hominin communities together, promoting warm feelings and mutual support.

The australopithecines were the first hominin to 'break the 400 cc threshold for brain size'.[17] They had ape-like characteristics: for example, there is considerable difference in size between males and females. Lucy, the famous australopithecine from Ethiopia, was only just over 1 m (3 ft) tall. Her male admirers were more formidable, which suggests that sexual activity was organized on the 'harem' model: one big dominant male together with several smaller females and their children, like present-day gorillas. The male would also act as a bodyguard. Small ground dwellers, like australopithecine females and their offspring, were very vulnerable to predatory big cats and hyaenas. They were not yet top of the food chain. More developed hominins such as *Homo ergaster,* with brain sizes of over 900 cc, appeared in Africa between two million and one million years ago. As brain size increased, the quality of the food must have been a vital factor in fuelling this hungry organ (the modern brain forms 2% of the body weight of humans, but consumes 20% of the body's energy budget).

The decreasing size of the gut in evolving hominins saved energy, which could be diverted to brain growth, but the 'expensive tissue hypothesis' predicts improvement in the quality of the diet. This can partly be explained by the quality of tools, which gave their owners a big advantage in the quest for tubers, roots and vegetables and valuable animal fats. Even before they began to hunt large prey, scavenging hominins could smash tough bones to access rich bone marrow and the brain inside the skull, even when top predators had stripped the carcass.

Richard Wrangham, a primate specialist at Harvard University's Peabody Museum, has taken the 'expensive tissue hypothesis' a stage further. He argues that rather than simply moving from a largely vegetarian to a more carnivorous diet, our ancestors developed the controlled use of fire for cooking – what Darwin called 'probably the greatest [discovery], excepting language, ever made by man'. Wrangham proposes that cooking improved our food, making it tastier, more tender and easier to digest. Increasing the amount of energy we gain from food, cooking promoted the growth of our brain. 'It made us physically human.'[18] Highlighting the significance of controlled fire and cooking is not new,[19] but Wrangham puts its inception earlier in the human story than others have done: from about 1.8 million years ago when *H. ergaster* arrives on the scene, making it a prime mover in the development of the brain and the human mind. Others disagree on the timing and the contribution to brain growth, notably the *Thinking Big* team.[20]

It is not difficult to appreciate the potential of fire. Not long ago I was walking in the remote mountains in the south of France and I came across an enormous area of blackened tree stumps. The ground was littered with charcoal and fragments of animal bone – mainly sheep. Overhead vultures soared on the rising thermals. The ramparts of a prehistoric fortification, previously masked by forest, now stood out on the skyline. Fierce fires are common on the dry mountainsides, frequently caused by lightning strikes. In the savannah of Africa, lightning is spectacular, and fires are visible from far away. Vultures appreciate the possibilities, and so would early hominins. Wild fires often leave a bounty of charred carcasses, nuts and tubers.

The problem for archaeologists is to identify controlled fire. Opportunistic barbecues have probably been around for millions of years – but hearths and the knowledge of how to kindle fire? When I was based in Oxford our teams of archaeologists excavated dozens of local prehistoric settlements, a mere three thousand to two thousand years old. Hearths were as rare as hens' teeth, even though these communities clearly were expert manipulators of fire and pyrotechnics. The physical traces of hearths are easily destroyed by erosion of one sort or another so finding convincing evidence hundreds of thousands of years old is no easy matter. Claims have been made for burnt patches, about 1.6 million years old, from Kenya, and *H. ergaster* was alive and well at the time. But there is no consistency in the archaeological record, only a gap of half a million years or more.

Some of the most convincing evidence for controlled fire has been uncovered in Israel. The lakeside settlements at Gesher Benot Ya'aqov, occupied about 700,000 years ago, have repeated traces of burning along with fragments of burnt stone tools.[21] In Kenya, slightly earlier, there is evidence for controlled fire in cave sites, along with butchered and burnt animal bones.[22] In lower levels of the cave, many bones show that small-brained australopithecines had fallen victim to predators. With their smaller brains and limited imaginations perhaps they were fortunate enough not to have nightmares about the horrors that stalked in the dark. The rulers of fire, however, had moved up the food chain. The scarcity of their bones suggests that with fire and probably weapons they were able to defend themselves. The cave became a home rather than a trap.

The cranial capacity of *H. ergaster* increased by 280 cc (58%) over the australopithecines and then up to as much as 930 cc in the later *H. erectus* fossils. They had also become taller and more efficient runners, and about 40% larger than the australopith. As Robin Dunbar points out, large brains, bigger bodies and larger communities necessitate more time for feeding and social interactions: 'they must have found ways to circumvent the time budget bottleneck'.[23] The use of fire allowed hominins to extend the day, sitting around the campfire and enjoying more time together.

Dunbar is sceptical about Wrangham's emphasis on routine cooking as long as 1.5 million years ago. Having made calculations for factors such as the cooling climate in Africa and longer legs reducing travelling time, Dunbar returns to his favourite subject: the amount of time hominins spent socializing or bonding with each other. So how could *H. ergaster,* without controlled fire and cooking, both save time and find a more efficient way of 'grooming' within a larger group? His answer is, perhaps surprisingly, laughter, an activity that sends endorphins rushing to the brain and makes us feel good. That does not mean *H. ergaster/erectus* was a stand-up comedian. Speech may have been slowly developing, but almost certainly not language (a more formal version of verbal communication). Humour was probably physical: hominins slipping on banana skins or kicking hyaenas up the backside. Good novelists are sometimes ahead of scientists in the perception stakes. In 1953 in *Officers and Gentlemen*, Evelyn Waugh wrote: 'Men who have endured danger and privation together often separate and forget one another…if they laugh together…orgiastically they seal their friendship on a plane rarer and loftier than normal human intercourse.'

The question of how these capable early hominins solved their evolutionary challenges will continue to be debated. One major achievement is already clear from the archaeological record: some of them moved out of Africa into a wider world of grass and large, vulnerable animals.

CHAPTER TWO
# Following the herds:
# Heidelbergs and Neanderthals

**Hominins on the move**

A couple of years ago, I collected my grandson, then aged seven, from school. 'Do anything interesting today?' I asked. 'Yeah, we're studying dinosaurs. Someone asked my teacher what they ate and she said, "Grass". I told her, "There was no grass over sixty-six million years ago. They ate leaves and each other."' And he was right – we take grass for granted, but the first major grass-lands only appeared on Earth about eight million years ago. When a cold spell set in, the tropical forests then in the northern hemisphere disappeared, to be replaced by broad-leaved woodland. Carbon dioxide levels continued to fall and new plants evolved that could absorb the gas more effectively. These included grasses, and great swathes stretched across Eurasia.

Eating grass is not straightforward – it is packed with harsh cellulose and slivers of glass-like silica. Grazing animals adapted different strategies to tackle the stuff – horses evolved high-crowned grinding teeth, sheep have teeth like scissors. Cattle ancestors developed a digestive system that used bacteria to break down these rough, hard-to-digest plants. While other animals went extinct, the successful grazers spread across the savannah, the prairie and the steppe. There was, in fact, a boom in species diversity. Hominins came on the scene at a time when Earth was abundant with life, particularly large, meaty, grass-eating mammals. The primates of the shrinking tropical forest continued to browse on soft leaves and fruit, while hominins increasingly exploited those animals that could capture energy by digesting the scarcely digestible – grass.

At Boxgrove, northeast of Chichester in West Sussex, Mark Roberts, of University College London, and his team uncovered one of Britain's most remarkable archaeological sites. Painstakingly, they revealed a half-a-million-year-old land surface, buried at the foot of a chalk cliff. The cliff had been cut by the sea, which receded as a result of climatic cooling, so today it is 10 km (6 miles) further south. As the waters retreated they left behind a coastal plain, grazed by horses, bison and red deer. It was a predators' paradise. Lions, hyaenas and wolves stalked the herds across an English landscape that resembled the Serengeti plain – a sea of grass. But there was another animal present, a hominin who walked on two legs and knapped Acheulean axes from nodules of flint prised from the chalk cliff face. At Boxgrove the ground surface is so well preserved that it is possible to identify where a single individual sat and chipped out a handaxe, spraying the flakes of flint debris in a small arc between his or her legs. This is archaeology at its most vivid, capturing a moment 500,000 years ago.[1]

We left hominins in the ancestral homeland of Africa. So what are they doing in Britain? It is now clear that almost two million years ago the first hominins – probably *Homo ergaster/erectus* – began the long march out of Africa.[2] At the start of the Ice Age, Africa experienced drier conditions, woodland shrank, grassland savannah became increasingly parched and animals moved in search of food. The bigger-brained, long-legged hominins went with them. Over centuries, or probably millennia, they reached as far as China and Indonesia. In the late 19th century, a Dutchman, Eugène Dubois, went in search of the 'missing link' and found the remains known as 'Java Man'; in

A reconstruction of *Homo heidelbergensis* activity at Boxgrove, West Sussex, about half a million years ago. In the foreground, one knaps a handaxe, while behind a group butchers a rhino.

the 1920s 'Peking Man' appeared. As a result, the argument raged for decades about where humans originated. Did they evolve in Africa, Asia or both? Genetic studies have now settled the question in favour of Africa.

In the early 1980s, archaeologists excavating the medieval village at Dmanisi in Georgia had a surprise. They found a rhinoceros tooth, then the remains of five hominins, which dated to between 1.8 million and 1.7 million years ago. These bones have fuelled arguments among palaeoanthropologists. Do they belong to *H. erectus,* a predecessor such as *H. habilis*, or are they new kids on the block? What is beyond doubt, however, is that hominins were beginning to spread around the world. Until relatively recently, it was believed that they did not reach western Europe at this early time, but that has all changed as a result of work since the 1990s in Spain and Britain.

In the Atapuerca Hills of northern Spain several collapsed caves (revealed by a railway cutting) have produced bones indicating the most ancient hominin occupation in Europe almost one million years ago. These caves overlooked rich grazing grounds and the migratory routes along two river valleys at a time when the environment was still temperate. By about 100,000 years later hominins had reached Britain. Along the soft, eroding coast of East Anglia, at Pakefield and Happisburgh (pronounced 'Haze-boro'), the sea continuously exposes geological layers belonging to an ancient river valley known as Bytham, which was the predecessor of the River Thames. The clues are few – mainly a few dozen pieces of worked flint – but enough to show that hominins were present, at what is, so far, their northernmost limit. At the time, 900,000 to 700,000 years ago, Britain was attached to the Continent.

A temperate Britain, swarming with animal life, was an attractive place for hominins. A little later (relatively speaking) it was not. From just over 650,000 years ago Europe went into the refrigerator; it entered the 40,000-year-long cold spell of an ice age glacial period. The hominins retreated. When conditions improved again, they reappeared. This time it was a new, larger-brained species, who had probably evolved in Africa, but was named after a town in Germany because in 1903 a jawbone was found in a quarry outside Heidelberg. At the time, there was something of an arms and status race going on in Europe between the leading imperial nations not only in battleships and guns, but also for the prestige of having the oldest humans. France had its Cro-Magnon artists in the Dordogne region; Germany could counter with its Neanderthals, and now Heidelberg Man. Britain resorted to a forgery: someone cobbled together 'Piltdown Man'.[3]

*Homo heidelbergensis* is an important actor on the human stage. In Africa, *H. ergaster* was the dominant hominin for just over a million years (from 1.8 million years ago). Although they expanded out of Africa, in that time there was relatively little development, physically or culturally, probably because there were few additional selection pressures, such as environmental change.[4] Then, about 800,000 to 600,000 years ago, *H. heidelbergensis* appeared. Soon they also occupied Europe and Western Asia, and probably beyond. There is an unresolved argument about where *H. heidelbergensis* originated: in Africa or in Eurasia – and the direction in which they subsequently spread. A tiny bone fragment discovered in 2009 in the Denisova region of the Altai Mountains of southeast Russia has proved to be genetically different from modern humans and Neanderthals. Is this a new species, a descendant of *H. heidelbergensis*?[5]

## Bones, bodies and brains

These new hominins represent a major hike in the big-brain stakes, averaging 1210 cc in Africa and later 1240 cc in Europe, half as big again as the *H. ergaster* brain (about 760 cc). Of course, to mean something, brain size has to be compared with body mass. For increased intelligence brain growth has to exceed growth in body size, which it does in Heidelbergs. The spectacular bone collections from the Atapuerca cave deposit known as Sima de los Huesos (Pit of Bones) include the remains of thirty-two individuals (arguably *H. heidelbergensis* or a close relative). These are tough-looking, heavy-boned characters, the males around 1.75 m (5 ft 9 in.) tall and the women slightly less. However, they died young (half were under eighteen years of age) and led violent lives. One individual had the scars of thirteen blows on his bones, and it takes more than an occasional slap or fall to impact the bone. Other physical problems ranged from deafness and arthritis to painful septicaemia in the teeth and face. Yet this was a successful species. Robin Dunbar estimates an average group size of about 110, almost 75% bigger than an *H. ergaster* community. He also argues that the Heidelberg brain grew considerably after about 300,000 years ago, and points now to the control of fire and cooking as a principal factor to explain how Heidelbergs balanced the demands of the larger brain and increased body size and managed their hectic social lives.[6]

Cooking increases the calorific value of food, helping to stoke both muscles and grey matter, and fire lengthens the day. When we sit and eat together round the campfire we trigger an endorphin rush that makes us feel companionable.

We literally get a warm feeling. The campfire also keeps the dark at bay and allows us to stay awake. The extra calories and the extra hours of light for social interaction probably helped the large Heidelberg groups balance their daily time budget and hence ensure their evolutionary viability.

Members of an *H. heidelbergensis* clan left their traces across the land surface at Boxgrove. These powerful hominins posed a severe threat to other animals. At Boxgrove they fashioned handaxes and left more than three hundred of them discarded on the ground. These were butchery tools, and the bones of the victims (horses, bison and rhinoceros) lay nearby – incised by the sharp edges of the flint as their flesh was sliced off. Coincidentally, as I was writing these words, there was a knock at the door. It was Jeannot, my French neighbour, who keeps goats and two packs of hunting hounds. Like my friend in Woodstock, he had also brought a gift in a bag. This time it was part of the bloody carcass of a wild boar. I spent the evening cutting the meat from the ribs and the spine with a razor-sharp Japanese knife. It was hard work for someone who spends much of his day at a desk. It made me appreciate just how tough a job it must have been to carve up a rhinoceros with flint tools. It also takes considerable concentration. The butchers would certainly have needed their compatriots to frighten off the scavengers while they worked. Eventually, the scavenging hyaenas were allowed their turn at the feast. The marks of their gnawing teeth are all over the bones – but superimposed on the butchery marks. It was clear who the top dog was at Boxgrove.

Clearly, the Heidelbergs had access to the rhinoceros carcass before the slavering hyaenas, but did they kill this powerful beast? Archaeologists have argued for some time about when hominins became hunters. Given the impressive muscularity and strength, intelligence and group size of these Heidelbergs there seems no obvious reason why they should not have been serious predators. There is further evidence at other sites; organic materials of such age rarely survive – but occasionally they do. At Schöningen in Germany a charred wooden spear was found, dating to about 400,000 years ago, and another came from Clacton in Essex. These are stabbing, not throwing spears, whose owners had to get up close and personal with their prey. The hunters led dangerous lives. It is not surprising that they carried the marks of their encounters on their bones, and often died young.

Boxgrove was a butchery site. After collecting up the meat, the hominins left the remains to the scavengers, who had been kept at bay by the perimeter guards, yelling, gesticulating, wielding their long spears and hurling rocks.

About this time, hearths become more frequent in the archaeological record; they were found, for example, near the burnt spear at Schöningen. At Beeches Pit in eastern England someone sat by a fire knapping a handaxe from a lump of flint. Most of the flakes fell around him or her, but a couple shot into the fire and were burnt red. Hearths were centres of activity, places where people gathered and ate together. The Boxgrove hominins climbed up the chalk cliffs to some more sheltered spot where they could cook and share the meat and other foodstuffs – fruit, nuts and plants brought in by other members of the band.

We modern humans mostly sleep about eight hours a day, less than other apes, and in the evening we are still active when chimpanzees are taking to their tree nests to sleep. We can thank fire, not television, for this pattern of behaviour. Such rich food as slabs of grilled rhino flesh and horsemeat (to which the modern British, but not my French neighbours, now have a peculiar aversion) helps explain the evolutionary development of these powerful Boxgrove people.

Boxgrove delivered marvellous evidence of hominins at work. It was only after a decade of excavation that physical traces of the butchers themselves appeared. Mark Roberts, the site director, arranged for a mechanical excavator to strip part of the site. Roger Pederson, supervising the machine, spotted a bone in the ground. It turned out to be a shin bone from a tall (1.8 m/5 ft 11 in.), well-built hominin about forty years old: a male *H. heidelbergensis*. His shin bone had been gnawed by a wolf. Two teeth were the only other hominin remains. Marks etched into them showed that their owners had gripped meat or vegetation with their teeth, while slicing through the fibres with flint blades – held in the right hand.

## Neanderthals in Norfolk

Ancient humans continued to manufacture handaxes for millennia. In early 2002, John Lord, a local fieldworker, made another staggeringly rare find in the gravel quarry at Lynford in Norfolk. A cut-off meander of an old watercourse had created a hollow in the gravel, in which he spotted distinctive handaxes along with woolly mammoth bones and well-preserved environmental deposits. Fortunately, archaeologists at Norfolk County Council, recognizing the importance of the discovery, contacted English Heritage, who immediately agreed to fund a research project.

I found that visiting Lynford was as impressive an experience as Olorgesailie and Boxgrove and provided the same immediate contact with the deep past. Here, forty-seven handaxes, many in almost mint condition, lay around the dismembered remains of animals, mostly woolly mammoth. The butchers had left behind massive tusks along with their tools.

You may have noticed that Olorgesailie, Boxgrove and Lynford have something in common: the hominins at all three sites seem to have been remarkably careless with their handaxes. Archaeologists have naturally speculated on the reason for this redundancy of axes. Were they left at butchery sites for future use, rather like I leave my steel axe near the woodpile? Or were they used and then abandoned? If so, was this because they were easy to replace (modern flint knappers estimate that it takes ten to twenty minutes to make a handaxe)? Or was the actual making of axes as important as their use? Did the individual hominins find satisfaction in the action of manufacture, and in this way help to establish their place in the group? Archaeologists seek to get into the minds of people in the past. The redundant axes issue shows that it is not easy, especially when we are not sure how their minds worked.[7]

Victor Papanek, an expert on craft and design, has reminded us that not all humans think alike about objects or things. Discussing the traditional Inuit, he emphasizes that design to them 'is an act, not an object; a ritual, not a possession'. The Inuit make small sculptures in great detail, reflecting their powers of observation. These are carried around, passed from hand to hand and often casually discarded. The coastal Inuit of Greenland carve ivory or stone figures known as *tupilak* ('harmful ghosts'). The function of these figures is to absorb any bad feelings or emotions from the carver (I find whittling wood does the trick). Once completed, such a beautifully detailed figure is often tossed into water, taking the carver's hatreds and aggression with it.[8]

Returning to Lynford, its deposits lie beyond the range of radiocarbon dating, so optical stimulated luminescence (OSL) dating was needed to estimate that the drama occurred about 67,000 to 57,000 years ago, admittedly not the sort of timescale that would satisfy a crime scene investigator. The landscape was dominated by grasses, sedge, scrub and sparse stands of birch and the climate was relatively mild: the mean midsummer temperature was up to 14°C (57°F) and the winters between -8°C (17.6°F) and -15°C (5°F).[9] This part of modern-day Norfolk has been described as a bleak and alien landscape, the English steppes, in which blasted heath predominate: the only place in Britain that stone curlews breed. It was harsher 60,000 years ago, but full of life. The hominins roamed here in one of the main intervals in the last great cold stage in Britain – not a full-blown cold phase, but not exactly balmy either. Winters were tough, but in early summer 60,000 years ago the Lynford pools were covered with water crowsfoot, a relative of the buttercup with masses of white and yellow flowers.

There were no human bone remains at Lynford, so who were the actors? The axe types point to Neanderthals.[10] These Lynford axes are very distinctive: small and heart-shaped with a flat base (what are known in the trade as *bout coupé* axes). I always think these are very elegant tools, quite at odds with the clichéd image of brutish, beetle-browed Neanderthals in popular culture. Their ancestors, *H. erectus*, had spread out of Africa and evolved into the impressive Heidelbergs; this species probably evolved into Neanderthals about 250,000 years ago.[11]

Neanderthals are often wrongly portrayed as shuffling cavemen because of a fundamental misunderstanding. A well-preserved Neanderthal skeleton, found in 1908 at La Chapelle-aux-Saints, France, was riddled with a degenerative disease. This was not appreciated at the time and instead the arthritic, stooped, elderly individual, lacking most of his teeth, was taken

The excavation of the Neanderthal site at Lynford, Norfolk. A mammoth tusk lies to the right of the excavator.

as typical. The popular image of Neanderthals was born – and still survives: the US Republican politician, Sarah Palin, referred to one of her opponents as a 'knuckle-dragging Neanderthal'. In fact, not only did Neanderthals walk upright, but the survival of the poor crippled Neanderthal into relative old age also suggests that his community took care of him.

Neanderthals also achieved a new record for hominins – an average brain size of about 1320 cc, and larger in some males, such as the skull from the Amud Cave in Israel, at a whopping 1750 cc. However, Neanderthals were hefty characters, bulkier than modern humans whose brain size varies between about 1200 and 1700 cc, averaging 1350 cc.[12] Studies of modern humans have not established a straightforward link between brain size and intelligence. A big brain alone does not make you Einstein.

Another factor influencing Neanderthal brain size had little to do with intelligence. This species evolved in Eurasia, not in Africa, so developed to cope with the low light levels of short, winter days and relatively dull summers in the northern hemisphere. This created a problem of time-budgeting – getting everything done that needed to be done, from feeding to social activity. Dull light is particularly a problem for hunters. I have noticed myself, when trying to observe animals such as wild boar, pine martens, deer and lynx on the edge of the forest, that in midsummer near the Mediterranean I can spot them in the crepuscular light at 9.45 p.m.; a few minutes later the light thickens, their forms blur and they disappear in the deepening gloom.

The Neanderthal evolutionary solution was to enlarge the visual processing system: increasing the size of the retina to capture more light, which required a bigger eyeball, and developing a bigger visual-systems area in the brain. Neanderthals had eyes about 20% larger than ours and a bulge at the back of their brain evolved to cope with the needs of visual processing. Modern humans, on the other hand, grew the frontal part of the brain that increases social intelligence. As Clive Gamble and the *Thinking Big* team have emphasized: 'Neanderthals inhabited northern regions critically too early to be able to develop the full-scale social brains that characterize *Homo sapiens*.'[13] The big Neanderthal brain, then, is a response to visual issues more than an increase in intelligence, and Neanderthal community sizes probably remained similar to those of the Heidelbergs, at about 110–120 individuals.[14]

The Neanderthals have often had a bad press as primitives who went extinct. Recently, however, their public relations have improved considerably. It is now fashionable to see their good side – they were a species that, from before 200,000 years ago, spread across Eurasia – from Wales to the edges of Siberia and as far south as Gibraltar – before they finally disappeared around 40,000 years ago. To a certain extent, Neanderthals live on. Their genes make up 1–4% of non-African humans today. This suggests that when humans first came out of Africa into the Middle East some interbred with Neanderthals, then carried the Neanderthal genes to regions the Neanderthals themselves never reached.[15]

Neanderthals had stocky bodies, like weightlifters or prop-forwards in rugby. They had the strength of the Heidelbergs but were more adapted to the cold climate of higher latitudes, especially so that they would experience less heat loss in winter. Life in the chilly northern world of Lynford would have been tough. Yet this steppe environment, spreading further south than similar areas today, was rich in animal life. Neanderthals shared their world with herds of large mammals such as mammoths and woolly rhinoceros, reindeer and horses. As these animals migrated with the seasons, and on a large scale with climatic change, the Neanderthals probably kept pace, tracking the movements of the herd or lying in wait at favourable locations in the landscape, like Lynford.

Encounters were brutal; Neanderthal hunting still involved close contact. Injuries observed in Neanderthal males resemble those seen today in rodeo riders. Their heavily muscled bodies suggest a protein-rich diet and this is confirmed by isotopic studies of bone collagen indicating that Neanderthals relied substantially on meat much like wolves, their fellow predators and competitors. Yet they were, in the right circumstances, capable of some flexibility in their diet. From the plaque in Neanderthal teeth, evidence has come from northern Spain and Shanidar in Iraq that Neanderthals roasted vegetables and ate wild grain. Some of the last generations of Neanderthals, in Gibraltar, even caught rabbits, ibex and tortoises, collected shellfish such as cockles and mussels, and consumed dolphins and monk seals. Seafood, vegetables, tortoises and plants were on the menu of the Neanderthal Mediterranean diet.

## Neanderthal limits

The capabilities of Neanderthals were clearly superior to what was once imagined. However, although their toolkit improved from that of their hominin ancestors, they did not colonize the world; neither the harshest environments of the north and south, nor Australia and America. According to the social brain hypothesis, group size was probably a factor. Communities of about 110–120 individuals were divided into bands of about 30 people who would interact and cooperate with, perhaps, three other groups. Modern humans, as we will see, found ways of extending the chain of communication and network of interactions. Neanderthal expansion might have been limited by the scale of their contacts, and life can be impossible for isolated groups of any species.

How Neanderthals communicated with each other has been a subject of much debate. Modern human societies all have language, but sophisticated language, with grammar and great flexibility, a means for us to tell stories and plan future behaviour, is a relatively late arrival on the communication scene. Hominins probably began with gestures, limited sounds and laughter, rhythmic clapping and dancing. In view of Neanderthal achievements it is likely that they were capable of language of some kind, albeit less sophisticated than that of modern humans.

In 1962 the Oxford classicist Sir Maurice Bowra imagined that dancing and songs might go back as far as the societies that painted the walls of Palaeolithic caves. He was right, but in 1962 it was inconceivable to plunge back even further into deep time.[16] A generation or two later, Steven Mithen of Reading University proposed that music, singing and dance acted as the glue to help bind Neanderthals together.[17] Even without language, communal rhythmic chanting and stomping triggers endorphin release – bringing people together. Trying to make friends with Darwin's companions, the Yámana people of Tierra del Fuego roped in two of the crew of HMS *Beagle* to join their dance. Holding hands they jumped up and down, happily and interminably singing, Ha ma la ha ma la ha ma la ha ma la, O la la la la la la la la. Primitive speech, like primitive forms of the eye, may not seem sophisticated, but it can nevertheless fulfil a vital purpose.

Sixty thousand years ago, Lynford was close to the northern limit of the Neanderthal world. Archaeologists suggest that in the northwest peninsula of Eurasia Neanderthals were never more than thin on the ground and probably exploited the area seasonally, as a summer hunting ground. Nevertheless, other Neanderthal territories ('local operational areas' in the academic jargon) have been recognized in Britain, and some of the evidence both indicates Neanderthal capabilities and adds to our story of the axe.

There were Neanderthal territories in the south of Britain, notably around the valleys of the River Axe in Somerset and the Solent in Hampshire, and intrepid Neanderthals pushed even further north. The toughest reached the wilds of Yorkshire, and a related clan left remains in a cave at Pontnewydd, North Wales. Here there are objects that echo our greenstone axe – a scraper and flakes made of a distinctive stone. This is andesite, which, like our greenstone, is found in the Lake District – over 100 km (60 miles) north of the Pontnewydd cave. Andesite can be found in Ennerdale and Eskdale, a little to the southwest of Langdale, the home of our Neolithic axe. The exploitation of this material may even predate Neanderthals. Andesite axes have turned up near Coventry, in the English Midlands, associated with the extinct Bytham River that flowed eastwards past the sites at Pakefield and Happisburgh, sites with the earliest evidence of hominins in Britain. This was the traditional routeway for early hominins following the seasonal migrations from inland Europe across the lowlands, now known to archaeologists as Doggerland, which were subsequently flooded by rising sea levels to form the North Sea. Even at the limits of colonization hominins were searching out exotic stone.

By roughly 41,000 years ago, with another period of deepening cold, even the hardiest Neanderthals had given up on Britain, as did the hyaenas. In fact, across Eurasia the Neanderthal populations slid into decline and became isolated in small groups. The sabre-toothed cat prowled the cold, windswept steppes of Britain, undisturbed by hominins.

## CHAPTER THREE

# Great minds think alike:
# The emergence of modern humans

## Living with the Ice Age

Today 'climate change' or 'global warming' is rightly a topic of global concern. The issues now are to what extent we humans are influencing the Earth's climate and what we can do about it. Climate change, in the long view, is nothing new. Humans in the past learnt to cope with enormous climatic variation. As the climatologist Bill Burroughs wrote: 'The climate is deeply etched into our genetic make-up. It may also lurk within our psyche.'[1]

It was another of the great scientific breakthroughs of the 19th century that revealed the ebb and flow of ice ages. In the 1830s, the Swiss biologist Louis Agassiz concluded that glaciers had once been much more extensive, carving out valleys, polishing and scratching rock surfaces and depositing moraines, eskers and erratics. Agassiz coined the name for it: *die Eiszeit* – the Ice Age.

More recent scientific techniques have helped to provide a much more detailed picture of the Earth's climatic history: information from ocean sediment cores has revealed a persistent temperature decrease over the past 50 million years, with the temperature sometimes falling rapidly and then rising again. Coring into the polar ice also tells us about the Earth's ancient atmosphere and the levels of greenhouse gases ($CO_2$), which vary with the regular shifts in the Earth's orbit.[2]

The Earth has undergone several major ice ages in the deep past, some of which have taken life on the planet to the brink of extinction. About 750 million to 600 million years ago (geologically speaking, the late Precambrian) the cold was so severe that large areas of the oceans froze and produced what climatologists memorably label 'Snowball Earth'. But benefits can come out of the deep freeze. It was followed by the Cambrian explosion of life.[3] Humans, like the rest of life, have evolved on an Earth subject to natural selection pressures. These can take the form of gradual or rapid change or even sudden impacts from meteorites or volcanoes. Environmental change can be disastrous for species that cannot adapt with sufficient rapidity. It can also lead to periods of branching and experimentation in life forms. Such shocks, notably climatic stress, may have stimulated innovation in our ancestral evolution: the first apes in the Miocene 23 million years ago (when the Antarctic ice sheet formed) or *Homo erectus* two million years ago.

At about 2.5 million years ago the tilt of the Earth generated a change in the world's climate. Gradually the ice sheets of the northern hemisphere expanded as the warm wet climate of the Pliocene succumbed to a new (the latest) Ice Age. But this was not 'Snowball Earth'. The ice sheets of the northern hemisphere expanded southwards covering, at their maximum, what is now Canada, part of the American Midwest as far south as St. Louis, Scandinavia and most of Britain and Ireland.

Ice ages are not that straightforward. The study of marine sediments shows that the graph of Earth's temperature resembles the teeth of a saw. In the past 2.5 million years, during the latest Ice Age, there have been fifty troughs of extreme cold (glacial periods), interspersed with the peaks of warmer intervals (and just to complicate matters, there can be sudden colder spells during the warm intervals). These cycles are influenced by the Earth's orbit around the Sun. For 1.5 million years, glacials and warm intervals (interglacials) see-sawed every 41,000 years, then for the next million years the cycle slowed so that the fluctuations took place every 100,000 years.

So if most of the ice was in the north, how did the Ice Age affect our ancestors, who were confined, in the earlier stages at least, to the African continent? The fundamental issue for them was water. Ice ages are extremely dry because so much water is locked up in the glaciers. Massive deposits of windblown dust (loess) across Eurasia and central and northeast Africa testify to the dry conditions, as does the shrinkage of the tropical African forest. African hominins came under stress as their ancient habitats were reduced and fragmented.

The chimpanzee family adapted by staying put and reducing their numbers. Our hominin ancestors evolved relatively rapidly, developed their tool and fire-making skills and expanded into any new habitats that they could exploit. This does not mean that big-brained hominins necessarily flourished. Genetic evidence indicates that there was a bottleneck in the population of modern humans approximately 80,000 to 70,000 years ago. Geneticists have also noted a bottleneck in the population of the human louse at about this time. We became as rare as gorillas are today: probably 15,000–40,000 people in total survived in scattered bands. Because genetic 'dating' is imprecise, we cannot be sure what caused this crisis. Yet climate change must be the prime suspect – either one of the usual oscillations, or the volcanic winter resulting from the huge volcanic eruption of Mount Toba in Indonesia at 71,000 years ago.

Less water also meant that sea levels were drastically reduced by 120 m (394 ft) or more. The geography of coastlines changed and archipelagos, such as Indonesia and Britain, became attached to their mainlands. When hominins (probably *H. erectus* and *H. heidelbergensis)* expanded out of Africa and into Eurasia, they were able to walk into many areas that are islands today.

It is not my intention here to give a detailed account of the horrendously complicated ups and downs of the Ice Age. The point I want to make is that the 'climatic rollercoaster', to borrow Brian Fagan's phrase, created pressures and opportunities that stimulated human evolution and cultural adaptation, and in the long run benefited the lucky ones – us! Other species were less fortunate: monkeys disappeared from Italy 250,000 years ago and the last Neanderthal probably died about 40,000 years ago, the victim of coincidental pressures, such as climatic change and competition from the more versatile modern humans.[4]

## The arrival of modern humans

The climate had a major impact on the biosphere. The huge ice fields – inexorable, groaning juggernauts a mile high – ground away plant life in the northern lands. The atmosphere itself changed: there was a major reduction in greenhouse gases such as carbon dioxide and methane, which allowed heat to escape constantly and the planet to cool even further. This meant that the quantity of plants on land shrank by a half. Nevertheless, during the intervals when the land warmed, mosses, lichens, grassland plants, shrubs and trees colonized new territories and in their wake came the herds of grazers and their predators. While the Lynford Neanderthals were briefly occupying Britain, a new potential competitor was emerging in Africa, a hominin who would eventually be defined as *Homo sapiens*, anatomically modern humans (AMH). Surprisingly, perhaps, *H. sapiens* is one of the most poorly defined species in the animal kingdom.[5] The great biological classifier, Linnaeus, avoided the problem: '*Homo* know for yourself', he said. Generally, however, if you want to identify an AMH by his or her skull, look for a prominent chin, a flattish mid-face region, a steep forehead, minimal brow-ridge and a rounded cranium. Such traits appear in African bones from about 260,000 years ago and became more fully developed over the next 60,000 years.

In the absence of bones (and they are usually absent at these early dates), archaeologists look for evidence of supposedly modern human behaviour. The big question is: exactly what is modern behaviour? And when do its traits appear? For example, modern humans eventually learned some very clever new tricks with stone, but in the early days they made tools not unlike those of the Neanderthals and based on traditions that were many millennia old.[6] As with earlier hominins, we took time to develop our potential.

We can observe the size of the human brain and measure the significant increase in its cranial capacity. However, there is also the issue of the brain's capabilities, of the human mind. Modern humans have some sophisticated abilities that put them apart from most other animals: for example, figuring out how our own behaviour might influence the future actions of other people.

I mentioned earlier that Jeannot, my neighbour from down the valley, had given me a large chunk of wild boar (it made an excellent stew). I did not mention that a few weeks before, I had unblocked the aqueduct that waters his meadow. He noticed and thanked me. Following the gift of the boar meat I decided that, as soon as the biblical rains plaguing our village stopped, I would take him a bottle of whisky. I have to admit that I was not unaware that I may want to borrow his tractor in the future. So I want to keep this reciprocal thing going. This is what psychologists call 'Theory of Mind' – putting yourself in someone else's mind as well as your own. Human children develop the knack about the age of five. They might, as a result, learn to play nicely. They also learn to tell fibs and stories. Human adults can take this further.

If knowing your own mind is 'first order intentionality', and my having a belief about your belief is 'second order intentionality', then most people can take 'Theory of Mind' to five orders (and some even further). The *Thinking Big* team express this as: 'I *wonder* whether you *suppose* that I *intend* that you *think* that I *believe* X to be true.'[7] We need these mentalizing cognitive skills to function effectively in the adult world. It is also what allowed us to develop myth, legends and religious beliefs – to appreciate that we all die, practise elaborate burial rites and comfort or scare ourselves with the concept of an afterlife.

One outcome of this evolution of mental capability is that we learnt to think symbolically, to relate to our environment, including artefacts, in a different way. Tools such as our Neolithic axe become sources of memory and a means of conveying messages about the carrier. But this ability to live in the imagination began before the Neolithic. Archaeologists regard attempts at bodily decoration as signs of the modern mind in action, communicating messages or identity (our gender, status or group affiliation) to others. Pierced shells designed to be strung on necklaces are some of the earliest indicators, dating in South Africa to about 120,000 years ago. At Blombos Cave, South Africa, humans were mixing paint in shell containers 100,000 years ago. The obsidian block sitting on my desk came from near Lake Naivasha in Kenya, also the source of spectacular red and brown obsidian – from about 200,000 years ago, AMH transported this material in increasing quantities over considerable distances to sites such as Kilombe, 100 km (60 miles) to the north.

## The 'Human Revolution'

Archaeologists and historians love to be able to identify a 'revolution' – whether it is cultural, technical or political. Thirty years ago, the 'Human Revolution' – the appearance of the modern mind in action, represented by art, burials and complex tools – was seen as a European phenomenon, occurring first about 40,000 years ago in places like the Dordogne. More recent discoveries now propel it further back in time to our African homeland: there we developed our minds as well as our bodies.[8] The discovery of rock art in Southeast Asia has also further undermined the Eurocentric revolution: hand stencils and depictions of animals have been shown by uranium-series dating to be as much as 40,000 years old, the oldest at Leang Timpuseng, Sulawesi, Indonesia.[9]

Nevertheless, some of the most spectacular evidence of the cultural development of humans comes from Europe, where archaeologists have been searching intensively for almost two centuries. A cave site in South Wales revealed the burial of a person famously known as the 'Red Lady of Paviland', who had the fully developed characteristics of an early modern human both physically and culturally, though the 'Red Lady' is in fact a 'he'. On 15 February 1823, William Buckland, Oxford University's first Professor of Geology, gave a special lecture at the Ashmolean Museum to announce his discoveries at Goat's Hole, Paviland, one of a series of caves in the rugged coastal cliffs of the Gower Peninsula. Today the entrance to the cave is only accessible at low tide. When the 'Red Lady' was buried, the sea level was about 80 m (260 ft) lower than today; the Bristol Channel did not exist, except as a coastal plain, and the sea was over 50 km (30 miles) to the west. Buckland knew none of this. He belonged to the catastrophist school of geology and looked to the Bible, the Flood and a short chronology – his geology had to fit into Genesis 6–8. The Paviland burial was nicknamed the 'Red Lady' because

A cross-section of Goat's Hole Cave, Paviland, South Wales, where William Buckland found Britain's earliest modern human remains, the so-called 'Red Lady', buried at least 28,000 years ago.

the bones were stained with red ochre, or 'ruddle', as Buckland called it. He assumed that 'she' belonged to the Roman period and was associated with the promontory fort (now known to be Iron Age) on the clifftop above the caves.

In the 1990s the Paviland caves were subject to a major re-evaluation. A team led by Stephen Aldhouse-Green of the University of Wales, Newport, attacked the surviving material with every scientific technique they could get their hands on and produced something rare: an excavation report that is a good read.[10] We now know that the 'Red Lady' is a young man, a *Homo sapiens* who was buried on the remote extreme northwestern peninsula of Eurasia at least 28,000 years ago. His mitochondrial DNA sequence matches the most common extant lineage in Europe, showing that he belongs to the first group of modern humans, ultimately from Africa, who rather belatedly colonized northwest Europe, long after others of their kind had reached Australia by 40,000 years ago.

The 'Red Lady' is physically and genetically modern. His burial also shows that he belonged to a highly developed culture, revealing distinctive characteristics of modern behaviour and mental or cognitive development. In other words, he was like us and so were the people who buried him. His burial in the cave seems to have been part of an elaborate ritual. The characteristics of the ceremony are seen at other sites across Europe at this time, displaying a level of creativity and use of symbolic material that was beyond earlier hominins.[11] Here we have brains that work like ours and, it is assumed, people communicating with a fully functioning language. They understood metaphor. The brain size, particularly the well-developed neocortex, suggests a social group size of 150, the largest of any hominin.

The burial of the young man in Paviland Cave demonstrates the thinking of modern humans. His compatriots covered his lower body with red ochre, which stained his bones. As a child I used to say that red was my favourite colour. I did not know then that red is the brightest colour that humans can perceive or that it is of enormous symbolic significance in societies around the world, from the Kalahari Desert to Tasmania.[12] Red is associated with blood, thus with life, rebirth and power. Julius Caesar, Catholic cardinals and many military organizations understood the force of red and so, it seems, did the Paviland people.

Near to the head of the burial lay the complete skull of an adult mammoth – a massive object weighing over 300 kg (660 lb). Was this part of the funerary ritual? Certainly, ivory was valued. At Lynford, the Neanderthals had simply left ivory tusks with the abandoned carcass; to them it had no value. Early modern humans collected, worked and exchanged ivory. To them it meant something: aesthetically, practically and symbolically. Our continuing fascination with this beautiful material could yet drive elephants to extinction.

At Paviland many small cylinder-shaped ivory rods lay by the ribs of the 'Red Lady', probably originally stitched onto clothing. He also wore ivory bracelets and perforated periwinkle shells. Modern humans, characteristically, are fond of the exotic and are able to arrange the exchange of these materials over long distances. The ability to make needles and sew tailored clothing (and make shoes) was fundamental to their success in a cold climate. Across Europe there are burials with similar characteristics to that at Paviland, which reflect widespread use of materials like ivory, body decoration and probably common ritual practices.

Modern humans had lightly built bodies adapted to the warmer climate of Africa, but with warm clothing they could deal with the cold. Heading north was no problem. Even in tough climatic conditions there was a corridor: the mammoth steppe, a dry tundra bursting with life that stretched southwards between Scandinavian and Alpine ice sheets from Britain to Russia. Today the Siberian steppe is inhospitable, boggy and acidic, grazed mainly by reindeer who survive on a diet of moss. Yet the bones and even the preserved bodies of grass-eating mammoths, giant elk, musk ox, bison and horses show that life on the Ice Age steppe was much more prolific than it is today.

The mammoth was designed for this environment, powerful enough to bulldoze snow and open up patches of grass to feed, letting in smaller herbivores. The steppe was bitingly cold, yet it was productive. Today, vegetation on the tundra becomes waterlogged, freezes and forms acidic peat, and below is permafrost – permanently frozen ground that grips hold of its nutrients. Not many plants thrive in this environment. Although the climate is not as extreme as in the Ice Age, the growing season is shorter (peat acts as a chilly blanket, insulating the ground and blocking the sun's rays). The Ice Age steppe was prolific because the herds, particularly mammoths, ate the vegetation before it could become peat and recycled the plant material as a constant stream of fertilizer. Mammoth dung made the northern world go round. As Tim Flannery wrote, 'If ever a creature deserved the epithet of biological banker it was the mammoth...it kept a climatically formidable environment productive and alive.'[13]

The herds trundled across the steppe followed by the new humans, hunters armed with stone-tipped spears and atlatls – spear-throwing devices designed to increase the arm length and impart more energy and distance into the missile. The steppe was a bonanza of meat, skins, fur and bones. Large herbivores in Africa had lived alongside these super-hunters for millennia and adapted to the danger. The sudden appearance of *Homo sapiens* in continents like Australia, and later America, coincided with a catastrophic decline and extinction of many species of large herbivorous animals. Even the mammoth eventually succumbed. Many coincidences point the finger at humans as congenital serial killers throughout our history. However, the dramatic environmental changes at this time make it hard to pin the blame principally on humans as the cause of mammoth extinction.

With developed language, larger groups and increased networking these people could spread new ideas and new technology. The more they clustered together, the more ideas they had; the more they expanded into new territory, the more the ideas and technologies spread. That is not to say good ideas and innovative technology are always adopted or maintained.

Isolation, environmental change, disease or even belief systems can condemn them to oblivion. History is littered with failed colonizations, from the Vikings in America and Greenland to the first British in Roanoke, Virginia. We will never know how many Polynesian crews failed to reach remote Pacific islands. The earliest recorded European to sail into the Atlantic, heading around Africa, simply disappeared.

## Coping with the cold

In this period of the Ice Age, about 33,000 to 24,000 years ago, we see humans in Europe spreading common ideas, fashions and beliefs. Archaeologists have labelled these societies Gravettian, after the French site at La Gravette in the Périgord. These are the inventive people who adapted to the cold, making their own shelters from the howling gales with mammoth bones, hides and turf.[14] Some of these substantial dwellings were used over long periods. Předmostí, in the Czech Republic, a natural, forested hollow in the tundra sited on an animal migration route, was a place to which hunting bands regularly returned and congregated over many millennia. If this was not quite 'settling down' in the sense usually associated with Neolithic farmers, it was not far off. Here, the Předmostí people, gathered around their hearths, could eat, tell stories, pass on ideas and experiences, bond with family and make new friends and allies.

Another nearby settlement, at Dolní Věstonice, is one of the most important Upper Palaeolithic sites in Europe, where the alkaline soils are good for the preservation of bone. Excavations have revealed dozens of dwellings and many artefacts. Most remarkable at this early period was the discovery of two kilns that had been used for firing clay pellets and figurines, showing an understanding of the properties of clay and ceramic technology 15,000 years before the advent of the Neolithic. At this stage clay was not being used to manufacture pots, however; instead, it was used as a material to create models of living figures.[15]

A fired clay figurine made about 26,000 years ago at Dolní Věstonice, Czech Republic.

The most evocative are those of women with exaggerated female form – the substantial breasts, buttocks and hips, which would never be seen today on the fashion catwalk. Perhaps male Gravettians admired women bursting with fertility, figures that felt good in the hand. Alternatively, women may have made the figurines, emphasizing what they saw as desirable characteristics.

Unlike Neanderthals, the Gravettians were expert at catching smaller swift animals, such as foxes and hares for their furs and birds for their feathers, as well as meat. Archaeologists spend a lot of time trying to wring information out of stone tools, but the bones of these animals remind us that organic materials were highly important to hominins (as we saw earlier with the Schöningen spear, see page 42). The Gravettians were certainly expert at making and setting traps and must have been skilled at twisting and knotting fibres to make nets and snares. Their weapons also included spears tipped with fine flint blades glued and bound onto specially shaped wooden hafts. They made spears designed to split on impact so that the haft could be collected and reused.

These Ice Age hunters were skilled at catching small animals, but they were also supreme hunters of big game. They worked cooperatively, utilizing the lie of the land to drive herds of horses or reindeer into deliberately designed funnels or corrals, where the animals could more easily be killed. Following the mass slaughter, butchery was highly organized, probably with well-defined rules for the division of the spoils. The aim was to provide storable meat through the winter. Such organization has been recorded at Upper Palaeolithic sites from Siberia to France. As Paul Pettitt, a Palaeolithic specialist at Durham University, writes: 'People of the Palaeolithic come to the fore, not as the hot air of archaeological theorizing over the "individual" but as real people, preserved forever in the remains of their domesticity.'[16]

The black flint used by the Czech hunters was beautiful stuff, brought from a Russian source 150 km (94 miles) away. Other stone came from southern Poland, while radiolarite stone from Austria and Slovakia was used to make burins, specialist chisel-like tools used for working ivory and bone. Clearly these people were part of a very extensive social network – far more elaborate than the Neanderthals'. In the Gravettian world, people transported material such as amber and shells over hundreds of kilometres from sources in the Baltic, the Atlantic coast, the Mediterranean and the Black Sea. They incorporated these objects into artefacts, which were not only functional but must also have been entangled in a web of relationships, memories and myths.

### Dogs: the first domesticated animal

Some Gravettian hunters may have already domesticated the dog. Genetics shows us that all modern dogs are descended from the Eurasian grey wolf – hard to imagine if you could see the small bundle of fur (Lulu, a Shih Tzu) asleep on the chair next to mine. Genetic 'dating' suggests that dogs emerged from wolves over 20,000 years ago. However, such calculations are contentious. It is clear from skeletal evidence that domestic dogs were widespread by 14,000 to 12,000 years ago, appearing in Europe, the Americas and Southeast Asia. At Eliseevich in Russia the skull of a husky-like dog was buried near to a pile of mammoth skulls about 14,000 years ago. More recent discoveries potentially push man's best friend into a deeper past. At Goyet in Belgium the remains of a large dog were found that are said to be 31,000 years old. It is possible that there were many failed or short-lived attempts to domesticate wolves, which might explain the anomaly of Goyet and the absence of dogs in much of the Ice Age.

There is another evocative (if perhaps inconclusive) piece of evidence. In the Chauvet Cave, in the Ardèche region of southern France, there are the oldest human footprints in Europe, those of a child of about ten years old. Alongside are the paw prints of a canid slightly smaller than a wolf. Radiocarbon dating suggests these tracks were possibly made 26,000 years ago (see below). Were these the footprints of an intrepid Stone Age Mowgli and his (or her – in ethnographic observations it is frequently women who make pets of small animals) dog descending into a vortex of mysterious paintings?

Whatever date is finally decided, the dog is certainly the most ancient domesticated animal and provided humans with enormous help – as a guard, herder, hunter, companion, pack animal and source of warmth, and sometimes meat and fur.[17] Dogs spread around the world with their human companions – it has been argued that the domestication of dogs and their use as hunting animals gave modern humans the edge over Neanderthals in Europe, and contributed to Neanderthal extinction.[18] At Koster, Illinois, they were present 8,500 years ago, and genetic studies confirm that these American dogs were descended from Eurasian grey wolves, like every other dog on the planet – even Lulu.

### Social complexity

The Gravettian burials on the Continent remind us of Paviland, but some are even more complex. At Sunghir in north Russia, a mere 150 km (94 miles) south of the ice about 27,000 years ago, a cemetery included the burials of two teenage boys and a woman, who between them had as many as 13,000 mammoth ivory beads to decorate their clothing. Each bead, it is estimated, involved an hour's work. These grave goods suggest their young owners were important people in their community; their impacted wisdom teeth indicate that they were related. Particularly significant is the burial of a young boy, aged about twelve years. He wore a belt decorated with 250 arctic fox canines and was accompanied in the grave by two carved ivory animal figurines, one representing a mammoth, the other possibly a horse. Most remarkably, the femur of an adult human, its cavity packed with red ochre, had been placed alongside the boy. It seems that already human relics were being circulated and used symbolically, accompanying the boy with a remarkable collection of grave goods. In an egalitarian society adults can earn status, which may be reflected in the objects in their graves. However, archaeologists see richly endowed children as evidence of inherited status and the emergence of hierarchies in society.[19]

Another burial of this period found near Brno in the Czech Republic contained the skeleton of a man buried with more than 600 dentalium shells and 16 discs carved from a variety of materials. Most remarkable were the head, body and left arm of a human figure carved out of ivory. These were perforated so that they could be strung together to form a marionette. This may have featured in a puppet-show for entertainment, but more probably in a form of ritual ceremony.

In 1994, remarkable cave paintings were discovered in the Chauvet-Pont-d'Arc Cave, in the Ardèche. The portrayal of animals such as lions and rhino is brilliantly vivid. In 2015, a superb reconstruction of the cave complex and its paintings was opened near the original site – to which, for conservation reasons, access is limited. The excavators argue, from radiocarbon dates, that the earliest paintings were made about 36,000 years ago, which is remarkably old and stylistically seems out of kilter with other examples of similar art. There are approximately one hundred published dates, which makes the cave, according to the French, *'le mieux daté du monde'* (the best-dated in the world). This is misleading, however, as the vast majority of the samples came from a single hearth and charcoal on the floor – irrelevant to the dating of the art. There are only eight measurements on charcoal from six images, and for technical reasons these are contentious. Paul Pettitt and Paul Bahn have challenged the 'official' dating and proposed a working alternative chronology until more reliable samples are taken from the artwork itself. They suggest that the major cave-art production post-dates 23,000 years ago, and is possibly considerably more recent.[20]

In 2002, David Lewis-Williams, of the University of the Witwatersrand in South Africa, wrote one of the most influential (at least in English) books on the hunters of the Ice Age.[21] In *The Mind in the Cave* he argues that the spectacular cave art found at such sites as Lascaux, in the Dordogne, Altamira, in northern Spain, and Chauvet Cave should be associated with ritual specialists (often called 'shamans', the word for such people in the Tungus language of Central Asia; see page 201). Shamans undergo various types of altered states of consciousness brought about through repetitive dancing, chanting, drumming or sensory deprivation, or with the help of drugs. Shamans have the power and skills to explore alternative realities, in particular to enter spirit realms, which are usually perceived as above or below those of everyday life.[22] The rock walls of caves act as a kind of membrane that can be penetrated to enter the spirit world, often with the help of animals as spirit guides. So the bison, lions and horses painted on the cave walls are not meant to represent real animals out there in the landscape, rather the spirit animals who live beyond the rock surface.

The human nervous system, in various altered states, generates an illusion of out-of-body experiences, often associated with flying, crawling down dark tunnels or entering an underwater world. In recent hunter-gatherer communities, from Central Asia to Lappland, South America and South Africa, shaman-like figures are believed to be able to contact and communicate with spirits and supernatural beings, control animals, alter the weather and heal the sick. Lewis-Williams proposes that in the Palaeolithic caves we are witnessing the origins of religious ritual. In contrast, Palaeolithic art expert Paul Bahn emphasizes the complexities of human symbolism and motivation – there can be many reasons for practising cave art – and attacks sloppy analogies based on recent ethnographies in no uncertain terms.[23]

To return to the man buried near Brno with his puppet; he was accompanied by some of the paraphernalia that is often associated with shamans, such as a costume covered in shells, and twirling and glittery discs. Sometimes figures like the ivory marionette are used in shamanistic healing rituals. At any rate these very remarkable Gravettian burials occur over an enormous area of Europe from Paviland in South Wales to Italy and Portugal, Moravia and Russia. Modern humans scatter ideas, some of them strange, like seeds. And their artefacts become things with which to think and influence others.

With modern humans we see the appearance of the modern mind, the ability to empathize, communicate and tell stories through the use of language, and stretch the 'chains of social connection' across continents. Objects imbued with symbolism demonstrate the common links, alliances and cooperation between communities. Humans learnt to exploit a wide variety of plants and animals for food in different environments. They also figured out how to store or cache food for future use. So the hunters of Předmostí were able to stay in one place for much of the time. On the other hand, alliances with distant communities, indicated by exotic stone, shells or portable carved figurines, allowed people to travel with greater security. If ideas spread quickly, so did the humans themselves – through Eurasia to Australia, and eventually to the Americas and across the islands of the Pacific. The planet's most deadly hunters made an impact everywhere they set foot.

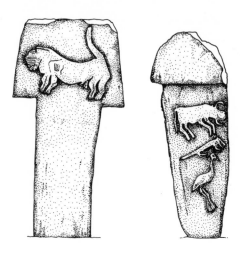

# PART TWO

## The first farmers

Carved pillars from Göbekli Tepe
(see page 87).

CHAPTER FOUR

# Gathering the abundance: Creating futures

## Gordon Childe, Revolutionary

In 1936 Gordon Childe produced a little book that made a big impact, entitled *Man Makes Himself* (gender awareness was not strong in the 1930s). This was no archaeological textbook, thick with descriptions of pots, typologies, house plans and the stuff that defined Childe's idea of archaeological 'cultures'. The editor of the leading archaeological journal *Antiquity* described the book as 'the most stimulating, original and convincing contribution to the history of civilization which we have ever read'.

In the dark days of the thirties and faced with the rise of fascism, Childe wrote *Man Makes Himself* to stimulate the general public. He wanted to emphasize the progress of humanity, taking the 'long and wide view' provided by prehistory.

Childe was fond of revolutionary analogies. During his travels in the Middle East in the early 1930s he had been impressed by the way ancient villages like Ur had grown into substantial towns. It reminded him of how the Industrial Revolution in Britain had generated the massive expansion of Glasgow, Manchester, Leeds and Birmingham. He saw this as a Darwinian success story, a demographic upsurge that would clearly stand out in the archaeological record. In *New Light on the Most Ancient East* (1934) he had explained his idea of two fundamental revolutions in humanity's prehistoric past: the transformation from food gathering to food production by domesticating selected plants and animals (the Neolithic Revolution) and the emergence of towns or cities based on trade and craft specialization, particularly metalworking (the Urban Revolution). Unfortunately, in Childe's view, the latter also elevated the power of priests, kings and pharaohs. This was a class for whom Childe, a Marxist and the son of a Victorian clergyman, had little time. He wrote, 'It is hoped that a consideration of revolutions, so remote that it is impossible to get angry or enthusiastic about them, may help to indicate the idea of progress against sentimentalists and mystics.' The mystics included German Nazis peddling notions of racial superiority.[1]

Professor Vere Gordon Childe (1892–1957), the eminent prehistorian who launched the concept of the 'Neolithic Revolution', here with a companion.

In the 1930s not all archaeologists agreed with Childe's Marxist philosophy, his emphasis on technology and society rather than the individual, nor his sympathy for Soviet Russia. Professor Grahame Clark, probably along with Gordon Childe the most distinguished prehistorian in Britain, retaliated with 'Russian archaeology: the other side of the picture', in which he pointed out the extent of state control over Russian archaeology (he called it 'Bolshevik propaganda') and Russian archaeologists. Several notable ones had been 'disappeared'.[2]

Nevertheless, Childe's approachable ideas helped to generate post-war research. The Neolithic was not now simply a period of new stone technology; it was associated with the transformation of humans from hunters to farmers. The big question was where and when it first occurred. American and British archaeologists seized the opportunity to head for the Near East (the countries of Western Asia from Iran and Iraq to Syria, Jordan, Israel, Lebanon and Turkey). From 1948, Robert J. Braidwood of the University of Chicago's Oriental Institute focused on what he called 'the hilly flanks of the fertile crescent' in search of the origins of domestication. Braidwood set new standards at the time by carrying out surveys in areas where the wild prototypes of wheat, barley and sheep were likely to have been found. He then selected sites (notably Jarmo in northeast Iraq) that might answer his research questions and over the next decade tackled them with multidisciplinary teams of scientists who specialized in the study of pollen, soils, animal bones and ethnobotany (the human use of plants).

Only a year after the start of Braidwood's project, another Chicago scientist, Willard F. Libby, published the first radiocarbon dates – the most significant breakthrough in the study of the past since the 19th century. While Muddy Waters, father of the West Side Chicago blues, laid the foundations for 1960s British pop music, another band of Chicagoans were putting the ideas of Gordon Childe to the test. They were armed with scientific techniques that came a generation too late for Childe himself.

### Digging mounds in Israel

When I was a student in the mid 1960s, the study of the 'Neolithic Revolution' was one of the most exciting and contested areas of archaeological research, and this was partly why I found myself in the Levant. I joined the excavation of an ancient settlement mound in Israel – Tell Lachish, southwest of Jerusalem – being undertaken by the universities of Haifa and North Carolina. Lachish had had an eventful history. Most famously, it was sacked by the awesome Assyrian army of Sennacherib in 701 BC. When English children learnt verse by heart at school everyone knew about 'The Assyrian', from Byron's 'The Destruction of Sennacherib', who 'came down like the wolf on the fold/ And his cohorts were gleaming in purple and gold.'

The biblical levels were relatively high in the stratigraphy of the tell. To explore the origins of farming (if they existed) would have meant digging much deeper, and through millennia of occupation. Not an easy task. In the Bible, Lachish appeared to be a city that was regularly sacked and whose rulers never died in their own beds.[3] Childe was not overly fond of archaeology as the handmaiden of history. The Bible gives us the name of important men and dramatic events – it is not the stuff of his prehistory: of social change, and economic, environmental and technological development.

In 1968, however, Lachish was all over the Israeli media. On a break from the excavation I hitchhiked to Herod's Masada, the fortress and palace that towers over the Dead Sea. The recent excavation, led by Yigael Yadin, emphasized a story of Jewish resistance and sacrifice. Masada remains a place of pilgrimage, Israel's national shrine. I was picked up by a lorry-driver, who looked at me quite carefully and then said, 'Your picture's in the paper.' Later in the day, after climbing up Masada, I arrived at the oasis of Ein Gedi, halfway along the

Dead Sea. I went into the kibbutz dining room, for the Shabbat meal. A group of kibbutzniks looked up from their chicken salad. 'You're in the paper,' they said, pushing over a double page spread that showed photos of the excavation at Lachish. The largest one featured me, 'an English hippy archaeologist', alongside Miriam, a conscript into the Israeli army, heroically and fetchingly wearing her fatigues. It was amusing to have five minutes of fame, but I was uneasy that in Israel archaeology was so closely linked with the creation of national identity. Politics continue to affect the study of early farming. While Israel still produces important new evidence, many other Middle Eastern countries are inaccessible, as a result of war and severe security problems.

From Ein Gedi I hitched a ride in a boat northwards, along the Dead Sea, reaching another tell site, Tell es Sultan, better known as Jericho, arguably the oldest and, at 258 m (846 ft) below sea level, the lowest town on Earth. This is also an oasis, whose prolific springs irrigate the soils of the Jordan Valley. Sheltered by the Judaean hills to the west and lying within the Rift Valley, Jericho's climate is tropical in summer and mild in winter: an ideal place to grow crops and fruit.

Childe's Neolithic hypothesis proposed that it was in this general area that the wild prototypes of wheat and barley were to be found, along with sheep and goats. He argued that a Neolithic Revolution had to take place where there were wild species of plants and animals that were capable of domestication. As the Urban Revolution developed first in the Near East, it was highly likely that the Neolithic Revolution preceded it. At the end of the Pleistocene, he argued, the weather changed across Eurasia and the Near East became desiccated. In this dry landscape, people, plants and animals would focus on oases. Proximity would help to domesticate all of them, according to Childe's 'oasis hypothesis'. If you wanted to find the origins of the Neolithic, Jericho should be the ideal place to look.

This was an idea taken up by the English archaeologist Kathleen Kenyon, who worked there between 1951 and 1958 with an army of diggers. Kenyon was what you might call a formidable woman, a fully paid-up member of the English intellectual establishment. She was the eldest daughter of Sir Frederic Kenyon, director of the British Museum, grew up in Bloomsbury and went on to study at Oxford University. Dame Kathleen, as she predictably became, honed her digging skills in the strictly controlled stratigraphic excavations of Mortimer and Tessa Wheeler, at the Romano-British city of Verulamium (St Albans) in the 1930s. After the war she worked alongside Gordon Childe at the Institute of Archaeology in London. Jericho was the site that made her world-famous and vice versa.

Kathleen Kenyon's heroic investigations had shown the potential of archaeology to provide data both to support and question Childe's hypothesis. She proposed that hunter-gatherers had first settled by a spring now at the base of the 'man-made tell' at Jericho, about 10,000 BC. These so-called 'Natufians' established a cult sanctuary and, economically, were in a 'transitional stage' towards domestication. The Natufians entered history thanks to another Englishwoman, Dorothy Garrod, the first woman to become professor of archaeology at Cambridge University. She excavated at Mount Carmel, near Haifa, in the 1930s and found evidence of foragers gathering wild cereals with flint sickles. She named the culture 'Natufian' after the local Wadi an-Natuf.

The Natufians at Jericho were in the process of establishing a permanent settlement of circular mud-brick houses with domed roofs, which Kenyon

The excavation of the early aceramic Neolithic stone-and-mortar tower at Jericho, which was attached to the inside of the settlement walls.

suggested were derived from an earlier tradition of temporary, slightly built shelters. These were big claims: for the first time in human history people were gathering plants, then domesticating them and living in sedentary communities. The shift towards plant gathering and processing was indicated by plant remains, such as carbonized seeds, and by the tools: polished axes and adzes; mortars and pestles; flint-bladed sickles and hammerstones. But there were no ceramic vessels; pottery, one of the icons of Neolithic communities, was not yet present. Hence, Kenyon called this phase at Jericho the 'pre-pottery Neolithic A culture' (PPNA). By 8000 BC the densely packed houses of Jericho were surrounded by a substantial wall, and most remarkable, a great stone tower built inside the wall, at its base 8.5 m (28 ft) in diameter and surviving almost 8 m (26 ft) high. At Jericho, Kenyon also found human skulls – covered with plaster and with cowrie shells set into the eye sockets – which people had cared for within their houses. Archaeologists would find this obsession with human body parts, particularly skulls, occurring again and again in proto-Neolithic and Neolithic communities.

In the 19th and 20th centuries, archaeologists and anthropologists were accustomed to referring to societies of hunter-gatherers, and even early farmers, as in states of 'savagery' and 'barbarism' – a model of society promoted by the 19th-century American sociologist Lewis Morgan and adopted by Marx, Engels and, not surprisingly, Gordon Childe. At Jericho, however, Kenyon's excavations revealed what appeared to be the origins of civilization.[4]

## Moving from food procurement to food production

Childe may have adopted anthropological terms like 'savagery', but this did not mean he had a low opinion of hunter-gatherers. He wrote of the 'dazzling culture' of Upper Palaeolithic Europe 'that supported a substantially increased population'. He understood that the mammoth steppe, stretching further south than similar environments today, was exceptionally productive, a walking larder of large, meat-rich animals. Upper Palaeolithic hunters might be classed as 'savages' by anthropologists, but they had produced superb art – cave paintings and sculpture – and lived in semi-permanent settlements such as Dolní Věstonice (see Chapter 3). They were overtaken by environmental change just as the mammoths and reindeer were. The herbivores' choices were limited: move in pursuit of familiar environments, or die. Humans were more adaptable and versatile.

According to the great Dutch naturalist and geologist Geerat J. Vermeij, 'the ability to create a future has been intrinsic to living things for billions of years'.[5] Humans, however, were more adept at creating futures than any other species. As we have seen, *Homo sapiens* crossed a communications threshold with the development of large brains, language and complex toolmaking. However, as Vermeij explains, 'humans are at one end of a continuum of emergent meaning and control, not one side of a steep ravine that separates us from the rest of the animal world'.

After the Last Glacial Maximum, about 14,500 years ago, humans were faced with dramatic change, the shrinkage of the mammoth steppe, the retreat and even extinction of their traditional herds, rising sea level and the flooding of productive areas. In much of northern Europe, tundra gave way to expanding forests, although the climate was less harsh. Childe believed that in the Middle East, there was drought and desiccation – hence his 'oasis hypothesis'. In fact, he was wrong. There was no desiccation at this time. However, he was right that this was a place to seek the origins of agriculture.

There is a question: if humans over the past million years had developed such big brains, communication and cooperation skills and technical know-how, why did we take so long to domesticate other species? It is not as if it is a new phenomenon, 'the cultivation of one species by another'.[6] In the past hundred million years on Earth, various animals have successfully adopted the farming way of life, notably the New World attine or leafcutter ants, who collect and shred the juiciest leaves from living plants to feed to domesticated fungi, which they rear in underground chambers.[7] Various animals, besides ants, have learnt the trick of domestication including species of termites, beetles, fish, snails and crustaceans. All, apparently, select domesticates for higher yields, easier handling, disease resistance and probably reduced toxicity. For any human gardener this sounds familiar.

For humans, the domestication of other species happened very recently in our history. Yet when humans developed this new lifestyle they did it almost simultaneously, and independently, in many different areas across the world. Modern humans spread across the planet from Africa to Southeast Asia, Australia, Europe and the Americas, relying on their abilities as hunter-gatherers. Yet over the course of a few thousand years, starting about 14,000 years ago, agriculture became the principal means of livelihood for the vast majority of human beings. We switched from procuring to producing food. From South and Central America, Western Asia and tropical Africa to southern and northern China and New Guinea, in environments as varied as seasonally dry grasslands and tropical rainforests, people began to exploit the different plants and animals that were available locally, particularly those, it should be emphasized, that had the potential to be domesticated. The demand for local domesticates, whether wheat and barley, sorghum, squash, chilli peppers, avocado, maize, millet, pulses, rice, taro, yams or sweet potato, spread rapidly. New foodstuffs have been moving round the planet ever since, and as a result of controlling its food supply, the population of humans on Earth has skyrocketed.

Humans had managed their food procurement for millennia: using fire to promote grazing or encourage desirable plants such as wild yams; and corralling wild animals, horses and reindeer with natural and artificial barriers. And, as we saw in Chapter 3, dogs had been domesticated by hunters as early as 14,000 years ago, if not earlier. Modern humans had the cognitive ability (probably for at least 100,000 years) to manipulate their environment and society in ways that Neanderthals and earlier hominins could not. During the Ice Age, however, climatic fluctuations, which could be rapid and extreme, and low levels of atmospheric carbon dioxide, which limited photosynthesis, made reliance on plant horticulture a very risky strategy. Yet soon after the Last Glacial Maximum, about 20,000 years ago, people began to diversify their food sources and rely more on wild plants. It was not that humans became more intelligent. Rather, circumstances changed and humans adapted. As the world warmed, environments had increasing productive potential and climatic conditions became much less variable outside of the tropics. Plant gathering and then agriculture became feasible strategies.[8]

The origins of farming and domestication can be studied in many parts of the world. Fortunately, archaeology is back on the agenda in China and the Americas have long been a major subject of study. It seems there were at least ten regions worldwide that independently developed domesticated plants (and animals) in the early Holocene, with the emphasis on staples such as wheat, barley and rye in Western Asia, rice and millet in East Asia, and maize, beans and squash in the Americas. Rice farming in China could be as early as, or even earlier than, domestication in the Middle East. The evidence is disputed and there are wild claims. However, domesticates of wild rice probably appear in the lower and middle Yangtze river valley or the upland slopes by the ninth millennium BC.[9] But it is in the Middle East/Levant (the countries and islands of the eastern Mediterranean) that archaeologists, palaeobotanists and zoologists have most intensively pursued the origin and development of early agriculture, and, on present evidence, this seems to be the part of the world where humans first adopted farming. It is from the Middle East that Europe and Britain ultimately derived the principal elements of their first agricultural systems.

## Varied diets and trophic levels

It is worth emphasizing that hunter-gatherer populations are generally small – the ecologist Paul A. Colinvaux made this clear with the book title: *Why Big Fierce Animals Are Rare*.[10] Big-game hunters like Neanderthals and modern humans living on the mammoth steppe had small populations for the same reason as polar bears, tigers and great white sharks. Ecologists express the food chain as a pyramid of usually four or five trophic (from the Greek *trophe*, meaning 'food' or 'feeding') levels. To put it simply, plants form the broad base of the pyramid at trophic level 1, with herbivores at level 2, predators at level 3 and carnivores or apex predators forming the peak. Even though real life is complicated by the fact that many animals have more varied diets – for example, wolves and foxes occasionally eat fruit as well as the flesh of herbivores – the basic rule is that the consumers at one trophic level convert only about 10% of the energy of the level below into their own organic tissue, so apex predators are relatively inefficient consumers and must be rarer than the species below them.

This is inevitable for tigers and great white sharks, but humans sometimes make a choice – with environmental changes and population pressure these top predators can change their habits and, for example, start to consume a larger amount of vegetable matter – leaves, seeds, nuts, fruit or tubers. Humans found that with the help of their technology – grinding, pounding and cooking – they could transform and digest unpalatable foodstuffs. If we move down the trophic levels and improve the efficiency of food production, the population can potentially rise.

So what is the benchmark: how many human beings were there in Eurasia at the Last Glacial Maximum, before the beginnings of the Neolithic Revolution? One reasonable estimate suggests an average population of one person per 60 sq. km (23 sq. miles).[11] These people would almost certainly have clustered in favoured terrains, such as the Dordogne region of France, with great barren lands between. Steven Mithen, Professor of Early Prehistory at Reading University, has made a stab at estimating the human population of the planet soon after 30,000 BC. He reminds us that no one then lived in the Americas, the climate was harsh in much of the world (reducing human lifespan) and that genetic evidence points to a population bottleneck of only about ten thousand modern humans alive 130,000 years ago. So his best 'guess' (his word) is one million people at 30,000 BC[12] (compare that with seven billion today). In many parts of the world, humans must have frequently faced extinction. In contrast, there were also the favoured areas, or refuges, of relatively mild microclimates, where people clustered and, because of the climatic restrictions, developed a more sedentary way of life.

## By the waters of Galilee

Archaeologists sometimes need to have luck on their side, and this happened in 1989 when a local man strolled along the shores of the Sea of Galilee near the village of Kinneret (in Israel the Sea of Galilee is known as Lake Kinneret). The water level had recently dropped dramatically by almost 4 m (13 ft), and in the newly exposed lakeside mud he spotted oval outlines marked out with charcoal. Israel is a country where archaeology is virtually a national sport, so the man reported his discovery. The site, known as Ohalo II, is now world-famous because it provides stunningly good evidence of how people lived during the late Ice Age, in a relatively favourable refuge, 23,000 years ago.

The charcoal-lined marks proved to be the remains of six huts of a hunter-gatherer camp. Shortly after the camp was abandoned the waters rose and silt enfolded the remains, preserving vast quantities of organic debris, wood, leaves, seeds and animal bones in the waterlogged, anaerobic conditions. Fortunately, the Ohalo II people were not house-proud and left behind the debris of their activities both in the hollow floors of their huts and outside. The huts themselves were simple, domed structures made from the branches of willow, pistachio, oak and tamarisk interwoven with smaller branches, leaves and grass. They are the oldest of their kind to survive anywhere in the world. In the hollowed-out floors, bundles of grass provided bedding, and there were fragments of twisted fibre from nets and rope.

The inhabitants used different parts of the site for different purposes. Just inside the hut doorways, where the light fell, flint knappers made micro-lithic blades for compound tools such as arrows and spears. As we have seen, stone tools are the stuff of Palaeolithic archaeology because they are durable and survive the rigours of time. The Ohalo tools are particularly interesting. Whereas in the ancient past hominins took a block of flint and made a handaxe or a few large blades, now a similarly sized piece of stone provided humans with dozens of microliths, small blades that could be stuck with resin into a spear or arrow shaft, or used to make a fishing harpoon. The flint knappers had learnt to be more productive, getting more versatile, multipurpose tools from a given quantity of stone. Eventually, microliths would be hafted to make reaping tools, with sawlike blades, to harvest cereals. These small versatile points were particularly good for hunting small animals. The Ohalo stone toolmakers also developed the knack of polishing the sharp edges of axes and adzes, which was more efficient than flaking them. Their techniques would appear in Europe, and in Britain, thousands of years later. Here are the roots of our polished stone axe.

Elsewhere in the camp they processed plants and stored food, and cooked around outdoor hearths. The huts had been rebuilt, which suggests that the Ohalo II settlement was not a brief seasonal stopover. The plant and animal remains also told a more complex story, and these were the great treasure of the site.

The environmental evidence indicates that the Ohalo II people lived in a varied mosaic landscape. The shores around the lake were a parkland with oak, olive trees, almond, pistachio and fig, familiar productive species around the Mediterranean today. Beyond there was savannah and woodland. These different ecological niches provided rich resources at different times of year. Hunter-gatherers are often assumed to be mobile, but here there were resources on the doorstep, if you knew how to find, catch and process them. These hunter-gatherers did not need to move regularly; in this favoured territory they had everything they needed to survive.

A man in his late thirties or early forties was buried at the camp. He had reached a good age by the standards of the time, and the pronounced musculature in his right arm suggested that in his prime he was no mean spear-thrower. He was the kind of experienced hunter who could advise the community on where to find gazelle, ass and wild goat in the open country, or wild cattle (aurochs) or boar in the woodland.[13]

Many years ago in spring, I travelled down the Israeli Rift Valley and into the Galilean hills with Martin Jones, an archaeobotanist, who has since become the George Pitt-Rivers Professor of Archaeological Science at Cambridge University. He pointed out the stands of wild grasses that were prototypes of today's domesticated cereals. The real drama was overhead: convoys of migrating birds – thousands of white storks, using the thermals of the Rift Valley to carry them out of Africa. Huge numbers of buzzards, kites and eagles accompanied the flocks. In his book *Feast*, Martin Jones suggests that the Ohalo II people used their knowledge of the stars to predict the arrival of the birds; that the moon and the Dog Star acted as important elements in their calendar, and inspired their myths. The Dog Star – Sirius – is one of the principal celestial players in Egyptian mythology, heralding the onset of the New Year and Nile floods.

The Ohalo people caught about eighty different varieties of bird, from marshland waders to raptors. They also took fish from the lake, harvesting shoals of small fish with nets. Plants formed an important part of the diet. By sieving out seeds, nuts, roots and berries from the settlement debris, archaeobotanists identified more than 140 varieties of edible plants. They did not know it, but these people were inventing the future. As Martin Jones emphasized, while many inhabitants of modern urban communities have a minimal knowledge of plant species, 'It is clear that communities remote from Western civilization have rich and complex taxonomies of nature.'[14]

The Ohalo II people were exploiting plants that would, in future, provide the staples of domesticated agriculture: grasses with small, hard seeds such as wild barley and wheat. Collecting this stuff was back-breaking work: not only were the seeds tiny, the grasses were relatively low and adapted to scattering their seeds in order to reproduce. At Ohalo II, there was a technical solution: the seeds could be shaken into woven baskets. The importance of simple, especially organic, artefacts on the road to civilization is often forgotten. Weaving baskets, ropes and nets allowed the Ohaloans to exploit the varying resources around their camp throughout the seasons.

At Lynford in Norfolk (another lucky discovery for archaeologists), as we saw in Chapter 2, Neanderthals focused on large, meaty animals. Isotopic studies across Europe confirm them as top predators consuming horse, reindeer and bison as well as mammoth, with an isotopic balance similar to wolves and hyaenas.[15] Modern humans, inhabiting the cold mammoth steppe of the north, also relied principally on hunting animals, although they exploited a wider range of species (and plants) than Neanderthals.

At Ohalo, in a less cold environment, people had access to a huge range of potential food species. This shift to a more varied diet has been called the 'broad spectrum revolution' (another revolution!).[16] It is sometimes assumed that this shift was an immediate precursor to the Neolithic Revolution, when domestication began to take place. Ohalo II has shown that, under pressure from climate, diminishing territories and growing population, modern humans can be incredibly versatile – even figuring out how to exploit apparently unattractive food sources, notably wild grasses, such as wheat and barley. That they processed the seeds into flour or porridge has been confirmed by the analysis of material adhering to the surface of a carefully set up large grinding stone in the camp (another indicator of more than short-term commitment to the site). The grinding stone was impregnated with the starch from cereals. This set in train habits of food consumption that may have had a direct influence on the way that plant domestication progressed.

Ohalo II has transformed our awareness of just how broad the food spectrum was at such an early date, especially of plants, birds and fish. Already, by 23,000 years ago, humans, with their technological development, had developed a food web much more complicated than the simple trophic levels described on page 74 – what Martin Jones has described as 'an entirely new engagement with nature in the course of the food quest'.[17] On the parkland/steppe, the Ohalo people occupied both the second trophic level (eating seeds, nuts, fruit and acorns) and the third (hunting gazelle and wild goat). By catching and eating raptors and larger fish, the feeding chain extended to six levels (humans ate big birds that ate smaller birds, that ate frogs, that ate insects, that fed on algae – reminiscent of the children's song, 'I know an old lady who swallowed a fly').

What Ohalo II tells us is that at a point when the climate was still relatively cold and dry (though worse further north) humans could exploit favourable refuges, squeezing their environment for all it was worth. They exploited every niche thanks to a detailed seasonal knowledge of plants and animals, on land, in the air and in water. Equipped with fine, microlith technology, they made compound tools, containers, nets and the grinding equipment to render unpalatable seeds edible. Nothing much could escape them. Such a wide variety of resources gave the Ohalo people the incentive to stay in one place throughout the year.

Anthropologists stress that all human societies, even the technologically and socially most simple, know that plants grow from seeds, that mighty oaks from little acorns grow. The Ohalo hunter-gatherers had most of the elements in place to develop domestication and farming, except the climate. As they gathered around their hearths the Ohalo people would have shared their knowledge with their families and neighbours, and passed it on to the next generations and to guests. (Mediterranean seashells were evidence of contact with the coast.) Although the climate meant that carbon dioxide levels were still low and sources of food could be erratic, these people had options and exploited them. Building alternative futures was a new evolutionary strategy.

When Dorothy Garrod and Kathleen Kenyon discovered Natufians, with their proto-Neolithic culture, they appeared, archaeologically speaking, to have come from nowhere. Thanks to Ohalo II we can now see them as part of a long human tradition of interacting with nature in the Near East over thousands of years.

## The ups and downs of climate

Since Gordon Childe's time we have a much more detailed picture of climate change after the Last Glacial Maximum and the beginning of the Holocene. In outline it goes like this. About 16,500 years ago there was a collapse of the great Laurentide ice sheet in North America. This thrust legions of clashing icebergs into the North Atlantic and locked Europe into the freezer (the last such Heinrich event). Then, about 14,500 years ago, both pollen and oxygen isotope records show that there was a sudden and substantial warming of the climate in Europe and Asia (the Bølling-Allerød Interstadial). In the Near East, this warmer, damper climate promoted the growth of plants beyond favourable refuges and the spread of ecological diversity over a wider area. The Garden of Eden was reopened. The hunter-gatherer populations expanded and the interaction with plants became even more 'thoroughgoing, active and culturally embracing'.[18]

The early Natufians (about 14,500 to 13,500 years ago) encouraged natural stands of cereals by burning off the competition, and by exploiting the cereals at different altitudes they could extend the harvest. At the Cave of Shukbah, at about 300 m (1,000 ft) in the mountains of Judea, Dorothy Garrod found evidence of wild cereal harvesting but few traces of processing or storage – the Natufians were probably collecting the late harvest at altitude and taking it to a lower, semi-permanent camp. To harvest cereals, the Natufians made the first purpose-made sickles, using microlith technology. Traces of silica on the stone blades confirm that they were used for harvesting cereals (which contain silica to discourage grazing animals). The adult Natufians had noticeably worn-down teeth as a result of a tough diet, which included gritty seeds.

Porridge or gruel may have been on the menu, as well as bread. At Abu Hureyra on the Euphrates, Gordon Hillman, a palaeobotanist formerly at University College London's Institute of Archaeology, identified 150 plant species. Isotope studies confirm the importance of plants in the diet at this time.

The early Natufians tended to settle in long-term camps, with circular huts, storage pits and heavy-duty grinding equipment. Some of their mortars were carved out of the bedrock, which suggests these were people who intended to stay put. So much so that they attracted unwelcome visitors, 'commensals' such as house mice – small animals evolved to live alongside humans in their stable settlements. And somewhere along the line (the date is uncertain) cats adopted humans and helped to control the mice as their part of the bargain.

## Natufian networking

Like the Ohalo II people, the early Natufians were also skilled hunters, catching sizeable animals: boar, deer, sheep and the massive wild aurochs, and their favourite, gazelle. More nimble prey, such as small mammals and birds, fell victim to their nets and arrows. The evidence of teeth and bones suggests that hunting parties brought animals such as gazelles back, all year round, to the camp. Some migratory species were culled en route, and during the winter waterfowl provided welcome meat. The populations of some prey animals were probably coming under pressure.

The Natufians themselves thrived, and not simply in terms of calorific intake. Beautifully carved bone sickle hafts, body decoration and ornaments such as exotic seashells, and elaborate burials in unprecedented numbers indicate lives that were socially complex and symbolically rich. At the Cave of Hayonim, in the hills of Galilee, Israeli archaeologists found Natufian burials inside and outside the cave. These people decorated themselves with large numbers of dentalium shells, some of which came from the nearby Mediterranean, only two hours' walk to the west. Many, however, were species found in the Red Sea, over 500 km (300 miles) to the south. Here again, as with the Langdale axe, we see people going to what seems like enormous lengths to acquire materials that are more easily or even locally available. Do these Red Sea shells have some deeper symbolic value? And were these objects physical expressions of social relations, friendships and alliances involved in the exchange of these shells, contacts along the routeway from the Gulf of Aqaba, through the Rift/Jordan Valley to Galilee? New settlement and ways of living must have generated new encounters between people. Networking is fundamental to humans, who with their big brains, could juggle with such complexities.[19]

In their large communities, Natufians were developing new ways of living. Disney Professor of Archaeology at Cambridge University, Cyprian Broodbank, echoing British Prime Minister Harold Macmillan, concluded that 'humanity in its modern guise had never had it so good'.[20] The early Natufians had taken the exploitation of wild plants, animals and marine resources to an unprecedented level. Any intensification from here could launch new future trajectories. We seem to be on the threshold of farming.

## The climate strikes back – and relents

Yet it was not to happen immediately. The climate had one more bad hand to play – and again it was dealt by the North American ice sheet. Now shrinking, its glacial meltwaters swept into the North Atlantic, switching off the conveyor belt of balmy tropical waters and imposing, from about 13,000 years ago, a twelve-hundred-year-long grip of fierce cold and drought known, rather charmingly, as the Younger Dryas. In Scotland, glaciers were on the march again (the Loch Lomond Readvance) and possibly human beings evacuated Britain completely. In the Near East life became a challenge. The Natufians, like earlier generations, had to resort to searching out the least inhospitable refuges – places such as Jericho.

Refuges, by definition, however, could not house what had been a burgeoning population. It seems likely that in these stressful times people close to the Mediterranean took to the waters in unprecedented numbers. There are no boats surviving in the archaeological record from this time, though there is other evidence for sea-voyaging as desperate migrants sought new, more favourable land. Cyprus, for example, received its first colony of humans, who celebrated by eating all the resident pygmy hippopotamus.[21] Voyagers also reached the Greek island of Melos and carried its volcanic glass, obsidian – even better than flint for making cutting tools – back to the Greek mainland. The seafarers who reached Melos had presumably explored many other islands, some with resources that leave no archaeological trace.

The Younger Dryas may have been inhospitable, yet it launched the first, full-blown seafaring expeditions onto the Mediterranean in the eleventh millennium BC. With desperation came new opportunities to find new places and exploit new resources. There is evidence at Hatoula, Israel, that the Natufians took to sea-fishing. What had been a barrier, an obstacle to movement, became a channel of communication, a new frontier. The peninsulas, islands and oases of the Mediterranean now had the potential to be part of a wider world. Hardship may have launched the first seafarers onto the Mediterranean, yet it was another key to a new future.

The opportunities returned as suddenly as they had been switched off when the Younger Dryas released its icy grip. From about 9600 BC temperatures rose by 7°C (12.5°F) in a matter of decades. This was the start of the Holocene, the most recent and relatively stable period (a warm interlude in the current ice age) in which we are still living. (Geologists and climatologists, however, suggest that we are currently living in a new era, the Anthropocene: an era influenced by humans – see page 388).

Conditions were similar to 100,000 years ago, except now, in the tenth millennium BC, modern humans had highly developed technological, cultural and social experiences. The Near East became warmer and wetter. Fresh water was abundant. Mixed forests of oak, lime and hazel spread up the slopes. In the Levant, almond, pistachio and terebinth dotted the savannah. As the warmer conditions persisted the great ice sheets of the north continued to melt – sea levels rose, at their peak, by almost 4 m (13 ft) a century. New islands were formed and coastal plains disappeared below the sea. It was this process that created the North Sea and the English Channel, making Great Britain an island by about 6500 BC.

It is important to appreciate that there is nothing inevitable about human 'progress'. We are not on a ladder, on which the only way is up – the Natufians learned that from the Younger Dryas. In the tenth millennium BC there was a coming together of factors that created the Neolithic farming communities of the Near East. As we have seen, modern humans had evolved large brains and developed language, and had control of fire and the technology of projectiles, traps, containers and food processing. They had, in places, developed settled communities with sophisticated belief systems. They had superb knowledge of plants and animals passed down through generations, and exchanged goods and ideas over long distances. Now, with a stable climate, better conditions for plant growth and a particularly fortunate collection of plants and animals capable of being domesticated, the conditions were aligned for a breakthrough in how humans would occupy the Earth.

## CHAPTER FIVE

# The seeds of farming

## The light bulbs of history

For Gordon Childe, humanity's shift to agriculture was 'the idea-driven revolution that created mankind'. He wrote in *Man Makes Himself*: 'Throughout the vast eras of the Ice Ages man had made no fundamental change in his attitude to external Nature. He had remained content to take what he could get....Soon after the end of the Ice Age man's attitude (or rather that of a few communities) to environment underwent a radical change fraught with revolutionary consequences for the whole species...in the last twentieth of his history, man has begun to control Nature.'[1]

This was an attractive thought, popular with historians in the succeeding decades, who liked the idea of 'Man' the heroic inventor, and history as a series of light bulbs, providing sudden and decisive illumination. It was also an excuse for many to ignore the first couple of million years of human prehistory, when, according to Childe, not much changed. The emphasis on sudden breaks and transformations has also led many archaeologists and prehistorians to pigeon-hole themselves into periods and regions, thus hindering the understanding of long-term change. The emphasis of research is often placed on the accessible, the visible and the spectacular.[2]

So, in trying to understand the emergence of domestication, it is important to appreciate that we are peering into a past that has only been partially illuminated. Childe was a great thinker and synthesizer – not a notable field archaeologist. He theorized his way to the Fertile Crescent (Western Asia) and so influential was his work that, as we have seen, many archaeologists literally followed him there. Evidence of early domestication was duly revealed, and the Fertile Crescent entered history as the heartland of farming.

We need to be aware that much still remains in darkness – unfortunately, many areas of the Middle East today are inaccessible war zones; in other regions a lack of spectacular discoveries has failed to attract archaeologists, who, in spite of what they often say, do tend to like a treasure trove of one sort or another. Even where there has been substantial expenditure of resources on attention-grabbing sites, the total sample excavated is usually quite small; for example, up to 2010 only 5% of the world-famous Turkish site of Çatalhöyük had been investigated and even that was to varying standards. In spite of the difficulties, significant advances have taken place in the past fifty or sixty years, particularly in our understanding of climate change, in radiometric dating and in archaeobotany, zoology, genetics and the hominin mind.

Graeme Barker, formerly the Disney Professor of Archaeology at the University of Cambridge, said of the debate about the origins of agriculture: 'The number of suggested causes that has been proposed over the years for why prehistoric foragers might have become farmers appears almost endless, with everybody joining the party including the lunatic fringe.'[3] So this is contentious stuff. Barker lists some of the causes proposed for the transition from foraging to farming: thirty-nine in total. For the sake of the sanity of my readers I will not go into them in detail, though some 'causes' seem to make more sense than others, such as broad spectrum adaptation (eating a wide variety of foodstuffs), climatic change, the domesticability of plants and animals, population growth and pressure, and technological innovation. However, there can be no one simple driver; many factors have to be taken into account, and these can be different, at different times and places. Even in southwest Asia large areas remain in the shadows, archaeologically unexplored. The discovery of the spectacular monumental complex at Göbekli Tepe, in southeastern Turkey (see page 87), shows how suddenly the spotlight can swing to new areas, shift the focus of archaeologists and promote new hypotheses.

Archaeologists need to thoroughly explore varied regions, with their settlements – large and small, permanent and seasonal – activity areas and botanical and zoological deposits, in the context of cultural landscapes. That way we may begin to appreciate the range of inventive ways that different people around the world have contributed to the story of farming.


**Why farm when we have the mongongo nut?**

In the 1960s, the usual explanation for the adoption of farming was a kind of 'common-sense' approach taking its 'obvious' benefits for granted: a more secure food supply, allowing people to settle down, produce more children, enjoy more leisure time and develop specialized activities. Why would you not choose to be a farmer?

I was digging in Israel in 1968 and I remember the impact of a book that appeared that year. It was called *Man the Hunter*[4] and it was another firework from Chicago, which, this time, questioned the Western, 'common-sense' attitudes regarding hunter-gatherers' lives: were they really so insecure, nasty, brutish and short? Richard Lee's work, in particular, altered perceptions of hunter-gatherers. He focused on the nomadic !Kung-San 'bushmen' of the northwest Kalahari Desert and showed that their year was highly organized – a scheduled series of seasonal movements dictated by the availability of food sources. The biggest surprise was that in this toughest of environments, the !Kung-San spent only a few hours a day gathering food. Mostly they slept, chatted to each other, gambled, told stories and visited friends and relatives and carried out trance rituals. As Robin Dunbar has more recently pointed out, social life is as important as food gathering if communities are to stay together.[5]

The !Kung-San knew that other people farmed but their attitude was 'Why bother, when we have the mongongo nut?' The bushmen have eighty-five species of edible plants available to them; however, the mongongo nut (*Ricinodendron rautanenii schinz*) is nutritionally remarkable. It accounts for 50% of the vegetable diet by weight, and an average daily intake of 300 nuts provides 1,260 calories and 56 g (2 oz) of protein per person, five times the calories and ten times the proteins per cooked weight of cereal crops.

Of course, the foraging way of life has certain implications: regular mobility is a necessity; mobility means having few possessions; and the natural bounty of nature (the carrying capacity) limits the population (births are spaced and infanticide common). However, the *Man the Hunter* scenario changed the common perception that hunter-gatherers teetered on the brink of survival, that they were vulnerable primitives, pushed and pulled by the forces of nature, rather than being inventive manipulators of their world.

*Man the Hunter* and other anthropological studies also seriously undermined the argument that farming was a better, obviously advantageous way of life. In fact, experimental archaeologists, at about the same time, confirmed the benefits of collecting wild plants. The palaeobotanist Jack Harlan, armed with a prehistoric sickle, harvested wild einkorn in Turkey. He calculated that it would take a family only three weeks to harvest a year's supply of their daily bread from the wild grass. So if gathering from the wild was so prolific, why turn to agriculture with all the extra work of soil preparation, sowing, watering, protection, processing and storage? In contrast to the previous 'agriculture is obviously good' view, archaeologists now assumed that farming must be a last resort for foragers, the only solution to pressures of climate change or population growth. Foragers thus fell into a web of work, obligation and dependency.

### Learning to live together

The !Kung-San live in small, relatively simple groups but this is not the case with all hunter-gatherers. Around the world circumstances occur that encourage the development of super-groups: larger, more socially complex communities with access to rich, broad-based natural resources, living in permanent or semi-permanent settlements, where group rituals and feasting occur, prestige goods are increasingly important and socio-economic inequalities appear.

Such communities existed in the recent past on the northwest coast of North America and in prehistory on the coast of Peru and in Japan – and we could also include the Natufians of the Middle East. The hardships of the Younger Dryas hit the Natufians hard. Their communities were fragmented, food became scarcer and population fell. For about a thousand years they were hobbled by the harsh climate, then suddenly the world warmed and became wetter. The rapidity of the humans' response in the Holocene suggests that the Natufian cultural and technical knowledge had survived through this long (in human terms) interval.

I have so far explained the importance of climate, technology, long-distance contacts and people gathering into larger, socially complex semi-permanent communities to exploit varied landscapes. Other archaeologists and anthropologists prefer to focus on the role of beliefs and rituals in the emergence of farming. The French archaeologist Jacques Cauvin, who excavated the Syrian site of Mureybit, questioned 'the naïve materialism of science'. Whereas the Natufians principally carved and modelled animals, particularly their favourite prey, the gazelle, the inhabitants of Mureybit in the period between about 9500 BC and 9000 BC made stone and baked-clay figurines of women. Some of these were rather abstract but their sex was clearly indicated. Over a longer period, the Mureybit people buried the horns of bulls within the walls of their settlement. While Cauvin used the term 'Neolithic', he prioritized cultural rather than economic change: the advent of divinities and the 'revolution of symbols', manifested especially in images of 'the Woman and the Bull'.[6] Cauvin argued that it was this transformation in symbolic thinking that created the preconditions for domestication.

Some archaeologists feel that Cauvin has overstated his case. It is a chicken-and-egg argument: which comes first, the farming way of life or the religious beliefs? Cauvin certainly has a point: there is more to the Neolithic than domestication of plants and animals. The *Thinking Big* team argues that domestication is the straightforward part, not in itself a giant step for human-kind familiar for tens of thousands of years with the natural world. The hard part was for hominins, with brains wired to living in communities of about 150, to learn to cope with much larger, more complex societies. To do this they needed new cultural mechanisms.[7]

About 9000 BC in the Near East, people increasingly began to live in settled communities. This was made possible, firstly, by the availability of a wide range of wild resources. However, a recent discovery in southeast Turkey at Göbekli Tepe has blown wide-open the argument about hunter-gatherer capabilities and the complexity of their communities. Traditionally, big ritual sites are associated with farmers, as we will see in Britain at Stonehenge. Foragers were supposed to step lightly on the earth, making little impact and certainly not building monuments. So what is going on at Göbekli Tepe? Here, foragers created a remarkable hilltop ritual centre, erecting T-shaped pillars up to 50 tonnes in weight and 6 m (20 ft) tall. On the pillars they carved relief sculptures: a bestiary of bulls, a lion, wild boar, a canid (a fox?), snakes, scorpions and a long-legged wading bird and ducks (see page 146).[8] Some of these carvings were in high relief, and there were three-dimensional sculptures of other animals. Some of the great T-shaped pillars were abstract representations of people: they have relief carvings of arms and hands down the sides, apparently wearing clothing, as if standing to attention. Behind all this must lie a highly complex mythology, the imagination of fertile minds surviving in stone. These megaliths were quarried nearby, yet their sheer scale suggests that hunter-gatherer communities came together to harness a substantial labour force and with a great communal effort created a prominent ritual centre of more than local significance.[9]

The German team investigating Göbekli Tepe has come up with the interesting idea that wild cereals were used here for brewing on a grand scale in large-capacity stone vessels. If they are right then this would be the earliest evidence for beer production in the world. Nutritionally, there is a lot going for beer and it is less perishable than many cereal products. Of course, its biggest advantage is that it is alcoholic and gets people drunk (what anthropologists like to call 'an altered state of consciousness'). There are also lots of animal bones at Göbekli Tepe, mainly from gazelle, aurochs and wild ass, often smashed to get at the nutritious marrow. As well as creating a cult centre, these foragers enjoyed feasting and drinking. No doubt there was some serious bonding going on. The remains of cereals are limited, though there are many grinders, mortars and pestles; those cereal fragments that have been found are from wild varieties of wheat and barley. These all grew in abundance in the hinterland of Göbekli Tepe, between the Tigris and Euphrates rivers, and were soon to appear in domesticated forms.[10]

Was Göbekli Tepe a new kind of place? A place with the power to draw together people who now lived in larger groups: a cultural response to the limitations of the brain? Did these substantial gatherings, and collective feasts at cult centres, also act as an incentive to intensify the production of cereals? Cauvin argues that this concentration of people, charged with new beliefs and ideologies, sparked the development of formalized agriculture. Most researchers prefer to see these things entangled together: beliefs and symbolism developing along with socio-economic change, rather than driving it.[11] During the long process of domestication, people's anxieties, fears and priorities changed; these were mirrored in their religion.

Sometimes an unusual and rare discovery can shed light into unknown corners, giving some sense of the varied communities that occupied the Near East between 10,000 BC and 8000 BC. Whereas waterlogging preserved the remarkable deposits at Ohalo II by the Sea of Galilee, not far away the Nahal Hemar Cave, above the Dead Sea, had a bone-dry environment. There, in 1983, archaeologists Ofer Bar-Yosef and David Alon came upon a remarkable collection of material. They found well-preserved woven baskets, wooden objects, nets, wooden arrows, a sickle and a weaving spatula. Some of these things were held together or waterproofed with the oldest glue found anywhere in the world, made from the collagen in animal skins and sinews, probably treated with an alkaline solution (radiocarbon-dated to 8310–8110 BC, four thousand years before the Egyptians are known to have done the same thing). This was one technological breakthrough. Another was the lime plaster used to line the baskets, and also make beads and figurines. Here, before the use of pottery, people had mixed materials together and heated them to create a chemical transformation. These were skills not usually associated with foragers.

Polished limestone masks found in the Nahal Hemar Cave, Israel, from about ten thousand years ago. Remarkable evidence of ritual dramas at the dawn of agriculture.

There were also other very special objects: plastered human skulls, like those at Jericho, criss-crossed with patterns made of the glue. More unusual were the polished limestone masks, in the form of weird human faces, with cavities for eyes and prominent teeth. These had holes perforated around the edges so that they could be tied on, presumably during ritual performances. It seems likely that the shamans or priests of a cult honouring the ancestors had deposited their ritual paraphernalia in this cave, evidence of the sophistication of their technology and religious lives.[12]

## Unpacking the Neolithic

Gordon Childe saw the Neolithic as a package: tools, domesticated plants and animals, settled communities and pottery, which certain communities, in a limited area, adopted relatively quickly. It is now clear, particularly thanks to more precise scientific dating techniques, that different elements were developed at different times and places over long periods. As a revolution it was prolonged. Foragers began to manipulate plants by suppressing competitor plants (weeds), sowing seed in prepared plots and watering plants. It is worth remembering that innovation need not be dramatic. We can arrive at a new place as a result of an accumulation of advances based on old technology. These advances need not be the result of planning and forethought.

Dorian Fuller, Professor of Archaeobotany at the Institute of Archaeology, University College London, and colleagues take the view that cultivation by humans was a new technique that had unintended consequences, in favouring genetic innovations in cultivated plant populations. When domestication traits appear, they themselves would encourage 'further human behavioural innovations', which 'in turn will have altered the selection pressures on genetic variants within the crop populations and selected for further genetic innovation in the cultivated species. So early domestication involves an entangled process of behavioural and genetic innovations.'[13] These pathways to domestication could have taken centuries or even millennia, involving plants that were 'semi-domesticated', and economies that occupied shifting ground between that of foragers and full-blown agriculturalists.

By the time archaeobotanists recognize domestication in the archaeological record – for example, from the presence of non-shattering cereals (grasses that have evolved not to voluntarily shed their seeds) – then the process of cultivation will have been underway for generations. Cultivation may involve preparation of the soil, irrigation and the application of manure. This results in further genetic changes to plants, such as the increasing size of the grains in cereal crops. These genetic changes have implications for the farmer. Cereals that cling to their seeds rather than scattering them are dependent upon humans for their dispersal. They now need to be threshed and sown. The farmer gains higher yields at the expense of extra work. Protecting crops from grazing animals can also stimulate genetic changes: cereals may ripen more evenly and the whole crop is ready at the same time. This puts the farmer under pressure and causes a 'labour bottleneck'; certainly, a period of intensive work. These protected cereals may also grow taller, which has implications for harvesting methods.

The unintended genetic consequences of cultivation led the farmer into the trap of extra work and this had to be scheduled. People still involved in foraging had to make difficult either/or decisions: in China, should they harvest early rice or collect acorns? In the Near East, should they gather the wheat and barley crop or hunt gazelle and onagers (wild asses)? In Britain, the farmer may not have had time to pursue migratory species of fish – if they were not already a taboo food.

Farmers seem to have discovered relatively early that soil preparation, manuring and careful sowing or thinning of crops led to greater productivity. But these activities spring the trap of extra work. Hence cultivation gradually becomes a high-pressure activity that draws the farmer away from wild sources of foodstuffs, which themselves may become scarcer in the competition for land. As Fuller and his co-authors state, 'farmers became increasingly entangled into more labour-demanding food-production regimes', notably soil preparation and post-harvest labour. The result was the increased reliability of the harvest, greater yields and control and ownership of resources by farmers. Humans, plants and animals were drawn into a new way of life that had some advantages and certainly some major disadvantages for all the entangled parties. But, like being enticed into a Venus flytrap, there was usually no way out, either for the peasant farmer, the domestic sheep or the non-shattering cereal.

At some stage foragers did become farmers. Yet farming covers a multitude of activities. Leaving aside the enormous differences between, for example, cultivation in the Andes, New Guinea and Thailand, even in Eurasia – with the well-known local domesticates wheat, barley, cattle, sheep, goats and pigs – the permutations are considerable. Here in the mountains of the Cévennes, where I live, I am surrounded by expanding forest. Jeannot, the only farmer remaining in the valley below, keeps goats, which live under cover, to make cheese. He also keeps sheep – the young ones are mainly culled for meat – and irrigates a small area of pasture so they can graze all year round. A few kilometres to the south, on the dry limestone garrigue, there are more sheep, although since flocks were hit by disease their numbers have declined; farmers planted vines and many abandoned farming altogether.

The seasonal movement of sheep from the lowlands of southern France into the mountains of the Cévennes for summer grazing. The *drailles*, or transhumance, routes have probably been in use for millennia.

It is also important to appreciate that food is not mere sustenance; it plays a large part in the identity of individuals and the community, and can have an emotional resonance. On the granite hills where I live, huge numbers of sweet chestnut trees provided the traditional local staple. An elderly inhabitant of our local village, Lasalle, has stressed to me, with tears in his eyes, the importance of the sweet chestnuts during World War II when they kept him and his family alive, and provided the country people with something to trade in the local towns. Today, the economic importance of sweet chestnuts is limited, but the symbolic contribution to local identity is enormous – loaves of chestnut flour are still sold and chestnut festivals are held every autumn. In the West, we pray: 'Give us this day our daily bread', but in other parts of the world maize, rice and fufu (powdered cassava, plantain or yam) are as significant from both a dietary and a cultural point of view.

Food habits die hard: the Ohalo fondness for ground cereals containing gluten and therefore suitable for baking bread may have set in motion a long-term continuity in food processing.[14] Foodstuffs also became closely aligned with rituals and cosmological beliefs. The ingrained habit of baking at the origins of domestication may have led to the selection of cereals, notably wheat and barley, which were appropriate for these long-established cultural traditions. In contrast, when the Chinese acquired cereal flour they boiled it.

As archaeologists unearth the evidence for early farming around the world they are finding that it is not straightforward; there is no simple 'boundary between foraging and farming'.[15] Some people adopt elements of the 'agricultural package' while continuing to forage; others make the transition rapidly; a few communities, having tried agriculture, revert to a foraging way of life (at least for a time). People's motivation for acquiring domesticates can be complicated: not merely economic or dietary. At Göbekli Tepe we can see a community experimenting with ritual activity, and plants probably played an important part.


### Recognizing domestication

So how do archaeologists identify the shift from foraging to farming? The principal clues lie in the physical remains of plants and animals, establishing if physical and genetic changes have taken place that mark them as domesticated. Robert Braidwood, an early researcher into domestication, slogged across the foothills of the Zagros Mountains in Iraq in the 1940s and

1950s in search of pioneer farming settlements (see page 67). At Jarmo he found a cluster of mud-built houses dated about 7000 BC and from the debris filtered out the fragments of domesticated wheat (einkorn and emmer) and barley. These people had also domesticated cattle, sheep, goats, pigs and dogs, domesticating the goat about a millennium after the first domesticated cereals appeared, further west in the Levant. As well as making pottery vessels, large numbers of figurines in the form of animals were manufactured. Now animals and plants were coming together.

Some species are naturally more amenable to domestication than others. Wild sheep live in the mountains. They are agile, flock together and will follow an older female. Early farmers could exploit this behaviour. In contrast, the gazelle, the Natufians' favourite source of meat, lived on the open steppe. Its nervousness, speed and flight instinct provided a defence against predators, but were not characteristics favourable to domestication. Animals need to be manageable so that breeding individuals might be selected to produce smaller offspring and improve temperament, meatiness or woolliness (eventually). Some of these traits can be seen in the bones found: for example, the shift from large wild aurochs to smaller domestic cattle. The age at which the animals died, and their sex, can also indicate the management patterns of domesticated animals. In dairy herds most males are slaughtered at an early age, to provide meat, and only a few are kept for breeding or as traction animals.

Bones do not always survive in the archaeological record, however, particularly in acidic soils. Sometimes archaeologists rely on 'proxies' to detect the presence of animals. In the 1970s and 1980s at the Oxford Archaeological Unit, my colleagues and I excavated a number of late prehistoric and Roman settlements in the Thames Valley in order to establish whether there was a settlement hierarchy, and related differences in subsistence patterns. There were lots of potsherds, coins and metalwork, but we were hunting biological evidence. At one site, which we believed to be a cattle ranch, there were very few bones for the simple reason that the herds had been marched off the site to market. The 'proxies' provided clues: plant pollen indicated open grassland; some weed species suggested that the land was overgrazed; and large numbers of dung beetles told us that the animals, probably cattle, had been there. To find their bones we had to look elsewhere, to the towns such as Corinium (modern Cirencester) where they had been butchered and eaten.

To recover evidence of crops in dry conditions also requires sieving of the soils. What is found can depend on how and where the crops are processed:

from harvesting to threshing, winnowing, storage and cooking. If cereals come into contact with fire they may be burnt completely and destroyed, but if some are carbonized then they can survive indefinitely in the ground. The application of heat, fortunately, is often part of the processing of nuts and cereal grains. Other plants – for example, leafier vegetables like cabbage (brassicas) – may survive in waterlogged conditions, such as in wells, waterholes or deep drainage ditches. Similarly, crops such as flax, where water is involved in the processing, usually turn up in wet conditions. Of course, in deserts dryness is the archaeologist's best friend, and in cold conditions organic material will survive in the deep freeze, such as the mammoths of Siberia or the so-called Iceman, Ötzi, whose five-thousand-year-old body, clothing and weapons were incredibly well preserved in an Alpine glacier (see page 357). In the Near East and Europe the conditions mostly vary between dry and temperate, though there are extremes – the Dead Sea Scrolls survived in the ultra-dry prehistoric caves in limestone cliffs overlooking the Dead Sea, as the ritual paraphernalia did at Nahal Hemar Cave.

Aside from the remains of plants and animals, the activities of farmers can be detected in other ways, notably their impact on the landscape. Polished stone axes and adzes were used to fell trees and dig out scrub; with burning, irrigating, making enclosures, turning the soil, grazing and even unwittingly introducing disease, farmers alter the landscape. By excavating settlements we might find what farmers grew, ate, traded or even offered to their gods, but techniques such as pollen and soil analysis can give us a better idea of the scale of their activities in the landscape at large. The appearance of agriculture in a pollen diagram is often marked by the decline of tree pollen as the forest is cleared, accompanied by the rise of arable weed species, or grass pollen where pasture develops. As agriculture becomes more expansive it is reflected in the composition of the pollen diagrams.

## The process of domestication

At sites such as Ohalo II it is evident that for thousands of years foragers had a sophisticated and detailed knowledge of the wild resources in their environment. Domestication occurs when these resources are cultivated, genetically and physically changed and ultimately come to depend upon their human manipulators. Domesticated plants, for example, have to be sown and tended by farmers. This marks the beginning of the Neolithic proper. As we have seen, the earliest domesticate, the dog, is not the product of farmers at all and appears well before the Neolithic (see page 60). The dog has probably altered more than any other species of animal, in body size and shape, and also in temperament and behaviour. The biologist and dog expert John Bradshaw of Bristol University wrote, 'dogs have coexisted and co-evolved with us. Essentially, they domesticated themselves as much as we domesticated them.'[16] Some ecologists have also made this point. An alternative view to the 'humans invented agriculture and new species of domesticated plants and animals' is that plants and animals adapted and evolved, exploiting the opportunities provided by the behaviour of *Homo sapiens*: according to the author Michael Pollan this was 'the grand co-evolutionary bargain with humans we call agriculture'.[17]

In searching for the roots of agriculture, archaeologists usually focus, as Childe suggested, on regions with wild plants and animals amenable to domestication. The Near East was particularly well endowed: its wild animals included sheep, goats, pigs and cattle, all of which flock or herd and are reasonably sociable. Today their descendants are our most prolific domestic animals. The Near East combines a Mediterranean climate (hot dry summers and cool wet winters) with considerable variation of altitude. It is the richest area in the world for varied species of wild, large-seeded cereals, and legumes such as chickpeas, lentils, peas and broad beans. These are genetically programmed to germinate and grow in the wetter seasons and lie dormant in the ground through the hot summer. (For a list of wild prototypes and their distribution, see the Appendix.)

A telltale fingerprint of domestication, which palaeobotanists immediately recognize, is the physical alterations in the plants themselves. Grains, being grasses, form spikelets with a seed inside and a husk or glume, which protects the seed from predators. These are attached to the plant by a short stem, known as a rachis. Wild grains have evolved a brittle rachis, which easily snaps when the plants are ripe and allows the seeds to scatter. This is a nuisance to human foragers: grab a bundle of ripe stalks, whack through it with a sickle and the seed shoots everywhere. Natufian harvesters got round the problem by gathering the wild cereals while they were still green and then drying or roasting the grass before grinding the seeds. Alternatively, holding a basket under the ears of the cereal helped to counteract the problem of scattering grains. With domestication, the rachis ceased to be brittle; the seeds held onto the ear and did not scatter on the ground when harvested. The ears of grain and the individual seeds also became larger and more attractive to farmers. And, for good measure, the ears ripened at the same time instead of in a delayed sequence, making the harvest possible, although, as we have seen, this was at the expense of extra work and timetabling.

Gordon Hillman and Stuart Davies suggested that, in wheat and barley, the genomes for non-shattering rachis would have been selected quickly, and that 'domestication could be achieved within 20 to 30 years if the crop is harvested near-ripe by sickle reaping or uprooting, and if it is sown on virgin land every year...with seed...taken from last year's plots'.[18] The tough rachis occurs from natural mutations, so harvesters cutting ripe ears with a stone sickle would have lost more brittle grains and naturally selected for the tough rachis in wheat and barley. However, this theory is not matched by the actual evidence. As better-dated samples have accumulated it seems that the manipulation of cereals went on for two thousand or three thousand years before non-shattering cereals became the norm.

On the pathway to agriculture foragers began by collecting wild plants, then probably sowed wild seed, created cultivation plots and watered or irrigated plants to improve growth in dry ground. Domestication was a long-drawn-out process, but it certainly had two results: the domesticated species – plants or animals – became dependent on human farmers; and productivity increased in return for increasing human labour. With more food, the human population could expand, and although there are some societies where farmers went back to foraging, most were entangled in a web of domestication that made it difficult to revert to the older way of life.

### The first farmers appear

We can see the development of farming from the results of important excavations in north Syria. The Natufian sites at Mureybit produced remains of wild barley, einkorn and lentils at about 10,500 BC. Nearby at Abu Hureyra, on the Middle Euphrates, Gordon Hillman and his team did detailed studies of the well-preserved plant remains. They suggested that after 11,000 BC, and the Younger Dryas cold, dry phase, woodland disappeared and the Abu Hureyrans also took to harvesting wild cereals as well as hunting. Rye shows signs of domestication as early as 10,700 BC and there is an increase in arable weeds. However, conditions probably proved too harsh and the site was more or less abandoned for a thousand years.

Then about 8500 BC a full-blown farming community appeared at Abu Hureyra cultivating domesticated cereals. If the population had been some 100–200 people in the earlier phase, now in the 'proper' Neolithic (Abu Hureyra 2) it rose to several thousand. Here we see for the first time the implications of farming for the human population. Abu Hureyra is, of course, only one well-excavated site. Archaeologists have, understandably, a habit of latching on to the known and drawing conclusions from it. As I have explained before, real life was probably more complicated. Recent DNA studies of wild barley provide a warning. Peter Morrell and Michael Clegg of the University of California compared 10,500-year-old barley from the Near East with 9,000-year-old samples from Central Asia (1,500–3,000 km/900–1,800 miles further east). They then compared these with wild barley growing in Central Asia and found that the domesticated crops most closely matched the local wild species.[19] This suggests that domestication of barley occurred at least twice.

In fact, from the east Mediterranean to Pakistan we have a huge area, barely explored, in which people were adapting and experimenting with plants and animals 12,000 to 10,000 years ago. Lacking massive supplies of meat on the hoof, these communities learnt to exploit plants and smaller animals. Those that cooperated with humans entered a mutual bargain. We call this farming.

Martin Jones and his colleagues also point to the role of interaction, trade or exchange.[20] We can see that the Rift Valley provided a routeway for people as well as migrating birds. Other routes and networks are indicated by the spread of identifiable materials, particularly the volcanic glass obsidian, used for millennia to make fine stone tools. Obsidian is not only beautiful and practical (if you can knap stone tools), but also very helpful for archaeologists. Firstly, it has relatively few sources, coming from youngish volcanic rocks. Secondly, it has a distinctive chemical fingerprint so the source can be identified. Finally, it was desirable: Stone Age people clearly loved obsidian. In Anatolia (modern-day Turkey) there were two major areas where obsidian could be found: northeast of Çatalhöyük and further east towards Lake Van. The central Anatolian obsidian is found in sites in the Levant such as Jericho and Beidha, while the eastern obsidian found its way into the Zagros Mountains and the Tigris and Euphrates valley (modern-day Iraq). These were, probably, long-established lines of communication.

Professor Jones suggests that seeds would have been carried along the obsidian routes, as items for exchange or gift-giving. In this way people would have experimented, trying out plants in new environments. Over several millennia plants moved to and fro across Eurasia and into Africa. This included starchy cereals such as millet, which are fast-growing, multi-cropping and help the farmer to reduce the risk of crop failure. Some foods are also high status, associated with elites like oysters and caviar today; others are presumed to be medicinal or even have a religious function. They are desirable acquisitions for social reasons.[21] Some of the most valued plant products, such as tobacco, opium and frankincense, have no food value, and may even be harmful.

At Jericho, Kathleen Kenyon found some of the earliest evidence of the pathways to domestication (see Chapter 4); since then the paths have become a little more distinct. Over several millennia humans, plants and animals increasingly interacted. In the Zagros Mountains, people first herded sheep and goats: the number of animals increased as their size decreased. In other areas, like Jericho itself, people planted emmer and hulled two-row barley, or peas and lentils. Later, cattle and pigs joined the mix of domesticates. Around the Near East people traded and swapped different species, although increased rainfall and warmer conditions also promoted the spread of the wild cereal prototypes across the Near Eastern steppes.

About 8500 BC the essential elements of farming came together and, in the words of Graeme Barker, 'there was a veritable explosion in agricultural settlement throughout South-West Asia and beyond to the west and east'. The human population boomed. Settlements increased in size; some, such as Jericho and Beidha (Jordan) and Abu Hureyra (Syria), with as many as two thousand occupants.[22] Beidha is one of the best preserved of these permanent agricultural settlements and it illustrates the typical features of the new farming communities. Its square stone buildings survive to roof height, some with plastered floors and internal hearths. The storage pits and silos suggest that work and consumption was based around the household unit. People were skilled at flaking stone tools – microliths for sickle blades, tanged arrowheads, axes and fine tools for leatherwork and carpentry. Stone querns and rubbing stones were necessities for processing grain. Large communities needed to be near water, and chose to plant cereals in moisture-retentive alluvial soils.

Big, fierce Neanderthals and early *Homo sapiens* got by on a diet that included considerable quantities of meat; now Eurasian farmers thrived on porridge, bread and lentils. The new way of life was not without its problems, yet it would take over the world.

CHAPTER SIX
# Entangled in the farming web

## Warming up and taking off

In the past half-century or more archaeologists have successfully shovelled, trowelled and sieved into the past to reveal the origins of farming across the world, notably in southwest Asia. More recently, thanks to discoveries like Ohalo II, it has become clear that the Neolithic Revolution was not a sudden transformation; instead there was a complex and lengthy series of interactions between humans, plants and animals. From about 13,000 BC, in a period of warm climate, the Natufians developed systems of foraging that 'verged on husbandry'.[1] The counterpunch delivered by the cold snap known as the Younger Dryas (around 11,000–9500 BC) was both a setback and an incentive to adapt, migrate and exploit new territories and focus on more intensive ways of managing resources. People had to make many tough decisions to survive in a world of dramatic climate change.

When the climate suddenly warmed again about 9600 BC at the beginning of the current interglacial – the Holocene, in which we are living today – some communities in the Near East chose to manage cereals and livestock more intensively. They were helped not only by climatic warming, but also by a 50% increase in the amount of carbon dioxide in the atmosphere. Plants absorb carbon dioxide, mostly during the day, to promote photosynthesis and so create their own food from the sun's energy. Modern experiments confirm that elevated carbon dioxide levels speed up the growth of important food crops such as wheat, rice and soybeans. Significantly for the Middle Eastern farmers, increased carbon dioxide levels also reduce a plant's usage of water.

So in the tenth millennium BC some Near Eastern communities were heading rapidly towards full-blown agriculture. The move to cultivation required little innovation because the 'toolkit' was already in place: foragers had exploited the natural cycle of plants and animals for millennia.[2] However, not all the principal elements of farming were to be found in the same place (see Appendix). Cereals such as einkorn and emmer wheat were probably first domesticated in southeastern Anatolia and grown in the Jordan Valley in the mid tenth millennium BC. Several centuries later, hill people in the

Zagros Mountains in Iran shifted from hunting and herding sheep and goats to full-scale domestication. These animals were rapidly carried to farming communities further afield.

As previously explained in Chapter 5, restricted archaeological exploration across Western and Central Asia limits our understanding of this probably complicated story, but some claims for the independent development of agriculture beyond the conventional 'heartland of domestication' in the Levant and Mesopotamia (the land between the rivers Tigris and Euphrates, principally modern-day Iraq) are based on assumptions that have since proved wrong. For example, so-called 'goats' in the Mediterranean areas to the west were, in fact, ibex, an animal that has never been domesticated. Wild sheep, identified on some Mediterranean islands, have proved to be domesticates gone feral. Genetic studies confirm that cattle, goat and sheep were all first domesticated in the Near East and spread from there. As were pigs – although they continued to interbreed with wild boar in areas subsequently colonized by farmers. Wild einkorn is found in the Balkans to the west of the 'heartland', but genetic studies confirm that domestication first occurred in southeast Turkey, alongside emmer wheat, and provided the seed for cereal farming.[3]

What is clear is that in the tenth millennium BC people lived in interesting times: they swapped new ideas, exchanged materials, experimented and created new, not necessarily predictable, futures. The law of unintended consequences was always present. People appreciated the qualities of different species: for example, goats will eat almost anything, pigs consume domestic rubbish and barley is more tolerant of dry-upland steppe soils than wheat. By 8500 BC they had put together a mixed farming package that would prove to be incredibly powerful. In varying forms it spread across Eurasia and transformed human societies.

Mixed farming developed in southwest Asia in part because of the presence of a particularly suitable cohort of wild plants and animals, a long tradition of interaction with humans and the onset of a period of stable, mild climate. But why did this way of life spread into less favoured areas and oust the foraging lifestyle?

One possible answer is population growth. This is another contentious 'chicken-and-egg' subject. Which came first: population rise or farming? Did one promote the other? I am not particularly concerned to inflict the arguments on readers. However, the archaeological record strongly suggests that settling down promoted human fertility. There was a trend to settled communities before full-blown farming, but with farming many settlements expanded in number and in size. Abu Hureyra, for example, grew to 16 hectares (40 acres); to the south, 'Ain Ghazal in the Jordan Valley doubled in size to 10 hectares (25 acres), and Jericho's population may have reached two thousand souls (see page 98).

Mobile foragers tend to restrict their fertility. Mothers carry their youngest and wean them relatively late. Breastfeeding promotes the hormone prolactin, which tends to suppress fertility, so the gap between forager children is usually greater than that between those of agriculturalists. In forager communities more children meant more mouths to feed and bundles to carry as they moved from camp to camp; for farmers, extra children meant extra labour to extend cultivation and look after animals and ageing parents. Agriculturalist mothers could also wean their children at a younger age because they had available mushy, easily digestible porridge-type foods that could be made from cereals. When the milk of sheep, goats and cattle came on stream the diet of both children and adults improved, even with the risk of tuberculosis (though for the development of lactose tolerance, see page 209).

## Out of Eden

Early farming, however, was not all burgeoning fertility and rejoicing while bringing in the sheaves. Since the 'Man the Hunter' conference more than forty years ago, it has been fashionable among many researchers to shift from the Hobbesian view of foragers (life was 'nasty, brutish and short') to a more Rousseau-ish image – the 'noble savage', in touch with her environment, gathering nature's bounty. Recently, the downside of farming has been more widely recognized – and perhaps overplayed. Yet this is hardly a new approach. The authors of Genesis – the biblical origin story – describe a fecund and bountiful Garden of Eden, where Adam and his 'woman' (Eve is only named later) can simply gather their food. Then they eat of the forbidden fruit of the Tree of Knowledge, and a furious deity sentences them to a life in the vale of tears. The first foragers must now settle for hard toil: they are sentenced to a lifetime of farming. God gives it to them straight: 'Cursed is the ground for thy sake; in sorrow shalt thou eat of it all the days of thy life; Thorns also and thistles shall it bring forth to thee; and thou shalt eat the herb of the field; In the sweat of thy face shalt thou eat bread, till thou return unto the ground' (Genesis 3:17–19). The authors of Genesis, probably living in Canaan, in the Levantine lands between the Mediterranean and the River Jordan where agriculture began in the tenth millennium BC, saw farming as a life of continuous and repetitive hard work, a treadmill that ended only with death. This is a long way from later Christianity's sacramental image, where 'we plough the field and scatter the good seed on the land'.[4]

The harsh view of the Neolithic in Genesis is echoed in another bible, that of Marxist anthropology written by Friedrich Engels in 1884, *Origin of the Family, Private Property and the State.* For Engels, 'the domestication of animals and the breeding of herds...developed a hitherto unsuspected source of wealth and created entirely new relations' – thanks to farming we got private property, men obsessed with accumulating, keeping and passing on wealth – and 'the world historical defeat of the female sex'.

If that was not enough, recent commentators have emphasized other disadvantages of farming. For example, living in close proximity to live animals increases the chances of catching new diseases. William McNeill's influential book *Plagues and Peoples* could scare us to death. He tells us that we share forty-two diseases with pigs, forty-six with sheep and goats and twenty-six with chickens (probably more since he wrote in 1976). The media frequently carry horror stories of new strains of flu hitching a ride with a human host, usually on a plane from China to North America or Europe. We can thank farm animals for measles, brucellosis, smallpox, chickenpox, influenza and tuberculosis. All have emerged from the Pandora's Box that is farming.[5] Farmers in the Old World have, over millennia, adapted to many of these diseases, so that some of them are now seen as relatively mild infections of childhood. The indigenous people of the New World and Australia discovered, to their cost, the scourge of these Old World pathogens, which scythed through populations that had not had the time to develop immunity. At present it is difficult to estimate the impact of these zoonotic (literally in Greek, 'animal disease') infections when they first appeared among early, often densely crowded, farming communities.

Farmers had more than infectious diseases to contend with: hard labour brought on arthritis, and women developed the first repetitive stress injuries from grinding cereals.[6] A mushy carbohydrate diet brought on some of the earliest known cases of dental caries – though bad teeth became much more prevalent with the widespread use of industrially produced sucrose in the modern world. We tend to underestimate the significance of poor oral health, and the role of such a soft sticky substance as bread in promoting it.[7]

In harsh contrast to the soft, starchy food, flour processed on some stone querns contained grit, which wore teeth down dramatically and promoted abscesses. However, early farmers were not stupid – when hard, smooth, grit-free stone was available for grinding they used it.

The farming life took its toll: farmers became physically smaller as they adapted to sedentary life and continuous labour. Their children often died at birth or during infancy. The division between men and women probably became more pronounced as women were tied to the daily grind of the kitchen and the household while men worked the fields or hunted. For Samson, grinding corn was an exceptional punishment; for Neolithic women it was a routine chore.[8] To quote the Cambridge University archaeologist Cyprian Broodbank: 'Farming reflected an entrapment as much as a triumph and by boosting population to levels that could not be sustained in any other way, it caused the spectre of future crises should conditions deteriorate.'[9]

Peter Bellwood, Professor of Archaeology at the Australian National University, makes an interesting observation. Usually, he points out, the concept of the Neolithic Revolution is applied to the earliest evidence for the domestication of plants about 9000–8500 BC. However, 'the real turning point' in the revolution was the spread of agriculture beyond its homeland. After 8000 BC 'events came together' to blow the lid off the agricultural pressure cooker.[10] A major factor was the expansion of both human and domesticated animal populations. Specialized sheep and goat pastoralism developed alongside the cultivation of legumes on a large scale, which provided animal fodder. Flocks now relied on humans to feed them. By 6000 BC farmers skilled in the use of irrigation had colonized the Tigris/Euphrates lowlands. These trends laid the foundations for the earliest cities such as Uruk and the great Mesopotamian civilizations of Sumer and Akkad and the development of writing.

At the same time, farmers live with risk. Their actions, as we saw in the previous chapter, can have unintended consequences. The disastrous US agricultural policies on the Great Plains led to the dust-storms of the 1930s. The plight of Okie share-croppers has been engraved into the memory by John Steinbeck's book *The Grapes of Wrath* and even more so by John Ford's film of the same name and Dorothea Lange's photographs. The soil blew away from 400,000 sq. km (100 million acres) in Oklahoma and neighbouring states, and 3.5 million people went with it. Many, like the Joad family in *The Grapes of Wrath*, took to their beaten-up jalopies and headed down Route 66 to California.

As Peter Bellwood emphasizes, early farming had its environmental consequences. At 'Ain Ghazal, in the Jordan Valley, as on the Great Plains, agriculture, increasing population, a fragile ecosystem and decreasing rainfall combined disastrously at about 6500 BC. As mentioned earlier, the 'Ain Ghazal community had grown rapidly in size: woodland was denuded, cereal agriculture declined and pasture was overgrazed. Increasing numbers of children died young, probably malnourished. Around 'Ain Ghazal other communities abandoned their settlements and left for more promising futures – perhaps in northern Arabia. Other regions had similar problems. Abu Hureyra shrank dramatically and in northern Syria communities in drier areas abandoned their homes.

So, as on the Great Plains, floods of optimistic farmers can be followed by environmental degradation, depopulation and migration. A shift to sheep and goat herding in the Near East may have also promoted increasing mobility in previously settled communities. After about two thousand years of farming a combination of pressures, cultural and climatic, propelled the agricultural revolution out of its heartland and into Egypt, Europe and Central Asia and towards the Indus Valley (present-day Pakistan). The Neolithic Revolution was on the move.

## Invaders or indigenous adopters?

An earlier generation of archaeologists was attached to the idea that invasions and migrations were a major cause of cultural change; hardly surprising when the imperial powers of Europe, like Rome two millennia earlier, had invaded, swamped and controlled weaker peoples across the world. As a result it was usually assumed that numerically and culturally superior agriculturalists gradually spread out, advancing like an unstoppable wave across Eurasia, transporting their cargo of domesticated plants and animals, clearing the forests and transforming the land into arable and pasture.

During my career as an archaeologist the tide turned: it became the norm to assume that local foragers took it upon themselves to adopt the farming way of life. I have always had difficulty in accepting this orthodoxy. After all, in recent centuries many hunter-gatherers have lived alongside alien farmers – in the Americas, Central Asia, Central Africa, Southeast Asia and Australia. These communities may maintain different ways of life, yet have something to offer the other, for example, exchanging agricultural and pastoral products for furs, bush-meat, ivory, medicinal plants, honey, fish, craft products, seasonal labour, slaves – even wives. Many foragers have a rather biblical view of farming – it's too much like hard work, it's boring and not a proper job for a hunter. Having said that, across the world most foragers have become farmers, as their way of life has come under pressure – through loss of habitat and decline of their prey species, through decimation by disease, by force or many other less obvious factors. For example, one African forager group claimed that they converted to cattle pastoralism because without cattle, the standard commodity required to pay a bride-price in the region, they could not acquire women. I will return to this contentious subject as we cross Europe into the British Isles. It is clear, however, that in the Near East we are dealing with forager groups who had transformed themselves into farmers and then spread into neighbouring areas, usually relatively sparsely populated, introducing new species and a new way of life. At the same time, interaction with foragers could create vibrant new cultures.

## The Neolithic in 3D

The results can be seen most dramatically at a world-famous site in central Turkey – Çatalhöyük in the Konya Plain of Anatolia. Çatalhöyük is not the only, or even the earliest, Neolithic site in central Turkey,[11] but it is the most dramatic, and one of the largest – a real mega-site. This mound (*höyük*), 21 m (69 ft) high and covering 13.5 hectares (33.5 acres), has been the subject of two large-scale excavation campaigns: the first in 1961–65 by James Mellaart, and the current, ongoing excavations (since 1993) by an international team led by Ian Hodder of Stanford University. Mellaart's bravura excavations, rapid and incisive, revealed about 160 buildings (400 rooms) spread through 18 levels of occupation (these successive building levels created the *höyük*, or tell). In contrast, the Hodder approach is meticulous, analytical and inevitably slow. The mound is peeled with enormous attention to detail. Nevertheless, it is important to appreciate that only a little over 5% of this huge site has been excavated – so generalizations must be modified by the unknowns that still lie within the mound.

I met James Mellaart in 1967, when as a student I attended seminars about his research. He had just published an amazing book, *Çatal Hüyük: A Neolithic Town in Anatolia.* In studying the Neolithic we were accustomed to stone tools, potsherds, bones and seeds, spiced with megalithic monuments: mostly dry, colourless and forensic stuff – the chaff of the past. Here, suddenly, a Neolithic community came to life. These people had wild imaginations and lived in a world of symbols – coloured and in 3D. Inside their packed buildings were models or reliefs of wild animals, particularly paired leopards; bulls' heads and horns (bucrania) emerged from their walls, and skulls of foxes and weasels were embedded within them; female breasts had implanted animal skulls. There were paintings of vultures and headless corpses; men clad in leopard skins baiting a huge bull (see page 147); even an image of the settlement itself and the neighbouring volcano at Hasan Daği. No wonder Çatalhöyük was the most famous new excavation in the world in the mid 1960s.[12]

The settlement at Çatalhöyük emerged from about 7400 BC on a fan of fertile alluvial soil close to a water supply in an area where hunter-gatherers still roamed the land. Its rapid growth into a massive mounded settlement – more than 1 million cu. m (35 million cu. ft) of material were piled up – could be explained partly by incoming farmers successfully recruiting the local population. In eastern and central Anatolia there were many small Neolithic settlements with estimated populations of about 250–300 people, often only a few kilometres apart – perhaps at Çatalhöyük several such groups fused together. One advantage is that with such a large population the settlement could be endogamous – meaning people married within their own community. (I cannot begin to remember how many stories, novels and films feature the problem of isolated farmers seeking wives, but *Seven Brides for Seven Brothers* and *The Rape of the Sabine Women* spring to mind.)

As Robin Dunbar points out, big communities also need ways of dividing themselves into smaller groups in which people can interact at a personal level.[13] Division into neighbourhoods, clans or religious societies would be possible solutions at Çatalhöyük. Microliths in the lowest levels of the mound indicate the presence of hunter-gatherers and the obsession with wild animals suggests the hunters' mythology took hold of the community. As the *Thinking Big* team proposed, such powerful mythology, beliefs and rituals would have acted as the glue binding together the potentially fissile community.

The farmers raised wheat (emmer and einkorn), lentils and peas, which were stored in smallish household bins. Isotopic studies of human bones confirm the importance of plants in the diet. Wild sheep and goats had previously been managed and herded in Neolithic Anatolia – for example, at Aşikli Höyük – but at Çatalhöyük these animals were fully domesticated and provided the majority of the meat diet. Çatalhöyük became home to full-blown, dedicated farmers, yet their imaginations dwelt on the wild and the savage. Paintings and the bucrania show the importance of wild cattle (aurochs). In one image, young men wearing leopard skins seem to goad an enormous bull. Is this a mythical scene, a portrayal of some male initiation rite or the display of bravery, agility and marriageability? Even today, my local paper in the south of France regularly reports on the sport known as *la Course Camarguaise* where young men dressed all in white compete to grab rosettes from the horns of large, fast and agile cattle.

The cattle bones on the site are also from wild animals. Beef was consumed to a much lesser extent than mutton, but it was the preferred meat for special feasts. Dogs lived at Çatalhöyük, but not in the houses. Gnawed bone evidence suggests that they stayed outside. (Hardly surprising – my farming and hunting neighbours regard me as a soft city-type for letting my dogs sleep in the house.) The Çatalhöyük wall paintings show dogs in hunting scenes with humans, and isotope analysis indicates that their diet was similar to that of their owners. The dogs probably squabbled over leftovers and prowled the rubbish dumps.

The community was well embedded in the daily grind of farming, yet its imagery tells another story, emphasizing wild animals and what seem to be elements of danger and violence. Mellaart interpreted some of the closely packed, mud-brick, Lego-like buildings that contained cultic elements as shrines. Ian Hodder's team, however, suggests that all these buildings were houses. Yet it is evident that some contained more elaborate cultic elements than others. Through time these buildings accrued symbolic power and greater ritual significance. The famous French anthropologist Claude Lévi-Strauss described this phenomenon.[14] Such buildings become 'lineage houses' and reflect the acquisition of status and wealth among some sections of society. Out of the Neolithic obsession with ancestors and lineage emerged an increasingly hierarchical society.

In the early stages, especially, Çatalhöyük seems to have been an egalitarian and tolerant place. A community where people rubbed along very well. The flat roofs provided spaces for everyday activities and were the means for movement around the settlement. Entry to the houses was through holes in the roof, accessed by ladders. Inside, household activities took place on the south side of the main room. This was the kitchen area with its oven and hearth. Sometimes caches of obsidian were kept beneath the floor. The other, northern, part of the room was cleaner, less charcoal-strewn. Instead it was

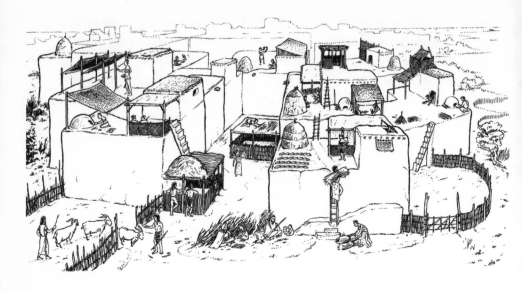

Part of the 'pueblo'-style Neolithic community at Çatalhöyük, Turkey, with its small yards and animal pens at ground level. Activities also took place on the flat roofs of the mud-brick houses.

A cross-section of a Neolithic house at Çatalhöyük. Ovens and drying areas sit on the flat roof, from which entrance is gained into the house below. Within the house there is room for both domestic and ritual activities.

plastered in white with a slightly elevated floor, or divided by a plaster ridge from the work area. The wall paintings, animal reliefs and bulls' horns decorate some of these areas. And remarkably, human adult burials lay beneath some of the floors.[15]

The Çatalhöyük people participated in an attitude to human remains, including a 'skull cult', which was widespread in the Near East and Anatolia in the early Neolithic. In previous chapters, I mentioned the plastered skulls at Jericho and Nahal Hemar Cave. At 'Ain Ghazal bodies buried beneath lime-plaster floors were later exposed so that the heads could be removed. At Çatalhöyük skulls were found in various locations: one was placed in a basket below a bull's head, two others on a platform below the vulture painting. But what is the story behind the burial of a young woman, placed crouched in a pit as part of the construction of a new building? She lay with her arms around a skull, its face close to hers. The skull had been plastered over its face many times and each time painted red.[16] The skull must have been an heirloom, kept for many years as an ancestral relic, before being so carefully placed with the woman. Deposition of valuable objects and burials as foundation deposits, to protect new households, is common in many societies. Polished greenstone axes, similar to the British axe head from Langdale, were also used in this way, and miniature greenstone axes were placed in burials. At Çatalhöyük the source of the greenstone remains uncertain.[17]

## Living together

To modern eyes Çatalhöyük may seem an alien society. Its crowded, packed dwellings with no streets, smelly rubbish dumps and communal roofs look like an experiment in Neolithic living doomed to failure. Yet it lasted a thousand years – about the same as the longest, continuously occupied settlement in North America, the pueblo of Acoma in New Mexico. The pueblos of America's southwest are architecturally similar to Çatalhöyük and reveal how such communities can be successfully bound together. Very different Native American groups – agriculturalists, such as the Hopi, Zuni and Tewa – occupy these pueblos and are particularly noted for their rich ceremonial lives. Dolls, masks and fetishes, music and dancing play a significant part in the cycle of rituals re-enacting a cosmic cycle and origin myth. In this way, pueblo dwellers seek to reconcile and bring together male and female, human and animal, temporal and eternal, social and psychological to re-create the primordial harmony in which spirits, people and animals lived together and death was unknown.[18]

The household and family are the focus of everyday activities, but the pueblo communities are divided into clans (as Dunbar would predict), responsible for ritual and communal activities. The symbols of the clans are often animals, such as the snake and coyote. These dedicated agricultural-ists still clung to elements of the wild in their symbolism, which inevitably reminds us of Göbekli Tepe's or Çatalhöyük's emphasis on wild creatures. In spite of huge pressures, from desiccation, hostility from Apache and Navajo raiders, conquistadores, Franciscan missionaries and, most dangerous of all, Anglo-Americans, the native American pueblo cultures have proved remark-ably resilient and adaptable.

### Entangled in a web of things

The pueblo people, concentrated together, have a rich material culture. At Çatalhöyük we see that these Neolithic people crowded together and also developed craft and technical skills in stonework, basketry, weaving, bead-making, housebuilding and ceramics. As Colin Renfrew has emphasized, the Neolithic is a time when people began to accumulate and develop a relation-ship with things. Their houses become repositories of material objects in a way that was impossible for mobile foragers. At its peak Çatalhöyük was home to as many as eight thousand people. It was not yet a 'town' in the sense of a place with specialized buildings (so far as we know), but it was a place that thrummed with activities, and perhaps that was part of the attraction. As they sang after World War I: 'How we gonna keep 'em down on the farm now that they've seen Paree?' With its crowds, rituals, music and dancing, Çatalhöyük was the place to be. Ian Hodder has also stressed that by congregating together in large numbers the Çatalhöyük people were able to build extensive networks, develop contacts and ideas and become a cultural driving force. However, he underplays the need for protection. A community full of material goods and, for that matter, women and children, might well be a target for raiders.

Not only did they exploit the land immediately around their Neolithic 'pueblo', the people of Çatalhöyük also gathered material from near and far. Obsidian, for example, travelled 170 km (105 miles) from Cappadocia in the east, and timber sources, clay pits and grazing were some distance away. To exploit these, they probably sent out specialist bands. Hodder uses the concept of 'entanglement'[19] – a term from quantum theory, where multiple objects exist in states that are linked together.[20] It is a useful metaphor because it conveys the idea that as people become dependent on things they also entangle or entrap themselves in a web of relationships. The pace of change – social, economic and technological – shifts up a gear as interactions constantly speed through this complex network of relationships.

Aside from polished stone axes, another icon of the Neolithic is pottery. Most of the earliest farming societies we have seen so far in the Near East did not, in fact, make or use pottery – hence archaeologists use off-putting jargon like pre-pottery Neolithic A and B (PPNA, PPNB) to describe these cultures. The earliest pottery in the world, about 16,000 BC from Yuchanyan Cave in China, and in Japan's Jōmon culture about 10,000 BC, was made by foragers, not by agriculturalists. However, pottery makes its appearance at Çatalhöyük and brings with it interesting implications about the entanglement of people, material and things. As we have already seen in previous chapters, pyrotechnic abilities had been around for a long time. At Çatalhöyük, there were fired clay objects in the earliest levels at around 7400 BC. The earliest pots appeared about 400–500 years later. These were thick-walled vessels, made of clay tempered with straw. There are no signs of burning on the exterior of the vessels, so they were not used for cooking. This is hardly surprising: organic-tempered pots will fracture if you put them on the fire. These first pots were used for storage – handy vessels for keeping the pests at bay, particularly the mice that infested the settlement.

So how did they cook in their gloomy kitchens? With ovens certainly, and also by placing heated clay balls into water in wooden or basketry containers.[21] Around the world many societies have used this awkward but effective method of boiling and simmering food. About 6500 BC the Çatalhöyük kitchen underwent a revolution: out with the old cooking balls and in with new, thick-walled, mineral-tempered pots that did not shatter on the fire. Now the Neolithic cook could, like me when I made the wild boar daube, put meat into a stewpot and leave it to simmer for a few hours. The cook, almost certainly a woman, was 'liberated' to get on with other work or even that vital Dunbar activity, chatting to the neighbours, instead of fiddling with those wretched balls. There are other implications in the production of cooking pots. Around this time houses were built of brick using sandy clay, the same material that appears in the new pots. This meant the development of a new supply chain. Analysis of the lipids embedded in these vessels shows that they were also used in rendering down fat from the bones of sheep and goats, which represented another substantial time saving in the kitchen.

The cooking pots are plain and undecorated. In Çatalhöyük society, decoration is reserved for the spiritual world, the symbolic world of ancestral histories. So pots never appear in burials – except one that has a modelled face on it (like the skull with the young woman). This pot seems to be a special artefact of the skull cult.

Towards the end of Çatalhöyük's life as a settlement, times were changing. Domestic cattle replaced wild aurochs (had they been hunted to extinction?). Houses became bigger and the hearths shifted to the centre of the room. Pots were routinely decorated with paint and not only used for storage and cooking, but also as serving vessels, displayed before the family and guests.

There is one final point to make about pots. Once they were used for cooking, they could also become containers for gifts: sending a stew to a sick neighbour or presenting food to someone as a reciprocal gesture. The advantage of a pot is that it is long-lasting and extends time. After the food has been consumed the pot remains as a reminder, a memory of the action.

Most of the crowded Neolithic communities of the Near East functioned well for centuries. In history, as the influential French scholar Fernand Braudel emphasized, there are deep trends influenced by the environment, but also 'stuff happens' – or as British Prime Minister Harold Macmillan said more elegantly: 'Events, dear boy, events.' The first farmers had taken advantage of a Holocene climate that had been relatively stable, but an unforeseen climatic lurch was about to unsettle them. This is known as the 6200 BC cold event after its approximate date.[22]

The cause was a sudden, massive outpouring of cold water, released when the last North American ice dams collapsed. The pent-up glacial meltwater flooded into the Atlantic. In Europe and Western Asia temperatures fell by about 6°C (11°F) on land and many areas were also stricken by drought. Fortunately, this cold interlude 'only' lasted about 150 years, but it was enough seriously to unsettle the farming communities – many places like Çatalhöyük shrank in size or were abandoned around this time. Communities fractured and dispersed, and there was no Dorothea Lange to record the distress. But farmers were desperate for new lands and opportunities, and they would take risks to find them.

CHAPTER SEVEN

# Taking to the water:
# Leapfrogging along the Mediterranean

### Land ahoy

The clearest evidence that early farmers were willing and able to colonize new lands comes from the east Mediterranean island of Cyprus. We have already seen in Chapter 4 that as a result of the climate crisis of the Younger Dryas, hard-pressed foragers from areas of previously burgeoning population took to the sea in search of more favoured environments. Desperation promoted new habits. Instead of an obstacle, the Mediterranean Sea gradually became a routeway. Foragers were free to explore, and to find islands such as volcanic Melos with its rich obsidian supplies. At this time, the late Natufians took to sea fishing. Seafaring had the potential to revolutionize the logic of Mediterranean space and erode the nearly two-million-year-old tyranny of the basin's 'negative geography' – a world of barriers, long peninsulas, maritime cul-de-sacs and isolated islands.[1]

The first farmers in the Levant inherited this tradition of seagoing from their forager ancestors. Archaeologists have found no physical remains of boats in the east Mediterranean at this early date and so speculate that large dugout canoes, skin-covered boats or craft made of rushes must have existed. Farmers who colonized the Italian peninsula a thousand years later left evidence in the form of an impressive 10 m (33 ft) dugout canoe from the lake settlement of La Marmotta, near Rome, dated to 5450 BC. A reconstruction of this vessel was capable of carrying a crew of ten people, with space for cargo and domestic animals, as far as 30 km (18 miles) a day.[2]

The farmers who made landfall in Cyprus brought with them the material to transpose their way of life: seeds to sow crops, half-wild cattle, goats, and later, sheep, cats and dogs. More remarkably, they carried wild boar and wild fallow deer. These Noah's arks of wild, semi-domesticated and domesticated animals had to negotiate some 70 km (45 miles) of open sea from their starting point on the Anatolian coast. It would take a couple of days of stiff rowing to accomplish the voyage, and desperate appeals to their equivalent of temperamental Poseidon to keep the sea placid.

In the Bible, Noah only made one voyage with a vessel full of animals. The first Cypriots probably shuttled between their new island home and the mainland with some regularity. Animal bone evidence from the Cypriot settlement of Shillourokambos tells of many phases of restocking from the original homeland communities. There is one particularly nice clue: the molars of Cypriot house mice reveal that the island mice did not vary from the mainland norms. In other words, the island mice regularly interbred with newly arrived stowaway mice hitching a lift from Anatolia. With the mice, came cats: one was buried with a human at Shillourokambos in about 7500 BC.[3]

However, all this toing and froing did not last. Gradually, the descendants of the pioneering farmers became insular, literally and metaphorically. Cypriots survived by hunting the imported wild deer, which ran free across the island, and catching large tuna. They became isolated from the mainland communities and the massive changes that took place there, as new kingdoms and empires emerged out of farming.

Nevertheless, Cyprus shows us what early farmers were capable of when they set their sights on new lands – pulled by the promise of a better future and pushed by the stresses at home. Some archaeologists think first of over-population and climatic deterioration as prime movers. It is salutary, however, to remember that in more recent times people launched themselves (or were pushed onto the terrors of the deep) for the sake of religion (Protestants to America; or Irish monks who sailed to isolated islands), as reluctant prisoners to Australia, slaves to the Americas or as the contemporary victims of civil war from Syria. With their expanding populations and sometimes deteriorating conditions, farmers had an incentive to move. Beyond Anatolia to the north and east lay the vast continental expanse of Eurasia. To the west was the coastline of the Mediterranean, accessible by boats that could take advantage of westerly flowing currents. Lawrence Durrell wrote in his novel *Balthazar*: 'The Mediterranean is an absurdly small sea; the length and greatness of its history make us dream it larger than it is.' That is not to underestimate, however, the achievements of the first people to take to the sea in small boats.

## Heading west

The advantage of going west, along the coast, was not just relative ease of transport – the farmers also remained in a familiar latitude. The lands of the Mediterranean are very fragmented, forming a mosaic that required colonists to be adaptable.[4] However, like future winegrowers in California, Australia, Chile and South Africa, they found similar conditions in the new lands, which suited the domesticated plants and animals from the Near East. Following the climatic shock of the 6200 BC cold event we can imagine a bunch of Neolithic wiseacres proclaiming (and predicting the advice of US newspaperman Horace Greeley): 'Go West, young man!' Not everyone agrees that the 6200 BC cold event had a major impact in Anatolia. Bleda Düring of Leiden University speculates that there were social forces at work even a century earlier, such as the emergence of dominant hierarchies, which led to the break-up of communities and the emergence of pioneering groups – a kind of 'Mayflower' model.[5]

We have a problem in understanding the development and spread of farming from its heartland; the tendency for archaeologists is to focus on origins. The Neolithic did not make a single revolution – it kept turning. Over time we see the emergence of new plants and animals, so-called 'secondary' products, such as milk, cheese and wool, and technologies like the plough and the wheel. The archaeological focus on the 'beginning' has led to the relative neglect of the development of the later Neolithic in the Near East. Nevertheless, it is clear that between 6400 BC and 6050 BC new agricultural settlements were sprouting across mainland Greece and far outnumber hunter-gatherer sites. They were accompanied by the Neolithic package of domestic animals, grain, pulses, pottery and polished stone tools. Even before farmers got to work on the Greek mainland, a group of colonizers had landed on the north coast of Crete in the first half of the seventh millennium BC. They followed a stream inland and established a modest pioneering settlement on the site that, four thousand years later, became the Minoan palace of Knossos.

For the past four decades a big issue for archaeologists has been whether Anatolian farmers trekked or sailed into new lands and literally transplanted their way of life or local foragers gradually adopt and modify agriculture and herding. As discussed earlier, partly as a result of modifications to chronology by radiocarbon dating, we now know that the origins of farming in most places are earlier than previously assumed. Archaeologists also came to promote the creativity and independence of indigenous people, rather than explain change by the overused invasion hypotheses, and most accepted the local adaptation theory. Now opinions are swinging towards a more mixed view, involving agricultural colonists and interaction with foragers where they existed. Clearly, however, on many uninhabited Mediterranean islands incoming farmers had the land to themselves.

## It's in the blood

In recent decades theories about agricultural expansion have been assisted, and complicated, by the emergence of genetic studies. The human genetic data have, not surprisingly, been the subject of lengthy and often technical arguments and I will not try to untangle them in any detail here.[6] However, as early as 1971, Albert Ammerman and Luca Cavalli-Sforza proposed on genetic grounds that migrant farmers from the east had spread agriculture across Europe. With further research to buttress the case, in 1984 Cavalli-Sforza and colleagues published *The Neolithic Transition and the Genetics of Populations in Europe*. Their argument in favour of the westward migration of early farmers hardened when in 1994 they published another book that promoted the 'wave of advance' theory – that rapidly breeding farmers overwhelmed the scanty and scattered populations of foragers.[7] Actually, it seemed more like a tsunami than a wave.

Inevitably, there was a reaction, first from archaeologists. A proliferation of radiocarbon dates showed that the wave of farming did not advance smoothly, or systematically. In some areas farming remained doggedly absent for many generations. Archaeologists also argued (sometimes wrongly as it turned out) that foragers often adopted elements of the farming package, but retained much of their traditional way of life. Then the geneticists provided more information. Researchers chipped in with their work on mitochondrial DNA – inherited through the mother – and claimed that modern Europeans inherited as much as 80–90% of their lineage from indigenous foragers. Only a small proportion came from immigrant farmers and that contribution was highest in southeast Europe, in areas like Greece.[8]

Something of a compromise was reached among the tribes of geneticists when Cavalli-Sforza's lab came back with further work on the Y chromosome, which more or less agreed with this picture. Most native Europeans, it seemed, were descended from Upper Palaeolithic/Mesolithic ancestors with a smaller proportion of eastern incomers. Anyone looking for a straightforward story, however, should bear in mind the words of geneticist Martin Richards: 'In the study of demographic history, the truth is rarely pure and never simple.'[9]

The sophistication of genetic data has also developed enormously in recent years, thanks to technical advances. In the early 2000s mitochondrial DNA analysis was suggesting that most living Europeans were descended from Palaeolithic or Mesolithic ancestors. When I wrote a popular account of this in 2005 it was picked up by the extreme right wing National Front party to emphasize the deep ancestry of white Britons. Predictably, they ignored my other message: 'We all came from Africa'!

If most Europeans had Palaeolithic ancestry, as seemed to be the case in the 2000s, then the Neolithic migration from Anatolia could not have amounted to much in terms of numbers. In the 21st century, there has been much more ancient DNA analysis taken directly from Neolithic bodies, so we are less reliant on samples from modern Europeans. In fact, DNA has been analysed from more ancient European (including Neanderthal) populations than from the rest of the world. The Y chromosome has also entered the picture (though it survives less well than mitochondrial DNA in ancient remains) and shows a strong link between Neolithic Western Asia, Europe and North Africa.[10] Incoming farmers from the southeast have made a greater contribution to the genetic make-up of Europeans than was previously thought.

There have also been genetic studies of the scale of mutations taking place in early Neolithic Europe and Asia. The increase in mutations indicates considerable population growth among agriculturalists – in contrast to hunter-gatherers.[11] In Europe this spurt is estimated to have taken place around 5700 BC, just as farming began to spread in the Carpathian Basin, so the genetics supports the archaeological evidence: farmers went forth and multiplied.

The position I take is that foragers adapted to farming and developed domesticated species in the Near East. Some of them migrated from their homeland into western Anatolia, Greece and some of the Mediterranean islands, taking with them their beliefs, attitudes and domesticated species. They interbred with foragers in some places. In other areas foragers maintained their traditional way of life for a time where conditions were particularly favourable or when the environment was unsuitable for farming. Other foragers, in close contact with people who already practised the farming way of life, adopted it, or aspects of it, themselves. People then as now were adaptable, innovative and creative: they made decisions about what suited their way of life and the landscape they inhabited. We should always remember the 'infinite variety of the human condition' (in the words of a British judge, reflecting Shakespeare's). Hunter-gatherers when confronted by the opportunities of farming will sometimes have seized them, and done things differently from the traditionalists – re-engineering or recombining elements in new ways – not just plants, animals and crafts, but origin myths and symbols.

North America provides an object lesson in how mobile foragers such as the Navajo and Apache took elements from neighbouring settled farmers, like the

Hopi, but retained a distinctive identity; or how the horticultural Lakota-Sioux domesticated the horse and reverted to mobile hunting on the Plains while creating new myths that fitted relatively new lifeways. Myths are not history. They are created, and re-created, to fit people's ideas about themselves. The result was a patchwork of cultures across Europe.

Most people, however, took up farming and stayed with it as a more efficient form of energy generation than was available to 'big, fierce' foragers in a diminishingly small wildscape. Farmers, with all their problems (and I have never met a farmer who didn't tell me about his or her problems) have natural advantages over foragers – they produce more – except in some of the Earth's harshest environments.

## Speaking in tongues

Another fascinating, if contentious issue is what language(s) the farmers spoke. 'Prehistory' means, by definition, a time before writing. Without writing there is limited evidence of language spoken by people in the past. So is it possible to tell what language flowed from the tongues of early farmers? As they moved into Europe farmers brought the Neolithic package of animals, plants and pots – did they also bring a new language?

Today, Europe has many languages but most of them belong to one family – so-called Indo-European. Even as long ago as the 16th century, scholars appreciated that there were similarities between Greek, Latin and Sanskrit, the ancient language of India. From Ireland across Asia there were many words that sounded more or less the same for similar concepts: mother, father, god, dogs, etc. This suggests that modern and recent languages are descended from a common ancestral language – the parent known as Proto-Indo-European (PIE).[12]

Languages are living entities and constantly change, especially when language communities physically separate.[13] It is often said Standard English and American English speakers are two people divided by a common language – not just pronunciation: 'I say tomayto and you say tomarto'; but also different meanings to words, for example: pants, yards, purses, fall and trunk. In England itself, the language has changed enormously over recent centuries from the tongue of Chaucer, to Shakespeare, to Tennyson and to Carol Ann Duffy, the current British Poet Laureate. Also, thanks to the British Empire in the 19th century, and American hegemony in the 20th, English – originally the language of a small remote Germanic tribe in AD 500 – has spread around the world and blossomed into many varieties, from Jamaica to Jaipur.

In Africa, Bantu-speaking farmers, expanding out of the tropics of Nigeria and Cameroon from 2000 BC, carried their language far to the east and south, swamping hunter-gatherers (and their languages) or confining them to zones inhospitable to farming, such as the Kalahari Desert. Colin Renfrew proposed a similar hypothesis for Europe: that Near Eastern farmers not only carried grain and sheep as they spread out of their homeland, but also PIE.[14] Not everyone agreed: J. P. Mallory and David Anthony, for example, argued that PIE contained words for later technological developments – ploughs, wheels, metals, wine and textiles – and so must belong to a later period. A more convincing scenario, Mallory and Anthony believed, was that PIE originated in the Pontic/Caspian steppes, through which flow the rivers Don and Dnieper, and spread with the invention and development of metallurgy in the early Copper Ages, carried by horse-riding pastoralists after about 4300 BC and into Europe around 3000 BC.[15]

My simple account barely does credit to this enormously complex, multi-disciplinary argument. For an outsider, like me, it is rather like standing on a hill and watching a chaotic, bloody battlefield, masked by dust and cannon smoke. It can take a long time to figure out who is winning the argument. At the moment, the 'Neolithic farmers out of Anatolia' hypothesis looks strong: genetics, radiocarbon dating and linguistic evidence seem to be coming to its support, like the Prussians arriving at Waterloo. Archaeology and genetics indicate widespread migration, the dispersal of people ultimately from Anatolia, into Greece, central Europe and around the Mediterranean – as well as eastwards to India. The linguistic arguments also increasingly point to Anatolia as the PIE homeland; and the technical words for horses and wagons may not be the obstacle they seemed.[16] In the earliest form of the language (PIE), the presence in the vocabulary of mountains, but not the sea, and of words for farming – plants such as wheat, barley and flax; words for sowing and rearing animals: cattle, sheep, goats and pigs; terms for milking, wool and weaving – all are compatible with an Anatolian origin. It seems likely that as farmers spread into Europe they brought PIE with them, gradually driving out the varied and different tongues of the hunter-gatherers.

## Leapfrogging round the pond

Nowadays, when referring to the movement of farmers, the image of 'leapfrogging' is more often used than the older 'wave of advance'.[17] If farmers could reach Cyprus and Crete then clearly they could explore the Mediterranean coast for suitable places to settle. In the mosaic of landscapes some areas were inhospitable – with cliffs, mountains or marsh close to the shore. Victor Hugo called it 'a stern, tawny coast' and the authors of *The Corrupting Sea* stressed the Mediterranean's 'micro-ecologies', its connectedness and its risks: sickness, earthquakes, volcanoes, floods, landslides, tsunamis, drought and disease.[18]

In some places foragers were few in number, but elsewhere they still thrived, with healthy populations, especially in resource-rich areas such as river deltas and in some of the forested mountains. So farmer-navigators meeting natural or human obstacles leapfrogged past them. The earliest Neolithic pottery on Corfu, at the mouth of the Adriatic, appears about 6500 BC, and is arguably a rare case in this area of foragers choosing to use pottery. It has been suggested that farming, spread by seagoing migrants, took many centuries to spread through the Adriatic.[19] However, further radiocarbon dating now indicates a much more rapid process, in a landscape devoid of forager groups. In Dalmatia, as in Greece, the Neolithic suite of domesticates arrived abruptly and 'the transition to farming seems to have been both wholesale and rapid'.[20]

Anthony Legge and Andrew Moore, archaeologists researching the Dalmatian coast of Croatia, made the interesting observation that pollen sequences from Mediterranean Italy show an intensive use of fire to control the landscape from the Neolithic onwards. Forest declined drastically at about 5700 BC, to be replaced by open country plants, such as plantains, chenopods and artemisia (all of which are growing as typical weeds, as I write, on the disturbed open ground of my cultivated terraces in the south of France). Much of the Mediterranean zone was relatively unattractive to foragers and, once cleared by the use of fire, farming had a 'catastrophic impact' on the wild.[21] The Mediterranean shores became a domesticated landscape, eventually dominated by cereals, vines, olives and sheep. Millennia later the great Roman poet Virgil, in *The Georgics* (book 1.12), his hymn to the gods of fertility and the productivity of the Italian countryside, would write '*Munera vestra cano*' – 'it is of your bounties that I sing'.

The key to understanding the spread of agriculture here, as in most parts of Europe, is a greater knowledge of 'the density and social organization of

Late Mesolithic people'.[22] This is not easy. Foragers often tread lightly on the land, and farmers do not; the result can be forest clearance and soil erosion that buries the traces of these earlier forager groups as valleys fill with alluvium (soil washed into the river systems as a result of erosion), pushing the sea further away (as in eastern Greece, where the soil was deposited along the coast). At the same time, the sea was rising and in many areas the remains of coastal-dwelling foragers may now be under the water, and difficult, though not impossible, to find.

On the western side of the Adriatic, in Italy, it is becoming clear that Mesolithic foragers exploited the forests and crags of the Apennines (and the Alps to the north) in the late sixth millennium BC. Even in the Po valley traces of late forager groups are now emerging from beneath the thick blanket of flood silts. However, there is a major contrast in the known distribution of Mesolithic and Neolithic sites: the former are found mainly above 500 m (1,600 ft), the latter below.[23] The Italian archaeologist, Paolo Biagi, points out the scarcity of evidence of Mesolithic hunter-gatherers: 'One possibility that we may have to consider in certain parts of Italy is that of decline in population numbers'; he raises the issue of 'new diseases and epidemics' similar to those that struck Native Americans with the arrival of Europeans.[24] Did the farmers transmit their zoonotic diseases to vulnerable foragers? This is still an open question.

In contrast, farmers flourished when they reached the desirable arable lands of southeast Italy. Aerial reconnaissance by the Royal Air Force in 1943–45 captured remarkable images of several hundred or more previously unknown Neolithic settlement enclosures. About 6000 BC incoming farmers discovered the extensive plain today known as the Tavoliere, in northern Apulia. The landscape was forested but crossed by rivers flowing from the Apennines to the Adriatic Sea. The soils in areas cleared of trees were fertile, light and free-draining, ideal for early farmers equipped with hoes, or possibly simple scratch ploughs (ards). The farmers obviously had an eye for soil (or felt it in their hands). They located 90% of their settlements on what are, today, called 'crosta' soils, with a subsoil of calcium carbonate.

This highly desirable new land supported a rapidly increasing population who cultivated plants and reared animals similar to those found in Greece: cereals, legumes, goats and sheep and, in fewer numbers, cattle and pigs. As in Thessaly (see Chapter 8) the landscape itself became domesticated and the 'wild' banished to the margins. The Tavoliere competes with Thessaly as

Aerial photograph of an early Neolithic settlement at the Tavoliere plain, Italy. A double-ditched enclosure surrounds circular house sites. Aerial investigation of the Tavoliere has produced evidence of many hundreds of such sites.

Europe's densest concentration of early Neolithic settlements. Unfortunately, we know relatively little about their character. In recent decades, as in much of Europe, senseless agricultural policies have led to the deep ploughing of the Tavoliere subsoils and the wholesale destruction of archaeological evidence: cultural vandalism on a massive scale. The starved Tavoliere soils produce durum wheat only because they are drenched in chemicals. And, as the watercourses are desiccated, water, while it lasts, has to be pumped from 40 m (130 ft) below the ground.

That is not to say that Neolithic farmers were environmental angels. Once they had cleared the forest, the soils, nurtured by generations of trees, began to lose nutrients and organic matter. The Tavoliere was, however, watered by year-round streams and the farmers needed to dig wells only 6 m (20 ft) deep to tap the water beneath their feet. (Today, there has been a massive drop in the water table and the streams are seasonal.) Nevertheless, the soils gradually became exhausted; the land – stripped of forest – dried out and erosion set in. By about 4800 BC, nine out of ten of the Tavoliere settlements were abandoned. Today's farmers solve their problems with agro-chemicals; the Neolithic farmers simply upped and left.[25]

To the west, the leapfrogging gained pace. 'Expansion in and beyond Tyrrhenia, Italy was astonishingly fast', in the words of Cyprian Broodbank.[26] Farmers reached Corsica and Sardinia by 5700 BC and left their traces in the important northwest Italian cave site of Arene Candide about two centuries earlier. On the Italian coast the first farmers made distinctive pottery impressed with seashells: so-called Cardial Wares from Tuscany, Sardinia and Corsica, decorated with triangles and chevrons, and a Ligurian style found at Arene Candide, decorated with grooves. These pots provide a fascinating insight into the movement westwards of farmer-colonists.

On the rocky, inhospitable coast of southern France the Neolithic farmers made landfalls at suitable bays. Like Classical Greek colonists, who five millennia later established settlements at Nice, Antibes and Marseilles, the Ligurians spread into Provence, bringing the suite of Near Eastern domesticates with them. The farmers seem to have sailed beyond the marshes of the Rhône delta and the lagoons near present-day Montpellier. These marshy areas may have been dominated by foragers at that time. Further south, about 5700 BC, they identified the rich plain where several rivers – the Hérault, the Orb and the Aude – disgorge into the Gulf of Lion – ideal country for raising sheep and cereals.

Two early Neolithic sites, only 3 km (2 miles) apart, point to parallels with later Classical Greek colonies (for example, migrants from the 'mother-city' of Chalcis in eastern Greece founded Cumae in western Italy about 730 BC, and their descendants went on to establish Neapolis, modern-day Naples). One of these Neolithic sites, Pont de Roque-Haute, had clear links with central Tyrrhenian Italy – its inhabitants were using the distinctive impressed Cardial Wares, as well as obsidian from the only recently exploited Lipari in the volcanic Aeolian islands, which jut steeply from the sea just north of Sicily. In contrast, Pont de Roque-Haute's near neighbour, the site of Peiro Signado, was settled by farmers connected to the Provence-Ligurian network.

The distinctive pottery, Cardial Ware, of the first farmers in the western Mediterranean.

It seems that these people were imbued with a pioneering spirit. As local pockets of good farmland were exploited, others set off in search of new territories from the Gulf of Lion along France's river systems – the Aude (past modern-day Carcassonne), the Tarn and the Garonne – to reach the Atlantic near modern-day Bordeaux. They brought with them the usual package of plants and animals, and the distinctive impressed wares. Others discovered France's great north–south corridor, the Rhône River, and expanded along it, while some headed south around the Spanish coast.

### Into the Atlantic

In many areas where farmers settled there were no signs of Mesolithic foragers.[27] Where indigenous people still remained, they sometimes maintained a separate way of life. The distinguished Portuguese archaeologist João Zilhão has shown that by about 5500–5250 BC Cardial Ware settlers were established on the Algarve coast of southern Portugal, west of the Strait of Gibraltar (the ancient Greeks' Pillars of Hercules). These people had escaped the confines of the Mediterranean and ventured onto the great, tidal ocean. To the north, forager groups still occupied the Atlantic coast and the valleys of the rivers Sado and Tagus, creating massive and monumental shell middens – the debris from centuries of gathering shellfish – which marked their settlements and where they also buried their dead.

The pioneer farmers sailed beyond these estuaries to the empty limestone massifs of Estremadura, which lay 300 km (180 miles) north of the Algarve. They brought Cardial pottery similar to that found in Spain and France and polished stone, both technologies unknown to the local foragers. They also put up menhirs (large stone memorials), some of Europe's earliest megaliths. Sheep were their principal domestic animal and isotopic analysis reveals they had a 'terrestrial' diet – farmers ate what they grew and reared, avoiding the maritime diet of the foragers. This was a dietary taboo that spread into Britain, as we shall see. The indigenous foragers were clearly under pressure. Something, perhaps disease or environmental change, had caused them to abandon much of the forested interior. By about 4800 BC their way of life had ceased.[28]

The Atlantic coast of southwest Europe was in the hands of farmers, who soon colonized inland Iberia as well. From here farmers probably linked up with those in western France and may, ultimately, have contributed to the arrival of the Neolithic in Britain and Ireland along the western seaways.[29]

CHAPTER EIGHT

# Across the river and into the trees: Farming spreads north[1]

## The mound builders

So what of the rest of Europe – the continental land mass west and north of the Black Sea? To trace the spread of farming through central Europe, Germany and northern France to Britain we need to return to Greece. A few years ago I took part in an archaeological fieldwork project that involved following a transect of land from Cape Sounion, south of Athens (where Lord Byron carved his name on the spectacular temple), up the eastern side of Greece, as far as the border with Bulgaria – the area that is Greece's large fertile breadbasket. As we crossed Thessaly, I was surprised at the scale and intensity of arable farming – no land was wasted on fences, walls or ditches and small villages clung to elevated slopes above the plain. At best, field boundaries were marked with a stick or stones painted white. The Greek farmers had obviously never heard that good fences make good neighbours.

It was this fertile area that attracted early Neolithic farmers from Anatolia.[2] Genetic evidence indicates immigration from Anatolia,[3] but we cannot entirely discount some interbreeding with local foragers. However, archaeological evidence for foragers has proved remarkably elusive in this area.

In Thessaly and the northern Greek plains the landscape is dotted with settlement mounds – the tell of the Near East and Çatalhöyük of Anatolia is known as 'magoule' in Thessaly and 'toumba' further north. Here, the Anatolian tradition of building in clay still survives today. Outside one village, actually called Toumba, I noticed that the surface of the ploughed field was covered in Neolithic pottery sherds. Literally tens of thousands of them. I walked about 400 m (1,300 ft) with my eyes fixed on the ground (this odd behaviour is typical of archaeologists when 'field walking'). As I reached the edge of the village my eyes rose upwards. The walls of the modern, yet still mud-brick houses were studded with Neolithic pottery. The villagers must have dug their clay from the fields and with it the eight-thousand-year-old potsherds.

Farmers arrived in this area about 7000 BC, rapidly colonizing the plain of Thessaly and the coast to the northwest, which leads past present-day Thessaloniki to Istanbul. It is most likely that the Anatolian seagoing farmers island-hopped, avoiding the enclaves of hunter-gatherers that existed close to the Bosphorus, and targeted the sort of promising land that suited their mixed agro-pastoral way of life. For whatever reason they wished to escape Anatolia (and explanations have varied from environmental to socio-political), the newcomers obviously struck it rich when they found Thessaly – a land of patchy forest relatively easily cleared, crossed by rivers and with few native inhabitants.[4] Had some Anatolian Erik the Red, exploring the west, returned home with the news that he had discovered the land of opportunity? If so, he was right. The settlers poured in and eventually established about 120 tell sites, mostly no more than an hour's walk apart, each reaching estimated populations of between 50 and 250 people. These tells reflect both permanent and restricted occupation. This is the first time in European history that people had routinely settled in one place.

Archaeologists were relatively slow to take an interest in the Neolithic of Greece – initially, the emphasis was very much on the achievements of Classical Greece and the spectacular palaces, tombs and fortifications of the Bronze Age, such as Knossos, Tiryns and Mycenae. Then, in the late 1950s and 1960s, the Serbian and Greek archaeologists Vladimir Milojčić and Demetrios Theocharis excavated, respectively, at the prominent tell sites of Argissa and Sesklo. These became flagship sites – permanent settlements with rich material culture forming a bridgehead between Anatolia and Europe.[5]

Mounded settlements are a fascinating phenomenon: why did people create places that were so restricted in terms of space and potentially restricting from a social point of view? One suggestion is that they were a means of elevating their inhabitants above potential floods. There are problems with this interpretation. First, some tells are on elevated ground where flooding was never a problem. Secondly, tells did not start as mounds; they are the result of successive generations demolishing or burning down their clay-walled buildings and reconstructing on the same spot, often with remarkable continuity of space and design. Clay buildings do not automatically result in mound creation. People have to want to stick to the same place, and there can be many reasons for this – an attachment to ancestral origins, the ownership of land, defence, status or trading opportunities. In a surprisingly large number of cases, houses were burnt down, sometimes as ritual acts of memorialization, burning the place into the fabric of the mound, as the house clay was transformed into durable ceramic.[6]

Tells usually control areas of productive land in lowland valleys and the edges of old lakes or watercourses. The creation of the mounds indicates, in itself, that these were long-lived settlements – the farmers probably maintained the fertility of their land, not by shifting around, as used to be suggested, but by manuring and crop rotation. Some farmers had already learnt how to keep land in good health.

Life in a tell involved living on top of the neighbours – and the inevitable potential for friction. As already mentioned in Chapter 6, in relation to Çatalhöyük, the probability is that larger groups subdivided themselves, like the pueblo people, into ritual 'clubs'. The presence of burials in and around households and the prevalence of human clay figurines have encouraged archaeologists to see these societies as very much concerned with their ancestors, and so attached to these special places, bound together by an ideology rooted in the tell settlement. The longer these places were occupied the higher status they became – and literally higher and more prominent. In these crowded landscapes there may have been vertical competition, a phenomenon that has persisted with the towers of medieval Tuscany and southern Greece (the Mani) or, for that matter, with modern skyscrapers.

Gordon Childe and many other archaeologists accepted that tells personified the Neolithic tendency to settle down, to live in one place. Of course, when an idea becomes almost routine doctrine, others will inevitably tilt at it. Many have argued for a more mobile Neolithic – that tells may have been seasonally occupied. In contrast, the Sheffield University archaeologist Paul Halstead has made a strong case for permanent occupation by analysing the evidence of animal bones – for example, the age at slaughter – and the remains of plants to show an active presence of occupants at virtually all the seasons of the year on a large sample of tells.[7] This does not mean, of course, that tell dwellers did not travel with their flocks and herds, to gather fuel, stone and clay, or to trade, visit relations and cement alliances.

In Neolithic Thessaly, sites such as the tell of Sesklo, covering less than 1 hectare (2½ acres), may have acquired status from their age and continuity. Sesklo is one of the few sites where excavation has extended beyond the tell itself – and by the middle Neolithic the contrast between the mound and its periphery was notable. The houses on the tell were substantial and well built, well equipped and within clearly defined spaces; the outer lower settlement had flimsier buildings, joined together with shared walls. While the tell build-ings were regularly rebuilt, those outside were short-lived. One possibility is that there was a social difference between those elevated on the mound and those that clustered below. Friedrich Engels believed that with farming came class differences. In a sense he was right, as farming eventually led to the growth of towns, temples, kings and priesthoods, but he was also being anachronistic in that the earliest farming communities emphasized belief in ancestors more than individual status. Archaeologists are also always on the hunt for evidence of social inequality, like pigs seeking truffles, but they do not have much luck in these Neolithic settlements: there is little differentia-tion apparent in burials, and tell houses are usually similar in size and layout. Houses, however, loomed large in the thinking of early farmers.[8]

We get our word 'domestic' from *domus*, Latin for 'house' – and it was not only animals that were domesticated. These people were developing and adapting to new ways of living, crowded together, yet growing and storing their own food in family dwellings. The significance of the house is implied by a fascinating clay model, buried beneath the floor of a house at Platia Magoula Zarkou (a tell in the northwest of Thessaly, which did flood in its early stages). This looks like a foundation offering representing a single-room house, partly divided by a partition with one external door. As in the real houses the model has a platform and oven against the back wall. It also contains eight stylized human figures. We can only speculate: are these ancestors; two idealized nuclear families (two couples and four children)? The space looks crowded, but Western ideas of privacy and space are not the norm even today and cer-tainly not in the past. At any rate, this and other clay model houses found in tells demonstrate the significance of the household in early Neolithic society.

The Neolithic settlements in southeast Greece became so prolific that the surrounding land itself must have been domesticated. Such intensive exploitation of the land partly explains why there is so little evidence for the consumption of wild plants and animals. There was little space left for them in a landscape devoted to grazing flocks or sown with emmer wheat, einkorn, peas, grass peas and bitter vetch (the last two are today used as fodder crops). Paul Halstead has suggested that on the good soils selected by the first farmers, cereal yields could reach up to 1,000 kg per hectare (890 lb per acre). Even with considerably lower yields, 50–60 hectares (125–150 acres) of land could have supported 200 people, assuming an annual consumption of cereals and pulses per person of 200 kg (440 lb).[9]

Sheep were the dominant domestic animal in terms of numbers, well adapted to their new, dry, open European homeland. Mostly they were kept for meat in this early period and slaughtered predominantly between six months and three years of age. Cattle were fewer, but each beast supplied far more meat than a sheep. Pigs were also a regular feature of the diet.

The scale and longevity of these Greek settlements demonstrates the success of farmers when they expanded beyond the Anatolian/Near Eastern heartland of agriculture. Clearly, these farmers reproduced themselves as successfully as did their flocks and herds. Nevertheless, it is salutary to bear in mind the mean age of death: in early Neolithic Turkey and Greece it was 29.8 years for females (possibly an underestimate) and 33.6 years for males. Burials of newborns and young children are frequently found. For women, giving birth was hazardous both for themselves and their babies; nevertheless, they reproduced frequently, and continued to generate more farmers.[10] Communities were numerically dominated by the young. Grandparents would have been respected for their knowledge – sacred and profane – and perhaps because there were not very many of them around. Grandparents were also, no doubt, useful carers when women played an active role in cultivating, tending animals, gathering fuel, cooking and craft activities, such as weaving.

It would be misleading to assume everyone lived in tell settlements. Well-known tell sites like Sesklo and Nea Nikomedeia attracted archaeologists because they were (and are) the most obvious features of the Neolithic landscape. Nevertheless, as in Turkey, only small proportions of these sites have been investigated – for example, less than one-eighth of Nea Nikomedeia's 2.4-hectare (6-acre) site. In addition, other less obvious Neolithic sites – flat, extended settlements, seasonal or short-lived sites and cave dwellings – have been largely ignored. Clearly, the prominent tells are not the only settlements or activity areas in the Neolithic landscape. One advantage of development-led archaeology is that it leads to the excavation of largely ignored site types. In the mid 1990s, for example, the flat site of Makriyalos, found during road and rail construction south of Thessaloniki, showed that there is more to early farming settlements in Greece than tells. It is beginning to appear that flat sites represent farmsteads, while tells began and continued as villages.[11]

## Objects of clay and stone

As farmers spread into Europe they adapted to changing conditions and modified their material culture: for example, clay for building in the east gave way
to timber in the north and west. Ceramics were also used in different ways:
strongly regional in style in some areas, less so in others. In the early Neolithic
in Greece, the emphasis seems to have been on grilling, baking and roasting
food on large hearths. Pots were not used much, if at all, for cooking. Instead
they were vessels reserved mainly for serving food and drink, for display – ceremonial and prestige items. In contrast, further north, in Bulgaria, farming
settlements were littered with pottery sherds – everyday items, which were
frequently broken and discarded after serving as cooking pots.

In Greece, clay was not simply for making houses and pots. Large numbers
of bullet- or egg-shaped clay missiles were used as slingstones. Sometimes
they are found in clusters near the hearths, where they had been laid to dry
and harden (they were not fired). Gordon Childe was the first to note their
frequency; he wrote that Neolithic Greece belonged to the 'sling era', and
considered the sling to be an important weapon of war – 'David's weapon'.[12]
But David, when he first appeared on the scene, was a shepherd not a warrior,
and it is still common in the Middle East for shepherds to use slings to control
recalcitrant sheep. Unfired clay slingstones deliver a sharp warning, but they
don't fell giants.

In considering variations in the material culture of early farmers we might
also return to our Neolithic icon, the polished stone axe. One archaeologist
stated that in Greece 'the stone axe was the most useful and necessary working
tool in the life of the Stone Age.'[13] Unfortunately, the archaeological evidence
does not support this statement. Stone axes do turn up in Greek Neolithic
sites – there were as many as thirteen from the excavations of the Sesklo
settlement – but generally they are sparse. Further north in Europe pioneer
farmers had to tackle forested landscapes and their heavier stone axes or adzes
were certainly important tools. Yet in Greece and in Mediterranean France
they were far less prevalent. The Mediterranean ecology may be a factor.
The open, dry woodland can be cleared by a combination of ring-barking and
burning, and smaller cutting tools are handy for dealing with rejuvenated
scrub in grazed landscapes.

Where dried clay and mud-brick architecture predominated there was
also less need for large timbers in building, so polished stone tools were
generally smaller, such as adzes, more suited to carpentry. Was the status

and symbolic importance of the axe therefore less in southern Europe than in the north, where, in Germany for example, larger stone axes accompanied men to the grave? In northern Europe axes were certainly prestige objects, made of exceptionally fine materials and transported across half a continent. Yet it would be unwise to dismiss the, albeit relatively rare, stone axes of Greece as mere tools. Two fine greenstone axes were deposited, with many other unusual artefacts, inside an exceptionally large building, which was, unusually, constructed with big timbers (a shrine or a men's house?) at the tell site of Nea Nikomedeia. At the tell of Achilleion in southern Thessaly the distinguished archaeologist Marija Gimbutas recorded unusual clay replicas of axes. The axe, then, seems to have had symbolic significance in Greece long before the famous 'double-axe' (labrys) symbol appeared in Minoan Crete.

The significance of the axe in early Neolithic Europe is not simply a matter of function. Its material is also significant. John Chapman of Durham University proposed that certain materials were, in many societies, intrinsically 'enchanting', especially when they were well crafted, and so reinforced ritual connotations and became charged with cosmological power. He suggests that there is 'a Neolithic aesthetic based on colour and brilliance, light and luminosity'.[14] The materials he identifies are observed in similar roles around the world (for example, among Native Americans), particularly objects made of greenstone, shells, burnished and slip-decorated pottery – and later metalwork, particularly gold. We might add that the Gravettian grave goods of the Upper Palaeolithic (see Chapter 3) reflect similar qualities. Such exotic and harmonious materials can also evoke distant places and mythic events. The Neolithic traveller who returned with stories of far-flung lands, new ideas and new materials – a prehistoric Odysseus or Marco Polo – could become a heroic figure in the community.[15]

The tell way of life obviously had great appeal to the farming communities of southeast Europe. From northern Greece, tell settlements spread north and west along the river systems into more forested and marshy environments. When I drove northwards with my Greek geologist colleague we crossed the eastward-flowing rivers of Thessaly (I think only the river Pineiós was actually flowing that summer), and, beyond Thessaloniki, we followed the Strimon River northwards towards the Bulgarian border. The Strimon is one of several rivers that emerge from the mountains of the Balkans and provide natural routeways between the north Aegean Sea and the Danube – the great axis of central Europe.

## Expanding northwards

In the centuries following the establishment of the first tell settlements in central and northern Greece, farming communities spread northwards into Macedonia, south Serbia, Bosnia, Bulgaria and Romania. By about 4800 BC they had reached their northernmost limits in the Great Hungarian Plain, concentrated particularly along the Tisza River. The distribution of Slovakian obsidian and decorated pottery from southeast Hungary indicates contact between communities over a very wide area. The tells were often sited close to rivers, and in Romania many were small, located on the edge of the flood-plains, and discreetly placed (almost hidden).

In the changing environments further north farmers adapted, but also made mistakes – for example, trying to rear sheep and goats in unsuitable territory. Forested and marshy areas were less suited to these Near Eastern animals. In the marshy Tisza valley, farming was small-scale and fishing remained important. Settlements were littered with dumps of fish bones – of monster pike and catfish as well as the remains of turtles, waterfowl and fishnet weights. These settlers were adapting to an environment that was different from the Mediterranean hinterland: more heavily forested and better supplied with wild animals. The elevated tells provided views across the broad floodplain and at Vitănești (in the Teleorman valley of south Romania) half of the animal bones came from wild species, including beaver. Hunting was a much more significant activity than in the south, and the site locations suggest that defence mattered. In these areas of central Europe, farmers and foragers may have learnt from each other, either amicably with intermarriage, or the hard way through conflict – and enforced intermarriage.

Archaeologists sometimes gain benefit from ancient disasters and the mis-fortune of those that they are trying to study. Volcanic eruptions at Pompeii, Herculaneum or the Greek island of Santorini are obvious examples. Instead of buildings eroding through time they are suddenly caught in the moment, like flies in amber. At the fortified tell site of Uivar in the Carpathian Basin of southwest Romania, fire swept through at least ten houses.[16] Here we are at the geographical limits of tell settlement, where they were relatively late arrivals. However, Uivar discloses rare evidence. First of all, the charred house remains provide details of their construction. The best preserved is dated to about 4900 BC and measures 12 × 4.5 m (40 × 15 ft). Its walls consisted of round wooden posts interlinked by wattle-and-daub panels. There were three ground-floor rooms and, at the western end opposite the doorway, an upstairs room. The floors were surprisingly complex, made of horizontal logs, overlain with vegetable matter and then plastered with a loamy earth. The evidence of many different types of wood (hazel, ash, poplar and alder) shows that the local forests were being managed and coppiced to produce suitable timber for construction and tools.

There are strong hints of ritual activities associated with this house building. For example, one foundation trench was packed with large cattle bones, probably the remains of a foundation ritual, which included animal sacrifice. In another foundation there was a complete female figurine – a domestic goddess? – and in another, half of a clay life-sized human face mask with modelled eyebrows and an open eye and mouth: an echo perhaps of ritual dramas that accompanied the setting up of the house, with the deliberate breaking of the mask at the conclusion. Over fifty years ago a German archaeologist suggested that some of the human figurines found at tell sites represented people in masks. It seems that he was right.

Here on the tell frontier the settlement was enclosed within a fortified boundary. At the entrance, the ditch terminals contained great concentrations of large animal bones, mostly from wild animals, including the skulls and horn cores of aurochs and red deer antlers. These trophies may have hung over the entrance gate. Were they simply displays of hunting prowess and power, like the antlers sprouting from some Scottish baronial hall, or were they apotropaic (protective) symbols announcing to both visitors and the inhabitants that the wild and the dangerous stops here, that this is the entrance to the domestic realm?

## Living with the wild

In many areas, as previously discussed, late Mesolithic foragers were notably thin on the ground or even absent. However, in parts of the Danube, Mesolithic foragers continued to thrive while not far away farming communities established themselves. In the Danubian Gorge, around the Iron Gates, foragers were spectacularly present. Here, on the present-day Romania/Serbia border, the Danube flows for over 100 km (60 miles) between hills and in dramatic gorges. In this favourable environment, with a mild microclimate and prolific supplies of fish, hunters routinely occupied a range of locations, such as Icoana (on the Romanian bank), Vlasac and, most well known, Lepenski Vir (on the Serbian bank). These settlement sites were in regular danger of seasonal flooding, so the inhabitants probably withdrew to higher ground where wild pigs, cattle, deer and chamois, as well as plants, could supplement their diet. In spite of the relatively rich wild resources, the teeth of these foragers (their irregular enamel growth) testify to episodes of malnutrition. Even here the foragers' life seems to have been under pressure. Their reaction was to exert their identity.

Unusually for Mesolithic foragers, the Lepenski Vir people left distinctive remains of a rich cultural life. In the early phases of the settlement there were at least twenty trapezoidal structures regularly laid out so that the wide ends faced the river. Many contain one or more human burials, usually placed at the back of the building behind a rectangular stone-lined hearth. Remains of wild animals, including antlers, and fish were deposited in a formalized and structured fashion, also at the back of the house. Most distinctive of all were carved stones, some of which resemble fish-faced humans, which were normally placed on the long axis of the structures. Although these odd buildings are usually interpreted as houses, their shape and interior deposits beg the question – could they be shrines?

Shrines and temples often exploit dramatic locations. This is certainly true of Lepenski Vir, which faced a powerful whirlpool in the Danube and the spectacular, distinctively shaped trapezoidal Treskavec Mountain on the opposite bank. The structures not only seem to mirror the shape of the mountain, but their dimensions also obey mathematical rules. The excavator D. Srejović (who dug the site in advance of a new dam flooding the area) noted that the trapezoidal structures possessed harmonious proportions resembling the golden section and suggesting that the builders used a system of triangulation in their layout that resulted in an isosceles

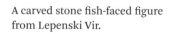

A carved stone fish-faced figure from Lepenski Vir.

triangle.[17] At Çatalhöyük, Ian Hodder interprets the symbol-laden buildings as houses. At Lepenski Vir, he observes that death and the wild were also closely entangled, with symbolic material and burials in the darker rear of the house, while daylight, the hearth and everyday, particularly female, activities occur at the front.[18]

None of this is behaviour usually associated with Mesolithic foragers. In the Danube Gorges, however, they developed a distinctive culture, marking their place in an equally distinctive landscape: emphasizing their identity. Symbolic burials, ritual deposits and memorialization are usually associated with the Neolithic. As at Göbekli Tepe, here at Lepenski Vir we see foragers intimately concerned with death and the images of the wild in a focal gathering place. At the same time, about 5000 BC, farmers were moving into the neighbourhood.

## Flexible farming

For the most part, the mound builders in Greece and the southern Balkans replicated a farming system similar to that in Anatolia, and in similar environmental conditions. However, as farming spread northwards things changed. Surplus water became more of an issue than drought, cold winters more of a problem than hot summers. Forests were thicker; daytimes and the growing season were shorter. Even the Romans regarded this area of the Danube as a significant frontier. In 74 BC the Roman general Caius Scribonius Curio coaxed his army up the Vardar River, as far as the Danube. The dark forest and looming mountains on the opposite bank persuaded him that this was the end of the line for any sensible empire builder. Almost 180 years later the emperor Trajan, backed by 120,000 men, had more confidence – or more incentive: there was gold in them there hills. He left a memorial at the Iron Gates, marking his bridging of the Danube (between present-day Serbia and Romania) and ultimate conquest of Dacia (modern-day Romania), the land beyond. In Rome he had his exploits carved in stone on the spiralling *bande dessinée* that is Trajan's Column. Even for the Romans this marked a thrust into new and strange lands.

Nevertheless, this area of the Danube (known as Transdanubia) marks an important crossroads in Eurasian history, vital for the spread of farming from the southeast into northwest Europe. From here, the Danube provides a route westwards to the Upper Rhine into Germany and France, northwards along the Oder and Vistula to the Baltic Sea, and along the Elbe to the North Sea.

Environmental evidence tells us that there was a densely wooded landscape in much of central Europe, often choked with undergrowth. Europe's main rivers provided arteries, as vital to movement as the Mediterranean was in the south. From about 5500 BC there was a major Neolithic surge from this area – what Peter Bogucki, of Princeton University, called 'a fundamental and irreversible commitment to agriculture'.[19] Farming proved to be sustainable in different environments because of its enormous flexibility. The Neolithic could be 'un-packed' to provide the right elements for the right place, with new ones added as farmers gained experience.

As I noted in the previous chapter, it is at this period that geneticists observe an increase in mutations in the human genome, and associate the phenomenon with the growth of population (see page 117). Farmers worked hard, on a restricted diet, but had bigger families. In most of Europe there was a major genetic breach between local Mesolithic hunter-gatherers and Neolithic farmers, whose genetic ancestry points to the southeast and ultimately Anatolia and the Fertile Crescent. It is probable that farming groups initially colonized suitable land, leaving hunter-gatherers to the mountains, forests and marshes, land less attractive to farmers.

Strontium analysis shows us that *Linearbandkeramik* farmers (see below), in spite of their long-term villages, were inveterate movers – constantly budding off to colonize new land and establish new settlements. Ethnographic evidence suggests that some hunter-gatherers on the margins of farming territory would innovate and adopt the new way of life – driven by economic, social or environmental factors. Their population would also rise on the demographic wave created by agriculture. As both groups increased in size it is likely that they would meet up and interact as humans inevitably do – complicating the European gene pool.

Peter Bellwood has pointed out that this process is not confined to humans. The first domestic pigs carried mtDNA haplogroups of Near Eastern origin. Yet by the time the first domestic pigs stepped ashore somewhere in the British Isles 'their DNA had become swamped by that of local and formerly wild European pigs'. In other words, pigs, like humans, first became domesticated in the Near East and subsequently spread into Europe where they found the rough, hairy locals irresistibly attractive.[20]

## The longhouse people

The farming communities of Transdanubia lived in impressive timber long-houses – the largest-known structures in Europe at that time. They spread north and west, eventually reaching the Paris Basin and the Netherlands. Large, open-area archaeological excavations, much more frequent on the Continent than in Britain in the pre- and early post-war periods, revealed settlements such as Köln-Lindenthal (Germany), Bylany (Czech Republic) and Elsloo and Sittard (Netherlands), all with rows of massive longhouses. For the most part, in this book I have tried to avoid the myriad, and rather confusing mishmash, of culture names that archaeologists use to label particular groups of people (or pots!).[21] But now, I must succumb to the jargon. These longhouse people are known by the far from inspiring name of *Linearbandkeramik* (LBK) because their settlements are littered with pots decorated with incised lines.

For many years the LBK was seen as a wave of farmers, emerging out of Anatolia and the Balkans, which spread rapidly and uniformly across Europe. Gordon Childe conveyed the idea in *The Dawn of European Civilization* when he wrote of a 'Neolithic population whose whole culture down to the finest details remains identical from the Drave to the Baltic and from the Dniester to the Meuse'. This is a monolithic Neolithic that sounds like a Napoleonic or EU bureaucrats' dream of European uniformity. In recent decades, however, there have been huge advances in LBK research, which shows that there is more regional and inter-site variation than Childe and many more recent researchers appreciated.[22]

These longhouse communities are undoubtedly a remarkable phenomenon that, emerging from western Hungary, spread the farming way of life and occupied a great swathe of Europe for the better part of a millennium (about 5500–4900 BC). In her admirably clear summary of the evidence available in 2013, Jean Manco concludes: 'Ancient mtDNA from the LBK showed *without*

An LBK (*Linearbandkeramik*) pot of the type found in the Neolithic longhouse settlements of central and northwestern Europe.

*doubt* that the first farmers of Central Europe were *not descended from local foragers* [italics my emphasis].'[23]

From Transdanubia, new LBK farming communities spread along the river networks, usually settling away from the major floodplains and mountains, on fertile soils in the secondary river valleys. The LBK sites are particularly associated with the broad band of loess (from the German for 'loose') soils that runs across Europe. These deep soils were deposited when dry particles were picked up and transported in huge quantities by glacial winds. In North America and China, loess soils result from winds blowing off deserts. Neolithic farmers appreciated that loess soils were fertile and well drained, especially when they were capped by organically rich brown earths. In Austria about 75% of LBK sites of all periods are sited on these soils.[24] Climatic conditions in continental Europe of the sixth millennium BC were slightly hotter and wetter than today and the LBK farmers favoured drier sites. However, there is still a lack of detailed evidence about the environments that confronted these pioneer farmers – especially the character of the woodland.

## Good farmers make good choices

Archaeologists frequently used to claim that forest clearance was by 'slash and burn' techniques, and that farmers regularly shifted their cereal plots as soil became exhausted. Both of these ideas are now discounted. The LBK plots were, in fact, intensively cultivated, fertilized and relatively stable. In the Near East and southeast Europe there was a clear set of founder crops (see the Appendix). The earliest LBK farmers were aware of these cereals, which occasionally turn up on LBK sites, but the majority grew the glume wheats, einkorn and emmer. As agriculture spread across central Europe the focus was on cultivating this narrower range of cereals. Of the five pulses (pea, lentil, chickpea, grass peas and bitter vetch) that were so important to early farmers in the south, only the pea remained significant. Why this reduction in plant diversity? The two obvious explanations – unsuitable environments further north or a bottleneck (species were not passed on) – are rejected by some researchers, who prefer a cultural explanation. In other words, farmers made a deliberate choice.

Environmental conditions should, however, be taken into account – some cereal species such as barley are more tolerant of drought. The LBK farmers favoured the glume wheats, although they are not in some ways the ideal candidates for central European conditions. However, einkorn has the advantage of standing upright in rainy conditions – it does not tend to fall over and lodge like some cereals. The glumes (the husk that encloses the grains) also provide protection from scavenging birds when the crop is in the fields and, in wetter conditions, inhibit insect and fungal attack. These might have been serious issues for farmers colonizing the forests of central Europe and explain why they favoured these particular wheats. Processing glume wheats is relatively time-consuming, but their advantages must have outweighed the downside – and they are a versatile if dull foodstuff, good for porridge, flat bread, gruel and beer. Even the waste products are valuable for fuel and fodder, bedding, thatch, basketry and tempering for clay.[25]

Other Mediterranean staples did not make the transition north. Chickpeas and lentils require too long a growing season. In contrast, the pea is happy in both the warm Mediterranean and cooler north and is, in fact, almost ubiquitous on LBK sites, even the most northerly. As farming spread northwards the lack of chickpeas and lentils was compensated for by the increasing importance of milk and milk products. The early LBK farmers reared sheep and cattle but they were not lactose tolerant. Like the vast majority of human adults at that time, after weaning they stopped producing the enzyme lactase, which allows babies to digest milk. So they may have consumed cheese and yoghurt made from the milk of the herds, products which are very low in lactose, but adults would not have enjoyed a jug of milk. There are a number of significant genetic differences, of which lactose tolerance is one, between LBK people and modern Europeans.[26] These were essential products for more northerly farmers and I will return to them when we reach Britain. Cattle and pigs became more economically important as the farmers moved into potentially richer grazing land. They may have also become significant in the social life of farmers – marks of wealth and status; necessities for bride wealth and public feasting.

Farmers chose which animals to rear. The southeast European attachment to sheep and goats proved unsustainable in more forested, wetter and marshy areas in Hungary, but pigs were ideally adapted. Central Europe remains the home of the sausage – when I worked in Romania, there was a running joke among the team at every mealtime, when someone would exclaim 'Ahh! More pork.' However, I am a believer in the French maxim '*Dans le cochon, tout est bon*', loosely equivalent to the British expression, 'Use everything but the squeal'.

Hunting also flourished again in some less intensively cultivated areas. And, as wild aurochs had not diminished in size by the later Neolithic, in the Hungarian marshland edges it seems that their population continued to flourish in spite of predation. The wild ass was less fortunate – it went extinct during the Neolithic on the Great Hungarian Plain. Smaller domesticated cattle increased in importance in continental Europe, for meat, and possibly for traction and milk. The origins of plough cultivation remain uncertain, though some osteozoologists claim to see evidence of castration in oxen and signs of stress in cattle bones of the kind associated with pulling ploughs and carts in the later sixth millennium BC.

The distinctive weeds that grew among LBK cereals show that cultivation was intensive, and cereals were often sown in autumn in fixed plots. Well-tended plots may have been the valued possessions of particular LBK longhouses and their occupants. For about a millennium the longhouses dominated the domestic architecture of Europe from the Carpathians to northern France and the Netherlands. Settlements vary in size. Many pioneering communities started small, with two to four houses, and then expanded into substantial villages. Other small settlements, of a single house, were offshoots of nearby villages, which themselves expanded into hamlets. Some pioneers made greater leaps. Settlement densities can be high in some areas as a result of population expansion, immigration and the recruitment of hunter-gatherers, some of whom may have been women, marrying into the farming group.

LBK settlements crossed the Rhine after 5300 BC. In one exceptionally well researched part of the Lower Rhine Basin, in the Aldenhovener Platte about 40 km (25 miles) west of Cologne, more than 120 LBK sites are known. Since the 1970s, lignite mining has stripped much of this area, so archaeologists could observe and investigate the exposed settlement remains. In the Merzbach valley area of the Aldenhovener Plateau archaeologists excavated six LBK settlements, a cemetery and three enclosures, and 3 km (2 miles) to the east, in the Schlangengraben valley, they investigated six more settlements, albeit on a smaller scale. Researchers have also located and studied another fifteen LBK settlements about 20 km (12 miles) to the northeast on the Titzer Plateau (another open-cast mining zone) in an area of almost 18 sq. km (7 sq. miles). This is seriously intensive archaeology. Few Neolithic settlement areas have received so much attention from researchers.[27]

Even here, however, the interpretation of the archaeology is not straight-forward. As I mentioned above, these early farmers chose to exploit fertile soils. Their successors have been doing the same thing for the past seven thousand years, hence the LBK remains have usually been severely eroded by ploughing. Unlike well-preserved, buried occupation levels within tells, in LBK settlements floor levels and building traces above foundation level have been scoured away. Archaeologists are faced with a kind of ink-blot test.

## Homes fit for heroes

The LBK settlements are very different from those of Anatolia and southeast Europe. The developed villages consist of rows of longhouses of varying sizes, from about 10 m (33 ft) to 40 m (130 ft) or even 60 m (200 ft) long. Usually the buildings are laid out more or less parallel, some distance apart, their position marked by long lines of substantial postholes, orientated northwest to southeast. Alongside, the builders dug borrow pits to provide clay with which to plaster the walls. These pits, over several years, accumulated settlement debris, potsherds and animal bones, and sometimes contained the burials of infants.[28]

It appears that when a house's life was finished, another was often built on the immediately adjacent plot. Generally, the dating of the houses is not very precise (we will see the use of radiocarbon techniques in a later chapter) – German archaeologists have argued for a household lifespan of about 25–30 years, which does not seem very much for such substantial structures (and modern reconstructions have proved capable of standing for much longer). If this lifespan proves to be correct when more precisely calibrated radiocarbon dates are available, then we have to ask: why so short? Perhaps buildings were abandoned on the death of a significant occupant. One suggestion is that the thatch roof would wear out in that time, though in my experience, old thatch is usually removed, spread on the fields as fertilizer and then replaced. Timber buildings can be taken apart and rebuilt on a new site, but in LBK sites they were apparently left to decompose, a constant reminder of previous generations.

Although archaeologists across Europe have excavated the sites of more than two thousand LBK houses, the interpretation of how they were constructed and used remains a problem. The buildings are outlined by smaller postholes and slots suggesting that the walls were not load-bearing. Inside there are usually three lines of massive postholes, often doubled-up and more closely spaced at the southeastern end, where the entrance was to be found.

In many reconstructions the interiors resemble a forest of poles, a cathedral of tree trunks. The large posts are more widely spaced in the central zone, providing an open area less cluttered with posts than at each end. Most interpretations assume that the larger longhouses were tripartite: a central dwelling zone (there is some evidence for hearths here) where a family lived, with storage at each end, possibly with elevated floors or platforms holding grain supplies, fodder and other materials. According to this interpretation, the LBK longhouses were barn-like structures with thatched roofs, housing a family of six or seven people, who stored their produce under their own roof and used the southeastern, more illuminated end of the building for work, craft activities or on ceremonial occasions.

When I first arrived in Oxford in the early 1970s archaeologists from the Institute of Archaeology, the Ashmolean Museum and its superb library used to cluster for lunch across Beaumont Street in the Playhouse Theatre. One of the research students, also a newcomer, was Bill Startin. He was trying to figure out how to construct Neolithic monuments: how many people were required, how much material and how long did it take to build a major henge, like Avebury, or an LBK longhouse? His work was very much about practicalities and function. He was a prehistoric time-and-motion expert. Bill estimated, for example, that the construction of a smaller LBK house required about 800 person-hours – and the larger ones about 2,600–3,200 person-hours. He concluded that LBK housebuilding was a communal activity.[29] I imagine something like the barn-raising scene in Peter Weir's film *Witness*, where Harrison Ford (fresh from playing Indiana Jones, the world's most famous 'archaeologist') joined the Amish, who gathered together in the warm sunlight of community spirit: the men cheerfully raising and fixing the big timbers, the children helping and the women preparing food.

In LBK communities, as with the Amish, it was probably the men who built the timber houses – at least, this is what is suggested by the stone axes and adzes placed in their graves and also found in large numbers in the houses. However, the skeletons of Neolithic women and children suggest that they, too, tackled heavy work. Bill Startin pointed out that LBK builders and carpenters had to rely on stone tools; they had no metal saws, awls or iron nails. I think he was inclined to underestimate the skill of LBK carpenters. He also assumed that the occupants lived at ground level.

Since then there has, in fact, been a great deal of speculation about the form and use of LBK houses, based on the evidence of their postholes

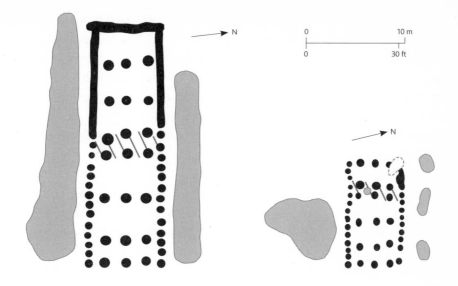

Plans of longhouses at Cuiry-lès-Chaudardes, northeastern France, showing post-built walls and internal divisions/supports. Wall trenches are evident at the western end of the larger house, and both houses have external quarries.

(or 'post molds' in North American terminology). The German archaeologist, Oliver Rück, pointed out that these houses are often sited on sloping ground above watercourses or at the edge of loess-covered river terraces, such as the extensively excavated settlements of Köln-Lindenthal, Cuiry-lès-Chaudardes in northeast France and Mold, Lower Austria.[30] He convincingly argues that the builders coped with the slope by elevating the house floor on substantial timber piles, and at the gable end there was an elevated veranda or plat-form. The sloping ground was advantageous for drainage, in a period when dendrochronology indicates that rainfall was high.[31] Gulleys and pits carried the water away from the houses and the dry space beneath would have been useful for storage. These massive structures suggest that LBK people were skilled carpenters and this is confirmed by the discovery of well-preserved and beautifully built timber well linings.

Any examination of standing traditional timber buildings around the world immediately demonstrates the problem that faces archaeologists relying on truncated postholes: the sheer exuberance and skill of carpenters and the outright barminess of their superstructures can be completely unpredictable. For example, on Sulawesi, an island north of Bali, the Toraja people practise a religion known as 'the way of the ancestors'. Their lives are focused on their huge soaring timber houses known as 'houses of origin' (see page 152). According to legend, the Toraja arrived on the island in boats, and, upturned, these provided their first shelters – hence the 'houses of origin' with their improbable gable ends are supposed to resemble boats. They are also built to face the north, the direction from which their ancestors came. The exterior walls of the houses are ornately carved and painted, according to strict rules that specify what designs are allowed according to the status of the occupants. The house is a symbol of family identity and the placentas of children born there are buried outside, in order to draw them back as adults.[32] In Southeast Asia many houses are built on piles with elevated floors, in the manner that Rück proposes for LBK buildings. Houses are imbued with symbolism – they reflect mythical stories and ritual practices – but they are also practical. The pile dwellings are a response to prevailing winds, heavy rainfall and flooding, they keep pests out and help air to circulate. In Europe, later prehistoric, Roman and medieval granaries were often built with elevated floors on piles.

LBK houses emerged in a European landscape that would be alien to many of us today; a landscape in which the wild existed just beyond the front door, where the forest was still home to bears, wolves, lynx, wild pigs and wild cattle. The huge LBK houses must have been a startling contrast when they first appeared, as islands of security, shelter and domesticity.

As we have seen, buildings are not merely functional. In traditional societies they often model the cosmology of their inhabitants; they can represent a universe in miniature, and convey ideas, beliefs and appropriate actions or behaviour – much as temples, mosques and churches do in many urbanized societies today. Gordon Childe, so often perspicacious, observed that the domains of the living and the dead are not entirely separate; that long barrows and mounds are similar in shape and size to many houses. In fact, sometimes the former replace the latter, as at the French site of Balloy, Seine-et-Marne (see page 216).

## The dead speak

For more than five centuries, LBK settlers built longhouses across Europe to remarkably similar plans. Where they do vary, however, is in the direction of their entrances. In Transdanubia they are orientated mainly to the south, then as LBK settlements spread to the northwest and west the longhouses,

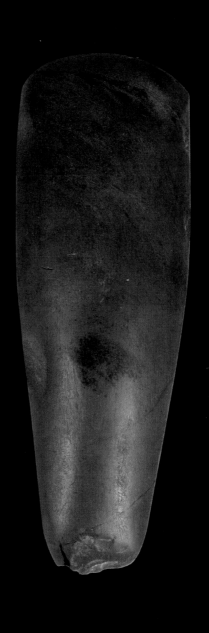

The Neolithic stone axe found near the Devil's
Quoits henge monument, Stanton Harcourt,
Oxfordshire. Made of Langdale tuff quarried
in the English Lake District nearly five thousand
years ago.

OPPOSITE A carved stone stele, engraved with scorpion and bird figures, from Göbekli Tepe, Turkey. These remarkable monuments were erected by hunter-gatherers on the eve of the origins of agriculture.

ABOVE A wall painting from Çatalhöyük. Excited human figures wearing leopard skins and clutching bows torment the giant figure of a bull. In the domesticated early Neolithic, the wild loomed large.

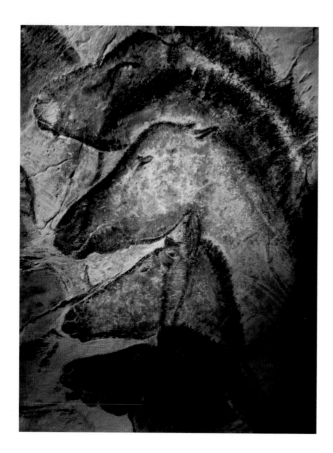

LEFT The beautifully painted heads of wild horses in the Chauvet Cave, Ardèche, France.

OPPOSITE
Some of ancient Egypt's finest and most informative wall paintings appear in the tombs of the great Middle Kingdom cemetery complex at Beni Hasan, dating to about 2000 BC. The wall paintings show a variety of domesticated and wild or tamed animals.
ABOVE: A Semitic figure brings a wild antelope as tribute.
BELOW: A domesticated donkey is used as a beast of burden.

BELOW Przewalski's horses, which closely resemble the Palaeolithic wild horses depicted in the Chauvet Cave, today run wild on the nearby Causse Méjean, having been introduced from Mongolia.

ABOVE An engraved stone in the Neolithic tomb at Gavr'Inis, Morbihan, Brittany. Among the carved patterns are the distinctive shapes of jadeitite axes.

BELOW The Grand Menhir Brisè, Brittany. The huge, axe-shaped stone, now fallen, was once the largest menhir in the region of imposing standing stones.

TOP  Monte Viso, dominating the skyline on the Italy/France border, and the source of the jadeitite stone used to create western Europe's most spectacular Neolithic polished axes.

ABOVE  A fine Monte Viso axe which found its way to Wiltshire, southern England, about six thousand years ago. Damaged when thrown out of a window by a farmer's wife, but now safe in the Wiltshire Museum.

ABOVE Timber houses can be spectacular and symbolic structures. The Toraja people of Sulawesi, Indonesia, build houses symbolizing ships, 'houses of origin', pointing towards their original homeland.

BELOW A basic reconstruction of an LBK longhouse gives a sense of the impressive size of these buildings, but may be lacking the more imaginative details and craftsmanship of the original architecture.

like the needle of a compass, swing consistently towards their point of origin. Some explain the house orientation in terms of prevailing wind and, of course, function and myth can complement each other. In the LBK cemeteries, bodies are also placed in the same way. Are LBK people looking backwards towards the homeland of their ancestors?[33]

Another clue is the fondness for *Spondylus* shells, which were made into amulets or bracelets and often buried with older members of the community. *Spondylus* is a genus of bivalve molluscs, which divers collect from rocks submerged beneath the Aegean Sea off Greece. Their reddish colour reminds us of the importance of red ochre in much earlier burials, and, in fact, red ochre is also scattered in LBK graves. The origin myths of LBK farmers may have reminded settlers in Germany or the Paris Basin that they owed their way of life to ancestors, the tell dwellers, who first colonized the shores of the Aegean, or by then they may have developed another myth to explain what had become a routine practice.

Fortunately, LBK burials are frequently found in and near their settlements. One of the most informative cemeteries for archaeologists is that at Aiterhofen in Bavaria, the largest in the region. LBK people began to bury their dead there about 5300 BC, a century after the first farmers began to cultivate local soils. Cattle rearing was particularly important to them, along with raising pigs and hunting. Over a period of about 400 years the Aiterhofen people placed their dead: 159 in inhumations (bodies placed in graves), 18 in double inhumations and 65 in cremations. About 65% of the burials had grave goods: shell and bone ornaments, pottery, flint tools and scatters of red ochre. This is the conventional stuff of archaeology that provides clues about age, gender and social differences in the Aiterhofen LBK community.

However, science allows us to probe deeper. Sixty-four individuals had molars that were sufficiently well preserved to provide samples from their tooth enamel for strontium isotope analysis. These can give us a geographic signature that indicates whether a particular person was raised in the local area or came in later from elsewhere. Carbon and nitrogen isotopes, from bone collagen, are a further source of information about diet or, at least, levels of protein consumption in the latter years of life. What all this tells us is that the Aiterhofen people ate a remarkably similar diet to each other. It was a community of equals, more or less, not of aristocrats and plebs, or nobles and serfs. With one exception: older men, those buried with polished stone axes, ate more meat and dairy products than the rest.

The only other person to stand out was a baby – still being breastfed when he or she died. The strontium isotope results suggest that the mother may have married into the Aiterhofen group from other LBK communities with a similar diet (rather than from forager groups). Many people, however, were locals, born and bred, and they produced the same mean isotopic values as the pigs, which were also locally reared. The Aiterhofen men seem to have travelled more routinely than the women – probably in the course of hunting, trading or taking their herds to seasonal grazing grounds.

Archaeologists obsessed with the forager/farmer dichotomy have seized on grave goods as badges of identity: river shell decoration equals Mesolithic foragers; polished stone tools or *Spondylus* shells equal Neolithic farmers. Aiterhofen's cemetery shows that such ideas are too simplistic. Some older women, for example, were buried with both river shells and *Spondylus* shells. Individuals do not always conform to categories created by archaeologists. They do, however, have rules that bind the community – for example, stone axes are routinely the attribute of mature men.[34]

## Peace and war

In 2008, Alasdair Whittle, Professor of Archaeology at Cardiff University, and colleagues produced a collection of academic papers that they entitled *Living Well Together?*.[35] In spite of the question mark, the underlying idea was that the period in which farming spread across Europe 'is best defined in terms of co-operation and collaboration, of success in community cohesion, or collaboration in large-scale activities such as field agriculture, and of a level of success developed enough to support specialized craft activities and the expansion of population'. Their ideas, independently, reflect some of those emphasized by Robin Dunbar: that good humour, companionship, love and affection are essential to stability. This is stating the obvious, perhaps, but academics in general, and human sciences in particular, suffer a severe case of 'gravitas'.[36] In contrast, Whittle and co. stress the importance of peaceful-ness, human interconnectedness, gift-sharing and the informal as opposed to the formal and institutional. This may seem idealistic, but it is how ethical groups live.

In practice, of course, communities also fracture and divide, sometimes because people fail to live up to the ideals of the society.[37] Where relation-ships break down irretrievably, mobility can be a solution. Hunter-gatherers frequently respond to their disagreements by moving out. For farmers this can be more difficult, especially if they are boxed in by intensive land use.

The LBK farming communities colonized much of Europe with relative rapidity and consistency. In spite of some regional differences there seems to have been considerable similarity of belief, identity and material culture. The way of life extended across Europe and for several centuries a boundary or frontier zone existed south of the Baltic and around the North Sea. Beyond, hunter-gatherers who clearly interacted with the farmers, remained doggedly resistant to change. Among the farmers, in the earlier fifth millennium BC there were increasing signs that LBK communities were fracturing, adopting new, more regionally distinct lifestyles. In the northwest, late LBK sites were sometimes surrounded with enclosures and ditches while areas between streams and lakes were blocked by palisades, suggesting a growing concern with defence and with separating themselves from the outside world. Deteriorating climate, irregular harvests and disease may have been destabilizing factors. It looks like things were changing for the worse.

Some of the most dramatic evidence of conflict within LBK society was unearthed in 1983–84 at Talheim in the Neckar valley, Germany. Here eleven men, seven women and sixteen children had been flung, unceremoniously, into a freshly dug pit. The forensic examination of the bones revealed the cause of death: two adults were pierced in the head by flint-tipped arrows; most of the others had been bludgeoned from behind with polished stone axes or adzes. At Talheim hostile raiders had used woodworking tools for more sinister purposes. Forensic examination of the wounds suggest that an LBK settlement was attacked by another LBK group, who beat the villagers to death as they fled. DNA and isotopic studies show that some of the dead were related to each other. There are no young women among the victims; they may have been dragged away by the raiders. Of course, one massacre does not indicate a totally dysfunctional society, but there is other evidence for a crisis in the late LBK.

At Asparn/Schletz in Austria several dozen people were killed – again with axes and arrows – and their bodies dumped in a ditch. In 2006, German scientists led by Christian Meyer of the University of Mainz announced that the examination of an LBK burial pit of about 5000 BC at Kilianstädten, 20 km (12 miles) northeast of Frankfurt, had revealed yet another LBK massacre. This mass grave contained the remains of twenty-four people, including thirteen children (ten of whom were under six years of age and one only six months old). The remainder of the victims were men and only two women. These people had also been brutally slain by axe blows to the head and by arrow-shot. Several had broken legs. The lack of female bodies again suggests that the attackers carried off the women while slaughtering the children and menfolk.[38]

The site of Herxheim in the Palatinate in southwest Germany is unusual. The settlement lies on the spur of a loess plateau, at the confluence of two rivers. It was inhabited from about 5300 BC to 4950 BC – the dying days of the LBK. The settlement evidence is not of much interest because it was almost scoured away by ploughing. However, the perimeter is a different matter: continuous elongated pits were regularly dug and infilled to form a symbolic, rather than a defensive, boundary. Altogether they formed an oval of 250 × 230 m (820 × 750 ft). In the latter stages of the settlement's life the open pits were filled with some very strange deposits: high-quality broken pots and other artefacts, the remains of many dogs and cattle horns – and the fragments of hundreds of human bodies.

One particular slot was almost 8 m (26 ft) long and packed with fragments of human bones, all placed there at the same time. Careful forensic analysis of the fragments showed that there were ten individuals: two perinatals (one aged about thirty-six weeks *in utero*); an infant of about five years; a youth of about fifteen years; and six adults of both sexes. The excavation exposed the remains of about 500 individuals in total, but the German archaeologists only investigated just under half of the site.

So what was going on at Herxheim? Further detailed analysis in 2009 came to some startling conclusions. The human bodies had been butchered like animals, processed to maximize the yield of meat and marrow. Huge numbers of cut marks showed how these people had been dissected and defleshed, their larger long bones split and the marrow extracted. The skulls were carefully split to remove the brains but the skullcaps preserved and deposited in nested groups in the open pits. The conclusion was that large numbers of people had been brought to this ceremonial centre over a short period, killed and cannibalized. The distinctive, high-quality pots and other artefacts came from a wide area – some originated in the Elbe region, 500 km (300 miles) away. Were these unfortunate people captives from long-distance raids?

Archaeologists tend to be reluctant to claim to have found cannibal rites. Often, in the past, accusations of cannibalism were exaggerated propaganda. However, cannibalism did, and does, happen: in a crisis when people are starving – for example, the infamous Chilean air crash of 1972, when passengers, justifiably in my opinion, resorted to eating the remains of dead companions. Anthropologists also record cannibalism as part of solemn funeral rites – consuming parts of relatives out of respect; or eating captured enemies, to show contempt, to literally consume their power and to appease one's own dead and the bereaved. The excavators of Herxheim initially interpreted the site as a place of specialized ritual, where the community's dead were dismembered, then more detailed analysis suggested that raiding or war cannibalism of prisoners, over a short and intensive period of time, is more probable.[39]

So there is accumulating evidence for a crisis at the end of the LBK era, and a dramatic transformation in the behaviour of LBK communities. Climate change may have been a factor. The peak of LBK settlement in central Europe coincided with a relatively high level of rainfall. Settlement numbers declined as rainfall decreased. The researchers at Herxheim concluded that there was 'a millennarist crisis' at the end of the LBK.

For centuries LBK societies had been essentially peaceable, familial and communal. They seemed to share joint values with the focus on impressive houses and cooperation, on land and ancestors. By the early fifth millennium BC the great longhouse societies had carried agriculture almost to Europe's northern seas. Yet they were about to fissure into smaller more regional groups, some of whose traditions came from the Cardial cultures formed in the Mediterranean, the south of France and the Atlantic coast. It was from these people that agriculture would spread to the shores of the Baltic and the North Sea – and beyond into the British Isles.

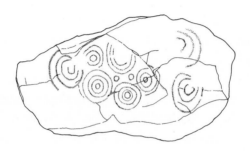

# PART THREE

Crossing the water to Britain

Kerbstone from the perimeter of Knowth tomb
(see page 316).

## CHAPTER NINE

# The remote foragers of Britain

## Looking across the Channel

On 11 August 1999, my wife and I made our way along the clifftops near Fécamp on the Normandy coast. We were two people among hundreds, gathering like lemmings on the northern lip of France. We all knew that this could be one of the best spots in Europe to observe an imminent full eclipse of the sun. As we walked towards the edge of the land the sky was spectre-grey; a grisaille canopy of thin cloud obscured the sun. Then, as the time for the eclipse approached, the veil parted. People gazed through protective spectacles at the glaring sun. A black arc began to bite across it as the moon moved into the sun's orbit, snuffing out its radiance. At first, a crepuscular light remained and then a vertical dark curtain appeared across the water, moving rapidly towards us. The day was closing down fast. In the deepening gloom, a sparkling train of light flickered along the coastline as thousands of cameras flashed, then for a few minutes darkness overwhelmed us. This was an amazing place to observe the eclipse because we were looking across the open sea, where the English Channel – France's La Manche ('the Sleeve') – widens out; it is about 105 km (65 miles) from coast to coast.

The British see themselves as islanders. Enemies – William the Conqueror, the Vikings, Napoleon and the Nazis – lay across the sea. But Britain has not always been an island – several hundred thousand years ago Britain and France were joined together by a chalk dome (the Weald-Artois Ridge). Beyond it to the north, rivers such as the Thames (on a more northerly course than today's), the Humber, Rhine, Meuse and Elbe flowed into the basin that is now the North Sea, and then drained northwards. To the south of the chalk upland, which attached the British peninsula to the Continent, rivers such as the Seine, the Somme and the Solent flowed into the English Channel basin.

In glacial periods an ice dam blocked the northwards flow and created a large lake. As these waters rose they flowed over the Weald-Artois Ridge, cutting through the soft, vulnerable chalk and creating a massive canyon. The cliffs on either side of the Strait of Dover, the White Cliffs and

Cap Blanc Nez, are today visible evidence of the great breach. The biblical torrents, fed by all the rivers and ice sheets of northwest Europe, flowed southwest and carved out a massive valley that, as sea levels rose, became the Strait of Dover and the English Channel.

There has been much debate about the timing of the breach. It seems most likely that it happened during the Anglian Glaciation (MIS 12) about 450,000 years ago when much of Britain was covered by ice and the River Thames was shoved southwards to its present course. The resulting English Channel river was such a fast-flowing torrent that it really did cut Britain off from the Continent for a time.[1]

## Exploring beneath the waves: the search for Doggerland

Until about 6000–5500 BC the lowlands and the southern North Sea basin were occupied by some of Europe's great rivers, notably the Seine, the Rhine and the Thames. Looking across its grey waters today at one of the world's busiest shipping lanes, it is hard to imagine the scene nine or ten thousand years ago. The person who has done most to bring it back to life is Professor Vince Gaffney. When I visited his office at Birmingham University in 2007 it resembled the bridge of the *Starship Enterprise*, dominated by a bank of large computer screens. At a flick of a few switches we began to boldly go beneath the waters of the southern North Sea, into the flooded region known as Doggerland.[2] Vince glided over never-before-seen terrain. As a fan of NASA's superb website I thought we could have been looking at the latest images from some distant planet. In fact, in front of us was the topography of the sea basin before it was inundated and buried in silt. Here was a landscape of lakes, marshes, small hills and valleys, steams and river channels, a Mesolithic (and earlier) Eden ideal for hunters, fishers, fowlers and plant-collectors.

As long ago as 1913, the remarkably prescient geologist Sir Clement Reid, in a book on submerged forests in England, noted the potential of flooded landscapes where 'the antiquary should find the remains of ancient races of man, sealed up with his weapons and tools' as well as 'implements of wood, basketwork or objects in leather, such as are so rarely preserved in deposits above water-level'.[3] Reid was ahead of his time. Most archaeologists tended to think in terms of a 'land bridge' between Britain and the Continent – a strip of land strictly for passing over, and of not much interest otherwise. We now know that the southern North Sea – from southern Scotland to the

English Channel and across to northern France, the Netherlands, Denmark and Germany – contains a prehistoric landscape of world-class importance, as long as it can be recorded and preserved in the face of intensive modern activities: oil-drilling, marine aggregates extraction, trawling and dredging.

In May 2003, English Heritage invited archaeologists from five countries bordering the North Sea to a workshop on the subject of submarine prehistory and relations with industry. As a relative newcomer to this field I was aston-ished by the images we were shown by continental maritime archaeologists. They were definitely ahead of us in this game. Particularly striking were the pictures of Dutch trawlers, their decks laden, not with fish, but the bones and fossils of prehistoric animals dragged from the seabed. These catches confirmed that the Palaeolithic mammoth steppe once stretched across the North Sea basin. One trawler, in waters off Rotterdam, hauled in the skull of an old male woolly mammoth with tusks 3.2 m (10 ft 6 in.) long. Another landed the jaw of a sabre-toothed cat, which radiocarbon dates later showed to be 28,000 years old.[4]

Between 1997 and 2003 the Dutch archaeologists involved in the North Sea Project collected 60,000 kg (60 tons) of bones from large and small mammals and eight thousand molars from woolly mammoths. Far more were probably sold on the fossil market. The Dutch images were striking; the implications horrendous. Modern beam trawlers, fishing for sole, plaice and turbot, liter-ally scour the seabed, their nets attached to heavy metal beams, 12 m (40 ft) long and strewn with chains. At the same time, they gouge through relict landscapes, harvesting ancient animal and human bones as well as prehistoric artefacts. If fishing has the biggest impact in the North Sea, it is not alone – oil pipelines, wind farms and aggregate dredging are all transforming the seabed. It seemed that we had rediscovered Doggerland just in time to see it shredded by modern maritime development. This drowned world, a real Atlantis, is being pulverized.

English Heritage was established in 1983 as the public body responsible for the protection and management of England's historic environment. When I joined in 1999 there was a gaping hole in our activities – an anomaly in the Act that established English Heritage meant that the underwater environment, off England's shores, was not part of its responsibilities. Hence archaeologi-cal research and the protection of wrecks and submerged landscapes were seriously neglected. This is why our continental colleagues were ahead of us in appreciating and tackling the conservation problems. Fortunately, an

RIGHT Map of Doggerland, 9000 BC. Great Britain was attached to the Continent by Doggerland. In about 6500 BC rising sea levels flooded the southern North Sea Basin and breached the Channel.

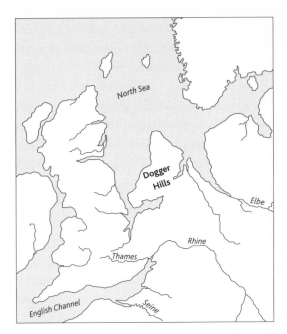

BELOW Petrified tree stumps, such as these examples from Borth, Aberystwyth, are evidence of the Mesolithic forests that once grew around Britain's contemporary coast, before they were flooded and submerged by rising sea levels.

opportunity to change this appeared, and the passing of the National Heritage Act with all-party support in May 2002 gave English Heritage the authority to deal with maritime archaeology.

We immediately established a small team of specialists, led by Ian Oxley, and then set about talking to as many people as possible with interests in the North Sea and the rest of British waters.[5] Fortunately, progress was rapid. Since the early 1970s archaeologists had developed excellent relations with the aggregates industry on land. It had also become routine to investigate archaeological landscapes in advance of quarrying. So in 2005, English Heritage archaeologists and the top brass of the British Marine Aggregate Producers Association (BMAPA) gathered on the deck of HMS *Belfast* in the Pool of London, overlooked by Tower Bridge, to launch a protocol. We agreed that companies involved in underwater dredging would cooperate with archaeologists.

In early February 2008 came the clearest evidence, so far, that the protocol was working.[6] The Dutch authorities sent word that twenty-eight Palaeolithic handaxes had turned up in aggregate deposits landed in Rotterdam, dredged from the waters off Great Yarmouth on England's east coast, in a zone known not very evocatively as Area 240. We then informed the operators that Area 240 was sensitive and they withdrew their dredgers. These machines are electronically monitored so it was possible to locate where the axes had come from (ironically, it was easier than locating the find spot of the Neolithic handaxe found near Oxford). Eventually seventy-five handaxes and other flint artefacts, and the remains of woolly rhinoceros, bison, mammoths, reindeer and horses were found. All this material came from deposits of different dates, but the discovery was a paradigm changer. It showed that beneath the North Sea there were surviving landscapes at least 300,000 years old. Here was evidence that deposits connected with early hominin activity, possibly even as early as those excavated on the eroding East Anglian coast at Pakefield and Happisburgh, and the channel of the ancient Bytham River, continued beneath the present-day North Sea towards Doggerland.

## Recolonizing Britain

About 24,000 years ago, temperatures in Europe began to plummet during what is known as the Last Glacial Maximum. Conditions in northern regions like Britain were too tough for human habitation. Then, about 16,000 years ago, the cold began to release its grip. Plants and animals took the opportunity to colonize the land that was emerging from the freezer. Herds of reindeer and horses moved north and west in Europe seeking out new grazing lands. Wolves and human hunters followed in their wake. These were the first modern humans to return to Britain since the ancestors of the Red Lady of Paviland had been driven out by the onset of the last big freeze.

The presence of the intrepid newcomers can be seen vividly at Creswell Crags on the Derbyshire/Nottinghamshire border. Here, a spectacular gorge, about 1 km (⅔ mile) long, cuts through the Magnesian Limestone. Its vertical cliffs are studded with caves, which provided shelter to bands of hunters. Creswell Crags is a smaller version of the well-watered gorges of central France, such as those in the Lot, Dordogne and Ardèche valleys, which acted as refuges to humans during the cold of the last glaciation (about 140,000 to 22,000 years ago).

Archaeologists call these groups Magdalenian, after the rock shelf of La Madeleine in the Dordogne. These are the people who produced the most spectacular Upper Palaeolithic art on the walls of the caves of Lascaux in France and Altamira in Spain. At La Madeleine itself hunter-artists beautifully evoked reindeer and horses by engraving their images on bone and antler. I managed recently to get close to a small herd of wild Przewalski's horses, cousins of the Upper Palaeolithic animals, which today graze on the 'steppe' of the Causse Méjean – a remote limestone plateau in southern France. Standing next to these stolid, calm animals, 'megalith-still', it was clear that the Magdalenian artists had perfectly captured their stocky build, blunt heads with Roman noses and distinctive upright, bristling manes.[7]

More than 36,000 years ago Neanderthals had discovered the potential of Creswell Crags for shelter and as a hunting base. Twenty thousand years later, modern humans moved in. They littered the caves and their entrances, known now as Church Hole Cave, Robin Hood Cave, Mother Grundy's Parlour and Pin Hole, with distinctive flint tools, many used as spearheads or as engraving tools. This flintwork has close affinities with material from sites in southwest Britain, such as Cheddar Gorge, and others on the edges of the uplands of Belgium and the Netherlands, and in the Paris Basin. It seems that these hunters were wide ranging. They emerged out of central France into the north, colonized Doggerland when the sea level was still about 48 m (157 ft) lower than today, and then spread into Britain. Magdalenian sites and material in Britain are scarce. These incomers were not numerous; their visits may even have been intermittent and seasonal.

They were certainly present in spring, following the migrating reindeer to their upland calving grounds and taking vulnerable young animals. Although summer temperatures were similar to today's, the landscape was still an open grassland. Wild horses and woolly mammoths also fell prey to the humans, whose isotope results confirm that they had a meat-rich diet. Arctic or mountain hare were systematically trapped. Their superb fur is at its most distinctive in winter when they don their white camouflage. It is probable that the hares were caught in spring and their fur used to supplement and repair warm winter clothing. To add insult to injury, the hares' own tibiae were made into awls in order to pierce the pelts and stitch them together. This genius for catching small animals and producing thermally efficient clothing made it possible for modern humans to colonize cold northern wastes.

The Upper Palaeolithic record of Britain has always looked a bit second-rate compared with its magnificent manifestation in France and northern Spain. In France the galleries of Lascaux and Chauvet are still taken as proof of the inherent superiority and antiquity of French culture. It seemed that there were no Picassos among British Ice Age hunters; then in 2003 archaeologists Paul Bahn, Paul Pettitt and Sergio Ripoll made the first discovery of Palaeolithic cave art in Britain.[8] These were not painted images like the famous bulls of Lascaux or lions of Chauvet. At Creswell Crags the hunter-artists engraved the outlines of bulls, deer and birds into the rock surface. Only when strong, raking light was played over the rock walls did the figures become more clearly visible.[9] The discoveries put Britain firmly into the Ice Age art club and showed that the people who recolonized Britain were firmly embedded in the Magdalenian orbit, the hunter bands who repopulated northwestern Europe.

Textbooks about Upper Palaeolithic Britain usually emphasize its apparent cultural links with France. Creswell Crags is portrayed as the ultimate frontier for the big game hunters. Scotland is often left off the map completely – and, it now seems, unfairly. From 2003 local fieldwalkers scouring the fields at Howburn Farm, northeast of Biggar in South Lanarkshire, found thousands of stone – mainly flint and chert – artefacts, probably brought to the surface by ploughing, and in 2005 they undertook a small excavation. The site was a palimpsest of stone objects, deposited at different periods over millennia. There were even fragments of Neolithic polished stone axes made of Langdale tuff.

The most important discoveries emerged when Alan Saville, of the National Museums of Scotland, and Torben Bjarke Ballin, both lithic experts, got to work on this massive stone jigsaw puzzle. Refitting broken fragments together, a kind of flint forensics, they identified a distinctive tanged projectile point. Along with this there were blades struck from cylindrical cores. What they had identified was an assemblage of tools more or less contemporary with the Creswell Crags late Palaeolithic occupation of about 14,000 years ago and Scotland's earliest-known occupants. However, while Creswell Crags's stone tools, and those found on contemporary sites in southern England, pointed to links with central France, Howburn had connections directly eastwards, across Doggerland to northern Germany and Denmark, where the Hamburgian culture took advantage of a warm period of the Ice Age. Similar tools had been excavated at sites such as Jels and Slotseng in southern Denmark, both prominent places where hunters could observe wild reindeer and horses approaching water. Howburn had similar topography, overlooking what was probably a well-watered valley on the migration routes.

It seems that as the climate improved and the Last Glacial Maximum went into retreat hunters moved along with animals into the empty peninsula of Britain both from modern-day France, and further north from Denmark and northern Germany. Turn west and keep walking; the southern uplands of Scotland were just about as far as Palaeolithic hunters could go.[10] Or might they have taken to the sea?

## In and out of the freezer – again

Once again, climate change delivered an unwelcome setback. Britain had been reoccupied by the Magdalenians when midwinter temperatures rose from -40°C (-40°F) to something close to today's, then about 13,000 years ago the glacial Lake Agassiz, in North America, released a vast quantity of cold fresh water into the Atlantic. This formed a cap on the denser, saltier waters of the Gulf Stream and switched off the warm Atlantic conveyor that bathes the British Isles. The outpourings of glacial meltwater from North America put Europe into the freezer, with the last great cold spell known as the Younger Dryas (see also Chapter 4). The climatic impact of the Gulf Stream shutdown was global. It not only affected the Near East, where the Natufians struggled to adapt, but also as far afield as New Zealand and South America. In Britain, the impact was drastic: glaciers reappeared in northwest Scotland and other uplands. The glacial winter dragged on for twelve hundred years, and the hunters may have retreated to more southerly refuges during the harshest times, as their ancestors had done before.

In 2015, the story of the Ice Age colonization of Scotland suddenly became more interesting thanks to a bunch of pigs grubbing on the coastline of the Isle of Islay, in the Inner Hebrides. The animals turned up several stone artefacts that were brought to the attention of Reading University's Steven Mithen and Karen Wicks. Their excavation at the site, Rubha Port an t-Seilich, revealed the remains of an exceptionally well-preserved early Mesolithic occupation, dating to about 9,300 years ago. More remarkable, however, was an earlier level (Layer 111), sealed beneath a Mesolithic hearth and containing sixty-five stone artefacts. These were unlike Mesolithic tools; instead they resembled those used by the Hamburgian reindeer hunters. Specialists provisionally identified them more closely to later reindeer hunting groups in Belgium and northern Germany known as Ahrensburgian. Layer 111 contained no organic material suitable for radiocarbon dating. Fortunately, however, there were microscopic horizons of tephra – volcanic ash from dated Icelandic eruptions. The stone tools lay sandwiched between two volcanic events known to have occurred 12,100 years ago and 8,300 years ago, and so belonged to the second half of the Younger Dryas and fitted the proposed Ahrensburgian context.[11]

This identification throws up an interesting idea about the settlement of Scotland. Ahrensburgian artefacts are rare in northern England, but have occasionally been found in Orkney, Shieldaig on the northwest coast of Scotland, and the island of Tiree (Inner Hebrides), and now, for the first time, in an undisturbed stratified layer at Rubha Port an t-Seilich. Felix Reide, an expert on this period at Aarhus University, Denmark, suggests that the Ahrensburgian reindeer hunters took to the sea in order to explore the coast of southern Scandinavia. It seems possible that these people followed the coast of Doggerland in their boats to the northward-projecting peninsula of Scotland, reached Orkney and then island-hopped at least as far south as Islay, exploring the fluctuating northern limits of the Ice Age world when glaciers still covered most of inland Scandinavia and a large area of the Highlands of Scotland. Humans in the north were engaged in a constant struggle, a game of cat-and-mouse with the climate. Any slackening in the grip of the ice opened new opportunities. The Scottish coastline and the islands of the northwest provided virgin hunting territory for the pioneers who risked the icy waters.

Then the Younger Dryas cold spell came to an end. About 11,500 years ago, subtropical water again poured into the North Atlantic and reanimated the Gulf Stream. This was the start of the Holocene, the interglacial period in which we live today.

The rewarming of the planet, with higher rainfall levels, had a drastic impact. Much of the Sahara bloomed; grasslands flourished in the Near East and trees spread northwards across Europe towards the North Pole. The hunters of the mammoth steppe were faced with a radical change in their way of life, as the great herds became extinct or retreated into limited ranges. The remains of four mammoths, which died about 12,700 years ago, were found in a gravel pit in Shropshire in the English West Midlands in 1987. These impressive beasts would not be seen for much longer in Britain, nor in most of northern Europe. Instead, different animals became the focus of attention for hungry humans.

In 1985, Tim Allen, one of my Oxford colleagues, was watching a water pipeline as it sliced across the fields of Gatehampton Farm, where the River Thames cuts through the narrow Goring Gap between the chalk uplands on either side. In the trench he spotted the line of an old watercourse, infilled with an ancient soil and containing superb-quality flint tools. Excavations over the next few years revealed what had been an island in the Thames. On it some of the last Palaeolithic hunters in Britain squatted and knapped flint nodules, from which they pressure-flaked superb long blades. This was an ideal spot. Flint was prolific in the nearby chalk and migrating reindeer and horses may have used the Goring Gap as a routeway between the valley and the chalk uplands. The Gatehampton hunters lay in wait at the river crossing. This is also the crossing point for the famous Ridgeway, a prehistoric trail that runs across southeastern England linking Wessex with East Anglia. I like to think that it was the Ice Age herds that first forged this route. It would have led them back towards the rich pastures of Doggerland. Unfortunately, animal bone did not survive at Gatehampton Farm; however, reindeer and horses, whose remains have been found at nearby contemporary sites, were probably still the target for these hunters living in Britain at the very end of the last glacial period.[12]

Sometimes, an unimpressive section through the soil can tell us a great deal. Here, at Gatehampton Farm, in the ancient soil deposits lying above the 'long blade' flint layer, there were traces of plant pollen only visible through the microscope. These pollen grains had been dispersed by warmth-loving trees. The way of life of Ice Age hunters was coming to an end. The newly arrived forests of the milder Holocene would attract different animals. Humans would have to adapt to a new way of life.

## Living in the wild wood

After 9500 BC temperatures in northwest Europe rose rapidly. As the tundra warmed new plant species colonized the land. We see the same effect today in reverse if we travel northwards, say from New York State through Canada to Alaska, or from lowlands into high mountains and beyond the treeline. In Britain, pollen samples – often taken by coring into bogs and marshes – indicate the presence or absence of plants through time. The first foothold of birch trees, with some willow and hazel, is seen in East Anglia after 9500 BC. These species probably spread out of the Netherlands, across Doggerland and into Britain.

By 7000 BC woodland was widespread in Britain, mostly conifers in the north, and mixed with deciduous species in the south: initially oak, elm and hazel, with alder and ash arriving about 6000 BC and lime a few centuries later. Lime (*Tilia cordata*), which has nothing to do with the fruit of that name, was ultimately an important species in the English forest. When I walked home in the early summer evenings in Oxford I routinely crossed Magdalen Bridge over the River Cherwell. By the bridge there was a group of lime trees. As I passed beneath I could hear the thrumming of thousands of bees. This is why the lime tree presents a problem for palaeobotanists. It is insect pollinated and so does not shed much pollen into the air and consequently into preserved deposits. As a result it can be under-represented in pollen diagrams compared with species like oak and hazel. It was, however, an important tree for the hunter-gatherers, who used it for making dugout canoes.

For the people who inhabited the newly forested Britain the nature of the woodland mattered. This was the environment that supplied them with the animals and plants for food and the raw materials upon which they depended for shelter, clothing and tools. In the early Holocene, Britain and northwest Europe became a very different place to that occupied by Upper Palaeolithic hunters. This new habitat attracted red deer, huge aurochs (wild cattle), wild boar, beavers and bears. Foxes and wolves, almost as adaptable as humans, also thrived.

However, much of what grows in temperate forest – wood, leaves and grass – is not edible for humans. Although there are nuts, berries, tubers and animals, particularly the browsing ungulates, a temperate forest is less of a carnivore's larder than the tundra. Forest animals are thinner on the ground, flightier and harder to track down and approach than great, shifting herds of reindeer, horses and mammoths. From my own experience of living surrounded by forest I know that wild pigs are the easiest target. I have, unfortunately, never had the privilege of confronting an auroch: for Mesolithic hunters this must have been the beast to seal their reputations in the clan. It was a magnificent, powerful and increasingly rare animal that would provide families with meat for weeks, as well as bone, horn, sinew, grease and leather.

Hunters who take more than 5% of ungulate prey population a year put future supplies of prey at risk. These animals also have to cope with disease, ageing and other predators, and their population can easily plummet. In the temperate forest it is important for hunter-gatherers to have territories close to rivers, lochs and lakes or coastlines so that fish, shellfish, birds and plants from the water margins play an important part in survival. It has been estimated that a hunter searching for prey consumes about 200 calories per hour (and needs to consume 2,200–3,000 plus calories a day depending upon the climate and topography) so surviving off the land can be a risky business, especially short-term fluctuations in food supply. There are also seasonal risks such as the shortage of animal fats in winter and early spring when prey are themselves lean – in the Mesolithic, a pressing problem could be too much protein and a shortage of carbohydrates as animals fattened for winter and the rutting season rapidly lost weight. Hunter-gatherers developed coping strategies – storing hazelnuts, smoking or drying fish and meat (further north, freezing and caching were possible), moving about in pursuit of fresh food supplies and limiting and maintaining the human population below the carrying capacity of their environment. Big, fierce animals are always relatively rare – and this applied to humans living in the temperate woodland of post-glacial Britain.

For most of the 20th century palaeobotanists portrayed a Mesolithic land covered in dense, close-canopy forest. This is now questioned.[13] It is increasingly appreciated that animals make an impact on their habitat. In areas like Britain, where we have driven aurochs, wolves, bears, boars and beavers to extinction, it is easy to forget the importance of such animals to the character and ecology of the ancient landscape. The pollen diagrams of the early Holocene show a preponderance of light-loving species such as hazel and oak. Larger animals, like the powerful aurochs, would have opened and maintained clearings in the woodland, providing opportunities for hazel to thrive around the edges, and grasses and other plants to grow where the light flooded in. Clearings would attract browsing deer, rodents and their predators, which would in turn restrict forest regeneration. Beavers also engineered their environment, cutting down trees, creating channels and building dams, which resulted in networks of wetland, so attracting fish, amphibians and birds.[14] In the river valleys, watercourses were still braided and irregular – littered with islands and sandbanks. As we will see later, farming – particularly ploughing – smoothed off the rough edges of this wildscape; forest clearance and erosion filled in the hollows; drainage systems dried out the land and canalized the rivers.

So ten thousand years ago in Britain, the hunter-gatherers occupied a mosaic of landscapes in which thrived the plants and animals that had colonized the peninsula from their European refuges, although some species never reached Britain under their own efforts – the number of native species of plants and animals is far fewer than in Mediterranean lands or the Near East. Temperature was still a barrier for some of them, while others were hindered by natural obstacles, such as the Alps.

The resources that nature provided to hunter-gatherers in northwest Europe were very different to those available to the Natufians and proto-farmers of the Near East, and they were particularly limited in Ireland. Today, the typical clichéd image of the Emerald Isle is of lush pasture and heavy-uddered cows, a land dripping with butter – what Nobel laureate poet Seamus Heaney called 'coagulated sunlight, heaped up like gilded gravel in the bowl'.[15] All this came later. Ten thousand years ago, Ireland looked like a wasteland, the ground striated and scarred by glaciers. The retreating ice left behind a landscape of lakes, hollows, eskers, dumps of gravel and bare, scoured rock. It took a time to heal this Mordor. And because Ireland was soon cut off by the sea from Britain and the Continent, many plants and animals did not make it there after the Ice Age. As J. P. Mallory says, 'in terms of prey for hunters, Ireland was one of the poorest places in Europe'.[16]

When I was a child, educated initially in St Patrick's School, West Vale, Yorkshire, a garish plaster statue of Ireland's patron saint dominated our classroom. He looked like a stern, bearded bishop in his yellow and green vestments – and his crozier pinned down the writhing body of a snake. As we were very regularly told by Father Hickey and the headmistress, Miss McAuliffe, St Patrick had banished the heathen serpents from godly Ireland. Unfortunately for the veracity of the myth, snakes didn't reach Ireland. And neither did humans until about 8000 BC – Ireland was one of the last places in Eurasia to be settled. The end result was that whereas France can claim about 3,500 native plants, Britain has fewer than 1,200 and Ireland a mere 815. Animal species are similarly depleted.

However, the theory of an Irish–French land bridge (or stepping stones) is given some support by the DNA analysis of native Irish fauna. From the window in my writer's cell in France, I sometimes see a family of pine martens scampering over the granite bounders along the edge of the river. Genetic evidence indicates that Irish pine martens are more closely related to my French neighbours than they are to the Scottish populations. The same applies to Irish house mice, stoats and mountain hares.[17] Stoats and hares, however, do not go a long way among a band of hungry hunter-gatherers. Big ungulates like reindeer can provide 50 kg (110 lb) of meat (or 135,000 calories) and red deer also come in large packages; neither of these was present in Ireland in the early Holocene. Nevertheless, as the climate warmed and sea levels rose, and as forests clothed the scarred glacial landscapes, bands of Mesolithic hunters, plant gatherers, fishers and seafarers explored and colonized the peninsula of Britain and its islands. They were learning to adapt to new environments; developing new lives in new landscapes.

## CHAPTER TEN

# The forested islands

## Inventing the Mesolithic

As the wildwood of the Holocene spread across northwest Europe and Britain, hunter-gatherers had to adapt to new habitats and develop new technologies. Archaeologists call this slice of human history (at least in Europe) the Mesolithic, or Middle Stone Age, distinguishing a period of prehistoric time between Sir John Lubbock's Palaeolithic and Neolithic. Sometimes, the Mesolithic can seem like a minor interlude, an *amuse-bouche* between the major courses when big game hunters decorated caves with spectacular paintings and humanity at last arrived at the road to civilization with the adoption of farming.

Penny Spikins, a Mesolithic specialist at York University, explains: 'One of the deep-seated concepts of the Mesolithic is as a time of cultural stagnation – passive societies in which little changed and social relationships were uncontested.' The root of such ideas is 'the long-standing view of Mesolithic societies as being dominated by their environment'.[1] Richard Bradley nailed the issue with a memorable bon mot: 'Successful farmers have social relations with one another, while hunter-gatherers have ecological relations with hazelnuts.'[2] The person most responsible for this image was the distinguished Cambridge archaeologist Sir Grahame Clark. This is not a criticism. As Clark (never a fan of Marxism) explained himself, when he began his research in 1930 the Mesolithic was a hazy concept. Gordon Childe, influenced by Russian archaeologists, 'found it hard to treat the transitional assemblages as anything more than the fag-end of the preceding era' and 'felt compelled to deny its status as marking a substantive phase in prehistory'.[3]

Clark argued for the integrity of the Mesolithic, though admitted that his own pioneering work on the period 'amounted to little more than a typological study of flint assemblages supplemented by occasional artifacts of antler and bone'.[4] Clark, partly as a result of his innovative work with palaeobotanists, zoologists and pollen specialists, succeeded in putting the Mesolithic on the map – with the emphasis on ecological adaptation. This made perfect sense at the time, and is still an essential element in archaeological research. In Britain he excavated the well-preserved, waterlogged site at Star Carr in Yorkshire, an early Mesolithic site that dominates its period perhaps like no other in British prehistory.

Yet the Mesolithic in Britain, and even more so in Europe, is a fascinating period, hardly a 'prelude', to quote Clark's own book title. In Britain, the Mesolithic stretches between about 9000 BC and 4000 BC – the temporal distance between ourselves and the early Bronze Age. This is a time of great change in the lifeways of humans. In Europe (as elsewhere) people demonstrated their flexibility and adaptability. They took to the waters to discover new lands, to catch fish and collect shellfish, and they pursued seals and other sea mammals almost to the Arctic Circle. They exploited the rivers, such as the Danube, which provided routeways into the forests that covered the Continent. Europe was a complex mosaic of specialist and generalist groups, intimate with their environment but hardly dominated by it. The people in the north of Europe were as flexible and inventive as those to the southeast who were pioneering agriculture at this time,[5] and were operating in different environments that provided very different opportunities.

## The neglected hunter-gatherers

To understand why and how the farming revolution reached Britain we need to know more about the people who occupied these islands (and the continent of Europe, for that matter) in the centuries and millennia before 4000 BC. But there is a problem. This 'period' labelled by prehistorians as the Mesolithic, has, until recently, been one of the least studied of all, especially in England, although in Wales, Scotland and Ireland the Mesolithic has fared distinctly better. The balance has been redressed to a limited extent in the past two decades, particularly by systematic surveys of the wetlands of both lowland and upland Britain, monitoring coastal erosion and undertaking offshore surveys of the landscapes flooded by prehistoric sea-level rise. However, we cannot avoid the fundamental issue: hunter-gatherers generally leave relatively little trace of their existence.

Hunter-gatherers made some impact on the landscape and we should not underestimate the extent to which they prepared the ground for the first farmers – for example, by burning areas deliberately, opening up and maintaining clearings to attract browsing animals, or even for ritual purposes, and creating trails and access to water. In some parts of the world they introduced new species, such as wild pigs, deer, dogs and other commensals. They probably also contributed to the decline and extinction of large animals stressed by climate change or disease. Nevertheless, in Britain, their camps and settlements leave slight traces. Burials are rare; ritual monuments scarce or non-existent. Shell middens are probably the most distinctive feature in some coastal areas. Their skills as craftsmen and craftswomen with wood, twine, leather and basketry are almost as ephemeral and transient as their language, song and myth. Yet there are traces, fragments of the past left behind for those who search diligently. Flakes of flint or chert, chips from stoneworking, sometimes recognizable axes, arrowheads, scrapers and piercing tools litter the landscape – resistant to decay.

For centuries, 'civilized' people who kept domestic animals – and fellow humans as slaves – built temples, churches and mosques, lived in cities and respected social hierarchies, tended to have a low opinion of hunter-gatherers, the people that culture had left behind. In 1832, Charles Darwin, during that voyage in the *Beagle* that has taken on a legendary significance almost on a par with Jason and the Argonauts or Ulysses, came across the Yámana – hunter-gatherers of Tierra del Fuego. He recorded the encounter: 'I could not have believed how wide was the difference, between savage and civilized man. It is greater than between a wild and domesticated animal.' Darwin continued: 'We have no reason to believe that they perform any sort of religious worship...no government or chief...the language scarcely deserves to be called articulate.' Darwin's view was that such people could not 'know the feeling of having a home, and still less that of domestic affection'.[6] The Fuegians were adapted to their foraging lifestyle, but this did not mean that they were trapped in some animal-like 'savagery' (until recently, a term much used by anthropologists). Early in the 20th century, the Reverend Thomas Bridges compiled a dictionary of the Yámana language. He lists 32,000 words, including many that describe kinship and home. The Yámana dwellings were slight, even short-lived, but the word they used for them meant 'the home where the family came together'. In fact, it also meant 'the family' itself: the community who clustered around the hearth, to eat, tell jokes and create stories and myths.

If such a thoughtful 19th-century man as Darwin failed, in part (not all his comments were as unsympathetic as the ones quoted above), to see the humanity of hunter-gatherers, to appreciate their skills, cosmology and cultural life, others could behave far worse. Even as Darwin wrote, and in the following decades, hunter-gatherers in North and South America, Africa, Australia and Tasmania were themselves hunted like wild animals. Unfortunately, the social skills of civilized farmers and town dwellers have rarely been applied to understanding or empathizing with those who continued to follow a two-million-year-old way of life. Even as recently as 1957, the distinguished American archaeologist and pioneering excavator of Neolithic Jarmo, Robert Braidwood, declared: 'A man who spends his whole life following animals just to kill them to eat, or moving from one berry patch to another is really living just like an animal himself.'[7]

More recently, the anthropologist Marshall Sahlins wrote of 'the original affluent society',[8] and attitudes in anthropological and archaeological circles have become more sympathetic to hunter-gatherers. These were, after all, our ancestors, who evolved large brains and sophisticated language, not to improve their foraging abilities, but as Kent Flannery and Joyce Marcus of the Museum of Anthropological Archaeology, University of Michigan, point out: 'to make us better at social networking'.[9] Sahlins described hunter-gatherers as 'affluent' because he believed that many were able to collect ample food in a relatively short time, which left them able to develop a rich, imaginative world of myths, music and dance. It was a way of life not burdened with cumbersome material possessions.

So archaeologists, who love litter and rubbish, were often slow to investigate the Mesolithic. Like everyone else, we are creatures of our own time. We like photogenic discoveries, the 'first', the 'unique', the relatively easy to get at and celebrity sites. For many of us the late hunter-gatherers of the Mesolithic do not quite hit the mark. Ancient farmers built impressive stone monuments, permanent villages, even cities. They simply made more stuff; their impact on the planet and on the world of archaeology was greater. Fortunately, though, some archaeologists like a challenge and persist in the search for those people who trod lightly on the earth.


## Tools for the job

One issue for humans in northern Eurasia 11,000 years ago was how to adapt from life on the open mammoth steppe or tundra to very different conditions, as temperate woodland colonized northern Europe and the British Isles. For the people of northwest Europe, a world dominated by trees required new technologies, and new mythologies we can only guess at. Timber became a

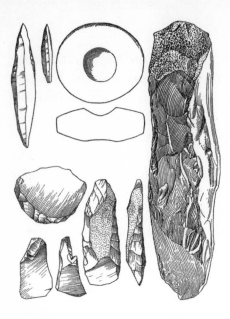

Mesolithic stone tools include the distinctive tranchet axe head on the right.

principal resource: for shelter, fuel, tools and transport. A new form of flint axe came into its own, designed to cut and trim timber. In archaeological illustrations the so-called tranchet axe looks superficially like the handaxe, which played such an important role during the long millennia of the Palaeolithic. In fact, the tranchet axe is very different. It was made by flaking a core and then sharpening (or resharpening) the edges with transverse blows to produce a tool that could function like a chisel or a chopping axe. Even when there are no axes, archaeologists with a sharp eye for such things can find their distinctive flakes left scattered around where Mesolithic knappers once worked. These axes were not held in the hand, but hafted with wooden handles, often inserted first into a red deer antler bole, to help absorb the blow when cutting timber. Tranchet axes are a distinctive feature through the British Mesolithic, except in Scotland where flint was in short supply (these axes required good-quality flint). Mesolithic hunter-gatherers did not usually transport heavy raw materials very far. Instead, they found alternative solutions. In Scotland they still needed axes, so they made them out of antler.[10]

In Wales and Ireland, however, inventive stoneworkers came up with another tool – the groundstone axe – which like our later Neolithic axe, was polished or ground rather than flaked. Nab Head, a promontory in western Pembrokeshire, is a place where such axes were manufactured. It struck me when walking on the nearby beach that many of the pebbles, washed slick and shining by the waves, actually looked like polished axes. Perhaps some innovative lithics worker had a 'Eureka moment' on that beach.

In southwest Ireland, at Ferriter's Cove, five axes were found actually made of elongated pebbles of black shale, deposited together in a cache. Others were placed with a cremation at Castleconnell on the bank of the Shannon and in the river itself. The axes were certainly functional but they may also have held a deeper meaning for Mesolithic people. It is probably their social and symbolic importance that explains why in Ireland (and in Britain and Scandinavia) such axes were buried in caches, deposited around lake edges and in rivers like the Shannon. The largest Irish group of tranchet axes and adzes, 750 in total, was found by the River Shannon, at Killaloe.[11] Rivers were also important places for ritual deposition of axes in southern Britain. Huge numbers were placed in the River Thames and its tributary, the Kennet (an elongated version of the tranchet axe, frequently found in the River Thames, is known as a 'Thames Pick').

Often these axes seem to be fresh, unused and somewhat larger than more utilitarian examples. This seems to be the start of a long tradition in northwest Europe of placing offerings, especially tools or weapons, in watery places.[12]


## Mesolithic angst

As an archaeologist, it is not unusual for people to ask me, 'If you could live in any period in the past, what would it be?' The honest answer is, 'I'll stay here, thanks. I quite like painkillers, modern dentistry, hot running water, flush toilets, books and my iPad.' But, so as not to sound like a boring materialist, I usually answer, 'The Mesolithic – not many humans and a pristine environment.' I am probably guilty of romanticism. In the Mesolithic we are still dealing with human beings in all their diversity, with their good and bad habits.

The hunter-gatherers at this time faced some serious challenges. One of the most significant was the rising sea level. If Doggerland was a hunter-gatherers' Eden, it was also one from which people were being cast out. Communities must, literally, have had to move as the waters visibly rose, with some presumably heading westwards into Britain. Resources such as fish, wildfowl and useful plants were often concentrated into restricted areas, such as river estuaries and lakesides. Mesolithic migrant bands would have to negotiate access and hunting rights with other potentially rival groups. With people on the move this may have led to stresses and to conflict.

These people were skilled hunters – they knew how to bring down large prey, which could include fellow humans. The iconic Mesolithic artefact is the microlith, a small triangular piece of flint or other stone, which in itself is not impressive. This microlithic technology was, however, a very efficient way of generating large numbers of elements from a nodule of stone. The sharp triangular point could be inserted and glued into a wood or bone handle, or at the end of a shaft to make a reaping tool, a projectile point or a harpoon. A serrated line of microliths looks like the jaw of a miniature shark or the blade of a saw. They could be used to reap, to slash or to stab.

One of the frequent uses was to make arrows and other projectiles. The sophistication of the bow and arrow is apparent at the reindeer hunting site of Stellmoor in Germany, where archaeologists found one hundred well-preserved arrows and parts of two bows, dating to about 8500 BC. These arrows were designed to break halfway along the shaft when they hit their target, so that the hunter could regain the flight end. Eighteen thousand reindeer bones testify to their effectiveness. In the early Mesolithic, microlith arrow-heads frequently turn up embedded in animal bone. At Loshult, in Sweden, a well-preserved shaft of pinewood had a microlith tip and a barb fixed in place with birch-bark resin. At Lydstep in Pembrokeshire, hunters at the very end of the Mesolithic, close to 4000 BC, had a frustrating day. At least one of their arrows hit the target – a wild boar – which kept running, disappeared into dense forest and died a pointless death. The body was found about six thousand years later, complete with the still-smoking gun – or in this case distinctive rod microliths that had penetrated the carcass and ultimately brought down the boar. The animal was found in one of the twelve areas of submerged forest that A. L. Leach identified during World War I along the Pembrokeshire coast, areas that decades later would provide much more detailed information about lives and landscape in the Mesolithic.[13]

## Nasty and brutish lives

My generation of archaeologists – mostly born in the late 1940s and 1950s – have been reluctant to see warfare and aggression as important factors in prehistoric societies. Most of us in the West had no direct experience of the military (except for Israeli colleagues and the relatively few American academics who served in Vietnam). In the British, French and German edu-cation systems, until the 1960s, youthful scholars absorbed Julius Caesar's *de Bello Gallico* (The Gallic Wars) and Homer's heroically gory *Iliad* with their school milk. In reacting against the obsession with warfare and invasion, archaeologists and anthropologists of my generation sometimes failed to consider evidence for human nastiness that lay, reeking fairly obviously, under our noses.

In fact, warfare was about to break out among the tweed-jacketed tribes of academia. A French anthropologist, with an appropriate name – Napoleon Chagnon – launched the hostilities. He studied the Yanomamö of Venezuela and Brazil and claimed that warfare and raiding were endemic among these hunter-gatherer people. His 1977 book meant what it said on the cover: *Yanomamö: The Fierce People*.[14] Then, some years later, he reported that warriors who had killed other men sired three times as many children as non-killers.

This really put the cat among the theoretical pigeons as it implied that homicide conveyed an evolutionary advantage. Chagnon argued that raiding was principally to gain access to young women – a 'Rape of the Sabine Women' scenario (in Rome's origin myth, its young men raided the Sabines in order to steal their women). Dr Chagnon interviewed a Yanomamö shaman about the reasons for village fissions into hostile groups. The impatient shaman barked in reply, 'Don't ask such stupid questions! Women! Women! Women! Women! Women!' Ironically, internecine warfare then spread to the American Anthropological Association. As a result of his challenge to the 'noble savage' concept, combined with accusations of spreading disease and exaggerating the locals' tendency to violence, Chagnon was banned from field research in Brazil.

Nevertheless, since the Yanomamö controversy, interest in the origins of human aggression has continued to grow.[15] Laurence Keeley stirred the controversy by accusing his fellow scholars of artificially pacifying the past. Steven Pinker has gone even further by claiming that hunter-gatherers and simple horticultural societies were often very violent indeed, and with the march to civilization, we have become more ordered and less aggressive (in relative terms). This is a controversial issue, especially for those who lived in a century that witnessed World Wars, the genocide of the Armenians, and the shocking actions and policies of Hitler, Stalin, Mao and Pol Pot. And, in spite of nonsensical claims that we have witnessed the 'End of History' with the fall of the USSR, the present century continues to experience its share of violence, warfare and intolerance.

Pinker's argument depends upon the accuracy of dubious statistics – for example, the rate of death in warfare in non-state and state societies. Nevertheless, he has clearly established that violence, raiding and homicide were routine among many 'non-state' tribal groups. The ones who avoided inter-community aggression tended to live in extreme isolation. It may be unfair to characterize such subtle philosophers as Hobbes and Rousseau by two short snappy stereotypes, but at the moment the evidence for 'nasty, brutish and short' prehistoric lives seems to be trumping the 'noble savage'.

The result of this changing perspective is that forensic archaeologists now look more carefully for evidence of violent trauma to human remains, particularly blows to the skull, fractures, cuts into the bone and piercing by spears or arrows. And they quite often find it.

One unfortunate young man, buried in a late Mesolithic cemetery at Téviec, Brittany, was found to have parts of two microlithic points embedded in his thoracic vertebrae. He had led a short, eventful life: his jaw had previously been fractured. There is also similar evidence of Mesolithic conflict along the Dnieper River in Ukraine. Were fishing rights at stake?

Mesolithic aggression is most gruesomely represented by the 'nest' of skulls and vertebrae from thirty-four or thirty-eight individuals, carefully stacked in two pits close to the entrance of Ofnet Cave, in Bavaria, about 6500 BC. Two-thirds were women, and many were children. The men, especially, showed signs of violent injury, blows to the head probably inflicted with stone axes. Cut marks indicated that people had been scalped and decapitated. Finally, those who deposited the bones sprinkled them with red ochre and placed pierced red deer teeth and four thousand seashells in the pits. All this could represent some strange funerary rite, but it has all the hallmarks of a trophy burial by a band of head-hunters.[16]

In France, the fragmented remains of eight people, adults and children were found among a collection of domestic refuse and animal bones in the cave of Perrats at Agris, in the Charente region of France. Cut marks on the human bones indicated that the bodies had been butchered and defleshed. Claims of cannibalism are always controversial, but the Perrats evidence points strongly in this direction.[17]

Although the evidence for violence is limited, such butchered and decapitated remains have led to speculation that the late Mesolithic saw increased competition for resources. The Yanomamö shaman quoted above claimed that in his society access to women was the cause of conflict. Elsewhere, and in the past, other factors might have provoked violence: competitions over access to fishing and hunting grounds or sources of stone or water, fear of witchcraft, blood feuds or pre-emptive strikes against potentially aggressive neighbours or newcomers. Lewis and Clark, on their pioneering trans-American journey of exploration, encountered the Shoshone and attempted to discourage them from constantly raiding neighbouring tribes. 'But how would we select our leaders if we did not prove ourselves in such encounters?' they replied. For many Plains Indians, raiding was the means by which young men achieved status. Besides, it was seen as great fun for the winners.[18]

In Britain, evidence of Mesolithic burials, let alone violence, is scanty (although it has been suggested that simple cremation burials may prove to be Mesolithic when radiocarbon-dated). However, if resource competition created problems, the British coastline with its constant marine incursions would have been a contested area. Natural disaster could also strike out of the blue. The Storegga incident of about 6100 BC witnessed the gigantic collapse of a chunk of Norway's coastal shelf.[19] This submarine landslide generated a series of tsunamis that swept across the North Sea area. Anyone still living on the low islands around Doggerland would probably have been swept away, and the wall of water hit the coast of Scotland. Archaeologists often find what they are not looking for, but rarely do Medievalists, digging 13th-century town houses, come across quite such a contrast as Jonathan Wordsworth and his team did in Inverness. Beneath the remains of the medieval town they found thousands of Mesolithic artefacts and bone. It seemed to be a place where hunters had camped by the coast. Perhaps they were after seals, or birds' eggs. We do not know if they were sitting or sleeping around their campfire when the tsunami struck. However, we can say that it dumped thousands of cubic kilometres of silt along the Scottish coast and inundated their campsite.

### The Star Carr problem

The best-known Mesolithic settlement in Britain is also one of the earliest. Grahame Clark, whom we met earlier, excavated at Star Carr in the Vale of Pickering, Yorkshire, between 1949 and 1951. The preservation in the water-logged conditions was excellent, and the prolific data has been argued about for the past sixty-odd years.[20] The excavation revealed a platform of brushwood and birch projecting into the water's edge. Today, the area is flat, drained agricultural land, probably a disappointment to those who come to see this world-famous prehistoric site. About 8700 BC, hunter-gatherers were living on a promontory projecting into the western end of a lake (about 4 km/2½ miles across and 2 km/1¼ miles wide), now known as Lake Flixton. More research since 1985 has discovered traces of Mesolithic activity all around the lake, and on islands within it, at some twenty-five different sites. Reed swamp fringed the lake, and beyond, birch forest covered the landscape. The chalk hills of the Yorkshire Wolds rise about 10 km (6 miles) to the south and the North York Moors a little further to the north.

Clark was ahead of his time in carefully recovering animal bone. He showed that red and roe deer were the hunters' principal target, then elk and aurochs, and to a lesser extent wild boar. The site also contained the bones of the earliest domestic dog yet found in Britain. Clark and the bone specialist came to the conclusion that Star Carr was occupied in winter and that in summer the band relocated to the nearby uplands, following the deer herds. It is this seasonality issue that has proved to be most contentious. Others subsequently argued that shed antler was collected and stored; that the excavation site was an antler workshop and could be part of a larger settlement complex that was occupied all year round. Then, in 1988, the animal bones were re-examined in more detail. The teeth came under the microscope. These showed that the red and roe deer were killed in early and late summer. So it is possible that the Star Carr band and their neighbours retreated into the Doggerland basin during the winter months. Today, the North Sea coast is less than 10 km (6 miles) away to the east along the Vale of Pickering. Detailed studies of Mesolithic settlements, camps and activity areas suggest that these hunter-gatherers led a structured way of life, exploiting different areas within their territorial range on a seasonal basis.

## Outward bound or housebound? Reaching Scotland

In 2013 my wife and I went to see an exhibition in one of my favourite museums, the Sir John Soane's Museum in London's Lincoln's Inn Fields. On show was the work of the underestimated English artist Alan Sorrell, probably Britain's finest archaeological reconstruction artist, who created a vivid image of Mesolithic life at Star Carr. He wanted to include dwellings in the painting but Clark, a stickler for the evidence, prevented him on the grounds that none had been found in the excavations. Excavations between 2004 and 2010 at Star Carr, however, confirmed Sorrell's hunch when, on drier land back from the lakeshore, the slight remains of a structure were found. The British press announced the discovery of the country's oldest house, dating to about 9000 BC. The traces consisted of an irregular oval hollow surrounded by

A reconstruction of the Star Carr Mesolithic settlement, with its busy inhabitants.

postholes. The latest reconstruction images of Star Carr, by Dominic Andrews, now show a group of oval, thatched dwellings beyond the reed-fringed lake.[21]

In the past decade, discoveries of Mesolithic houses have thrown doubt on the hypothesis that all hunter-gatherer groups were constantly, or at least seasonally, on the move. There appear, at least, to be places that were used regularly and repeatedly, even if not permanently occupied. At Howick, on the Northumberland coast, Clive Waddington found the relatively well-preserved remains of a house first occupied about 7850 BC.[22] There was a hollow in the ground, 6 m (20 ft) across, surrounded by postholes. In the centre was a hearth, and scattered around it were large quantities of scorched hazelnuts and animal bone. Richard Bradley was right that Mesolithic people had close relations with hazelnuts. At Howick, hazelnuts littered the site.

Charred hazelnuts seem to have been a favourite food. They appeared at the well-known site of Thatcham in Berkshire, and in large quantities at Staosnaig on Colonsay in the Inner Hebrides of Scotland. There, as at Howick, hazelnuts were intensively exploited as a major foodstuff. It is probable that hazelnuts were roasted in order to make them more palatable and to preserve and store them; the shells could also be used as fuel. The hazelnut is an obvious example of the potential food value of wild plants – it is possible to collect half a tonne of nuts from 1 hectare (2½ acres) of hazel woodland.

The people at Howick also knapped stone around the hearth, producing narrow-blade stone tools from local beach pebbles, especially what archaeologists call scalene triangles for classic microliths. This house was occupied for almost two hundred years and refurbished several times by the family that used it, who finally moved out about 7650 BC. If there were other houses or midden deposits nearby, they have been claimed by the sea. Howick now sits on the edge of an eroding cliff.

Mesolithic houses are rare in Britain but Howick conforms to similar structures from Mount Sandel, Northern Ireland, and Broom Hill at Braishfield, Hampshire. Shortly after the discovery of the Howick house an almost identical structure turned up 80 km (50 miles) to the north at East Barns, near Dunbar in East Lothian. There are also unpublished Mesolithic houses from Scotland at South Queensferry in Lothian, and Dunragit in Dumfries and Galloway. It is evident that hunter-gatherers moved into the northerly parts of Britain relatively rapidly after Britain's last glacier had melted away in the Northwest Highlands.

Scotland, compared with southern Britain, is not well supplied with flint. Alan Saville, who helped identify Scotland's first occupants, has also set out the evidence for Mesolithic artefacts and material culture in Scotland. Given the lack of resources, he quite rightly says: 'it is the resourcefulness with which flint and other appropriate rock were sought out and exploited, which is one of the triumphs of human endeavour at this period'.[23] Sources of useful stone were pursued with great diligence. However, compared with the Neolithic, the material was not moved or exchanged very far.

The site at Morton, in Fife, demonstrates the versatility and geological awareness of stoneworkers in Mesolithic Scotland in the face of adversity. They used quartz, quartzite, rock crystal, chalcedony, bloodstone, jasper, pitchstone, baked mudstone, agate, opal and silicified limestone. With these diverse materials they churned out small microburins (for piercing leather, wood and so on) as well as scrapers – shaped like half a tortoise shell and just big enough to be gripped in between thumb and forefingers. I once used a couple of them, effectively, to scrape clean the inside of a badger pelt (I peacefully share my garden with badgers; the one that provided the pelt, unfortunately, was roadkill). They are a handy little tool and continued in use until the Bronze Age, about six thousand years later.

By the late Mesolithic, on the eve of the arrival of farming, the south and central areas of Scotland and the eastern slopes of the Highlands were dominated by oak, elm and hazel woodland. Elm was far less significant to the west and north, and pine and birch predominated on higher ground and in the windswept northerly lowlands, such as Caithness, Orkney and Shetland. But, partly thanks to the activities of browsing animals and humans, the post-glacial landscape became a complex mosaic of woodlands, clearings, bogs and moorland.

By 8000 BC, early Mesolithic seafarers had crossed some of Europe's trickiest waters, such as the Pentland Firth to Orkney and the Minch to the Western Isles. They even went beyond, tackling the 80 km (50 miles) from Orkney to the Shetlands. Like the Cyprus colonists in the Mediterranean (see Chapter 7), they transported a living food supply: in this case wild deer to breed on the new islands. These seafarers may have used logboats and paddles, similar to examples found in Scandinavia and Lough Neagh in Ireland. However, maritime specialists question the seaworthiness of dugouts and speculate that skin-covered boats, like the Irish currach, or even more sophisticated timber boats, may have already existed. Decisive physical evidence may be lacking but clearly the hunters of northern Britain were skilled pilots and intrepid explorers, as familiar with the seaways as they were with the woodlands and rivers on land.

The earliest settlers reached Scotland about 8500 BC. By 7000 BC or even earlier they had colonized the Hebrides and so discovered a rare source of flint in the 'Rinns', the western peninsula of Islay, better known today for its throat-singeing, peaty whiskies. Fortunately, this was a small area that had remained free of ice and so the flint nodules that naturally occurred there had not been bulldozed away. At Coulerach, the hunter-gatherers camped alongside a beach covered in flint nodules and thanked whatever spirits brought them luck. However, some of their work and material used was so shoddy that lithic experts suggest that this was also a place where children learnt the trade. There were other attractions on Scottish islands, such as deer, migrating geese, gulls and their eggs, seals and otters. Mesolithic hunters explored the coast searching out things that were good to eat, to wear or to make into tools.

Colonsay is an island 20 km (12 miles) further out to sea than Islay. Large land mammals had not reached it in the Mesolithic; it had no obvious attractions to Mesolithic hunters. However, Steve Mithen persisted in searching the island for traces of Mesolithic activity. In 1994, he found them at Staosnaig: a large pit stuffed with charred hazelnuts and stone tools.[24] The pit was probably all that was left of a house site, and around it was a scatter of smaller pits. Careful analysis also revealed fragments of apple and lesser celandine, a plant used in traditional medicine, whose waxy yellow flowers, heralds of spring, are glowing in the meadow and woodland edge as I write. Its other name, pilewort, gives us an idea of its use. Small pits seem to have been ovens for roasting the hazelnuts, and the excavators found the shells of more than 300,000 of them. Around 6200 BC, hazelnut gathering and roasting was a major activity at Staosnaig. So the Mesolithic people probably made seasonal visits, paddling to Colonsay (whose name in Gaelic means 'hazelnut island') to exploit the harvest. Pollen evidence suggests that their activities were so intense that the hazel woods were eventually almost wiped out.

Oronsay was another island targeted by specialist collectors. Here on this tiny island in the later Mesolithic, about 5300–4300 BC, they gathered shellfish and left behind rubbish dumps, or middens, which accumulated bone pins for making skin clothes, beads of periwinkle shells, bones of seabirds and seals and also a few rare human remains. Most of these were the small bones of hands and feet, perhaps left behind when exposed bodies were removed for disposal elsewhere. There is a long tradition in western Britain of burial on islands, liminal places between the earth, sky and sea. On a more mundane level, marine fish, particularly the saithe (a type of cod) were a major prey for the visitors to Oronsay, caught on lines from boats. The issue of seasonal activity and settlement raised its troublesome head once again. The ear bones of the saithe provided an indication of the time of year that the fish were caught. The excavator, Paul Mellars of Cambridge University, noting that different middens were used at different times of the year, argued that the Mesolithic population lived on this tiny island all year round in permanent settlements at a time when nearby larger islands seem to have been abandoned. Not surprisingly, carbon isotope analysis of the human bones found in the middens indicated that these people subsisted on a diet made up almost entirely of marine products – from seals and seabirds to shellfish, fish and crabs.[25]

Scottish islands had varied resources and meat could also be on the menu. We saw in Chapter 9 that Steven Mithen's exploration of the Hebridean islands located late glacial activity at Rubha Port an t-Seilich on the east coast of Islay. These early stone tools lay beneath a Mesolithic hearth close to which lay fine microliths, made from rock crystal quartz, and hazelnut shells. Unusually for a Hebridean settlement site, animal bones also survived – previously, they had only turned up in shell middens. A few kilometres inland, Mithen's team also investigated another Mesolithic site at Storakaig. This proved to be an upland base from which to hunt red deer, roe deer and wild boar.

These Islay sites represent either end of the Mesolithic colonization of western Scotland, and both are well preserved and relatively rich in artefacts and biological evidence. Mesolithic Rubha Port an t-Seilich dates from about 9,300 years ago, while Storakaig's hunters prowled the forested landscape about 6,000 years ago. The site is that valuable rarity in Britain: a place of hunter-gatherer occupation that appears to overlap with the onset of the Neolithic.

The small trenches dug by Steven Mithen and Karen Wicks' team on Islay produced fascinating, detailed results. Their analysis of 137 Mesolithic radio-carbon results from western Scotland, using Bayesian statistics, revealed a remarkable big picture. From about 9,500 years ago Mesolithic activity rose rapidly to a peak about 8,400 years ago. The evidence of occupation, as indi-cated by the radiocarbon dates, then collapses drastically, leaving western Scotland with a very low Mesolithic population for over a thousand years. Then about 6,800 years ago there is evidence of recolonization. So what is going on?

I noted in Chapter 6 the impact of the 6200 BC cold event, visible in the Greenland ice-core record, on the early farmers of the Near East. Mithen and Wicks' radiocarbon 'trough' could not be clearer. The dramatic cooling of the climate at 8,200 years ago was too much for the hunter-gatherers of western Scotland. They retreated to the balmier south for more than a millennium.[26]

## If you go across the sea to Ireland

If Scotland was explored and exploited down to its smallest islands, what about the large island to the west? As a place of colonization by plants, animals and humans, Ireland is a fascinating case study. So far we have no evidence that modern humans managed to settle, or even reach Ireland before about 8000 BC. In other words, people tackled the Arctic and reached Patagonia before anyone settled the Emerald Isles. As already mentioned in Chapter 9, Ireland presented a no-get-to area for many animal species. Large herbivores had reached it during more favourable climatic interludes, but the cold snap of the Younger Dryas (known as the Nahanagan Interstadial in Ireland) put paid to the presence of reindeer, red deer and the impressive giant Irish elk.

When the first groups of people arrived in Ireland about 8000 BC they found a relatively restricted variety of prey species, and particularly a lack of large meaty animals: no red or roe deer, aurochs or elk.

The presence of Mesolithic hunter-gatherers is most frequently indicated by scatters of microliths and the slivers of material left behind during their manufacture. However, at Mount Sandel, County Londonderry, near the north coast, the archaeologist Peter Woodman discovered more substantial evidence of the early settlement of Ireland.[27] Here there was a series of oval huts, made of bent poles and up to about 6 m (20 ft) across. A small family probably occupied each hut, clustering around a central hearth. The small Mount Sandel clan may have moved round the landscape in the course of the year to exploit different food resources, returning to these huts seasonally. Wild pigs seem to have been an important part of the diet, with smaller animals, such as hares, adding variety. This contrasts with British Mesolithic sites such as Star Carr, where bones of deer and aurochs predominate. These animals typically provide two to four times as much meat as wild boar. It seems odd that wild boars could have reached Ireland under their own steam, when other good swimmers such as red deer did not. One plausible theory is that the early human colonists transported the pigs to run wild, breed rapidly and supplement Ireland's limited natural larder. In the words of J. P. Mallory, 'it suggests that Ireland was first colonized by a human population that deliberately attempted to engineer its native fauna to suit its economic needs.'[28]

At least Ireland was prolific in fish. At Mount Sandel and another early Mesolithic settlement at Lough Boora, County Offaly (in central Ireland), fish made up the vast majority of animal bones. Migratory species dominated: eels, salmon and trout swarmed up the rivers in summer and early autumn, using their sense of smell to relocate the waters in which they were born, providing a predictable target for predators. The eel is incredibly nutritious, packed with calories, fat and vitamins A and C, although it takes about 250 of them (with a huge number of bones) to deliver the same amount of food as a wild pig. At Mesolithic coastal sites such as Mount Sandel and Ferriter's Cove, County Kerry, the fish bones show that Mesolithic people took to the sea to catch a wide range of species: plaice, bass, flounder, wrasse, cod and whiting.

On archaeological sites with alkaline soils animal bones may be well preserved and even small fish bones can be routinely collected by sieving. Plants are another matter. Their importance in the Mesolithic diet can easily be over-looked as often they leave little trace, except of course for those hazelnuts and their shells, which are carbonized by proximity to the hearth. Ireland, despite its botanical paucity, has more than 120 species of edible native plants. There are fairly obvious delicacies – such as raspberries, crab apple, elderberries, nettles, dandelion and fungi – as well as resources that are lesser known to generations more used to grazing the aisles of supermarkets: plants such as edible bracken root, waterlily seeds, various types of seaweed and marsh samphire.

In most hunter-gatherer societies, in temperate and tropical zones, women and children collect such foodstuffs. Archaeologists sometimes overemphasize presumed male activities, such as hunting large animals, at the expense of the vital role played by women, who collected plants, firewood and water, made shelters and clothing, reared children and cooked. These are roles noted from ethnographic analogies, but not always obvious in the archaeological record. In rural England, families regularly gathered hazelnuts until World War I, and village schools closed on Holy Cross Day (14 September) to allow the children to help. Leave them much later and the nuts will be gathered by squirrels and jays.[29]

## Where did the settlers of Ireland come from?

One question that is not entirely resolved is where the first colonists in Ireland came from. The earliest Mesolithic sites in England are distinguished by stone tools, such as long blades and larger microliths, which show a marked resemblance to assemblages from the Netherlands, and date to about 9600 BC. By 8000 BC smaller microliths appear in Britain and these are the first tools to be found in Ireland. In Wales, Mesolithic communities were exploiting coastal resources about this time. The peninsula of Pembrokeshire is particularly rich in Mesolithic sites from about 8500 BC. Could Pembrokeshire populations have made the relatively short crossing to southeastern Ireland, mirroring today's Fishguard to Rosslare route? Lithic specialists have argued endlessly about the similarities and differences of Irish and Welsh material culture without resolving the question.

Geography and archaeology also point to a possible Scottish origin for the earliest settlers of Ireland. Today, the Mull of Kintyre to Torr Head (east of the Mount Sandel site) is the shortest crossing at about 20 km (12 miles); it would have been even shorter ten thousand years ago when sea levels were lower.

Ireland would have been clearly visible from the Mull of Kintyre, at least when it was not rainy or foggy. Surely the Mesolithic voyagers who could explore the Orkneys and the Hebrides would have been drawn to explore Ireland – even if its attractions proved to be limited? In fact, one attraction was compelling: Antrim, on Ireland's northeast coast, had an enormous supply of flint – material that, as noted earlier, is relatively rare in Scotland – and it was in Antrim that archaeologists first recognized Irish Mesolithic artefacts. So this link has been the most popular solution to the origins question for many decades.

However, since the late 1970s, metaphorical spanners have been thrown into the Mesolithic works: unfortunately, there is not a close match between Irish and Scottish stone toolkits, and early Mesolithic sites are now known across Ireland, not just in the northeast. So perhaps Ireland was colonized from several regions on the British mainland? Or, not from the mainland at all, but from what J. P. Mallory calls the 'Manx Atlantis'.

When flying from Scotland over the Isle of Man, from such a height it is striking how the Isle of Man stands out like a sentinel in the sea, closely surrounded by the coastlines of Ireland, Scotland, England and Wales. Ten thousand years ago, the island may have been attached to England (the seas today are shallow) and there are many Mesolithic sites on Man, especially on the west coast opposite Ireland (and wild pig was also the most important source of meat there). So with rising sea levels, the lower ground around Man could have been inundated, driving out the population and pushing them (with their wild pigs?) westwards to the new frontier of Ireland. Confirmation of this attractive hypothesis, if it exists, would lie beneath the waters of the Celtic Sea. So far these flooded lands have been little explored. However, a small number of determined archaeologists and palaeobotanists have doggedly pursued the evidence of the Mesolithic elsewhere around the coast even in the most difficult conditions.

## Exploring the drowned world

Conditions do not come much more inhospitable for archaeologists than in the Severn Estuary, the funnel-shaped body of water between the shorelines of South West England and South Wales. The estuary has a remarkable tidal range, the second highest in the world, which reaches 14.8 m (48 ft) at Avonmouth. When the tidal bore is at its maximum, surfers can ride the waves up the River Severn. Once, standing on the ramparts of Chepstow castle,

I watched a single seal swimming upriver. The estuary shorelines are exposed, at low tide, for as little as two hours or less. The mudflats are scoured by westerly winds, lashed by williwaws. The opportunities for archaeologists are fleeting and uncomfortable. The ground is shifting and gloopy. So I have nothing but admiration for Reading University's Martin Bell and his colleagues, who devoted themselves to exploring this cold, wet and frustratingly transient coast in pursuit of the fragile traces of Mesolithic people and their environment.

They were not the first to appreciate the interest of this shoreline. In the late 12th century, Gerald of Wales, from a family of Norman invaders who had intermarried with the Welsh, reported the siting of ancient tree stumps in the seashore following a storm. Gerald's Norman family diplomatically adopted the surname of 'Barry' from Barry Island, near Cardiff. It was there, during the excavations for Barry Docks in 1895, that another submerged forest appeared. Among the trees was a Neolithic polished stone axe, which indicated when this land surface was last dry. Further west at Whitesands Bay in Pembrokeshire, an exposed land surface revealed the skulls of aurochs and another polished stone axe. This one had its wooden handle intact.[30]

Credit for first recognizing the archaeological potential of the inhospitable Severn Estuary in the 1980s should go to the amateur archaeologist Derek Upton. As in many shifting and difficult environments, such as shorelines and gravel pits, it is local voluntary archaeologists who dedicate themselves to regularly pounding the beat – or trudging through the mud – in search of emerging evidence. Derek Upton not only found Mesolithic scatters of stone tools, he was also the first to spot human footprints in silts that proved to be overlain by peat dating to 5460–4960 BC.[31]

Martin Bell was well aware of the limited evidence from Mesolithic England and Wales, and, in particular, of the need for well-preserved organic deposits, rich in environmental evidence. He wrote, in the project report, about the experience of walking the estuary between Goldcliff and Redwick: 'One of the most evocative sights in the remarkable sediment sequence of the Severn Estuary is the great oak trunks and stumps exposed in the bed of the estuary. Here at low spring tides one has the experience of walking through a lost landscape of around 6000 BC.'[32]

The fragile remains of Mesolithic activity are often best preserved where they have been flooded by rising waters and buried by silt or in peat. So as well as on the shorelines, careful observation in river valleys can be productive. Important deposits have turned up in the valley of the River Kennet, a tributary of the Thames. Hunter-gatherers occupied what were, ten thousand or so years ago, dry islands in the wider, braided river valley. In more recent centuries most English rivers have been regularly dredged, canalized and controlled. In the Mesolithic these islands in the river would have been close to marshes and meandering watercourses that provided a ready supply of fish, as well as edible and useful plants. The surrounding woodland was a patchwork of pine, hazel, oak and elm. The main meat supply came from aurochs and red deer. At Thatcham the plentiful flint tools were analysed by lithic experts for what is known as 'use-wear' – the distinctive marks or traces left on the tools. These showed that while some were for hunting, most of the tools were used for gathering and processing plants, or making other tools from bone and antler.[33]

## Before Stonehenge

The Mesolithic camp at Blick Mead is an interesting recent discovery. It lies in a natural hollow fed by a spring, alongside the River Avon, about 3 km (2 miles) east of Stonehenge. Here there is a large quantity of worked flint, as much as 4,000 fragments in 1 sq. m (10 sq. ft) of the excavation. By summer 2014, archaeologists had collected over 31,000 fragments in total. This was clearly a place where serious flint knapping took place routinely, between the eighth millennium and the fifth millennium BC. Blick Mead could be one of a number of places that Mesolithic groups returned to persistently – in this case a sheltered area, close to boggy ground and surrounded by mature woodland.

Barry Bishop, who is analysing the flint tools, thinks that they were being made for use in a wide range of activities, from hunting and butchering animals to cutting reeds and making clothing. Unusually for the Mesolithic period, the stone tools indicate wide-ranging contacts. For example, there are distinctive projectile points, known as Horsham points, which are usually found further east in the Weald (Sussex and Kent); one of them is made from a green slate that came from the west of Britain. There are also chert tools and a unique smooth bar of red sandstone. It looks like the Blick Mead people had contacts both to the east and west.[34]

Blick Mead was an easy place to access. The River Avon would have provided a north–south routeway, and another regularly used site in the mid to late Mesolithic, at Downton, lies an estimated four hours' canoe journey downstream. Blick Mead may also have had both practical and 'magical' qualities that attracted hunter-gatherers. The constant water temperature in the spring (10–14°C/50–57°F) extended the growing season for plants upon which prey animals could graze. More unusually, flint that lay in the water developed a striking pink colour, as a result of the combination of light, water temperature and the algae present. As we have seen, prehistoric people seem to have been especially attracted to unusual colours and this exotic quality may have drawn them to Blick Mead for centuries.

Masses of animal bones from huge aurochs (the dominant food species), wild boar and red deer were left behind – carcasses capable of feeding large gatherings of people who, like the worked stones, may have come to Blick Mead from some distance across southern Britain. The cooks also provided for more exotic tastes, providing salmon and toad (but they were not, as the British press claimed, eating frogs eight thousand years before the French).

The excavators of Blick Mead believe that the site may have been a base from which to hunt aurochs, which would have grazed extensively across the open woodland of Salisbury Plain. West of Blick Mead there is a shallow valley, now dry but which once contained a watercourse. This runs past what was to become the site of Stonehenge. A natural routeway could funnel herds of animals to a fording point, which, like the island we excavated in the Goring Gap (see page 169), would be an obvious place for human hunters to lie in wait. When the now-removed Stonehenge car park was constructed in the 1960s archaeologists discovered a line of massive Mesolithic timber postholes alongside this routeway. This is a unique structure in the British Mesolithic. Can we call it a monument? Were the posts some kind of waymarker, signposts for hunters from afar? We can only speculate about their purpose. However, Blick Mead and these telegraph-pole-sized timbers show that this was a special place for several thousand years before Stonehenge itself was built.

## Back to the coast

Many hunter-gatherers lived by, or at least regularly visited, the coast alongside estuaries in order to harvest the opportunities of land, sea and the intertidal zone. But in the early Holocene this was a place of rapid transit and change. As the glaciers melted and retreated north, sea levels rose. At the end of the Ice Age, sea level was about 55 m (180 ft) lower than today, so the Bristol Channel and the Severn Estuary did not exist. Cardigan Bay was dry land, Anglesey was not an island and no one needed a ferry across the Mersey. At 11,000 years ago sea level was around 37 m (120 ft) below present-day levels, and by 9,500 years ago the sea had risen a further 22 m (72 ft); about 8,000 years ago it reached approximately the level we see today. In other words, during the Mesolithic a lot of British land (as well as the Doggerland North Sea basin) disappeared underwater and the peninsula became a group of islands with a long indented coast, separated from the European mainland.

Archaeologists logically assume the many hunter-gatherer sites and territories around Britain and Ireland were overwhelmed by the sea in the period between 11,500 and 8,000 years ago. I saw the evidence for this myself when I went to meet up with another hero of the wet zone on the coast of southern England in the western Solent. Marine archaeologist Garry Momber does not just explore the muddy, intertidal flats, he is truly amphibious and dives into what he describes as 'hostile, cold, dark "gravity-free" surroundings' where 'the perpetual movement' of the waters 'attempts to remove anything or anyone that isn't secure from site'. When I visited him he was perched in a small boat on the choppy, grey waters of the Solent, wearing a black rubber wetsuit and weighed down with gas cylinders and powerful lamps.

The western Solent is the narrow strip of sea between the great harbour of Southampton Water in the east and the Needles Channel in the west. Eleven thousand years ago the Solent would have been a sheltered valley fed by a number of small rivers with easy access to the sea, the uplands and sources of flint – ideal territory for hunter-gatherers, who left numerous scatters of worked flint on the nearby higher, dry ground. The valley bottom was probably even more attractive before the brackish salt marsh formed, before silts developed and finally the sea poured, or perhaps dribbled in about eight thousand years ago. The Solent became an arm of the English Channel: a departure point for Henry V heading an encounter with the French at Agincourt, and the *Titanic* heading for an encounter with an iceberg.

In 1985, Mike Jones was operating his fishing vessel *My Pat* in the Solent. Along with his harvest of oysters he hauled in a collection of distinctive Mesolithic flint tranchet axes and picks, which attracted the attention of archaeologists. Garry Momber quotes Mike Jones as saying that in the early 1960s, when licensed oyster trawling first started, huge quantities of archaeological objects were trawled from the sea. What this means is that an intact Mesolithic landscape, a whole valley preserved beneath a protective blanket of silt, has been – and continues to be – trashed in the lifetimes of most of us, ironically by oyster fishermen, some of Britain's last hunter-gatherers, equipped with modern, seabed scouring technology. Garry Momber hoped that fragments of this landscape might remain intact, especially close to land where the edges of the drowned Mesolithic world could have escaped destruction by trawlers.

One of the most promising areas was the eroding Bouldnor Cliff on the northwest coast of the Isle of Wight.[35] Here, Garry and his team dived into the murky waters of the Solent. About 4 m (13 ft) below the surface they found a layer cake of geologically recent deposits made up of bands of peat and silt deposited as the post-glacial sea level rose. The divers gathered core samples that contained pollen, forams and diatoms: evidence of the changing conditions. These showed that seawater had inundated mudflats and salt marsh. Below the marine silts, Garry discovered what he was looking for – with help from unexpected allies. A lobster had burrowed into peaty ground at about 11.5 m (38 ft) below the present sea level. It crouched in the entrance of its lair guarding, it seemed, a treasure trove of Mesolithic flints that it had conveniently excavated from what had once been the ground surface.

Detailed investigation of a very small area subsequently showed that this was a place where hunter-gatherers had camped and knapped flints when the land was dry. All around were the stumps of a submerged oak forest, which grew here about eight thousand years ago. The hunter-gatherers camped on a sandy riverbank and roamed a landscape dominated by oak, with elm, hazel and alder. Pine was in decline as the climate warmed, though still present. Almost inevitably there were fragments of charred hazelnut shells, but no other edible plant remains survived.

A rare discovery, however, was evidence of woodworking, in the form of woodchips, toolmarks on timber and even a flint blade embedded in a piece of alder wood. When archaeologists in England find prehistoric wood they usually send for Dr Maisie Taylor. Where ancient people have hacked and hewn, Maisie is the ultimate crime scene investigator. At Bouldnor Cliff she found the 'fingerprints', or cut marks, left by tranchet axes.[36] Close by were flint flakes discarded when woodworkers sharpened their blunted axes.

The most impressive fragment of timber from Bouldnor Cliff was a piece of oak almost 1 m (3 ft) long, which had been tangentially split from a large tree. This is a technique for producing massive planks. Before the Bouldnor Cliff discovery the earliest recorded such timbers were incorporated into Neolithic monumental structures, two thousand years later – for example, in the Haddenham long barrow (about 3600 BC) in Cambridgeshire.[37] But this is also a technique used in boatbuilding to produce planks 1–2 m (3–6 ft) wide and over 10 m (33 ft) long; the remaining tree bole can then be hollowed out. The resulting craft would be larger than any dugout, with a flatter bottom and steeper sides. Craft like this are known from the later Bronze Age, in the centuries before and after 1000 BC. One piece of Mesolithic wood does not make for a sophisticated vessel, but it does hint at the quality of Mesolithic carpentry, the technical abilities and degree of cooperation among hunter-gatherer bands. And it provides hope that early craft still await discovery; the type that could have voyaged to Shetland and Ireland.

## Footprints on the shore

Back on the shores of the Severn Estuary, Martin Bell and his team found that, while Mesolithic hunter-gatherers walked lightly on the earth, they certainly left footprints in the mud, particularly at Goldcliff, on a layer dated to about 5500–5200 BC. One trail of sixteen prints belonged to a barefooted, slim girl or boy, aged eleven or twelve, about 1.42 m (4 ft 8 in.) tall if a girl, and 1.47 m (4 ft 10 in.) if a boy. The youngster was walking briskly, parallel to the shoreline, and then halted for a moment, before continuing. Yes, you can tell all this from footprints – or Dr Rachel Scales of Reading University can. She rivals an Apache scout when it comes to interpreting tracks. Elsewhere, four young people walked together side by side. The clearest prints belonged to an eight- or nine-year-old with long toenails, who was about 1.34 m (4 ft 5 in.) tall. Not surprisingly, this child Friday was not walking purposefully – just laking about, scimaundering, to use Yorkshire words. Altogether the footprints of at least twenty-one people have been identified at Goldcliff. Four were adults, but most were youngsters between three and fourteen years old.

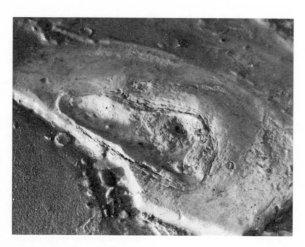

A Mesolithic human footprint in the mud of the foreshore of the Severn Estuary at Goldcliff.

They may have been foraging for food, wild fowling, hunting game or just playing in the mud. And not just at Goldcliff: similar sets of human footprints have also been found in Cardigan Bay in Wales and Formby in Lancashire.[38]

In hunter-gatherer societies children soon began to learn to forage, and even travelled considerable distances in pursuit of game. At Goldcliff and the other sites, along with human footprints there were many of red and roe deer, which grazed on the salt marsh. A few aurochs ventured out of the forest (though no wild boar) and a pair of wolves loped along the mudflats. Birds thronged the estuary: gulls, terns, oystercatchers, herons and summer visitors – exceptionally large cranes – left their prints, like cuneiform writing, in the mud.

The children's tracks are a reminder that Mesolithic groups were young by modern standards. As I mentioned earlier, human burials of this period are rare, compared with the later Neolithic. An exceptional site is Aveline's Hole, south of the Bristol Channel in the Mendip Hills. In the 18th and 19th centuries, antiquarians recovered the remains of more than fifty individuals, men, women and children, of which only twenty-one survive. Several children died between birth and the age of seven and showed signs of stress or anaemia. Poor diet and parasites were probably to blame. No one lived to the ripe old age of fifty in the Aveline's Hole sample.[39] So life was short and conditions not idyllic. Mother Nature was not always bountiful. In winter, food supplies could run short. Young children suffered especially. Adult hunter-gatherers tend to be lean and hardy; however, arthritis was common, cooking over wood fires caused eye disease and people aged quickly. The anthropologist Marshall Sahlins theorized about the 'affluent society' of foragers; in practice, life could be tough.

## Sea level and climate change

The hunter-gatherers of northwest Europe adapted to the major post-glacial environmental changes – warming temperatures, expanding forests and new prey species. Sea level rise could be dramatic on both sides of the North Sea: the Baltic, for example, rose about 2.3 m (7 ft) per century between 9,000 and 8,200 years ago.[40] The climate could be fickle, as we saw in the Near East, and in Scotland with the 6200 BC cold event.

In Europe and the Near East conditions became colder and drier for two or three centuries. The Greenland core shows a huge increase in carbon, probably caused by fires in the desiccated forests. It was one more thing for hunter-gatherers to cope with. In the following centuries, the sea level rose around southern Britain, encouraged also by the tilting effect known as isostatic readjustment: the removal of the massive weight of ice in northern Britain caused a rebound response – the land in northern Britain rose while, like a see-saw, southern Britain sank relative to the sea (and the process continues today) – so the seashore of southern Britain suffered a double whammy: as the sea level rose, the land lowered. The result at Goldcliff was that the forest was submerged. Over seventy of its trees have been analysed for dendrochronology (tree-ring dating), which provided a calendar of annual rings for more than 431 years. Unfortunately, this is still a floating (no pun intended!) chronology that cannot be precisely tied down, but radiocarbon dates indicate that the forest grew for a couple of centuries before and after eight thousand years ago, and overlaps with the forest found by the divers at Bouldnor (and other sites). So by 5600 BC the forest had given way to the silty coastline on which the hunter-gatherer children left their footprints.

The process of environmental change is not straightforward nor one directional (which causes confusion among ill-informed commentators on present-day climate change). For example, about 4500 BC sea level rise in southwest Britain went into reverse and fell. A forest of alder, birch and oak recolonized the shore of the Severn Estuary (from 4477 BC to 4239 BC), then the sea level began to rise again. In the marshes of the Somerset Levels, as we will see later in Chapter 13, some of the first Neolithic farmers responded by laying timber trackways across the increasingly boggy ground.

In the Severn Estuary, the Mesolithic shoreline activity was much reduced after 4800 BC. Archaeologists have a problem with the last centuries of the Mesolithic – there is relatively little evidence. Burials and well-dated, in-situ deposits are rare across much of the British Isles.

Through most of the Mesolithic period Britain and Ireland were occupied by small extended family groups who exploited annual territories that may have extended over distances of 30 km (18 miles), or as far as 90 km (56 miles), depending upon the richness and availability of resources.[41] Temporary camps may have been visited seasonally, or even several times a year, to fish, collect shellfish and plants, and hunt wildfowl and seals on the coast. River valleys also provided rich resources, though in the five millennia of the Mesolithic many British river valleys were reduced in length by as much as 40% as a result of coastal inundation. The rivers also provided routeways to the uplands in summer to which hunting bands would have travelled in pursuit of game, and where they could set fires to burn off scrub or gorse to promote browsing. By taking to the sea they discovered new lands, sources of food and stone. Their numbers, however, were limited by the availability of wild resources and the human hunter-gatherer population remained low, vulnerable to environmental change.

## The spiritual world

Mesolithic humans did not live by hazelnuts alone. All human beings create a cosmology: forms of belief and rituals that help them to explain and deal with the world and its physical and spiritual forces. Hunter-gatherers have usually lived in small, scattered, family-based communities that are more or less egalitarian and have an ethos of sharing. Certain members of the community, both men and women, across Eurasia, in the Americas and Africa, are accepted as intermediaries between the spirit and the human world, people who can pass through the veil enclosing this world, and descend into the underworld or ascend to the heavens. Anthropologists often call such people 'shamans', from the word used by the Tungus-speaking Evenk people of the Siberian forests.[42]

Because of the nature of the physical evidence that survives, archaeologists researching the Mesolithic in Britain tend to focus on the economic, environmental and physical aspects of life in the early Holocene. Elsewhere, evidence for a symbolic world can be more dramatic. Returning to Israel, for example, in the Hilazon Tachtit cave in Galilee there is a late Natufian burial that takes the breath away, even from the most hard-bitten archaeologist. An elderly, disabled woman was buried in a pit. The wing of a golden eagle was laid on her body, along with an aurochs' tail, a leopard's pelvis, a boar's leg and martens' skulls. A severed foot (not hers) was placed by her hand. And alongside the woman's body were fifty shells of tortoises, probably consumed in a funerary feast. The excavators were convinced they had discovered the burial of a shaman.[43]

The Hilazon Tachtit cave is a long way from Britain, but across Eurasia there are burials that provide us with clues as to how the hunter-gatherers thought about their world, and which have elements in common. As Richard Bradley emphasizes, 'the dominant symbols of Mesolithic burials are actually shared across large geographical areas'.[44] Perhaps there was a hunter-gatherer 'world view' in Europe that was transformed by the spread of Neolithic farming. Bradley notes two burials from Dragsholm in Zealand (Denmark). They lie 2 m (6 ft) apart in distance, and three centuries in time. One contains the bodies of two women and belongs to the late Mesolithic. The second is of a man, buried at the beginning of the Neolithic. There is no doubt about his Neolithic credentials: he had a pot, a stone axe, a battle-axe, ten flint arrowheads and several amber pendants. In a game of 'animal, vegetable and mineral', his grave goods were distinctly mineral. In contrast, the women had grave goods dominated by the animal: a dagger and an awl made of bone and many pendants made from wild pig and red deer teeth. There was also red ochre in the grave, a tradition that goes back millennia to the Red Lady of Paviland and the painted caves of France and Spain (see Chapter 3).

By themselves, the differences between the two graves may not look like much, and perhaps gender played a part. However, the Danish Mesolithic burial is not alone. Across Europe, Mesolithic grave goods are dominated by natural materials, particularly from animals. There was particular emphasis on the deposition of antlers with human bodies, often with red ochre. Did these represent regeneration, fertility, the continuity of the family? Animal images were also carved on antler, and on amber, a material that even today plays a significant symbolic role – amber found around the Baltic has been valued for millennia. Another repeated element is the burial of dogs in human graves, although dogs were also buried alone in their own graves – for example, in the Skateholm cemetery in southern Sweden. Man's best friend buried not only with him, but like him.

Bradley points out that there are 'five recurrent features' across Mesolithic Europe, from Scandinavia to Portugal. Four of these relate to human burials: the deposition of red ochre; placing antlers with the dead (often framing the body or the head); the burial of domesticated dogs; and the circulation of isolated human bones. The fifth symbolic element is the placing of material in ritual deposits in natural places – in water and among rocks. As in the Upper Palaeolithic, the ritual actions of the Mesolithic consistently relate to the natural world. Some anthropologists have observed that to many hunter-gatherers, the natural world is not seen so much as a place of danger as a 'giving environment', a world that provides humans with sustenance through the procreation of plants, animals and humans.[45]

Richard Bradley argues that Mesolithic symbolism emphasized life rather than death, and did not draw a distinction between culture and nature.

Humans were part of the natural world. Unlike farmers, hunter-gatherers did not 'own' resources. They were allowed by nature and its spirit guardians to take plants and animals for their own survival but they did not possess them. They were grateful to the prey animals that allowed themselves to be sacrificed. They did not lay claim to nature and the land by building monuments. Important artefacts were made of organic materials; significant places were natural outcrops of rocks, caves, springs, lakes and rivers. In most hunter-gatherer communities made up of small, often transient bands, ancestors did not play a significant role and burials are frequently not elaborate. The hunter-gatherer imagination may be vivid and creative, but it does not dwell on the past.

On the Continent there were people with a different world view, people who had attempted to dominate and control the land, manipulate plants and animals, and transform natural materials into pottery and polished stone axes. The shift from hunter to farmer was not just a matter of changing tasks and diets. Hunter-gatherers saw themselves as part of the natural environment and sought the cooperation of the animals they pursued. To farmers, plants and animals were commodities and possessions, and also a source of constant anxiety. New gods were required, along with a change of mentality. The cultural and economic tsunami of the Neolithic was about to break over the shores of Britain and Ireland.

## CHAPTER ELEVEN

# Farmers face the northern seas

## The spread of farmers: a matter of numbers

As scattered bands of hunter-gatherers in Britain and Ireland exploited the coasts, forests and uplands in the quest for food, on the continental mainland, trees succumbed to the polished stone axe. The ground was broken by the hoe and the plough. Animals, once at home in the Near East, grazed and toiled through the woodland and in newly cleared plots. Alien cereals sprouted and provided daily bread or, some would argue, porridge. The descendants of *Linearbandkeramik* (LBK) farmers, now fragmented into more varied groups, had spread across northern and western Europe. By 4500 BC they had brought their way of life almost to the coast of northern France, the Low Countries, Germany and Scandinavia. The means by which farming spread into south-western France are more contentious. There is very limited evidence for movement along the Atlantic coast from Iberia, although it is possible that the Cardial Ware peoples on the French Mediterranean coast spread northwest along the Garonne corridor, mixing with or acculturating the local hunter-gatherer groups.

In recent decades, archaeologists have endlessly argued: did migrations generate the spread of farming, or did local hunter-gatherer communities choose to change or adapt their way of life? Clues are constantly sought in the archaeological record that might indicate whether incoming farmers swamped the indigenous locals or whether hunters lived alongside farmers, and if so, for how long? Did the hunters lust after some of the farmers' possessions, such as pots, polished stone axes and other stone tools, domesticated foodstuffs, even their strange new animals? In exchange, hunters might provide furs, shells, amber, exotic stone, wild meat, honey or even their own labour or women. Hunter-gatherers did not necessarily see farming, with its endless labour, as an overwhelmingly attractive lifestyle choice. But sometimes they may have had no choice.

It is not difficult in recorded history and ethnology to find examples of all the above scenarios. Human life is complicated. Across Europe there must have been many and varied encounters, just as there were across North and South America in more recent centuries. But across Europe, and ultimately the world, the current certainly flowed in favour of farming. The gradual warming of the climate, the fragmentation of forests, the pressure on wild species of animals from increasing human populations: all promoted farming at the expense of hunters in the temperate zone. Once farmers move in, wild resources rapidly retreat; it is difficult to return to the hunter-gatherer way of life, even if it is more attractive and less back-breaking.[1]

Another powerful factor is that farmers outbred hunters. Hunter populations were limited: by their lifestyle, their beliefs and environmental factors. Nature in temperate Europe is seasonal and can be fickle. When food supplies became short in one area, hunter-gatherers routinely moved. Babies and very small children were a handicap to mobility. Hunter-gatherer women, lacking cereal and dairy products, also continued to breastfeed infants for about three years. In contrast, farmers' babies were weaned in half that time, so mothers became fertile again more quickly and could produce more children – who were welcome in farming families; children soon become productive little workers. Hunter-gatherer children carried out useful tasks but ethnographic studies show that in subsistence farming communities children work more systematically and for longer. They undertake more than just a few chores. The extra labour on the farm generated greater productivity, providing, of course, that land was available or had the potential for intensification of production. This was not a problem in the early Neolithic. Big families also had other advantages: more young members provided security and insurance for ageing parents and grandparents.

Hunter-gatherers accumulated sufficient food to maintain a small family. In contrast, it is estimated that early Neolithic farmers in Europe could harvest an average of 12,800 calories a day, enough to support a family of six. So it might seem that the advantages of farming are obvious, but not necessarily to hunter-gatherers. Their food was fresh and seasonally varied, and they usually ate many different things. Their meat came from wild animals who, they believed, cooperated in the hunt. Wild animals were not dumb victims; like humans, they were part of nature. The hunt may have seemed more like leisure than work. In contrast, farmers relied on staples – increasingly so as farming became universal. In Europe, bread or porridge dominated the diet, with some pulses and cheese (and eventually milk), a limited range of vegetables and fruit, a little meat, or lots on special feasting occasions.

To the average hunter-gatherer, farmers' fare may have seemed monotonous and dull, and their lives a repetitive routine of drudgery.

Subsistence farming also had other handicaps: periodic famine when crops failed, or were destroyed by enemies and bad weather; and diseases, brought about by proximity to animals, spread in more settled, crowded communities. Neolithic farmers probably sought support from their gods to help them with the uncertainties of a vicarious world. These new gods were demanding and fickle, requiring constant attention, rituals, sacrifice and respect. However, in the early Neolithic, farming was still small-scale and under the control of the family producers. Famine and disease may not yet have played such a major role in promoting human misery as it would in later centuries. Nevertheless, early farmers were on a treadmill of hard, repetitive work that resulted in more mouths to feed, a boring starchy diet and, always, the potential for disaster. Whether they liked it or not, human beings had launched themselves on a new trajectory, hoeing or ploughing a furrow from which they could not easily retreat. The consequence, intended or not, was that the wild diminished as domestic crops, domestic animals and domestic human beings spread across newly transformed landscapes.

## Changing attitudes: from persons to things

Did attitudes to animals, plants and even the landscape change with the shift to the Neolithic? This is a question that has recently concerned anthropologists as well as archaeologists, keen to understand how the world view of hunter-gatherers altered with the adoption of agriculture. Recent work among the Kattu (forest) Nayaka people of Nilgiris, southern India, throws up some interesting insights.

The Nayaka are not an especially isolated people, yet they retained a hunter-gatherer lifestyle until the late 20th century and only in recent years took up cultivation and animal husbandry – supplemented by hunting, fishing, collecting honey and wild plants, and wage labour. The anthropologist Tim Ingold famously proposed that with farming, people came to see themselves as dominant in relation to plants and animals. Rather than 'domestication' he prefers the term 'from trust to domination'.[2] The farmers and herders are now in control.

The hunter-gatherer Nayaka were animists: other animals, plants and even rocks had souls; they were 'who' not 'what', relatives or co-dwellers who shared the world. Even growing wood was not cut from trees, as this was hurtful to a living creature. Since the 1980s the Nayaka have come under pressure from increased deforestation, laws that restrict hunting and large-scale Tamil immigration from Sri Lanka, who competed for waged jobs. At the same time, government agencies encouraged the Nayaka to take up farming, offering seed, domestic animals and land rights. So in recent years they have taken to cultivating coffee, tea and pepper for sale, and rice as a staple foodstuff. Some of them keep cows and chickens. Secondary products such as milk and manure are exchanged. They maintain the Hindu taboo against eating beef, though they sometimes sell young cattle to Muslim neighbours. The dogs, which previously were kept for hunting, are now mainly used to guard the settlements.

Nayaka attitudes to both animals and plants – what Tim Ingold called 'dominated subjects' – have changed. The cattle and even the dogs are seen as 'things' that can be treated aggressively: living creatures and plants are not sentient beings, but objects of utilitarian interest, handled with less consideration. An attitude of respect has changed to one largely of exploitation, although not always: attitudes depend upon circumstances. The family cow giving milk may be regarded with more affection than animals reared for sale, for example. Attitudes to land have also changed. Before, it was personified – the rock and spring had a soul – but as land is extracted from the forest, cleared, cultivated and sown, it becomes a distinct, bounded space, 'someone's land'. Beyond, the forested hills are still seen as a place of spirits and invoked in Nayaka trance sessions. The Nayaka are just one example, which helps us to understand how circumstances affect the way hunter-gatherers think. Several thousand years ago in Europe, as the Neolithic introduced new ways of living, it also brought new ways of thinking: were plants and animals also objectified according to their usefulness and the land regarded as a possession? When attitudes change towards the rest of the world, they can also change towards fellow humans. All animals were equal, but now some become more important than others.[3]

I have lived and worked close to farmers all my life. Many will object to this rather negative view. Certainly, I know farmers who are devoted and generally kind to their beasts. However, the utilitarian view pervades farming.

## Guessing the numbers

It is impossible to assess prehistoric populations with any degree of precision, or even much confidence. It has been said, 'one estimate is as bad as another', and many archaeological textbooks avoid the issue of numbers completely.[4] Nowadays, we are accustomed to a world overrun with human beings. It is worth remembering, however, that for most of our species' existence we were thin on the ground and even, until relatively recently, completely absent in some parts of the world; human beings were certainly late arrivals in North and South America, and Ireland.

In the early Holocene the small hunter-gatherer populations grew as they spread across Eurasia into previously unoccupied territory. A rough estimate puts the world's population at about six million, rising by the end of the European Neolithic, four thousand years ago, to around fifteen million.[5] But, as I explained in the previous chapter, the environment and lifestyle set limits.

Christopher Smith of Newcastle University has bravely attempted to tackle the tricky subject of Mesolithic population statistics.[6] The vanishingly small number of hunter-gatherers that survive today (or until recently) do so in marginal areas: the far north, tropical forests or the deserts of southern Africa. There are no close, living analogies for the temperate forest dwellers of Europe. For that matter, the temperate forest itself no longer exists in its wild state, at least not in western Europe. However, Christopher Smith makes some useful generalizations: hunter-gatherers usually live in low densities (below 0.1 person/sq. km). They may cluster around favourable resources, such as estuaries where migrating fish arrive, but overall densities are still low. Their population growth rates are modest, from 0.001% to 0.1% in particularly favourable circumstances. Most humans have the sense to avoid incest, so in a world where people are few, hunter-gatherers find partners from a fairly wide area, without tight social restrictions: what is known in the jargon of anthropologists as an exogamous breeding network. This means that hunter-gatherers can be biologically homogeneous across substantial territories.

In 2012 I gave a talk with the geneticist Turi King at the Science Museum in London. I made the point that race was an irrelevance, biologically speaking; we might as well focus on eye or hair colour, or shoe size. Humans as a species are genetically incredibly similar, and recent research at Harvard University has emphasized the point.[7] The humans who emerged from Africa into Europe 45,000 years ago were dark-skinned because they were adapted to strong sunlight. Recent DNA analysis indicates that dark skin persisted in Europe until 8,500 years ago, when hunter-gatherers in Hungary, Spain and Luxembourg still lacked the two genes associated with lighter skin. The first 'white' genes, and that for blue eyes, occur among skeletons excavated at Motala, in Sweden, a mere 7,700 years ago. This makes sense; in northern climates paler skin provides an evolutionary advantage as vitamin D can be more easily synthesized. What human anguish has been generated for such a minor, recent change in the appearance of a few of us.

Some of the first farmers, coming into Europe from the Near East, were probably lighter-skinned and spread the gene. These people, however, were lactose intolerant (see Chapter 8). It took until the mid to late third millennium BC before the genetic ability to process lactose from animal milk was widespread in northern Europe. In southeast Europe, colonized by Near Eastern farmers, modern populations are still predominantly lactose intolerant, so milk is processed into cheese and yoghurt. From about 6000 BC, northern Europeans also became taller than those in the south. So evolutionary change in humans can be recent; and it has not stopped.

To return to the question of population numbers. Studies of Native Americans in North America indicate that hunter-gatherers were normally bound together as families (though family groups rarely stuck together for more than fifty years). Families linked together as bands, which could vary enormously in size, but averaged about three hundred. Such bands would move across relatively stable territories, though not necessarily exploiting every area every year. Bands allied into tribes, usually speaking the same language or dialect, to form mating networks. Native American tribes averaged about nine hundred members, although there was considerable variation.

Christopher Smith suggests that the closest analogies for Mesolithic communities in Britain may be the tribes of the Pacific Northwest Coast of America – people such as the Haida and Kwakiutl, known for their elaborately carved totem poles, large timber houses, complex social structure and elaborate rituals, including the potlatch, ceremonies at which gifts were distributed and destroyed. Personally, I doubt that people in post-glacial Mesolithic Britain had the time or resources to evolve such an elaborate culture. The Pacific hunter-gatherers had another six thousand years to develop their complex way of life.

Smith himself, with sensible caution, emphasizes the low population numbers in Britain. These grew as the Holocene climate initially warmed and Doggerland succumbed to the rising waters of the North Sea. Nevertheless, if hunter-gatherers in temperate deciduous woodland averaged 0.01–0.02 people per sq. km (⅜ sq. miles), then the population of Britain (as the land mass took more or less its present outline in the late seventh millennium BC, covering about 270,000 sq. km/104,000 sq. miles) can be estimated at up to five thousand people, possibly even reduced by the 6200 BC cold event.

In the fifth millennium BC, continental farmers approached the shores of the English Channel. Archaeological traces of hunter-gatherers in Britain at this time become scarce. Does this mean that there were even fewer people in the islands? Alan Saville issued a warning when I asked him about the missing late Mesolithic: 'absence of evidence is not necessarily evidence of absence'. He has a logical point. In recent years new discoveries have transformed our view of prehistory in many respects. However, at present, we might reasonably speculate that climatic and ecological factors had caused Britain's small Mesolithic population to decline even further in the fifth millennium BC.

There are glimpses of late fifth millennium occupation in Britain: the shell middens of Oronsay and new sites in the Inner Hebrides, of West Voe (on the southern extremity of the Shetlands), and those of southern Ireland; cave sites in the catchment area of the River Dart in Devon and upland summer hunting camps in the Pennines; mostly in what, today, would be regarded the more remote areas of Britain. Where we find the classic sites of the earlier Mesolithic in the lowland valleys, however, evidence is currently lacking for a thriving population of hunter-gatherers in the late fifth millennium BC.

When English Heritage commissioned a detailed field survey of the Fenland of East Anglia, lithic scatters left by hunter-gatherers (and by early farmers) were the most frequently identified type site.[8] These suggested mobility, indicating places where some transient activity took place, where stone was worked for a specific task as people moved through the landscape. It has often been suggested (based on Scandinavian evidence) that later Mesolithic communities became increasingly specialized, socially complex and more sedentary. In other words, foragers were themselves taking important steps towards the adoption of agriculture. Recent research in the southern Netherlands indicates precisely the opposite. There the late Mesolithic was a time of smaller settlements occupied for brief periods; farming seems to have arrived with LBK colonists.[9]

In southern Britain there are odd overlaps between foragers and farmers – for example, scatters of Mesolithic flint debris beneath Neolithic monuments, such as the burial cairn at Hazleton, Gloucestershire. Near the quaintly named village of Sixpenny Handley in Dorset the farmer-archaeologist Martin Green (who has heroically spent half a lifetime investigating his own land and neighbourhood) excavated a natural sinkhole in the chalk, known as the Fir Tree Field shaft.[10] Immediately beneath a layer of Neolithic debris, which included a fragment of polished axe and plain bowl pottery, was a deposit of late Mesolithic material including distinctive rod microliths, probably from a hafted arrow. Like Robinson Crusoe's startling discovery of a footprint on the beach, such evidence reminds us that hunter-gatherers were alive on the northwest fringes of Europe. However, they remain frustratingly silent about their role in the revolutionary change that was imminent: how and why their lifestyle came to an end.

## Farmers and foragers: the contact zone

On the Continent it is clear that Europe's major river systems, such as the Danube and Rhine, assisted the spread of LBK farmers across Europe, and similarly, water transport was vital to Cardial Ware farmers, who leap-frogged across the Mediterranean into the Rhône network and around the coast of Iberia. In contrast, the North Sea coast seems to have provided a barrier for longer.[11]

It was coastal Mesolithic communities that resisted the temptations of the farming life the longest, from Brittany to the Low Countries and southern Scandinavia. A lifestyle based on fishing, shellfish, seabirds, hunting seal, scavenging larger sea mammals and gathering the plants of the shoreline and the woodlands was arguably attractive and relatively secure. Archaeologists in the Netherlands have, in recent years, found interesting evidence for this northern contact zone. LBK farmers arrived in the south of the Netherlands about 5250 BC. There, on the fertile loess plateau of the River Meuse, they established small villages. This was a transformation to fully fledged sedentary agriculture, complete with domestic animals, cattle, sheep and pigs; crops such as emmer wheat, einkorn, linseed and legumes; and the paraphernalia of domesticity: grindstones and pots and, of course, polished stone axes or adzes.

Yet only a short distance to the west the farmers had hunter-gatherer neighbours: small groups living in scattered, briefly occupied camps. It took about three centuries, until 4850 BC, before these traditional people, nearer the coast, began to use pottery, influenced by contacts with LBK farmers and others in northern France. The use of pots, however, was restricted to hunter-gatherers close to the contact zone. Polished adzes were traded more widely; these were useful tools that fit the Mesolithic way of life. Then, in the mid fifth millennium BC, bones of domestic animals began to appear on hunter sites, mostly from joints of meat, not butchered carcasses. It is uncertain whether they had started rearing domestic animals themselves; more likely the hunters were trading with farmers. Evidently, cereals had less attraction – these only put in an appearance in the traditional hunting grounds of the west Netherlands about 4200 BC. It seems that here there was a slow adoption of Neolithic elements by scattered, small-scale hunter-gatherer groups. Along the continental North Sea coast different indigenous peoples reacted to the presence of farming communities in varied ways, influenced by their individual social and economic outlooks.

When it comes to understanding the change from foraging to farming across northern Europe the fundamental problem is the patchiness of data – some regions are better investigated by archaeologists than others. In my experience, I find that many people think that archaeologists have probably dug everything worth digging. That is far from being the case. Archaeologists often generalize on the basis of rubbish samples (in both senses of the word!). There are also regional and national variations in archaeological practice and approaches, which make it difficult to compare one area with another. One of these issues is imprecision in chronologies.[12] The lack of reasonably precise data seriously hinders our understanding of the rhythms and pulses of change in the prehistoric past across Europe. Fortunately, there are now welcome changes afoot with the development of multinational, multidisciplinary research projects.[13]

## We are what we eat

One area where the Mesolithic has been comparatively well studied is southern Scandinavia. As a result, archaeologists have often used this part of the world to generalize about forager groups and the transition to farming in other areas. If one thing is clear, however, it is that archaeologists need to develop a sense of scale, of regional variation and chronological precision if they are to explain our past. The so-called Ertebølle culture of southern Scandinavia is often portrayed as the most sophisticated hunter-gatherer society in the north – comparing it to those of the Pacific Northwest Coast of America in historic times. Once again, I believe this is a parallel that is overdone.

The Ertebølle people exploited the land and the sea. Red deer, roe deer and wild pigs were their principal sources of meat. By the late Mesolithic, they had hunted aurochs to the verge of extinction in this region. Foxes, wolves, beavers, bears, lynx, badgers and wild cats provided fur. Seals and small whales were hunted and scavenged on the coast. The rivers teemed with salmon, eel, catfish and many other species. Offshore, the Ertebølle fishers caught cod, mackerel and plaice. Shellfish was also prolific, notably oysters, mussels and cockles. Large shell middens dotted the coast. There were also specialized hunting sites targeting animals as varied as swans, pigs and pine martens. In this rich, natural environment the temptations of farming were resistible (although in the earlier phases, farming probably still lay beyond the horizon). Nevertheless, archaeologists' claims that the Ertebølle people lived in sedentary communities with large populations are probably exaggerated. Although there are many and varied recorded burials from the mid fifth millennium BC, these seem to be associated with camps or seasonal settlements rather than with distinctive cemeteries or funerary monuments such as became characteristic of the farmers of the Neolithic.

Contact with farming communities probably brought about some changes in Ertebølle society: for example, they began to make distinctive pots with pointed bases and shallow clay lamps fuelled by fatty blubber. Polished stone axes also appear in settlements, graves and in votive deposits. But it was another five hundred years at least before full-blown farming arrived in southern Scandinavia.[14] Peter Rowley-Conwy of Durham University is not impressed by pots and axes. He states bluntly: 'The way to stabilize and Neolithize hunter-gatherers is not to sell them axes but to encroach on their territory and steal their women.'[15]

Southern Scandinavia may have been a happy and fruitful hunting ground, at least for much of the Mesolithic period. Nevertheless, about 4000 BC there was an abrupt change. The appearance of the Neolithic *Trichterbecherkultur* (TRB), or Funnelbeaker, culture in Denmark and southern Norway[16] probably announces the arrival of immigrants from the burgeoning farming populations to the south. Along with their animals and crops, they also brought food taboos and ideas about what it was proper to eat. Stable isotopes from human bone show that seafood rapidly went out of fashion and terrestrial foods dominated the farmers' diet. Although a food taboo is one explanation, another is that fishing clashed with the demanding agricultural timetable. Perhaps 'a time to plant, and a time to pluck up that which is planted'[17] simply intruded on less productive activities and the rigours of farming pushed out some of the varieties of life.

I am inclined to favour the theory that it was the 'push' of population expansion from the south that brought farming to southern Scandinavia rather than the gradual transformation of sophisticated hunter-gatherers. But were there also factors 'pulling' farmers northwards? Was the climate involved? Peter Rowley-Conwy is one of the few archaeologists working in this area to suggest that the 6200 BC cold event (which we have already noted in the Mediterranean and Scotland) might have destabilized northern hunter-gatherers. Climatic improvements about 4000 BC could then have drawn farmers northwards into relatively underpopulated territory.

## The farming pioneer movement: in from the east, up from the south

Not all European farmers moved on the LBK tide from the Danube and the Rhineland. As mentioned in Chapter 7, farmers who cruised the coast and islands of the Mediterranean brought pots impressed with seashells – the Cardial Wares – into southern France, Spain and into Atlantic waters. Northern France – from the Loire estuary, Brittany and the Paris Basin up to the Pas-de-Calais – is an interesting zone in this period. It could, potentially, have been influenced by farming groups from three directions – the LBK from the east; the Epi-Cardial-Ware peoples along the Rhône–Saône corridor (which Greek traders and Roman conquerors used millennia later); and people moving along western sea routes from southwest France, and possibly Iberia.

The LBK spread into Alsace in eastern France (where it is known as 'the Rubané culture') and occupied valley-floor sites. The LBK tradition of farming then encroached into northern France where it is named after the site of Villeneuve-Saint-Germain (the VSG cultural group) and, by about 4950–4650 BC, stretched from the Marne and Seine valleys to the eastern borders of Brittany, the Normandy coast and the central Loire Valley. Impressive settlements like Vignely 'La Porte aux Bergers', in the Marne valley, had trapezoidal longhouses, orientated with their narrow ends to the west (facing into the prevailing winds) and laid out in rows. Thanks to rescue excavations in advance of new rail, road and other development projects, many Neolithic sites have been discovered in recent years.[18] These settlements were not just in valleys, but extended onto the higher plateaus. French archaeologists argue that the spread of farming generated considerable population growth in northern France.[19] The VSG farmers continued the LBK tradition of cultivating einkorn and emmer wheat, barley and peas. Cattle were probably the major domesticated animal, but pigs became increasingly important. They were kept in restricted pens and systematically reared for their meat. The ancestors of the French were already attempting to improve the dreary, restricted Neolithic diet.

There is some evidence that VSG farming communities had contact with foragers of the Atlantic seaboard. Le Haut Mée is one of their most westerly sites, just on the edge of Brittany. The farmers there had polished stone rings made from local schist. One of the rings, however, was more exotic. It had been carved out of serpentine, a rock available from the Île de Groix, off the south coast of Morbihan – the finger of Brittany that projects westwards out into the Atlantic. This was hunter-gatherer territory so it seems the farmers may have traded the stone from Mesolithic groups. It is also possible that the schist supplies may have depended upon such contacts. The well-established farming communities of the VSG, reflecting the Danubian tradition that had so successfully colonized central Europe, acted as an important bridgehead to the world of the remaining hunter-gatherers. It was probably through them that domesticated plants and animals first reached the northwest coast of the Atlantic, the Channel and the North Sea.

The British archaeologist Chris Scarre, of Durham University, has also recognized influences from other farming groups – those of southwest France: 'Les Ouchetta is one of the key sites in the development of Neolithic communities in western France and the character of its pottery indicates links with the south.'[20] Les Ouchetta lies close to the Charente River about 50 km (30 miles) inland from where the river debouches into the sea opposite Île d'Oléron. Groups of farmers could have colonized this area by boat, a continuation of the process of leapfrogging from the south, spreading the techniques, ideas and materials of farming along the west coast of France and into maritime Brittany. Between this area and Poitiers, further inland, are some of the earliest Neolithic burials, dating to around 4700 BC. Cists made of limestone slabs, partly sunken into the ground, contain multiple burials.

In the next couple of centuries, funerary monuments become more impressive, particularly at Prissé-la-Charrière, where a small megalithic tomb was enclosed by a stone rotunda and finally covered by a 100-m (330-ft) long mound that contained two passage graves. We will see this inflating monumentalism again in the British and Irish Neolithic but, in central France, the phenomenon occurs several centuries earlier, in the second half of the fifth millennium BC.

At more or less the same time in the Paris Basin and Normandy, farming groups, known as the Cerny culture, constructed distinctive long barrows, sometimes clustered together and possibly inspired by the earlier longhouses. At Balloy, seventeen barrows were erected over a group of VSG longhouses that had been lived in two hundred years before. Presumably, the outlines of the buildings still lay in the landscape, echoes of the ancestors, proclaiming a special place.

## The land of menhirs

So what of Brittany, the peninsula and archipelago between two seas, pressed by farming communities on its landward, eastern flanks and from the south? Shortly after 5500 BC distinctive Mesolithic burials were taking place at Téviec and Hoëdic, islands off the Armorican peninsula. At the same time, to the south of the Loire, farmers were starting to cultivate the land. There is some evidence of contact between these hunters and farmers. For example, some of the Neolithic techniques for making flint tools, first observed in the Mediterranean area, appear among the hunters further north; in particular, a distinctive arrowhead with the rather stylish moniker of 'L'armature du Châtelet'. More obvious evidence, at least to the vast majority of us who are not lithic specialists, was buried beneath the long mound of Er Grah, on the south Brittany coast of Morbihan, opposite the cemeteries at Téviec and Hoëdic. Here lay two complete, but defleshed, domestic cattle skeletons dating to the later part of the sixth millennium BC. As the VSG groups were not yet farming along the eastern flanks of Brittany, the most likely source for the cattle was the farmers south of the Loire, whose ancestors had burst the bounds of the Mediterranean, navigated the raw Atlantic coast of Iberia or penetrated France along its river systems.

One morning, as I was stood by our front gate, a herd of magnificent Aubrac cattle came trotting down the road making brute music with their hooves: white and blond cows accompanied by their perky calves and a single coffee-coloured bull, all muscle and testosterone. 'What beautiful animals,' I said to the woman who, with her dogs, brought up the rear. 'We're taking them to the meadow at Calviac,' she replied, as she and her charges swept past. I was impressed by these beasts. What must the hunters of Er Grah have made of the first domestic cattle to appear in their world? The fact is, they ate them, perhaps at a large, communal feast, and then gave the remains a special burial. These Brittany hunters may not yet have got the hang of domestication, but they did indulge in more elaborate funerals than many other hunters. The graves at Téviec and Hoëdic were communal, some marked by stone cairns, a standing stone in one case, or contained by stone slabs forming cists. The dead were boxed and presented in stone. Is this the start of a tradition picked up by farmers, competitive and stone obsessed, who for the next three thousand years marked the land of northwestern Europe with their megalithic monuments?

Brittany has some of the earliest and most spectacular monuments in Europe. As Chris Scarre wrote: 'Brittany is a land of many menhirs.' Who could argue: almost twelve hundred have been recorded. These monoliths stand like admonishing fingers in the landscape of the west, particularly in Morbihan, Finistère and Côtes d'Armor. When my children were little we all went to Brittany on holiday. For a week we religiously tracked down the menhirs and megalithic tombs. At Kerloas stood Europe's tallest still-erect menhir at 9.5 m (31 ft) high. The local Neolithic community, with commitment as massive as the rock, dragged this 90-tonne monster uphill for 2.5 km (1½ miles), painstakingly shaped the granite with hammerstones and set it in place. My four-year-old daughter was not quite so devoted to big stones. She was, however, diplomatic. After a week we arrived at the Grand Menhir Brisé, once Europe's largest standing stone, and part of the great complex of megalithic monuments at Locmariaquer. As its name implies, the Grand Menhir now lies broken, in four pieces. The giant was toppled, some say by an earthquake. But my daughter had had enough. 'Daddy,' she said, 'it's very nice looking at these stones. But could we do something else now?' We headed for the beach. Neither of my children became archaeologists.

Radiocarbon dates put the origins of megalith building in Brittany at around 5000 BC or a little later. It has been suggested that the impressive natural crags of Brittany inspired the first monument builders, and perhaps Mesolithic hunters, who revered natural places, erected rough and irregular stones in imitation of natural stones; then, in the Neolithic, the stones were shaped and the architecture became more elaborate. Unfortunately, the radiocarbon dates do not support this argument. There are three distinctive groups of shaped menhirs: the best known stand along the indented coast of the southern Morbihan, then there is the Bas-Léon group on the extreme western peninsula of Brittany, and another, northern group around the estuary at St-Malo. What they have in common is proximity and visibility from the sea.

The radiocarbon dates point to an outburst of enthusiasm for shaping, decorating and erecting massive rocks in prominent places – first in the south and then around the coast – all within a generation in the early fifth millennium BC. This looks like competitive construction among early Neolithic communities. But there must also have been cooperation – how else could the 350-tonne, 20-m (65-ft) high Grand Menhir Brisé have been quarried from an outcrop of distinctive rock (orthogneiss) 4 km (2½ miles) away, dragged to its site, beautifully shaped with hammerstones and erected – to stand prominently, not alone but the tallest of a line of eighteen stone sentinels?[21]

The Grand Menhir dwarfs the sarsen stones of Stonehenge, and was erected several centuries earlier. Early farmers in northwest Europe and down to the Mediterranean seem to have been obsessed with erecting monuments made of massive stone, a kind of megalithomania. Many archaeologists are equally obsessed with the question of who started the tradition. We cannot yet be sure, but the Bretons are candidates.

At Locmariaquer hundreds of people from small-scale farming communities must have come together for their ongoing *grand projet*. Ongoing because after the erection of the Grand Menhir and its companion stones, two massive tombs were subsequently built immediately adjacent – the long mound of Er Grah (site of the earlier cattle feast) and the oval tumulus known as the Table des Marchand.

### The force be with you

Some archaeologists assume that such monumental effort and achievement imply compulsion by dominant leaders. Many societies – from ancient Egypt to Central America and China – had powerful hereditary elites that coerced, or even paid, large cohorts of workers to erect monuments in honour of themselves and their gods. But this is not the only way people get things done. In simpler, less hierarchical agricultural societies some people, usually men, pursue personal status and honour. Kent Flannery and Joyce Marcus of the University of Michigan provide a cautionary tale for archaeologists.[22]

Assam, on India's eastern border with Myanmar (Burma), is best known today for its tea. Until the beginning of the 20th century, however, these forested mountains were home to traditional Naga hill people, farmers who raised cattle and pigs and grew rice and millet. They lived in self-governing villages, divided into clans, with dormitory-style houses for the men.

The Naga believed in a life force that promoted the growth of crops and animals. They could accumulate the force by sacrificing animals – and head-hunting. Successful warriors were allowed to display their prowess by wearing boars' tusks and special cloth, and with tattoos. The most successful head-hunters became war leaders (and no heads could mean no wife).

Another route to prestige in the community was as a sponsor of rituals. A man amassed wealth and then redistributed it through feasts that involved music, dancing, consuming sacrificial pigs and cattle, and lots of rice beer. This sounds like a hugely enjoyable knees-up, though the event was also highly ritualized and reflected the sponsor's ability to control the life force. As the sponsor promoted more and bigger feasts he was eventually allowed to decorate his house with distinctive wooden horns.

At this stage, the promoter of rituals could move on to an even more prestigious ritual act – 'chisu' or stone pulling. After organizing a massive month-long feast, the sponsor called on his fellow clansmen, members of his menshouse and villagers to haul a huge monolith from a distant quarry (and the distance was important) to the village. The stone haulers, who might number up to several hundred, dressed for the occasion in elaborate ceremonial kit: conch-shell necklaces, brass and ivory armlets and bird plumes. The stone was levered onto a sled of logs; wooden rollers were placed along the route and hundreds of men, pulling on ropes, hauled the sled and its load. They toiled for hours, all the time singing to encourage themselves and looking forward to the rice beer that awaited them at the end. At the sponsor's village, a hole was dug to take the monolith. Once erected the stone became both a dwelling for powerful spirits and a memorial to the sponsor. He was now a 'Kemovo', or holy man, and entitled to special burial with others of his kind. The 'chisu' stone-pulling ritual echoed the belief that natural, rocky landmarks were the abode of spirits. The community regarded the sponsor's success in promoting feasts and bringing the monolith to the village as an indication of his good relations with the spirits and his ability to channel the life force.

In the small-scale farming societies of the Naga, men achieved status: their power was limited, not inherited, and depended upon the cooperation of a community with common beliefs and values – they all thought alike, and together transported and erected huge stones.

## Axes again

The megalithic monuments of Neolithic Brittany and Europe involved taking rocks from natural places that may have been seen as sources of spiritual power. But the sculpted stones also speak of artifice, of growing confidence, even arrogance; of people shaping their world with the help of their gods. Humans develop a mind-boggling variety of myths and belief systems. Only those with a deep familiarity of a particular culture can translate their esoteric meanings. Brittany's megaliths remain reticent, yet they do speak of a new, and changing, world. Our modest polished stone axe is its icon; the Grand Menhir Brisé, which looks remarkably like an axe, may be its greatest manifestation – the announcement that farmers, their axes and a new way of life had arrived at the furthest northwestern tip of the Eurasian continent.

The continuing importance of the axe as a symbol can be seen in two of the great stone tombs. The Grand Tumulus de Saint-Michel at Carnac in Brittany is impressive by anyone's standards: 12.5 m (40 ft) long, 60 m (200 ft) wide and 10 m (33 ft) high. The tumulus incorporates earlier megaliths and seems to be a monument representing continuity. One of its chambers contained thirty-nine polished stone axes, eleven of them made from beautiful, green jadeitite brought 800 km (500 miles) from the Alps. The tomb of Mané er Hroëk at Locmariaquer also contained as many as 106 exotic axes, carefully carved from jadeitite and black fibrolite, a material quarried in Spain, which speaks of persisting maritime contacts. These axes were clearly valued, ritual objects, not standard tools for felling trees or splitting the firewood. In the Gavr'Inis tomb, now an island a kilometre to the east of the Locmariaquer peninsula, many of the stones that lined the long entrance passage were carved with abstract symbols. On one stone, however, the flowing decoration surrounded a central zone in which there were carved very precise depictions of eighteen elegant axe heads.

With farming in Brittany came a massive outpouring of energy and effort into the creation of monuments that are impressive even today: a demonstration of massive enthusiasm on the part of farming communities. It can be argued, as I noted at the beginning of the chapter, that farming was a trap for humanity, an endless cycle of hard work in return for poor food. Yet in Brittany, as we will see across the water in Britain and Ireland, farming communities were capable of far more than tilling the fields and milking their herds.

The limit of Brittany is today known as Finistère, which means 'land's end'. But beyond lie further possibilities: the temperate archipelago of Britain,

Ireland and the northern isles warmed by the Gulf Stream, with only a small, scattered population of hunter-gatherers. For axe traders who had tackled the Bay of Biscay, and even for hunters who had crossed to Ireland and explored the Hebrides and the Shetland islands, the Channel cannot have presented insuperable problems. Indeed, Duncan Garrow of Reading University and Fraser Sturt of Southampton University go so far as to speak of 'Grey waters bright with Neolithic Argonauts'.[23] They are part of a team researching the Atlantic seaways: the *Stepping Stones to the Neolithic* project, which includes studying the emergence and occupation of the Channel Islands and the Isles of Scilly.[24]

There are particularly interesting indications of sea travel at the Old Quarry site, St Mary's, in the Scillies. There are good flint sources on the island and it seems that people travelled there and manufactured microliths around 6000 BC. Yet the style of flint-working does not point to Cornwall, the nearest mainland (a mere 40 km/25 miles away). The flint knappers more likely originated in northeast France, over 500 km (300 miles) to the east, along La Manche, the English Channel. A few microliths are not a lot of evidence but they provide a tantalizing glimpse of what may have been a Mesolithic maritime network, criss-crossing the recently formed waterway of the Channel.

At a later date there is another possible link across the waters between France and Ireland. At Er Grah, in Brittany, we saw the remains of domestic cattle consumed and buried by hunter-gatherers. Ferriter's Cove, County Kerry, in southwest Ireland, is 500 km (300 miles) across the sea from Brittany (the Isles of Scilly are halfway between the two). Here, on the coast in the mid fifth millennium BC, people mainly relied on maritime resources for food. And yet they also consumed domestic cattle – anyway at least once, on what may have been a memorable occasion of exotic feasting. Remember, big wild meaty animals were rare in Mesolithic Ireland, so domestic cattle would have provided a culinary thrill for carnivores. The northwest French coast was the nearest source of such animals. Did the maritime Neolithic farmers transport the cattle alive, or perhaps already butchered and jointed before the crossing? With this beast came the news to Ireland of domesticated livestock, of compliant meat on the hoof and a different way of life. There is, however, another possibility: it is not unknown for archaeozoologists to have difficulty distinguishing between aurochs and domestic cattle. This is a cold case worth reinvestigating. If the bones proved to be wild aurochs then they would still have come across the water, but more likely from Wales or another part of the coast of western Britain.[25]

At Ferriter's Cove the excavators also found a cache of polished stone axes made of local stone. British archaeologists often portray late Mesolithic Ireland as an odd place with an unusual insular stone toolkit – they ground axes, reduced the use of microlith technology and made larger flint blades.[26] In fact, Ireland's lithics in some respects resemble those of the Continent. It is southern Britain that is out of kilter. Polished stone axes arrived in Ireland first. Ireland, though, was not ready to welcome full-blown farming in the mid fifth millennium BC. It was to wait another six or seven centuries for farming to take root.

## CHAPTER TWELVE

# Farming on the move: The arrival in Britain

## Living by the lakes

By the later fifth millennium BC the Neolithic package, in its varied forms, had spread across much of Europe. In some areas there were large settlements with substantial houses; their occupants tilled the soil and grew wheat and barley, reared animals and churned milk into cheese and yoghurt. Elsewhere, notably Brittany (and as we will see in Britain), impressive megalithic monuments stand out in the landscape and dominate the way archaeologists think about the past. As a result there are different research traditions in Europe. Some scholars emphasize economic and domestic factors: the Neolithic is about farming, usually brought by immigrants. In areas where such evidence is scarce (or has been until recently), the focus is on the monuments: this Neolithic supposes that hunter-gatherers adopted some aspects of domestication, particularly herding, remained highly mobile, occupied light, transportable dwellings and built impressive burial monuments as the community focal point. Thanks to advances in radiocarbon dating and huge numbers of archaeological excavations in advance of redevelopment schemes, these two contrasting and simplistic images of the Neolithic are beginning to shift and fragment. It is a reminder that archaeologists should not jump to conclusions on the basis of limited evidence or value theories above reliable data.

One area where the evidence is excellent is on the shores of the Alpine Foreland lakes of Germany and Switzerland. The so-called 'Lake Villages' have been famous since well-preserved, waterlogged timber piles were first recorded in the mid 19th century, when thanks to a run of dry summers they were exposed as lake levels fell. The discovery of a new European prehistory caused so much excitement that the Lake Villages featured in the 1867 Exposition Universelle in Paris. Swiss schoolchildren learnt, proudly, of their past in textbooks such as *La Patrie*. The schoolbook reported (in French): 'In 1854, Doctor Keller from Zurich on the shore at Meilen, saw some half-decayed piles [*des piquets*] and fragments of crude ceramic ware [*poterie grossiere*] and stone axes [*des haches de pierre*]'. It goes on to describe how following the Lake Zurich discoveries other Swiss lakes were rapidly explored and traces of further settlements were discovered know as *constructions lacustres* or palafittes (lake dwellings). Early reconstruction drawings show these settlements perched on piled platforms over the water. Now we know that, in fact, the buildings stood on solid ground by the lakeshore. In the early years of the fourth millennium BC climatic fluctuations caused the lake levels to rise, inundating and preserving the timbers and much else besides.

The settlement at Hornstaad-Hörnle on Lake Constance (or the Bodensee in German) is a good example of the superb-quality data that can survive in ideal archaeological circumstances – here, as a result of both waterlogging and burning. The survival of house timbers means that tree-ring dating provides remarkable chronological precision.[1] In 3917 BC, four new houses sprang up. This small community attracted others, and fourteen more houses appeared in the next two years. Then, between 3911 BC and 3910 BC, at least twenty-four more houses were built. The settlement was growing fast and clearly these farming families were drawn to live in densely clustered communities: perhaps they provided security, opportunities to cooperate with the workload or to have a more varied social life.

Of course, when people live on top of each other there can be problems – arguments about children, dogs, borrowed tools, wandering spouses or trivial slights. Clustered wooden buildings are also at risk from fire. At Hornstaad-Hörnle there was a devastating conflagration shortly after 3910 BC. Some of the villagers rolled up their sleeves and began rebuilding; others decided to start a new settlement nearby, putting some distance between themselves and the older cluster of houses, yet staying close enough to retain rights to the land. At Hornstaad-Hörnle the final house was completed in 3902 BC, but the community did not remain there for long. They shifted in the face of the rising water level that began to encroach on them and other lakeside communities about this time.[2]

The farmers at Hornstaad-Hörnle had more than their fair share of problems, yet their misfortunes were a godsend for archaeologists. For example, the fire after 3910 BC carbonized and preserved a wealth of plant remains. As a result, it is clear that each household stored large supplies of grain and routinely cultivated its own plots of land.[3] At other sites around the Alpine lakes, cattle bones indicate the wear and tear inflicted on beasts used for traction, and pots were impregnated with the fats (lipids) from dairying.

Evidently, these people operated a mature, mixed agricultural system, even if climatic variation and fluctuating water levels still buffeted them somewhat. They were flexible and adaptable.

The evidence from the Alpine Foreland and other areas in Europe shows that Neolithic communities were becoming more varied, and regionally distinct. The great regimented ranks of *Linearbandkeramik* (LBK) longhouses were no longer in fashion. It didn't do to be Danubian! People were moving into new landscapes and environments, exploiting a wider range of varied resources (judging from isotopic evidence of diet) and building in less uniform ways. This flexible and varied Neolithic may also have more easily absorbed and included hunter-gatherers, who as we have seen in Britain were attracted to lakesides and shorelines. However, archaeologists have a familiar problem in the Alpine Foreland. Well-dated, late Mesolithic sites are vanishingly rare and there is a gap of several centuries between the latest-known Mesolithic and the beginning of the Neolithic.

## Crossing the Channel

At this time (around 4100 BC), the frontiers of farming in Europe were on the move again – pulsing into the Alpine Foreland and, further north, colonizing the coasts of the Atlantic, North Sea and Baltic, pushing into Scandinavia and Poland.[4] The increasing population of farmers may have been a factor, and in some areas hunter-gatherers began to be receptive to the new way of life, whether attracted by the material benefits of farming, its belief systems and social norms or pushed by challenges to their own traditional routines. There were also climatic changes in northern Europe from about 4100 BC, which improved the conditions for agriculture, lengthening the growing season for cereals, lowering winter rainfall and making new lands attractive; at the same time, these drier conditions may have been detrimental to hunter-gatherers.

The British archipelago presented a specific challenge: in order to introduce farming, domesticated sheep, pigs and cattle, foodstuffs, seed and equipment, as well as farming families, had to be shipped across the water. As we saw earlier, farmers in the Mediterranean, along the Atlantic coast and the European river systems seem to have regarded the water as their highway. Cattle – or at least bits of them – may have reached southern Ireland, probably from northwestern France, centuries before. Mesolithic seafarers had explored and colonized islands all around Britain, reaching Ireland, the

Hebrides and Orkney. Neolithic farmers on the Continent – at least those who had settled the Atlantic seaboard – and the northern hunter-gatherers were competent navigators.

There is, however, not much evidence for regular communications across the Channel into England before 4100 BC. For example, on the continental mainland a number of hunter-gatherer groups took to importing, using and even making pottery. But not in Britain. British stone tools also remained distinctly insular. Nevertheless, the farming surge did reach Britain at the end of the fifth millennium BC.

The early Neolithic in Britain and Ireland is marked by the presence of impressive tombs. Several generations of archaeologists have exerted themselves categorizing, defining, measuring and mapping the houses of the dead: megalithic tombs of bewildering variety, long barrows, chambered cairns, cromlechs and dolmens, passage tombs, court tombs, portal tombs and wedge tombs – the seemingly infinite variety of the Neolithic necropolis. From Spain to Ireland it is often obvious where early farmers placed their ancestors. They went to enormous trouble to build monuments to house their bones: the earliest surviving man-made structures in Europe, which have lasted for millennia.

In England, especially, the problem for archaeologists was where the farmers lived themselves. On the Continent, the study of the Neolithic has routinely been about settlements and houses, while in England archaeologists had difficulty finding them. So until recently, it has been fashionable among English archaeologists to dismiss the idea of wholesale migration from the Continent and instead emphasize the role of the, albeit invisible, indigenous population.[5] According to this view of the origin of the Neolithic, British hunter-gatherers gradually selected and adopted elements of the Neolithic package. Domestic animals could fit relatively easily into the mobile, Mesolithic way of life. Continued mobility would explain the flint scatters, the limited evidence of cereals and, above all, the lack of continental-style houses. Around the world those who live tied to animal herds – people as varied as the Lapps (the Sami), Mongols, Plains Indians and Maasai – house themselves in slight, easily erected and mobile structures. They travel light and move frequently – early Neolithic communities in northwest Europe had not yet domesticated the horse, though cattle could be used for traction; Mesolithic communities simply had their own muscle power and dogs to help transport their relatively meagre possessions.

## The English house problem

On 14 November 2007, after about eight thousand years, Britain regained a solid link with the continent of Europe. The Channel Tunnel opened. Then, contentiously on the English side, the Channel Tunnel Rail Link (now known as High Speed 1) was built, joining Paris to London. In advance of the construction, across Kent and into London, archaeologists carried out a massive programme of excavations. They found Ice Age elephants, dug complete Roman villas and cemeteries and Anglo-Saxon graves, and recorded standing medieval houses before literally lifting and moving them to new sites. One day in 1998, the field team contacted me in Oxford to suggest that I come and look at something special at a site they called White Horse Stone. As I approached the workings I could see a herd of huge machines, browsing on the hill slope of the North Downs. It looked like a scene out of *Jurassic Park*. At first I thought this was the construction of the Rail Link itself, then, as I got closer, I realized that the archaeologists themselves were working on a scale scarcely before seen in Britain.

On the brow of the slope they had uncovered an Iron Age settlement – a fairly routine find. However, these later prehistoric farmers and their successors had ploughed the land for centuries and caused the bare soil to wash down the hill – 'colluvium' in the jargon. After peeling away tons of this stuff the team made the discovery that sent them to the telephone. Protected by the deep blanket of soil were the dark marks where timber posts had stood, forming the rectangular outline of a large house, 17.5 m (57 ft) long and 7 m (23 ft) wide. The fact that it was under the colluvium meant it had to be old; fragments of pottery, a few cereal grains and flint artefacts put the structure in the early Neolithic. So, at White Horse Stone, not far from the coast, and as close to the Continent as Britain gets, was a building with a distinctly continental appearance. Nothing like this would have ever been seen before in the Mesolithic woodland of Britain.[6]

A grid of dark marks, indicating where a building had stood, might not look like much – a brief semaphore from the past. It is as if the wooden structure, its contents and its inhabitants had been sucked into the sky, leaving only an imprint behind. Imagine spiriting away a house, a barn or a church. What could we tell of its use and meaning from its imprint alone? Archaeologists often have to work with frustratingly faint traces. Few places speak with the clarity of the Alpine lakeside villages. Yet these particular traces in Kent represented something new. As the building was not abandoned in a hurry, or burnt down, there was little left within to indicate its purpose: was it for storage, a place of security, a ritual centre or the multipurpose house of a pioneer group of farmers? Radiocarbon dates, assisted by Bayesian modelling, further emphasized its importance: the hall-like building was probably built between 4065 BC and 3940 BC, stayed in use for about three centuries and was abandoned in 3745–3635 BC. This is the earliest-known Neolithic building in Britain: the imprint of the first farmers. Ambiguous perhaps, but a place to start, for us and them.

Were these people strangers in a strange land? Was the White Horse Stone house built by innovating natives or by immigrants arriving from across the sea? In this part of Kent there is scarcely any evidence of late Mesolithic activity, and the building bears no resemblance to anything seen before. Its occupants left some traces, albeit slight, of cereals and pottery – markers of the Neolithic. These few sherds of pottery are unimpressive yet they are some of the earliest material to be transformed and manufactured in Britain. Stone and wooden tools were made simply by carving and chipping natural material. These potsherds represented a new technology, altering the character of clay by control of pyrotechnics. It seems possible that we are looking at the work of newcomers. So can we tell where they came from? Romans in Britain, some four thousand years later, would conveniently drop coins minted in Italy or sherds of shiny red pottery made just across the mountain from where I am writing in southern France; they even left inscriptions declaring their birthplace in Spain or Thrace. There was no such clear message at White Horse Stone. Instead, we have the building imprint to work with – not the most distinctive of clues.

So can we identify a home for this architecture, a place of origin perhaps? What were farmers building across the Channel in 4000 BC? Certainly not the big LBK longhouses – their heyday was a thousand years earlier. There had been longhouses, or hall-type buildings, in the Paris Basin and Normandy several centuries later, but these were antiques compared with White Horse Stone. The problem is that this is a period of considerable change and diversity in northern Europe and buildings are relatively rare in the archaeological record; when they do appear they are stylistically variable.[7]

Jonathan Last, a colleague at English Heritage, has scoured reports on both sides of the Channel to collect the evidence for Neolithic buildings and attempt to understand their role in early farming societies. He suggests that by 4000 BC the house was no longer so fundamental to the way farmers

ABOVE The excavations of the White Horse Stone early Neolithic site in Kent, England. On the lower slopes of the chalk scarp overlooking the Medway Valley to the west, the remains of the timber building were preserved beneath hillwash.

RIGHT Traces of the White Horse Stone longhouse, possibly the earliest Neolithic building in Britain.

across the Channel saw themselves; houses were smaller, more varied in style and construction, often not built to last. By 4000 BC, northern farmers had downsized.[8] However, archaeologists have found houses in northern France and on the North Sea coast as far as Denmark that bear a resemblance to White Horse Stone and other British examples. There were other changes in northern Europe: a greater emphasis on rearing pigs and hunting wild animals, sometimes from seasonal camps, and most evidently, a fondness for elaborate funerary monuments that contained the burials of only a few people.

The earlier LBK longhouse perhaps initially represented an ideology of equality. The house was a focal point as well as a home, a place for families to gather, surrounded by others like themselves, and to receive guests. The longhouse, however, was also a place to store produce, and accumulate wealth and influence in the community. There were signs of developing inequality, community aggression and the need for defence. In northern Europe by the late fifth millennium BC, houses were more modest and relatively isolated; people stressed their identity through the communal effort of building monuments for the dead. They also created new places: large causewayed enclosures, arenas where scattered groups could gather. These were not the family gatherings of the LBK longhouse but events that were larger and more complex. These trends eventually appeared in Neolithic Britain, but not all at the very beginning.

## The lie of the land

The White Horse Stone building – and its companion (a second timber building, the Pilgrim's Way site, was found 200 m/650 ft to the southeast) – cannot be precisely matched in the near Continent. This is hardly surprising at a time when people did not work to a blueprint. We also seem to be looking at a pioneer site, which throws up other questions: the Neolithic settlers may have come from northern France or the North Sea coast. It is likely that before deciding to settle, scouts would have gone ahead to explore the lie of the land, and the coastal waters. They evidently came into the Thames estuary, found the River Medway and a route inland into the present-day county of Kent. Perhaps they had local guides who saw potential advantages to be gained from cooperation with the newcomers. At this time, sea level rise had temporarily halted and the coast had developed a zone of marshland and peatbogs, so the shoreline extended further out than today and was not particularly hospitable to farmers arriving by boat. The Neolithic pioneers travelled upriver to the White Horse Stone site. Today it is 25 km (15 miles) from the sea but in 4000 BC the distance was twice as far. This was not some great invasion by a powerful force, arriving at a bridgehead – it is not the world of Julius Caesar in 55 BC or William the Conqueror in 1066, both of whom arrived with armies in fleets of ships.

The Neolithic arrivals probably came as small kin groups in a handful of boats, still leapfrogging in pursuit of new places to live, perhaps like some of the Viking crews, searchers for land in Iceland, Greenland and Vinland, or the Pilgrim Fathers from Britain and the Netherlands who arrived in America. These pioneers had to find suitable landfall and negotiate with the local inhabitants. Things did not always go well. Locals were curious; they could help, or turn hostile. Pioneers do not always select good places to settle. If it was practicable the pioneers kept in touch with the homeland, for supplies and reinforcements. Traffic criss-crossed the waters. Unfortunately, at present, we can only speculate about the motivation of any newcomers arriving in Britain six thousand years ago. Nor can we be precise about the location of their original homeland.

The White Horse Stone people moved inland. They did not stay by the River Medway or locate their large structures prominently on high ground. Instead, their radical buildings were tucked into a fold in the slope, relatively inconspicuous from afar, and not near water. Were the settlers trying to be discreet, avoiding being too obvious to native hunting parties? Or was there another reason?

When I arrived at the White Horse Stone site I was amazed to see that as the machines peeled off the thick layer of hillwash, a forgotten field of sarsen boulders was revealed. Sarsens are the hard, resistant sandstone rocks that were used in the most impressive megalithic monuments: similar stone would be dragged to Avebury, Stonehenge and the West Kennet chambered tomb. Sarsens naturally lie scattered in dry chalk valleys – in Wessex, local farmers call them 'grey wethers' because, from above, they look like flocks of sheep ('wether' is a dialect word for a sheep).

Did the White Horse Stone people erect their large building here because of the presence of the stones, a place of natural megaliths, a reminder of their homeland and of the potential of the new world? It is easy to consider pioneer farmers simply in terms of economic and demographic forces. However, human beings constantly weave threads of significance into the landscape and layer it with symbolic meaning. I have often been struck when travelling through America, the West Indies and Kenya how colonists manipulate the landscape to remind themselves of the 'Old Country'. There is every reason why Neolithic newcomers would have attached themselves to the land through myths, stories and memories.

## Gathering time

The work on Bayesian modelling of radiocarbon dates by the *Gathering Time* project is, arguably, the most important development in British (or anyone else's) prehistory in decades.[9] The work developed out of efforts to unravel the chronology of Stonehenge, then establish the dates of several long barrows in southern Britain, and subsequently of early Neolithic enclosures in Britain and Ireland. By introducing a new level of precision, Alex Bayliss, Alasdair Whittle and their colleagues sliced through the Gordian knot that had tied researchers of the Neolithic into a cycle of repetitive arguments.

For the first time we have a sense of the tempo of change – how long it took for Neolithic things and practices to become established in Britain. The package can be summarized as: cultivated cereals; animal domesticates; bowl pottery; distinctive stone tools, such as leaf-shaped arrowheads and ground axes; burial monuments; flint mines; rectangular timber buildings and enclosures. The *Gathering Time* team put the White Horse Stone building and other sites in the Thames estuary at the very beginning of the British Neolithic sequence. The estimated time of arrival is the late 41st century BC.[10]

So what about the rest of the British Isles and Ireland? The new Bayesian data suggest that farming then spread over the next hundred years into southern England. About 3800 BC it accelerated and in a generation had reached Cornwall and northeast Scotland, and a decade or so later farmers were in the Isle of Man and Ireland. In the course of two hundred to three hundred years, from its arrival in the Thames estuary, farming – with its new crops, animals, pots and artefacts, houses and monuments – had spread across the entire British Isles and Ireland. In this time the hunter-gatherer way of life completely disappeared. The transformation of the British landscape began, and, arguably, is still ongoing today.

In a number of areas of Britain the data remain poor, however. The start of the Neolithic in Ireland presents some problems. The Neolithic package of domesticated plants and animals, pottery, houses, fields, trackways, stone quarries and court and portal tombs is certainly distinctive in Ireland. The *Gathering Time* team, while admitting the difficulties and shortcomings of the Irish data, generally put the origins of most of the Neolithic elements around 3800–3750 BC.

Except there is the issue of Magheraboy. Causewayed enclosures are a feature of the early Neolithic, particularly in southern and central England (see page 231). However, in 2003 in advance of the construction of a new road south of Sligo town, Irish archaeologists discovered a causewayed enclosure with an internal palisade trench. There was no doubt about its early Neolithic status: the ditches contained fragments of Carinated Bowl pottery and three axe heads. A porcellanite axe seemed to have been deliberately broken and placed near to the butt of a limestone axe head. Pits within the enclosure contained deliberately broken pots, leaf-shaped arrowheads, burnt bone and carbonized cereals. Although the Neolithic package is clearly represented at Magheraboy, the radiocarbon dates put the construction of the enclosure ditch in the decades either side of 4000 BC. If this is to be believed, then the Neolithic was launched in England and northwest Ireland at roughly the same time. Further detailed analysis and modelling by the *Gathering Time* team emphasized the early dates for the construction of the enclosure (4065–3945 BC at 68% probability), which poses fundamental questions about the date of the start of the Neolithic in Ireland and is a major challenge.

Otherwise, the analysis of early features in Ireland suggests that the Neolithic began about 3800 BC or a little later. The Magheraboy enclosure stands out as an anomaly two hundred years too early. Does it, perhaps, represent a false start, an early attempt to import the farming culture from northwest France? An historical analogy would be the Norse settlement at L'Anse aux Meadows on Newfoundland, dating to about AD 1000, five hundred years before the start of the principal European colonization of the Americas. But this analogy does not work: the houses at L'Anse aux Meadows are typical Norse turf constructions similar to contemporary examples in Iceland and Greenland. At Magheraboy the material culture is typically Irish early Neolithic – for example, the Antrim porcellanite exploitation, like the porphyry on Lambay Island, is not otherwise recorded before the early 38th century BC. Similarly, the bowl ceramics date to about the same time.

The alternative explanation is that the radiocarbon dates were obtained from bulk samples and residual material. Could relatively old timbers have influenced the dates? This seems like special pleading. The *Gathering Time* team conclude: 'the fact remains that we still do not know when the Neolithic came to Ireland.'[11] What we can say, however, is that by around 3800 BC and in the following decades, farming and the paraphernalia of the Neolithic spread rapidly, probably introduced from Britain, with the local Mesolithic hunter-gatherers playing relatively little part – or at least making little impact on the archaeological record.

If the Neolithic first appeared in Britain in the region of the Thames/ Medway estuary, the questions remain: who brought it and from where? This has been the subject of heated debate in archaeology for several decades. In the 1950s, Stuart Piggott argued for multiple colonizations from areas such as Brittany, Normandy and the Pas-de-Calais, as well as Flanders and the southern Netherlands. To the next generation this smacked of the unfashionable 'invasion hypothesis'. Since the 1970s the 'indigenous hypothesis' model has held sway. In other words, British hunter-gatherers selectively adopted and adapted the Neolithic practices of people on the Continent.[12] However, as a result of the evidence from genetics, isotope analysis, lithics, diet and dating, more balanced approaches have developed, favouring the arrival of small groups from the Continent.

The homeland areas remain a matter of debate, shifting as new discoveries appear in France, Belgium and the Netherlands. These people brought their expertise in farming along with their own cultural practices and religious beliefs. The incomers were the prime movers, but inevitably there must have been interaction with the native population, which, on the basis of limited archaeological evidence may have been quite low. Newcomers and indigenous peoples may have intermarried, the hunter-gatherers pulled towards farming by new prerogatives, such as the need for cattle as bride-price and status, or pushed by environmental change and expanding farming populations with a richer material culture making inroads into the natural environment and laying claim to land and other resources.

New settlers would need to remain in contact with the homeland for further supplies of animals and plants, labour and marriage partners. Like the later Norse colonizers of Iceland and Greenland or the British in Virginia it would be in their interests to buttress their position in the new-found land by encouraging others to join them in their idyllic, supposedly green and pleasant home where there was lots of space and friendly locals.

There is still the issue of multiple sources and strands for the British Neolithic. Did migrant farmers setting out from different places arrive in different parts of the British Isles? Was the seed, literally, planted in different places, not just the Thames estuary? Alison Sheridan, of the National Museums of Scotland, has fought a determined campaign in favour of the multiple-strand argument.[13] She argues that one channel of migration was from Brittany in the years before 4000 BC, targeting west Wales, northern Ireland and western Scotland. The spotlight has focused on a simple passage tomb, supposedly a Breton type, at Achnacreebeag in Argyll and Bute, which contained fragments of pottery said to resemble Breton vessels. Sheridan compares the most complete of these, decorated with incised arches, with ceramics from the Table des Marchand at Locmariaquer, Brittany, in use about 4000 BC. This little pot is probably the most contentious vessel in British prehistory and its Breton links remain far from secure. Scottish archaeologists Graeme Ritchie (the excavator)[14] and Audrey Henshall place the pot in a regional tradition of decorated bowls, comparable with a vessel found in the Clyde cairn at Blasthill in Kintyre. Stylistic arguments tend to be difficult to sustain without firm independent dating evidence. The inverted arc, which characterizes the Achnacreebeag pot, also appears on the Irish passage tomb at Knowth (see Chapter 16) in a later Neolithic context. Simple design features do tend to get around.

The *Gathering Time* team question the dating of the Achnacreebeag pottery (the tomb itself has not been radiocarbon-dated) as well as its Breton connection. The Bayesian modelling fixes the start of the Neolithic in southern Scotland at about 3815–3780 BC, a timescale that allows the new influences to flow from the southeast of Britain into the north. If there were further colonizations into southern and southwestern Britain from Normandy and Brittany, then they would probably have occurred later, around 3800 BC.[15]

The Thames estuary and the southeast of England seem to be the initial point of entry for Neolithic immigrants. The fine Carinated bowls with round bottoms and leaf-shaped arrowheads found in the earliest Neolithic contexts in Britain point to a Continental homeland in northeast France, Belgium and the southern Netherlands. This was also an area in which people were skilled at digging and exploiting flint mines, specifically for the exchange of flint tools, especially axes.[16]

Six thousand years ago there are signs that the previously stable farming/forager frontier came tumbling down. The Dutch archaeologist L. P. Louwe Kooijmans put it this way: 'Major social changes were...taking place among the agricultural communities on the other side of the "frontier"...crises involving drastic transformation in the communities' culture. It is tempting to associate some, if not all, of these changes with the confrontation, contacts and exchange of knowledge with the northern native population...The outcome was a "Neolithic" that was apparently acceptable to the native population of large parts of northern Europe.'[17] At present, I do not think we are in a position to judge how 'acceptable' the natives found the change, particularly in Britain.

The detailed evidence is contentious or absent, yet offers exciting avenues for joint research between Ireland, Britain and mainland Europe.

## Ireland

In Ireland most archaeologists were reluctant to accept the theory that mobile native hunter-gatherers gradually adopted Neolithic traits, and for a very good reason. For a long time they had been finding the traces of Neolithic houses, which seemed to mark settled farming communities. Neolithic houses turned up at Lough Gur, County Limerick, in the 1930s;[18] across the Knockadoon peninsula in the 1940s and 1950s; and in the late 1960s at Ballynagilly, County Tyrone. Irish pollen diagrams also suggested that early Neolithic farmers had made significant impacts on the landscape: for example, there was evidence of permanent woodland clearance at Lough Sheeauns, Connemara.[19]

This was further supported by Seamus Caulfield's revelation of Ireland's earliest field system, preserved beneath up to 4 m (13 ft) of peatbogs at Céide, County Mayo.[20] Lines of stone in a boggy field may not match Tutankhamun's tomb but, to some of us, Seamus's discovery was exciting stuff. Here were rectangular fields of several hectares bounded by stone walls up to 2 km (1¼ miles) long and 150 m (490 ft) or more apart: a regular chequerboard of fields principally for the purpose of raising stock and controlling grazing, which covered more than 1,000 hectares (2,470 acres). A dozen megalithic tombs were firmly planted around them. Pollen analysis 16 km (10 miles) to the south of the Céide Fields further indicates extensive Neolithic forest clearance for farming. Seamus suggested that several Neolithic communities – families or small clans – had cooperated in clearing the land from about 3700 BC, and then farmed it for several centuries. However, by about 2700 BC, blanket bog began to spread across the area, making the land unfit for intensive farming yet preserving the evidence of the first fields to be discovered in the British Isles and Ireland.

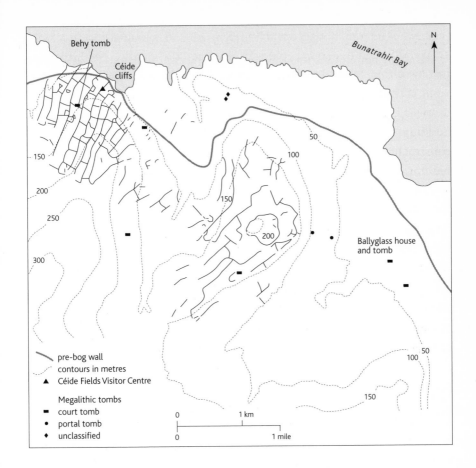

N

Behy tomb

Céide cliffs

Bunatrahir Bay

150

200

250

300

50

100

150

200

Ballyglass house
and tomb

50

100

150

pre-bog wall
contours in metres
▲ Céide Fields Visitor Centre

Megalithic tombs
■ court tomb
● portal tomb
♦ unclassified

0          1 km

0               1 mile

Plan of the Neolithic co-axial fields and megalithic tombs at Céide Fields,
County Mayo, Ireland.

So Irish archaeologists, like most of their continental colleagues, saw the
early Neolithic landscape as a place occupied by sedentary families in scattered farmsteads among clearly defined fields. Gabriel Cooney of University
College Dublin emphasized the importance of the homestead, domesticity
and commitment to place.[21] As the modern construction programme, driven by
what now seems the optimistically entitled 'Celtic Tiger Economy', advanced
across the country, more and more Neolithic houses turned up. In fact, the
rate of discovery peaked in 2006 when the total of early Neolithic houses in
2015 stood at about ninety, from more than fifty separate sites spread right
across the country (with the exception of the less well-explored midland area).[22]

Most of the Irish houses are relatively small and square or rectangular in shape. Although Irish archaeologists promoted the idea of a Neolithic typified by settled, family-based farmsteads, the picture is now more complex. Some of the houses seem to be isolated; others are in clusters, as at the site of Corbally, County Kildare, where there are at least seven buildings. Frequently, buildings occur in groups of two or three, possibly with varied functions, constructed of oak with vertical posts, horizontal planks and wattle panels of hazel and alder. At Ballyglass and Tankardstown there are unusual examples of larger rectangular houses with internal subdivisions. What seems clear is that settlers had arrived in Ireland by about 3800–3700 BC and farming, based on a variety of house types and small settlements, quickly took hold. What is surprising, however, is that this flush of housebuilding was short-lived. Within three or four generations – about a century – the Irish house boom came to an end. After about 3650 BC, houses became rarer in the archaeological record and when they are found they are of slighter, less regular construction. Instead, for the next six hundred years or so Neolithic communities put their effort into building monumental stone structures.

## Scotland: the towering halls

Until relatively recently, Scotland was seen as more or less building-free in the early Neolithic, but in the 1970s aerial surveys changed the picture when cropmarks of large rectangular structures were discovered. The initial response was to interpret them as early medieval in date. Big timber halls were well known from Anglo-Saxon England, thanks to excavations at Cheddar in Somerset and in the north at Yeavering. When Don Benson and I mapped the aerial photographs of the upper Thames Valley we identified Anglo-Saxon halls at Sutton Courtenay and Long Wittenham, south of Oxford. However, when excavated, the Scottish structures provided a surprise. The imposing timber buildings – at Balbridie and Warren Field, Crathes, both in Aberdeenshire; Claish in Stirling; Doon Hill in East Lothian; and Lockerbie Academy in Dumfries and Galloway – belonged to the beginning of the Neolithic. They were massive structures, mostly made with oak supports, about 22–24 m (72–79 ft) long and from 8 m (26 ft) to 11 m (36 ft) wide – similar proportions to the White Horse Stone building, though more substantial in construction with rounded ends and a series of internal divisions. These would have supported the roof and possibly a mezzanine floor for storage, as well as internal screening. Internally, the buildings were four times the height of a person, with a forest of big timber posts holding up the roof. These were impressive places; a statement of presence.

The neighbouring sites of Warren Field and Balbridie are worth considering in more detail. They stand a kilometre apart on the north (Crathes) and south (Balbridie) side of the River Dee – a well-known salmon and trout river whose Celtic name means 'the goddess'. The North Sea coast, at present-day sea levels, is 50 km (30 miles) to the east and both buildings lie on an obvious route inland. The *Gathering Time* analysis puts the construction of the houses in the first half of the 38th century BC (probably a decade or so either side of 3770 BC).[23] Crathes had gone out of use by 3700 BC, while Balbridie stood until the middle of the 37th century BC. The building at Claish, about 140 km (88 miles) to the southeast near the head of the Firth of Forth, has a remarkably similar ground plan to Balbridie, although it was probably built around 3700 BC and lasted for fifty years. Crathes was built first, prominently on the northern slope of the Dee Valley, and Balbridie most likely replaced it on the south bank, possibly built by the same people after they had ritually incinerated the earlier building. The burning of houses in Scotland and Ireland seems to be a frequent occurrence. If this was not carelessness, it may represent the deliberate destruction on an occasion such as the death of a clan elder.

In the Dee Valley, the builders of the first great house at Warren Field would have found a forested landscape, probably with small clearings and trails made by animals and the native foragers. Pollen analysis provides remarkable evidence of the energy of the pioneers at Warren Field: they cleared an area of trees several hundred metres across. A clear space with plenty of light is necessary to cultivate cereals, which evidently they did, including club/bread wheat. At the site, 365 cereal grains were found, a decent amount compared with most other sites, but a pittance compared with the 20,000 grains, possibly seed corn, preserved at Balbridie, across the river. There, emmer wheat was the dominant cereal.

The old geographical idea of a British Highland/Lowland zone – in which arable farming is dominant in southeastern England and pasture in the north and west – sometimes causes us to forget that there are potentially good arable soils in the north. The Dee-side pioneers had no such prejudices, and knew what they were looking for. This is not to say that the pioneers did not also exploit the wild landscape – after all, the vast majority of the land was forested, with extensive wetlands. Hazelnuts and wild fruit would have provided a useful supplement to the Neolithic diet, and hunting probably continued. The earliest bow to be found in Britain or Ireland turned up in the delightfully named Rotten Bottom, a boggy deposit high in the Tweedsmuir Hills, near Moffat in Dumfries and Galloway. This flat bow, made of yew, snapped and was discarded, probably while in action hunting deer. Archaeologists sometimes overlook the extent to which traditional farming communities also hunt. Three Neolithic bows have also been found in the Somerset Levels, two made of yew and the third, found next to the Sweet Track, of hazel wood. The Rotten Bottom bow was lighter than the others. All the bows were potentially deadly, especially the heavier ones, and would have fired arrows about 1 m (3 ft) long.

The Rotten Bottom bow leads us to other lines of enquiry. Radiocarbon-dated to 4040–3640 BC, it belongs to a fairly early period of the Neolithic, and it is made of yew wood – which does not grow in most of Scotland. The nearest place where it could have been acquired was Cumbria – the English Lake District. At this time, Scottish farmers were beginning to obtain polished greenstone axe heads from Great Langdale, also in Cumbria. Perhaps the bow is a rare example in the archaeological record of a wooden object on the move, travelling along the axe route.

It is time to bring out the stone axes again. Archaeologists have tested their effectiveness in the field: they rapidly cut through hardwood and softwood trees up to 35 cm (14 in.) in diameter. Big trees are harder work, yet unless they were dealing with regrowth in an earlier hunter-gatherer clearing the pioneers would have had to tackle substantial trees. The builders of the well-preserved timber mortuary chamber at Haddenham, Cambridgeshire, had access to oak 1.5 m (5 ft) in diameter and 10 m (33 ft) long, and about three hundred years old. A bog oak found in the peat in 1960 near Ely, also in Cambridgeshire, dating to the fourth millennium BC, was 21 m (69 ft) long and unbroken.[24] Britain's modern woodlands are a pale shadow of the ancient forests – the home of giants. In order to fell huge trees the farmers could first ringbark them or set fires around their bases. Dead and decayed trees could then be pulled over – leaving pits in the ground, or tree-throw holes, which are often found by archaeologists on Neolithic sites, marking where trees were removed during clearance or, in some cases, blown over in gales.

The settlers needed vast quantities of timber to construct the Warren Field and Balbridie buildings. Some of the posts were up to 1 m (3 ft) in diameter, and split timbers were used to make the walls and internal screens. As mentioned above, there is evidence of deliberate or accidental burning on Neolithic sites. The grain deposits at Balbridie survived, carbonized as a result of a fire. However, wooden posts were also charred deep into the ground. This is not to be expected as a result of a building fire so may have occurred when trees were burnt in the process of felling them or from a deliberate technique to make the post in the ground less vulnerable to decay.

Surprisingly, perhaps, there is little environmental evidence of pasture in the area, and the acidic soils are hard on any animal bones that might have existed. However, lipid analysis of the ceramics showed, as on other early Neolithic sites in Britain, that the pioneers produced dairy products and cooked pork in some of their vessels. The fine Carinated bowls may have played a part in the presentation of food at communal meals.

The fundamental question remains: what was the function of these buildings? The massive new structures reflect a fundamental and rapid change to the way of life in Britain. Their functions are not obvious: they may have been dwellings; alternatively, storage, ritual activities or seasonal gathering may have played a part. Certainly these were strong and secure architectural statements, declaring the presence of the newcomers and the creation of new places in the changing landscape.

The French anthropologist Claude Lévi-Strauss developed the idea of what he termed 'the house society' (*societés a maison*) while considering the case of the Kwakiutl on the Pacific Northwest Coast of America and Canada. He emphasized that the idea of the house extends to the occupants of the building and the members of a wider community.[25] Mary Helms further established the role of the house among communities exploiting a new environment as a way of establishing identity. Houses also have animate qualities; they are seen in terms of the human body and are born, live and die. The house is a way to bring a new community into being, a symbol of collective identity, unity and solidity. It need not be a dwelling house as such – though people might live there. It can also be a place for communal events, as were the Maori meeting houses constructed in response to the stress of European colonization.[26] Julian Thomas discussed 'the house society' at length and emphasized the relationships between houses and tombs.[27] 'Amongst house societies protracted funerary rites are common' with bodies being moved among the living. This form of ancestry serves to establish and maintain collective claims on property.

These 'towering structures' may not have been the only buildings. One problem is that archaeologists researching them have targeted excavations specifically at the large buildings visible on aerial photographs so we know little about their context. There may be Neolithic life beyond the buildings – for example, traces of activity were found 300 m (985 ft) north of Warren Field when the ground was stripped for a new car park in 2005. Were they subsidiary buildings, pathways, enclosures, shrines, watering holes? Other monuments appear soon afterwards, such as the Auchenlaich bank barrow near the Claish building, which began as a megalithic structure.

It is possible that the big building provided a community focal point while smaller ones also played a part – we have hints of less impressive structures in early Neolithic Scotland,[28] such as the site at Garthdee, Aberdeen, 20 km (12 miles) to the east near the mouth of the River Dee, which had an oval turf-walled building more or less contemporary with the Warren Field and Balbridie houses. Here there were thick deposits of occupation material – carbonized grain, pottery and flints – similar to material on the big sites, but discarded more prolifically. This suggests that farmers were living in more modest structures and using the big buildings for communal purposes.

## More buildings turn up

In England, the White Horse Stone houses are not alone.[29] Yarnton is a small village just north of Oxford. In recent years a large part of the parish has been gobbled up by one of the largest gravel quarries in the Thames Valley. As the floodplain alluvium was stripped away, a team of archaeologists led by Gill Hey recorded an underlying early Neolithic landscape.[30] Here, too, there was a large post-built house. The Yarnton team made another significant discovery: the earliest bread in Britain – albeit only consisting of two unprepossessing pieces of burnt toast that contained roughly ground cereal grains, including barley (*Hordeum* sp.) – radiocarbon-dated to between 3620 BC and 3350 BC.

Stone saddle querns found on Neolithic sites give some clue as to how cereals were processed. The stones are dished (Gordon Childe said 'saucer querns' was a better name) and can be used like a Roman (or modern) mortar to pound and crack grain. This was a trick learnt by hunter-gatherers at least 70,000 years before. In modern kitchens those of us who do not rely on electrically powered food processors usually use mortars to grind small quantities of spices – the Neolithic saddle quern was not a very efficient way to produce flour, but cracked grain could be eaten fresh or briefly roasted over a small fire. It is also ideal for making porridge to which fruits, nuts or even meat and broth can be added. Grain can also be germinated and malted, mixed with water to produce beer. It has been suggested that the Balbridie cache of cereals was for the purpose of making beer – the start of a distinguished Scots tradition perhaps. To make bread the grains have to be finely ground. Perhaps the rarity of querns after the start of the Neolithic (they reappear after almost two thousand years at the start of the Bronze Age) suggests that the Yarnton bread, and even cereal production itself, went out of fashion. Cheese, ale, porridge, brassicas and the occasional carnivorous feast probably fuelled the first farmers.[31]

Elsewhere on the site at Yarnton there were some traces of emmer wheat and barley, and wild plants such as apple and hazelnuts. These low-lying lands may also have favoured grazing. South of Oxford there is a marshy area known as Daisy Banks at Radley, which lies next to the Abingdon causewayed enclosure and Barrow Hills, a major Neolithic and Bronze Age burial complex (to which I will return). Pollen recovered from within the marsh indicated the presence of early Neolithic arable plots close by, on the well-drained gravel terrace, which has light soils ideal for cultivation.

The richest evidence for economic activity has come from another flood-plain site on the River Thames at Dorney. Here, archaeologists from Oxford cleared an enormous area, across the relict braided streams of the Thames, prior to the construction of the Olympic/Eton College Rowing Lake in the late 1990s. In one of the old river channels, early Neolithic farmers had dumped their rubbish. Such middens are rare and valuable, containing the type of evidence that is often missing at the house sites. Lipid analysis of the pottery fragments, mainly from Carinated Bowl types, showed that many vessels were used for processing milk products, probably from cows.[32] It is probably around this time that genetic changes occurred in northern Europe that eventually made most people lactose tolerant, and so able to consume milk as adults (see Chapter 11). Britain's population still has one of the highest levels of lactose tolerance in the world.

From about 4000 BC, and in the following centuries, life in Britain was transformed: not only how people worked and interacted in society and with nature, but also what they ate. When the Bible says Man 'cannot live by bread alone', it is not providing dietary advice. Nevertheless, it is also literally true – dairy products were an essential element in the new diet. The British diet was transformed with the shift to the Neolithic: isotope analysis of bone relies on the truism that 'we are what we eat' – and it reveals that from about 3800 BC people, even where they had access to marine resources in Ireland, Scotland, Wales and the English South West, still shifted dramatically to a terrestrial diet based on domesticated foodstuffs.[33]

The Eton midden provided traces of emmer wheat, hulled barley, bread wheat and the usual wild species. Environmental evidence in the Thames Valley shows that for the most part the land was still densely forested around 3800 BC. Hazelnuts, particularly at the woodland margins, continued to be a valuable food stuff – even for farmers. If we do not see many hazelnuts today on the trees it is because the recently introduced grey squirrels take them before they mature. Domesticated cattle and pigs would also have thrived in the woodlands, though possibly in demarcated areas. Studies of mitochondrial DNA show that domestic cattle, right across Europe, were descendants of Near Eastern animals. They were not domesticated in Europe and there is no evidence of cattle interbreeding with aurochs, which would soon become locally extinct, as eventually did beavers, wild boars, white-tailed eagles and any other large predators that dared to interfere with farming. The pigs enjoyed themselves grubbing for woodland fungi, which, according to the isotopic evidence, were a major part of their diet.[34] The Rowing Lake pots contained another first: the earliest evidence in Britain for the consumption of honey, although we cannot be certain whether this was gathered in the wild or from domesticated honey bees.

As farmers transformed their habitat their activities could have unintended consequences. Sheep, whose ancestors cropped the open grasslands of the Near East, were not at home in the forested Thames Valley at this time, and were rarely present. However, the forests gradually receded under attack from the axe, from fire and grazing domestic herds. Parkland or open grassland became more common. This attracted immigrants, originally natives of the continental steppes to the east: crows, ravens and rooks arrived in numbers. Farmers then had intelligent rivals to cope with, and the soundscape of the British countryside changed. The sheep flocks would safely graze as Neolithic farmers and their descendants created the downlands of England. In Ireland, lush pastures appeared for cattle. Grass would be a Neolithic monument as much as the megaliths.

## CHAPTER THIRTEEN

# Green treasure from the Magic Mountain

## The Devizes axe

The object that stimulated me to write this book, for better or worse, was a grey-green polished stone axe head, which appeared at my door years ago. It now demands to play a bigger role in the narrative. 'After all,' it says, 'I am an icon – I put the "Neo" into "Neolithic".'

However, I must first draw attention to one of its illustrious ancestors, an axe head on display at the museum in the Wiltshire market town of Devizes, along with a superb collection of material excavated from around Stonehenge. As part of the recent Stonehenge restoration project, the Heritage Lottery Fund agreed to fund the display of Devizes Museum's prehistoric collection, most of which had been hidden away in store for security reasons. When David Dawson, the museum's director, took me round the new galleries I felt a real tingle of excitement. I had only previously seen some of this amazing material in dingy photographs and small drawings. Now, here it was in all its physical reality – genuinely strange and exotic. This stuff still breathed life into the past.

Among the bling – there was plenty of gold – one object stood out: a glowing, green jadeitite axe head (see page 151). This was not an object born in Britain, and we are lucky to have it at all. The axe head was a stray find – picked from the soil by a farm labourer. For years it sat on the windowsill of the farm kitchen until, one day, the farmer's wife hurled it out of the window (was she angry with her husband, or the cat?), which is why there is a small chip in this otherwise pristine object. Fortunately, someone retrieved the axe head from the farmyard and eventually it found its way into the care of the museum.

## In search of the source

So where does this beautiful thing come from? Once again, I bring my long-suffering children into the tale. A few years after our holidays in Brittany we took to walking in the Alps – 'You are following in the footsteps of Hannibal and his elephants, and Napoleon', I said to encourage them on. We trekked in that very distinctive region known as the Queyras, where France borders on Italy – what might seem to be one of the most isolated and remote parts of western Europe. The huge fortifications at Château-Queyras tell another tale. These were first built in the 14th century, then, in 1692, the great French military engineer Vauban strengthened the fortress with impregnable angular walls. And all this for a good reason: the fortress controls the valley of the River Guil, which leads eastwards to the Italian border, and flows southwest into the heart of France. The high but sheltered valley often remains passable in winter.

From Château-Queyras we drove up the valley as far as L'Echalp, the last ill-fated hamlet, swamped by an avalanche in 1948. We walked by the river – ahead was a magnificent sight, the isolated pyramid of Monte Viso (see page 151). At 3,841 m (12,602 ft) this is not the highest mountain in the region, it just feels like it: a rocky sentinel silhouetted sharply against the blue sky. We climbed up its flank and in seconds we passed from summer to winter as a sudden, harsh storm thrashed us and the temperature plummeted. Eventually, we reached a crest. Below, the ground fell away into Italy. Behind, we could see the route back into France carved out by the Guil.

What I did not know at the time was that Monte Viso was a magnet to Neolithic stone seekers: the source of fabulous jadeitite axes, like the one in Devizes Museum, and even the inspiration for our Langdale axe.[1] Gustave Flaubert was not a fan of the Alps. After his disappointing holiday there in 1874, he wrote 'The Alps are out of all proportion to human existence. They are too big to be useful.' The great novelist was wrong.


## In pursuit of the axes

We now know much more thanks to the questioning persistence of Pierre and Anne-Marie Petréquin who spent twelve seasons searching for the sources of Alpine 'jades' in the massifs of Monte Viso and Monte Beigua, 100 km (60 miles) to the southeast. There was more to the project than dogged field-work. The Petréquins realized that a huge number of exotic 'jade' axes were distributed across northern Europe; beautiful objects that resemble things crafted in China or Mesoamerica.

Even in the later 19th century geologists had pointed to the southern Alps as a possible source of the raw material. By the 1970s geologists had become expert at identifying rock sources and the materials used to make stone axes; what they were asking was where the stone came from. The common assumption was that 'jade' material was probably scattered along many Alpine valleys and Neolithic prospectors found it in many places.

The Petréquins asked other questions: how had Neolithic people organized stone quarrying? Why did they value certain materials so highly? What role did these stones play in Neolithic society and its beliefs? The Petréquins looked for ideas in New Guinea, where farming communities were some of the last people on Earth to make, disperse and value polished stone axes – objects not only of practical value, but also charged with spiritual power, integrated into their social and spiritual lives.

The Petréquins appreciated that there was more to these stone axes than geology. Yet they were not desk-bound theoreticians. They put on their boots and tramped Monte Viso and the massifs beyond like devoted pilgrims, recruited a dedicated team, mapped the distribution of axes across the whole of western and northern Europe, and applied cutting-edge science. Project JADE is model research.[2]

The results, in summary, tell us that in the fifth and fourth millennia BC Neolithic prospectors systematically sought out and quarried exotic stone high in the Italian Alps around Monte Viso and Monte Beigua. These Alpine 'jades' varied in colour. The more common eclogites and omphacitites produced darker green material when cut and polished. The rarer, tougher jadeitite rocks were paler green, translucent and suffused with light. The darker materials tended to be used for axes that were used more locally in north Italy and France (though some found their way further north and into Britain). The distribution of the finer jadeitite was an eye-opener for prehistorians. Relatively few of these axes appeared locally, near to the quarry sites in the Alps. Instead, they turned up in large numbers in Brittany, especially in and around the megalithic tombs of the Morbihan; in Britain; and, most distant of all, Scotland, as far north as the Dee Valley, where we see big houses like Balbridie. Clearly, distinctive jadeitite axes played a special and highly valued role in northern societies.

The river systems of Europe – the Rhône–Saône, Loire, Seine, Meuse and Rhine – acted as corridors for the network of exchange. With artefact distribution, archaeologists often expect to see what are known as 'down-the-line' patterns: objects cluster around their source, while some are passed along by communities as trade items, gift exchange or bride wealth as the glue in social contracts. With distance, the objects should become rarer; their distribution thins and peters out. This was not the case with jadeitite axes. The people who controlled the supply of 'jade' stones targeted distant communities that especially valued them. They sent the stone northwards, often as roughed-out axe shapes (roughouts). Other groups, sometimes several hundred kilometres from the Alpine source, finished or reworked the stones, grinding and polishing them into forms favoured by local elites. There were fashions in axes, which changed through time and for different audiences.

The Petréquins found that specific sources of stone were valued and quarried. They located sites in the Alps where there were huge accumulations of flakes and roughouts. Here, the stoneworkers had knapped the precious rocks with hammerstones and fractured them deliberately with fire. It was even possible to identify individual boulders as the source for specific axes. Where the valuable, rare and extremely hard jadeitite was worked, the waste fragments were extremely small – this stuff was too precious to go to waste. The roughouts were then transported to places where they were further worked and polished into distinct shapes, which varied chronologically and regionally. Different styles were popular in different areas. For example, around 4500 BC at the peak of jadeitite production, mostly from Monte Viso, there were two distinct forms of axe head. These are known as the Altenstadt-Greenlaw type, with a broad blade and pointed butt, and the Chenoise type, which has the same configuration but a longer, slimmer body. Both of these types have a clearly northern distribution – from Brittany, across the Seine Valley into northern Germany and beyond into Britain.

It is at this time in the mid fifth millennium BC that we see the 'Carnac phenomenon': local people placed large numbers of these exotic axes in tombs in southern Brittany (the Morbihan/Carnac area); they perforated some for suspension, and carved their images onto megaliths, such as the walls of the Gavr'Inis tomb. On the Table des Marchand at Locmariaquer there is a famous carving of a hafted axe head in the form now known as a Bégude type; relatively early, dating to the first half of the fifth millennium BC, the form is slim with a rounded blade. Such axes are much more common to the south, closer to their Alpine source. The axe-head image was originally carved on a menhir or standing stone, then the stone was broken and reused in the great tomb. At some stage, around the mid fifth millennium BC, the image of the axe was recarved to represent the newer, more valued jadeitite (Altenstadt-Greenlaw type) axe. However, fashion never stands still – the Petréquins suggest that some Altenstadt-Greenlaw-type axes were reworked in the Morbihan, slimmed down to make them lighter and then perforated. To be hung, proudly, on the body perhaps – but where, and what did they symbolize? This new, beautiful, translucent material was rare and difficult to work. The further the green treasure from the magic mountain travelled north the greater its value – the valley of the River Dee in Scotland, where axes have been found, is 1,700 km (1,050 miles) from Monte Viso.

## Illumination from the Far East

The Petréquins looked at the use of polished stone axes in New Guinea to gain some understanding of their meaning in a traditional society. Instead, let us turn from old Scotland to New Caledonia. This is a group of islands in the middle of the Pacific Ocean, at the end of the chain that runs from New Guinea, New Britain, the Solomons and the New Hebrides. Obviously, these are names given by European colonists, not by the indigenous peoples, the Kanak. French anthropologists, missionaries and colonists recorded their way of life in the early contact years of the 19th century, but not usually with much sympathy or understanding.[3]

A few Kanaka got to speak for themselves, however. These small-scale cultivators grew edible tubers: taros and yams, plants that are more than staple foods; the Kanak referred to them as 'the flesh of our ancestors'. The yam, phallus-like, penetrates deeply into the ground to sow its seeds. The taro was vitalized by water from irrigated terraces. To the Kanak, this pair of plants represented opposite, masculine and feminine elements. They used long magical stones, which guaranteed fertility, to plant yams.

The Kanak, until relatively recently, possessed highly valued polished stone axes and discs. These were made of green, translucent nephrite, quarried on a small island to the south of their Great Island. The roughouts were then taken to the Loyalty Islands (about 200 km/125 miles east of the Great Island) where they were polished and transformed into various shapes, depending upon which community did the work. Different islands had different styles. The axes were the product of an ancient jade cycle known as 'the path to riches'. The initial transport of the axes was from west to east – from the setting sun to its rising; from night to day. After the finishing process the axes travelled in the reverse direction, east to west, and then became associated with sunlight. Some of the nephrite was carved into circular discs that resemble the sun, mounted on a wooden haft decorated with lengths of red, knotted twine.

These jade axes were prestige objects used in rituals and performances to invoke rain, fertility and describe the course of the sun and moon. They were exchanged between chieftains around 'the path to riches' on a route that circulated between the Great Island and the Loyalty Islands. Valued objects of jade, including bracelets and necklaces, were presented to visitors in a cycle of ritual offerings. Gift-giving strengthened alliances and the cycle of life. Maintaining these links could be vital in emergencies and at times of food shortage or warfare.[4] It is worth emphasizing that objects and materials can only be understood in the context of specific societies – whether these are Neolithic, Melanesian or our own. Early European contact with indigenous groups in the Pacific threw up fascinating differences of attitude to 'commodities', which could be bartered or traded for a price, and objects that had prestige and social or ritual ranking.

The Kanak believed in a world of spirits and ancestors (the *Pâ bèmu-vé*). The ancestors were the flesh of the clan; they had left this world yet remained attached to it. Unlike the ancestors, the spirits (*rhee*) were not human although they could exert a benevolent influence and take the form of animals or natural phenomena such as thunder. The Kanak invoked the ancestors and spirits through magic bundles made of plants and anthropomorphic statues of wood. They wore masks in ritual performances to represent and summon ancestors. The power of ancestors was conserved in megaliths carved with abstract animal designs and spirals. The power of these 'war stones', like some spiritual battery, could then be transferred to weapons, clubs and spears, when these came into contact.

Once, the Kanak claimed, the word '*kamo*' designated a person – any living being – human, animal or vegetable. They did not distinguish between them. Humans were one of the elements of life. Now humans are seen as unique. The Kanak blamed Western influence for this change of attitude. The 19th-century French colonists mostly had a very low opinion of the Kanak, while at the same time France celebrated its own prehistoric past. New Caledonia and Neolithic Scotland (and western Europe) are several thousand kilometres – and years – apart. Their physical environments are very different. However, the role of axes displays some striking similarities. Most of all, the Kanak remind us of the richness of the human mind and its ability to represent beliefs, myths and social relations through material objects; objects can take on a life and significance of their own. Early hominins had practical skills but only modern humans could create such a complex mental universe.

## The power of travel

Spectacular Alpine axe heads, like the one in Devizes Museum, found their way to Britain. The chronology suggests that they were quarried in the Alps in the mid fifth millennium BC. These valued objects, imbued with ancestral power, were carefully curated by their several 'owners', while being circulated among Neolithic elites. With age, further respect would accrue to them; they would develop a patina of myth, stories and association. Their distant origin would be a reminder of the excitement and physical and ritual dangers of travel; of the esoteric knowledge and status to be gained in remote and distant places. Around the world there are many examples, historical and mythical, of how both ritual and political power come from travel to, or from, remote places. There are also many cases of exotic newcomers establishing ruling elites in their guest communities, or young men who left their own communities to travel to strange, exotic places and learn the language, history, songs and traditions of other groups. On their return, their status could be enormously enhanced by their travels and learning.

In anthropology the best-known example of this phenomenon is the Kula Ring of the Trobriand Islands where through travel and ceremonial exchange men see themselves gaining ability, strength, esoteric knowledge and sophistication. Kula provides these men with the 'best potential avenue for immortality'. Ordinary men carry their names with them to the under-world after death. In contrast, the Kula men leave their names behind in this world, attached to the prominent shells that they acquired on their travels.[5] In future rituals their names would be chanted; their fame would echo in the ears of the unborn.

In Neolithic Britain, jadeitite axes fulfilled a role analogous to Kula shells. They probably arrived with the pioneers around 4000 BC or a century or two later – already objects of force and distinction, charged with spiritual power, perhaps capable of bestowing fertility on the efforts of Britain's first farmers. The first time I actually saw a 'jadeitite' axe was in Varna, Bulgaria. I was on a ship (travelling to exotic parts) that stopped briefly in the port and I decided to dash to the museum to see the famous burials that, dating to about 4500 BC, contained the world's earliest gold objects.[6] Finding the museum wasn't easy, but with the help of several locals, I gazed at last upon the most spectacular Varna burial. Here was a man who had died in his forties, accompanied to his grave by 990 gold objects – the earliest gold in the world. And what was the earliest gold used for? A gleaming penis sheath lay between the man's skeletal legs. Further extending his proud penis was a polished 'jade' axe or adze. The people who put that axe in the Varna grave were sending a clear message. They now had gold, yet I suspect 'green treasure from the magic mountain' still exerted power, even over fertility – of people, plants and animals – which must have loomed large in the concerns of European Neolithic farmers, as it did with the Kanak of the New Hebrides.

Around the time the Neolithic arrived in Britain, the supply of Alpine axes ceased for some reason. The ones that crossed the Channel were already old, and they served their purpose: the farming colonists became successfully rooted, from Kent to Cornwall and Wales, northern Scotland and Ireland. The axes promoted fertility and provided protection, and gave authority and status to those who possessed them.

## The meaning of stone

In the modern world it is easy to forget the multiple meanings and purposes that plants and minerals had for generations of humans. I once found myself sitting next to a bishop at a dinner at an Oxford college. He wore a distinctive ring mounted with an amethyst stone – a violet-coloured quartz. 'That must come in handy at college dinners,' I said. He looked puzzled. 'The Romans believed that amethyst kept drunkenness at bay,' I explained; *a-mathuien* in Greek literally means 'without being drunk'. (Oxford dinners can be remarkably boozy affairs.) To the Romans the colour of amethyst was a reminder of wine – and a cure for its effects. Early Christians adopted the stone, but significantly changed its meaning. Wine was associated with Christ at the wedding feast of Canaan and the Last Supper. The colour of amethyst became a reminder of the Kingdom of Heaven, hence its appearance even today on the hands of bishops.

Another example of the continuing and changing power of minerals came in an Anglo-Saxon cemetery I dug at Lechlade, Gloucestershire. Here the last generation of pagan women were swathed in strings of amber beads – reminders, perhaps, of a Germanic homeland (amber is commonly found around the Baltic Sea) and the power of the sun. According to the Roman writer Pliny, amber wards off tonsillitis and protects children. In contrast, in the same cemetery, the first generation of converted Christian women in the seventh century avoided amber. It had been condemned by the Church fathers in the sixth century because of its pagan associations. Instead, they wore amethyst and garnet beads – stones from the east that symbolized Christ and his blood.

So does any of this provide clues to the possible meanings of the green 'jade' stones that were used for the most impressive Neolithic axes? We could also consider the name. In 1595, Sir Walter Raleigh wrote of 'a kinde of green stones which the Spaniards call Piedras Hijadas and we use for spleene stones'. Chambers' Dictionary, in the mid 18th century, says, 'this stone applied to the reins (kidneys) is said to be a preservative from the nephritic colic'. In Spanish, '*hijadas*' means 'the sides', which in turn comes from the ancient Greek word for an 'internal obstruction'. The French borrowed the Spanish word, which became '*l'ejade*'. The English mistakenly took this to be '*le jade*' – hence the word in English: the stone to cure 'the stone'. As anyone knows who has read Samuel Pepys's diary – passing kidney stones, in an age before scientific medicine, was an excruciating experience. One jadeitite axe, of Altenstadt type from Monte Beigua, has a remarkable autobiography. It may have been found in Scotland and it is mentioned in G. F. Kunz's *The Curious Lore of Precious Stones*, published in 1913. It states that a Scottish officer and gentleman during the 1860s wore the axe – perforated and mounted in silver, tied like a sporran over his loins – as a 'cure' for kidney disease.[7]

This is not to say, of course, that Neolithic people held the same curative beliefs about 'jade' stones. As we saw with amethyst, ideas can shift as cultures develop and change. Yet the power of exotic stones is persistent.

## Finding stone in Neolithic Britain

Neolithic farmers had first to feed themselves. To do this they needed the tools for the job, and some supernatural or magical assistance; they had to look for supplies of stone to fulfil these needs, both practical and spiritual. The South Downs of East and West Sussex was one of the first areas to be systematically targeted for supplies of stone. This landscape is very different to Monte Viso. In 1930 the field archaeologist E. Cecil Curwen waxed lyrical, even erotic: 'There is something about the soft, sweeping curves of the chalk hills that delights the eye and soothes the soul, there are no rugged peaks or jagged rocks to overawe and amaze the beholder, but only curves – rising, fulling – swelling fading – soft, round and smooth.'[8]

Chalk may have stirred Curwen, but prehistoric people were attracted to what lay within: seams of hard flint, a micro-crystalline form of quartz that behaves like a super-cooled fluid. Flint is hard, yet can easily be fractured and flaked to produce blades, arrowheads or axes. In Chapter 1, I described ancient handaxes, like those from Saint-Acheul and Stanton Harcourt, made several hundred thousand years ago. Early hominins discovered the qualities of flint and flaked these axes from blocks that they discovered on or near the surface, eroded from the chalk. The Neolithic reveals a new relationship with flint and the earth: a willingness, even a necessity, to burrow in the systematic pursuit of the finest material. For the first time in Britain people mined into the ground, and ground out galleries in search of the black stuff.

In the early 19th century, hollow depressions were observed on the Downs by antiquarians who believed them to be the remains of ancient British pit dwellings. It was eventually realized that some of these hollows, especially where they were densely clustered, indicated the presence of Neolithic mine-shafts, which descended several metres into the ground.

Colonel Augustus Lane Fox (later Pitt-Rivers), the father of modern British archaeology, carried out some of the first excavations in 1867–68, at Cissbury. For Cecil Curwen the chalk downland was 'soft and sweeping', but at Cissbury it is about as dramatic as it gets – a prominent chalk spur (above present-day Worthing) that has soaring views of the sea and, in turn, can be seen from the Isle of Wight. The ramparts of a dominating Iron Age hillfort now cut across the pock-marked landscape where miners, almost three thousand years earlier, had hacked and hewn at least 270 shafts into the ground. Lane Fox was probably the first to appreciate that all this was 'for the purpose of obtaining flint', as he wrote in 1869. At about the same time Canon Greenwell began to explore the most extensive system of flint mines in Britain, at Grimes Graves, in Norfolk.

At Cissbury, and a group of neighbouring sites, Neolithic miners were first attracted by flint seams outcropping at the surface; they pursued them by digging shafts 6 m (20 ft) or more deep equipped with antler picks. From some mineshafts, they then dug sideways, excavating galleries to follow seams that could slope steeply. The extracted flint was not always of the highest quality, which has caused archaeologists to speculate that the location was more important than the standard of the material.

Flint mines are relatively rare in Britain. It is possible that they were dug by specialists who understood both the engineering techniques required and the essential rituals demanded by the spirits of the earth. Unfortunately, Neolithic flint mines have received relatively little attention from modern archaeologists, so the *Gathering Time* team were not blessed with an abundance of data when they attempted to date the workings. However, it does seem that

Reconstruction of a later Neolithic flint mine at Grimes Graves, Norfolk.

the Sussex Downland flint mines were the earliest in the country, beginning operations soon after 4000 BC. A Sussex axe head (probably from Cissbury) was ritually deposited on the Sweet Track, a Neolithic timber trackway crossing the Somerset Levels, before the end of the 39th century BC; there was also one from the Alps and another from Langdale, which gives us some of our best chronological evidence for the use of these axes.

The Somerset Levels trackways are the clearest demonstration of how people in the early Neolithic created pathways, here in marshland, by cutting vast numbers of timbers with stone axes and carefully laying them over the boggy surface. The tracks are physical evidence of people walking through the landscape, but this could be potentially hazardous, where rival groups met and confronted each other. The three axes were probably offerings laid on the track rather than lost tools.

Mining is a high-risk, skilled operation that tends to be restricted to experienced communities. It has, of course, to start somewhere and the Sussex miners may have learnt their trade among the continental flint miners of the Maastricht region, the Paris Basin or Limburg in Belgium. However, if flint axe heads were needed in Britain around 4000 BC it was not necessary to sink shafts and burrow beneath the earth – the surface material used for millennia was still available. For example, on the eroding North Norfolk coast, vast quantities of flint in good condition littered the beaches. Flint mining seems to be one of the earliest features of the Neolithic, yet it took place in a restricted area in Sussex. The vast majority of the chalklands, including Wessex, was ignored. The great Grimes Graves complex in Norfolk came into operation much later in the Neolithic. Perhaps what we are seeing in Sussex is the arrival of a group of specialist miners – possibly men, women and children[9] – from the Continent. Their operation was successful; when more than four hundred ground flint axe heads were analysed for trace elements – from objects found in Wessex, South East England and East Anglia – the biggest proportion came from the Sussex mines. Flint mining may have been undertaken not only to supply the local community but also to produce objects that could be traded, exchanged or given as gifts.

## Taking spiritual risks

Mining had a practical purpose, but it was also a highly ritualized activity. Not only was it physically dangerous, but miners also took psychic risks braving the transition between the layers of the cosmos. The mines were on Downland crests, close to the sky and the sea. They penetrated the earth and opened a portal to the underworld, with only a flickering lamp to illuminate the dark. Not surprisingly, the miners left offerings of meat, plants, carvings, pots and human remains, which probably marked locations of ritual activity at specific points along the workings. Perhaps it was the underworld source of the flint rather than its physical quality that provided a powerful attraction and made Sussex axes so desirable. Yet the mines were spiritually hazardous: the block of downland that contains Cissbury and the mines at Church Hill, Blackpatch and Harrow Hill is devoid of any other signs of activity. The mines appear to sit in their own sacred and reserved space.

The miners themselves may have been an exclusive group, who passed on their knowledge from one generation to the next, and from one locality to another as new resources had to be located. In the Roman world, specialist miners from the Balkans travelled with their skills – for example, to develop the amazingly sophisticated goldmines of Dacia (modern-day Romania). Cornish tin miners and Welsh coalminers similarly travelled around the world.

My colleague at English Heritage, Pete Topping, studied the rituals and techniques of stone and pipe-clay mining practised by Native Americans such as the Cheyenne, whose medicine arrows were the 'supreme tribal fetish' controlling hunting and warfare. The flint arrowheads were knapped by older men who garnered great prestige from their activities. The Red Pipestone Quarry of Minnesota, which has been exploited for at least seven hundred years and possibly much longer, is imbued with such religious significance that no one lived near the site. Both the miners and their tools were ritually purified; offerings were left to the spirits to placate them for the removal of the pipestone.[10]

In New Guinea the Petréquins record that ritual prayers and chanting constantly accompanied the process of quarrying for axe roughouts and clay for pottery: 'In each case the idea is the same: people are exploiting a sacred raw material which comes from the body, the humours or the blood of a Dream Time Being, in places that are sometimes secret and often barred to the uninitiated.'[11] If the wrong people try to exploit the quarry they will fall ill, as they have not been initiated into the essential rituals and chants. The axe heads are regarded as living beings from the time of the Ancestors that can be extracted from within the stone. The timing of axe production tends to be set by social demands such as the need for bride wealth, blood payments at the conclusion of a war, or alliances and festivals with other communities. Because the sources are remote and the axes or roughouts are heavy and difficult to carry, there tended to be a constant shortage of supplies. Nevertheless, there was an ever replenished flow to give to partners in these relatively egalitarian societies.

## Searching for the green stuff

A magnificent jadeitite axe left close to the River Avon at Breamore, Hampshire, must have come into Britain by sea. Its long, elegant form matches those carved on the walls of Gavr'Inis tomb in Brittany. Pierre Petréquin reckons that it is an unusual type that matches others deposited in the tumuli of

Brittany between 4500 BC and 4300 BC. It is unlikely to have arrived in Britain before the 39th century BC, by which time it must have been an heirloom of enormous prestige. Its elegance, colour and strength, let alone its autobiography, distinguished owners and mythical/supernatural origins on Monte Beigua all must have made an enormous impact in the early farming communities of southern England. If ethnographic observations in New Guinea and elsewhere are relevant – and the archaeological evidence suggests they are – then this was an object that could enhance the authority of its owner and the community, provide protection, power in war and fertility to the land. As the supply of Alpine jade axes closed up it is not surprising that Neolithic prospectors sought out alternative sources.

These sources were found among the igneous rocks of Cornwall, Wales and Ireland, but most prolifically some 350 km (220 miles) north of the Channel coast in the centre of the Lake District. From the northern shore of Lake Windermere, Scafell Pike, England's highest mountain, lies to the west, yet it is the prominent cairn-shaped bump of Pike o' Stickle that attracts the eye when it is not shrouded in mist. The glaciated valley of Great Langdale drew the stone prospectors deep into the mountains. Even today, Great Langdale feels remote – although the last time I was there I said 'Good afternoon' to a party of Chinese students cheerfully heading for Scafell Pike wearing trainers. They were probably unaware and unconcerned that the scree slope above them was the debris of the largest Neolithic axe 'factory' in Britain, and the source of the greenstone tuff from which the our axe head is made.

The 'remoteness' of Great Langdale is deceptive, rather like Monte Viso. In fact, look at a map or Google Earth and its position as a hub in the Lake District, penetrated by spoke-like valleys, is clear. The present-day landscape is also deceptive. Today the valley floor is highly managed, a viridian chequerboard of sheep pens, and the river is canalized. Along the valley floor and its sides there are traces of centuries of occupation. Above, the slopes are gnawed bare to the bone by sheep and the rocky skeleton of the land emerges. Six thousand years ago the stone seekers would have entered a 'dark and tangled' wooded valley of oak, rowan and birch, where browsing deer had to take their chances against wolves, bears and lynx. Trees flourished and farming had not yet scoured the land.[12]

The Neolithic prospectors would have used the beck as a rocky highway, their eyes scanning the bed for the gleam of telltale colours: not gold or copper – they desired green. Pebbles of the distinctive colour and sheen would have led them to the source: a band of stone eroding out of the cliffs of Pike o' Stickle, just above the treeline, above a sea of green. In 1872 Sir John Evans, with remarkable prescience, suggested that Cumbria was the source of a large group of distinctive Neolithic axes. He was right, though he knew less about the specifics of the geology than the practical Neolithic quarry-workers. Since the 1950s there has been systematic scientific research to find the sources of Neolithic axe stone.[13]

The Langdale axes were classified as Group VI (though with further research the picture becomes geologically more complex). The classic Group VI material comes from the Seathwaite Fell tuff formation, which coils in a band around the Great Langdale heights in the east, to Scafell Pike and then north-eastwards, a total of 19 km (12 miles). The Neolithic explorers must have tracked this line like bloodhounds; there are traces of their activities at dozens of favoured sites along it.

Richard Bradley and Mark Edmonds investigated the densest cluster of activity around Pike o' Stickle and the neighbouring Harrison Stickle.[14] Here the quarry-workers broke out lumps of the desired greenstone, sometimes by setting fires, and produced roughouts of more or less axe shape. The polishing of these roughouts required many hours or days of effort and took place at settlements on lower ground, in more hospitable valleys and near the coast. The miners chose some of the most inaccessible and difficult terrain from which to extract the greenstone itself. These locations may have had ritual significance, away from the everyday world, and distinctive high places were frequently selected as quarry sites. Or more practically, was it these difficult outcrops that produced the finest stone; stone of the right colour that harked back to the Alpine jades of Monte Viso? Stone that was recognizable to those who held it, even in Wessex, Ireland or the Fenlands of eastern England?

The axe quarries of Great Langdale are sometimes referred to as 'factories' and the movement of the axes as 'trade'. This is understandable but anachro-nistic. The distribution of roughouts suggests that they were taken along the spoke-like valleys, which radiate out from Great Langdale, to communities in every direction, to be polished and finished. These groups were attached to others by a network of alliances, friendships, marriages and even hostili-ties – blood debts had to be paid. The distribution of axes was an integral part of this social exchange, rather than the economic and often impersonal activity that the modern world calls 'trade'. Some axe production centres – for example, Graig Lwyd in North Wales, and Rathlin Island off the coast of

County Antrim – are positioned close to the sea. Clusters of Cornish axes found along the Thames have led to the suggestion of bulk transport by boat managed by independent traders. Certainly, axes crossed the sea, from Cumbria to Ireland and vice versa. About 100 Langdale axes have been found in Ireland and about 180 porcellanite axes from Antrim have turned up from Orkney to Wessex.

However, recent detailed modelling of axe distribution favours hand-to-hand exchange rather than the involvement of specialist traders. Finding axes in rivers probably tells us more about deposition than trade. High-value objects were frequently deposited as ritual offerings in rivers, lakes and bogs throughout prehistory and the Thames especially was the focus of such activities.

Similarly, the use of the term 'factory' suggests a place of routine, clock-watching, full-time specialist work. The Langdale miners were obviously skilled. At present, however, the evidence suggests that they probably came from a variety of places, at times of year when the weather was tolerable, to set up camp by the lakes or tarns close to the rock outcrops and undertake an activity imbued with physical difficulty and complex meanings.

There are problems in estimating when axe quarrying first began in the Lake District. The best current estimate places the start at roughly 3700 BC. The quarries lasted for more than a thousand years.[15] In the Alps, the Project JADE researchers 'fingerprinted' Alpine axes using geochemical methods.[16] This kind of detailed identification remains to be done for Cumbrian and many other British axes, so we cannot yet always pinpoint exact sources. Nevertheless, throughout the fourth millennium BC the central Cumbrian valleys rang to the sound of hammers on stone. It is not unreasonable to call this an industry, even if it was practised by people perched on vertigo-inducing ledges chanting ritual songs and relied solely on human muscle-power. Transportation of the roughout blocks must have been a slow and arduous business without horses or mules. Gradually, the miners would have worn or built trackways down the valleys from Great Langdale to places like Ehenside Tarn on the west coast of Cumbria. Here, people collected axe roughouts and turned them into finished, polished axes. In the waterlogged ground, one of the axe heads found was still mounted in its wooden haft.

The meagre British evidence for hafting bears no comparison with the incredible detail found at lakeside settlements in the Jura, France. Around Lake Chalain and Lake Clairvaux there are superbly well-dated deposits from the 43rd century BC. Here, stone axe heads were routinely mounted into sleeves of antler, which were then fixed onto the wooden hafts. The antler sleeve held the blade firmly, acted as a shock absorber and prevented the haft from splitting. These lakeside settlements began life surrounded by dense woodland. Marks on well-preserved timber and use-wear analysis of tools show that axes and adzes had multiple uses. The large ones could fell trees, split planks and butcher animals. Smaller tools were used for cutting poles, carving wood, building and craft activities. About 3040 BC, within a generation, the population tripled around the lakes. Woodland was in retreat and so were the deer. Decent antlers became hard to find. Axe-wielding humans were changing the environment.[17]

Around lowland sites in Britain, Neolithic farmers also used the axes to fell trees and clear the land for cultivation and grazing. The rare survival of the axe haft is a reminder, however, that the trees themselves were valuable. They could be coppiced and trained, cropped as a valuable resource for fuel, tools, fencing and building, and even laid as trackways across boggy ground. Neolithic people understood the qualities of wood as much as they appreciated the possibilities of stone. They transformed natural materials into cultural resources, used, in turn, to transform the natural landscape and create new places.

CHAPTER FOURTEEN
# Creating places

## Naming the land

One morning, I sat on the balcony drinking coffee as the sun rose and seeped along the valley, and it occurred to me that in the vast, tree-shrouded landscape in front of me there is only a single place that I could put a name to. There is an anonymity about the forest. A succession of ridges runs down into the valley, like green waves. In the valley bottom the river flickers in the sunlight, slithering between a chaos of silver granite boulders. The river, of course, has a name: La Salendrinque. River names are often extremely ancient.

We give names to places and features of the land that tell us how the landscape was settled. Sometimes names are attached to distinctive natural features – prominent rocks, hills or caves. Names reflect the physical and social environment, or at least the parts that interested the namers. A couple of hundred metres along the river from my balcony there is the Dark Pool, our own name for part of the river enclosed by vertical cliffs. We go swimming there. Mesolithic people may have associated such a place with their mythology. I once read about a similar feature in Australia where the Aborigines recounted how the pool had been hacked out with a stone axe by one of their powerful spirits. In Papua New Guinea there is a ridge named Yagenebo Sabe (Bird Dancing Ridge). It has this name not for ornithological reasons but because there is a longhouse there where men, elaborately decorated as birds, dance on ceremonial occasions. Perhaps the Neolithic longhouses by the River Dee had names, just as the hall was named 'Heorot' in the great Anglo-Saxon poem *Beowulf*.

I began by saying that the sea of forest in front of me has no formal cartographic names – except one. This is the ridge in the far east, which defines the horizon and where the sun rises (for us). It is known as La Grande Pallières – massive natural outcrops of granite mark the southern end of the ridge, not water-rounded boulders such as those in the river below me, but jutting, angular teeth. If we pass beyond the rocks, there is a line of prehistoric megalithic tombs that mark the ridge. Has an impressive natural feature – like the tors of Dartmoor or the bluestones of Preseli – been enhanced by the addition of megalithic tombs, and turned into a cultural place, a place of memory? It is a physical reminder of Simon Schama's words: 'landscape is the work of the mind. Its scenery is built up as much from the strata of memory as from layers of rock'.[1]

The linearity of the Grande Pallières ridge, the rocks and the tombs suggest movement. Today and for generations it has been the transhumance route along which flocks of sheep pass in early summer between the lowlands and the mountains, and it may have been for millennia. The route heads directly to the crossing of three rivers and into the mountain pastures. Six thousand years ago La Grande Pallières possibly had another name, now lost, something like 'the place where the ancestors are buried next to the great rocks' or perhaps a far more imaginative and poetic name: a name that contained a story and a myth. Keith Basso, an American anthropologist, undertook a survey of place names among the Western Apache in the USA and stated 'place names are arguably amongst the most highly charged and richly evocative of all linguistic symbols'.[2] The people who dwelt in the region probably built the tombs, which would both signify ancestral rights to the land and act as waymarkers and places for people to meet and congregate. These tombs acted as distinctive points in the landscape.

Many of the prehistoric monuments of Britain also seem to suggest motion; they form lines and avenues. They are often sited prominently and are places that acted as hubs and drew people in from distant communities. The inhabitants are not simply 'locals'. Archaeological excavations can make monuments seem isolated, by focusing on specific features. Actually, they were part of social networks – what the anthropologist Tim Ingold called 'knots', tied into lines of wayfaring that create a mesh of contacts.[3] The stone axes act as proxies for the Neolithic mesh, one which links Monte Viso with Brittany and Scotland. The links are not necessarily direct; nevertheless, across Europe there were farming communities with common concerns and ways of seeing the world.

The Australian anthropologist James F. Weiner emphasizes that 'Place-names create the world as a humanized, historicized space; but speech, like any other bodily activity, is conditioned and shaped by the tasks to which human interest directs it'.[4] The mouths of Neolithic farmers are silent, though their works still speak of their concerns. To build a society in the forested landscape of Britain they needed to create new places with names, to bind themselves together, express their fears and beliefs and to invigorate memories. The Neolithic is not simply a matter of economy. There also have to be a 'set of foundational ideas and practices that bind people together ("religion" comes from the Latin root *ligare*, to bind) in a cosmos, an ordered world, and that links them in community'.[5] In many religions, place matters.

## Altering the Earth

One of the most distinctive aspects of the Neolithic in Britain is the appearance of impressive monuments. For the first time communities created and constructed places that stood out in the landscape, that attracted people to them, were meant to endure and probably had names. A time-traveller crossing Neolithic Britain could, at various times and in different regions, have come across both massive and small buildings, megalithic tombs and cairns, earthen long barrows, causewayed enclosures, avenues bounded by ditches (cursuses), stone circles and henge monuments. In fact, many of them persist even today, dogged survivors whose meanings challenge our imagination.

Hunter-gatherers in Britain chopped down trees, created clearings and trackways, built shelters and small circular houses, constructed platforms by lakesides and accumulated shell middens near the shoreline. These were mostly slight, organic structures, however, not built to last. In contrast, Neolithic people more consistently set about 'altering the earth', making their contribution to a new sense of time and place by creating places to commemorate and endure.[6]

In the absence of chronological precision, archaeologists have tended to assume that monuments emerged with the beginning of the Neolithic; that they were constructed and utilized over long periods, made possible because farmers had the surpluses of food and time, as well as the inclination to indulge in such feats of construction. In Britain, the Neolithic monuments represent a transformation in how people lived in the world, but this did not happen all at once. The *Gathering Time* project now allows us to bring this transformation into chronological and regional focus, and actually, or at least potentially, see what was going on, rather than stir the elements into a Neolithic stew. We can now begin to see the relationships between Neolithic structures and sites; where and when they appeared and how their life cycles compare.

The arrival of the Neolithic in Britain is signalled by the long wooden buildings in the field of sarsen stones revealed during the construction of the Channel Tunnel Rail Link at White Horse Stone (see Chapter 12). The site also provided evidence of domesticated cereals and Carinated Bowl pottery, albeit in small quantities. The timber halls appeared within a generation or so of 4000 BC (4065–3940 BC). This area of Kent, close to the River Medway, was already well known to archaeologists for two groups of remarkable monuments, megalithic tombs made of sarsen stone that cluster on either side of the river where it cuts through the chalk between Rochester and Maidstone.

The group to the west of the Medway includes Coldrum, which sits just south of the downland escarpment; 2 km (1¼ miles) further south are the tombs of Addington and The Chestnuts. About 8 km (5 miles) away on the east side of the Medway is a second group of tombs, which include the megalithic sarsen structure of Kit's Coty House and the fragmentary remains of Upper White Horse Stone and Lower White Horse Stone. These last two are unusual in lying within sight of the early Neolithic timber buildings. However, only the Coldrum tomb is reliably dated. Here limited excavations in 1910 revealed disarticulated human remains including eleven skulls. One belonged to a woman killed by a blow from a stone axe. Analysis of the bones found that they came from at least sixteen individuals, buried in two separate phases in the tomb. Radiocarbon dating now puts the start of the monument at about 3960–3890 BC.[7] The first phase of burial was short-lived, lasting about one to three generations and ending in 3930–3745 BC. After an interval of two centuries (more or less), the second phase of burials probably began about 3665–3565 BC and lasted some three hundred to seven hundred years. The initial use of the monument was brief and the bones were interred soon after death, rather than being kept elsewhere. They belonged to some of the earliest farmers in Britain.

Elements that define the Neolithic appear early in the Thames estuary: cereals from Manor Way, Woolwich, date to 3920–3870 BC; a group of pits at Grovehurst, on the south side of the Swale from the Isle of Sheppey, contained over half a dozen polished flint axe heads, four flint sickles and Carinated Bowl pottery. A pattern is emerging of wooden structures and domesticated species appearing first, at the start of the Neolithic, then burial monuments, and subsequently causewayed enclosures.

These enclosures, which for the first time define areas of ground as special and separate, are another distinctive feature of the early Neolithic. Archaeologists came up with the name 'causewayed camps or enclosures' because their often concentric ditches, made up of short lengths, are punctuated by many causeways – possibly multiple entrances into the interior or gaps blocked by earthen banks rather than ditches. Thanks to aerial photography four such sites are now known in Kent, of which the most thoroughly investigated is Chalk Hill near Ramsgate. Today, the site overlooks Pegwell Bay, made famous by William Dyce's uneasy painting (1858–60) of diminutive Victorians confronted by nature. Archaeologists exposed a slice across the monument in advance of road building. Subsequently, radiocarbon dating indicated that it was built in three phases, starting about 3780–3680 BC and was in use for roughly a century. So Chalk Hill is the earliest-known causewayed enclosure in Kent and possibly in Britain.

The evidence consistently indicates that in Kent timber structures, cereals, polished axes, ceramic bowls, megalithic tombs and causewayed enclosures – all the fingerprints of the Neolithic – began early compared with the rest of Britain. The Thames estuary was a landfall for continental immigrants bringing new ideas and techniques, plants and animals into the country. Whether the Thames was the only point of entry, or whether other bridgeheads subsequently appeared in the south and west, is an argument that will continue until more precise dating evidence is forthcoming from other regions. It seems highly likely that the first colonists would have remained in contact with their homeland(s) and boatloads of new settlers would subsequently join them and boost the sparse population. Given the expected fertility rate of farmers in a new land the agricultural population could relatively quickly have outgrown or absorbed the native hunter-gatherers of Britain and Ireland.

Here in the southeast, farming began initially with small kin groups. As they became established and increased in numbers and confidence, a sufficiently large labour force could be mustered – first to construct long barrows after 3800 BC (similar to those that appeared on the Continent several centuries earlier), and then, a century later, the large causewayed enclosures or communal gathering places. Out of the forests new places emerged, built by communities attached to the land.

Thanks to the *Gathering Time* project we now have a reasonably reliable model showing date estimates for the 'appearance of Neolithic things and practices' across substantial areas (though not everywhere) in Britain and Ireland. If the Neolithic and its attributes first appeared in the southeast in the decades immediately before 4000 BC, then it spread into south-central and eastern Britain in the following century. Around 3800 BC, the rate of expansion increased and reached southern Scotland within a generation. Whatever was stimulating this move delivered the first Neolithic into north-eastern Scotland at the same time. It arrived there fully fledged, bringing the impressive timber halls of Crathes and Balbridie (see Chapter 12), crops such as wheat, barley, oats and flax, and Carinated Bowl pottery, and even burial monuments, whose appearance in the southeast had been delayed by a generation or two.

The decades immediately following 3800 BC were a period of impressive development across Britain and Ireland. The appearance of enclosures in southern Britain coincides with the start of regional networks of exchange. Polished stone axes from sources in Cornwall, Wales and Ireland as well as Cumbria appeared across the country. Distinctive pottery, made in the south-west from gabbroic clays, was also exchanged over long distances. In Ireland, smaller rectangular houses proliferate. There was a 'sizeable shift in the way society was organized at this time'.[8]

## Housing the dead

In the modern Western world, death is an event that tends to be hidden and even shunned. The dead are often kept at distance. In the state of human affairs this is unusual. In the Neolithic, death was familiar; it came early, through disease, child-bearing, accidents and violence. The dead were not avoided; they played an active part in life, and human bones were actors or props in the rituals of the living. The living were intimate with the dead; they sought their protection and help.

The first monuments built in Britain were memorials to the dead, and places where the dead and the living could interact. As with churches, mosques or synagogues, the architecture of megalithic tombs reproduced beliefs, cosmology, rituals and performances routinely practised, though we may have difficulty reading them. Megalithic tombs are found from Iberia through France, notably Brittany, to Scandinavia. In Britain there are several hundred, usually located where there is suitable stone. Elsewhere, for example in lowland Britain, timber mortuary enclosures, earthen long barrows or round barrows fulfil a similar purpose.

It is the megalithic tombs, however, that most impress us today. Some are simple, like King's Quoit in Pembrokeshire, which is ruggedly dramatic, perched above the sea between earth and sky. In County Sligo, the white stone cairn of Carrowkeel, which covers a passage tomb and its cremations, is silhouetted dramatically against the sky on top of sheer limestone cliffs. Pentre Ifan, in Pembrokeshire, is the most impressive of the portal dolmens – so-called because two large stones flank the entrance to the burial chamber, with a blocking stone between them. The Pentre Ifan chamber stands at the end of a long, now denuded, rectangular cairn. Most remarkable is the capping stone, which was dug from the ground where the monument now stands. Today, this huge stone (4.3 m/14 ft long and 2.4 m/8 ft wide) still seems to float in the air, delicately poised on the points of its slim support stones. This was not accidental or even easy: the Neolithic builders suspended the roof of the tomb between earth and sky.[9] They probably impressed the neighbours; they certainly impressed me.

Archaeologists have put a great deal of effort into classifying Neolithic tombs on the basis of their shapes and structure. Many forms have a distinctly regional distribution, emphasizing the variety of cultural differences between small-scale communities – for example, the court cairns of the northern part of Ireland, several of which were placed around the Céide Fields site. One of the finest is Creevykeel in County Sligo. Here, a low cairn defines an open court or arena, accessed by a narrow entrance. On the west side of the court, megaliths flank the entrance to a large burial chamber, with smaller

The portal dolmen of Pentre Ifan, Pembrokeshire, with its delicately balanced capping stone.

chambers beyond. The court acted as a theatre for mortuary and perhaps seasonal rituals; a place for drumming, blowing flutes, chanting the names of the illustrious dead, and consuming ale and mead. One of the court cairns, at Ballyglass, County Mayo, to the east of Céide Fields, has a megalithic chamber at each end of the court and was built partly over the site of a Neolithic house. Is this a deliberate link between the dwellings of the living and the dead? Certainly, many tombs resemble in form, at least superficially, the traditional longhouses of the Continent.

Jonathan Last has suggested that 'A switch from the investment in labour in houses to funerary monuments for a smaller number of people could therefore be interpreted as evidence of developing inequality.'[10] This could be the case if we were able to establish that the new funerary monuments were exclusive, retained for members of a particular elite kin group or high-status individuals. To establish that, we need well-preserved, recorded and dated funerary deposits in the context of well-excavated tomb structures. These circumstances are surprisingly rare.

## The tomb builders

First, let us look at the effort required to build tombs. The tomb of Tinkinswood in the Vale of Glamorgan is of a type known as a Cotswold-Severn tomb with a pronounced forecourt in front of the stone chamber. Some, however, are deliberately deceptive: architects built small burial chambers into the long sides of large mounds and placed a false forecourt at the narrow end. Did they have a problem with bone thieves? At Tinkinswood it is the capstone over the chamber that impresses, a 40-tonne monster, 6.5 × 4.5 m (21 × 15 ft) in size. The Neolithic farmers were expert at shifting rocks. There was a tradition going back several hundred years on the Continent of moving and lifting massive stones. It would culminate in transporting some of Pembrokeshire's finest to Stonehenge in about 2600 BC. Because these people were so skilled at raising and balancing massive rocks, a massive labour force was not required to build Tinkinswood.[11]

There are several hundred megalithic tombs from Kent, Cornwall, the Cotswolds and Wales to Orkney, the Hebrides and Ireland, representing an enormous effort for a small population. Archaeologists have found far more tombs than settlements. One of the most meticulously excavated is the tomb of Hazleton North in the Cotswolds, Gloucestershire (see page 300). This was a wedge-shaped long cairn which incorporated no massive stones, only a pile of limestone rocks 55 m (180 ft) long, 8–19 m (26–62 ft) wide and up to 2.5 m (8 ft) high. Actually, it is misleading to call it a 'pile'. The stone mound was bounded by beautifully constructed drystone walls and within there was a long 'spine' of stones with transverse ribs. This skeleton provided supporting coffers for the masses of stone rubble. No wonder the monument stood up for almost six thousand years. Alan Saville, the excavator, estimated that people equipped with antler picks, baskets and shovels of cattle shoulder blades quarried 742 cubic m (26,200 cubic ft) of stone from the ground alongside the cairn site and that the project in total, could have occupied a gang of ten people for about sixty-five eight-hour days.[12]

This was a substantial task, and one only undertaken for a good reason. Creating a visible and permanent resting place for some of the dead clearly mattered. Yet this was not an impossible task for a small community of farmers, and it does not necessarily imply direction from or on behalf of a social elite. The frequency and size of these monuments suggest we are seeing the effort of smallish clans – probably groups of related families working and thereby tied to the nearby land, cultivating cereals, herding cattle and perhaps sheep, keeping pigs and still exploiting wild resources. Unlike hunter-gatherers these farmers, by building such monuments, were laying visible claim to the land, putting down roots, creating a new place to which they would routinely return, and which reminded others of their presence and, perhaps most importantly, the presence of their ancestors.

By attempting to show the grand sweep of prehistory, from the Near East and across Europe, there is a danger of implying a sameness and uniformity about the Neolithic. While there are common factors – such as the exploitation of domesticated plants and animals, the use of appropriate tools, settling down, mythologies and monuments connected with agriculture and spiritual beliefs – there are also many variations in how these things were manipulated and expressed. These were small-scale societies. Most people would spend their lives close to where they were born; they generated enormous local diversity in how they built houses and monuments, and created and manipulated their material culture. Britain is fascinating at this time because, although farming spread rapidly, Neolithic people expressed themselves with considerable diversity in their daily lives. As Gabriel Cooney of University College Dublin wrote, there are 'local worlds linked by exotic elements'.[13]

## Histories of the dead

Thanks to the more precise chronologies developed by the *Gathering Time* project we can now begin to see the variations and actions of small-scale groups with greater precision.[14] Previously, archaeologists sweated blood over typologies of tombs. The distributions of tomb types are often interesting, marking out specific territories, but their chronologies remained frustratingly imprecise (and many still are). The impression was of a long-drawn-out prehistory in which change happened relatively slowly. So it is worth taking a look at a couple of sites whose histories have now come into sharper focus, thanks to Bayesian modelling.

There are two megalithic tombs (or long barrows) that I have personally visited more than any others. West Kennet in Wiltshire sits on a low ridge with wide views over the upper Kennet Valley and across the great sacred landscape of Avebury. Wayland's Smithy in Oxfordshire crouches on top of the chalk downlands alongside the Ridgeway, overlooking the scarp that plunges into the Vale of the White Horse (see page 300). Wayland's Smithy is an old name – or a new one, depending on your perspective. It was given by Old English speakers, between eleven hundred and fifteen hundred years ago, and is first mentioned in a charter of King Eadred of AD 955. The English renamers wove stories into this ancient landscape, thus claiming it as their own: about dragons, Till the archer god (as in William Tell, a later folk story), sacred ash trees – and Wayland, the lame smith god. To them the ancient tomb was mysterious, perhaps dangerous. They attached their own tales to it.

Wayland's Smithy lies about 25 km (15 miles) northeast of West Kennet, a good day's walk along the Ridgeway. Today the long-distance footpath is tightly constrained between barbed wire fences and a few hedgerows. The Downs are cultivated for cereals, their roots seriously soaked in nitrates to give them purchase in these thin, nutrient-poor chalky soils. There are a few isolated clumps of trees, tolerated as shelter for deer that emerge at their peril. Six thousand years ago, the land between West Kennet and Wayland's Smithy would have looked, felt and sounded very different: wooded, but perhaps more like the relatively open parkland that environmental scientists have identified elsewhere on the Wessex chalk. Water supplies are rare on the high chalk. Springs emerge below, at the foot of the escarpment, and feed streams where Roman villas and early English villages were later sited.

The two megalithic tombs of West Kennet and Wayland's Smithy look quite similar. Archaeologists such as Stuart Piggott believed that they were contemporary and in use probably for many centuries. Each consists of a long trapezoidal mound flanked by quarry ditches. Both have megalithic facades made of upright sarsen sentinels with stone-lined burial chambers behind. The facades enveloped areas used for ceremonies and feasting. West Kennet has a concave facade, and inside two pairs of opposing burials chambers with a fifth at the end of the passage. Wayland's Smithy is laid out in a similar way but with only one pair of opposing chambers. These chambers are distinct architectural features but their meaning remains obscure. Were they reserved, for example, for specific groups or segments within the clan?

The first excavations at Wayland's Smithy (or at least the first anyone admitted to) were in 1919–20, then in 1962–3 Stuart Piggott and Richard Atkinson took another crack at the site.[15] They found that beneath the long mound with its megalithic chamber, lay an earlier, smaller monument: an oval barrow with a central mortuary container made of timber. For many years, visiting the site, I told students the standard story. A small burial monument was used for several generations, then a much grander one was built on top. Here was a community proclaiming its authority, and then using its great monument for centuries. The Bayesian modelling of thirty-three radiocarbon results has thrown that little narrative into question.

Let's return to West Kennet. The long barrow was first excavated in 1859 by John Thurnham, a distinguished doctor with a fearsome set of mutton-chop whiskers and the medical superintendent of the Wiltshire County Asylum in Devizes. He used his patients as a labour force at West Kennet and his main interest was finding skulls. This was a period obsessed with the shape of the human cranium and Thurnham was a leading advocate of the idea that prehistoric Britons belonged to two races with different skull shapes: one the builders of long barrows, the other of round barrows. The problem with strongly held beliefs or theories is that they can influence sampling strategies. In Thurnham's case, the cranium was all that mattered, though his recording was reasonably good by the standards of the day. So for modern archaeologists, assessing old bones collected (or discarded) by antiquarians can be a problem. Fortunately, Thurnham found only one of West Kennet's five chambers.

The *Gathering Time* reanalysis of West Kennet dated its earliest burials to 3670–3635 BC. The first sequence of burials lasted ten to thirty years, then after a gap of just over a century – during which time the tomb deteriorated – bones were once again gradually placed in the chambers, a practice that continued

The long barrow of West Kennet, Wiltshire, with its imposing eastern facade of sarsen stones. The tomb lies on the downland crest overlooking the Kennet Valley and Silbury Hill.

into the second half of the third millennium BC. It has proved possible to analyse the human bones chamber by chamber. Many textbooks suggest that people were arranged by age and gender in West Kennet's five chambers, but that does not seem to be the case. Mostly men, women and children were massed together in the primary deposit, except in the west chamber, which contains four males only, aged under twenty-five. Was the west chamber retained for men? Four burials are not statistically convincing. In total, the tomb held the remains of thirty-six individuals (fifteen men, eleven women and several children).

The burials clearly do not represent anything as straightforward as high-status chieftains, and certainly not human sacrifices buried to accompany the clan chief, as Glyn Daniel suggested in the early 1950s. Archaeologists often rely on grave goods as an indicator of status, as in the spectacular Varna burial (see page 355), but generally, in British Neolithic tombs there are very few objects – the odd pot, a few modest items of jewelry, perhaps offerings of meat. If grave goods are a guide, then this was a relatively egalitarian society. All age groups and genders are represented. But were these people the whole community, or individuals selected for some reason for special burial, perhaps relatives of the pioneer kin group, a social elite?

Spectacular tombs housing a restricted number of the dead may be something other than routine burial sites. One possibility is that they were structures where the community paid its respect to its ancestors (the term 'ancestor' is used in anthropology to designate forebears who are remembered, either by names or as a collective). There has been justified criticism of the way British prehistorians reach for 'the ancestors' at every possibly opportunity.[16] However, I would not want to discard them entirely. Agriculturalists view the world differently to hunter-gatherer-fishers. The latter have an immediate return on their efforts, and their efforts alone. Farmers have a greater sense of time and continuity, investing effort for future returns (which also holds them together as a group) and an indebtedness to past generations. I have a smallholding that is held together by several kilometres of stone terracing. As we work the land we constantly refer to the efforts of those who went before – the people who cleared the forest, built the terraces, hauled especially huge blocks of granite into the terrace wall (or left them in situ) and installed irrigation ditches. For us, they are not ancestors – as I am a recent immigrant – but they are a constant presence and we appreciate the investment that they made, upon which we are still capitalizing. In contrast with hunter-gatherers, farmers are involved in a particularly 'ancestral' mode of production: they are indebted to the labour of their predecessors. Anthropologists have argued that it is because of this that ancestors feature so prominently in agricultural societies.

Richard Bradley discussed this issue in the 1980s when he emphasized not only 'that ancestors strengthen the cohesion of the community; they also establish that community's claim to the resources which they are controlling. For this reason there can be a close geographical relationship between a cemetery and a living area.'[17] This is true, but it is also true that ancestors are not always buried in the same way or place as everyone else. 'Ancestral' bodies are selected from within the community, and the factors behind the choice can be very varied – for example, some communities recognize their ancestry through the male line, others through the female. The number of burials in megalithic tombs is relatively small. The rest of the population might have been cremated, placed in rivers or in the innumerable smaller burial monuments that also occur in the British Neolithic.

At Wayland's Smithy, a different burial monument to that which we see today initially appeared in the landscape. This was a small oval barrow made of chalk rubble dug from two flanking ditches. Beneath the barrow was a container or chamber for burials, a wooden box laid on a sarsen pavement, marked at each end by a massive split timber post. The number of individuals in this phase of burial is estimated at fourteen: eleven males, two females and a child. Most of these skeletons were complete. It is frequently claimed that Neolithic bodies were defleshed and exposed before burial, but some here were certainly intact, laid in the chamber overlapping each other; intimate in death. Among the bones was the Neolithic equivalent of a smoking gun – three leaf-shaped arrowheads with broken tips. Another flint projectile point was embedded in the right pelvis of a man who had been shot through the abdomen. It seems that we have here the evidence for several victims slaughtered in a raid – perhaps attacked by a hostile group in pursuit of cattle and women – and then rapidly buried. The dead were placed in the wooden chamber before it was closed and then covered by the chalk mound.

The first burials in the Wayland's Smithy wooden chamber are now dated to 3610–3550 BC, several decades after the first burials in the big West Kennet tomb, and burials ceased in 3590–3520 BC. This means, statistically, that the burials could have taken place in as little as one year or as many as fifteen – at any rate what is, archaeologically, a very short period and possibly one individual event. We might say that men are represented in the burial because of their status. However, in the circumstances, we could simply be witnessing the burial of those who were the victims of a raid. The men were killed and, as at other Neolithic massacre sites, the women and children were taken away to stock the communities of the killers. The surviving members of the community piled a mound over the mortuary chamber about 3520–3420 BC and then left it for a few years. Vegetation began to encroach on the site, which was burnt off before the community began the construction of the impressive long barrow that we see today, in about 3460–3400 BC. The burials inside the visible Wayland's Smithy stone chambers were more or less trashed by looters. We can say, however, that the big monument was probably used as a place of burial for about a century.

Wayland's Smithy may look like West Kennet, but, in fact, it was built considerably later. While burials took place in the first wooden chamber, other long barrows were old or had fallen out of use – not only West Kennet but also other well-dated long barrows such as Ascott-under-Wychwood and Hazleton North in the Cotswolds. The first Wayland's Smithy mound is modest in size, yet it is not particularly early, as archaeologists have tended to claim as explanations of such things. Instead, we need to be aware of the discrepancies and differences between communities. Not everyone is an early adopter.

When the Wayland's Smithy people did build a large barrow, they copied the ancient one down the road at West Kennet. Was this a deliberate harking back to a heroic past during times of stress? From the evidence we currently have, it seems that some megalithic tombs were built and used as places of interment for a short period and for relatively few people. At that point they were completed monuments: memorials to ancestors, places for small communities to gather, to highlight their rights to land and resources. Judging from the number of tombs in areas such as the Cotswolds and Northern Ireland these communities were competitive, the tombs acting as banners: signs of fitness; stone memorials to the dead, and displays of the capabilities of the living.

Alasdair Whittle and his colleagues point out that the violent incident at Wayland's Smithy occurred after about 3650 BC when causewayed enclosures appear in the Thames Valley and Wessex.[18] As we will see, this was a time of tension and competition between communities. The first burial mounds may have been expressions of identity, new places to express self-awareness, then, as the population of farmers increased, new tensions demanded new places, where the living could gather to bond, to go forth and multiply.

## Forensics in the Cotswolds

We have compared the varied histories of West Kennet and Wayland's Smithy. Clearly, Neolithic people were as contrary and varied as anyone else. If we want to see good forensic evidence – how many men and women were buried, at what age, and even what killed them – we need well-preserved and recorded deposits; sites that did not attract antiquarians, or grave robbers, and have alkaline soils that preserve bone.

Two sites that fit these criteria lie to the north of West Kennet, on the limestone soils of the Cotswolds. The first long barrow is known as Ascott-under-Wychwood in Oxfordshire. When I began mapping the archaeology of the upper Thames Valley from aerial photographs in 1973 my partner-in-crime was Don Benson of the County Museum. On Friday evenings, as a reward for hours of poring over photographs, we would meet at Don's local pub, and afterwards retreat to the half-timbered medieval cottage that he called home. Inside, the place was like a Crime Scene Investigation Unit.

It was plastered with plans and photographs of stone chambers filled with human bones, all evidence of Don's recently completed excavation at the Ascott-under-Wychwood barrow. He didn't just take his work home with him, he slept with it. In those days, post-excavation work was often left to the site director. Nowadays, thank goodness, it is usually a team effort. However, it was obvious that Don had excavated the Ascott barrow with meticulous care, which is why it was eventually analysed and published in great detail.[19]

When Don Benson excavated the Ascott barrow, radiocarbon dating was still rather rough and ready. However, thanks to his careful recording, it has since been possible to assess the chronology with Bayesian modelling. The tomb, we now know, was probably built between 3760 and 3695 BC (two or three generations earlier than West Kennet). The Ascott barrow was extended very shortly afterwards in 3745–3670 BC. Bodies were inserted from the beginning, and the final ones interred in the 3640s or 3630s BC – so it is probable that Ascott was in use for three to five generations.

The second carefully excavated cairn is Hazleton North. It sat high on the Cotswolds, about 20 km (12 miles) west of Ascott-under-Wychwood. In the 1970s, Alan Saville, now at the National Museums of Scotland, recorded the burial mound and its contents with great precision.[20] Here two chambers were packed with bones before the entrance passage was finally blocked. The tomb was used for burial for an even shorter period than Ascott – probably only two or three generations, ending in the 3670s BC.

Interestingly, there were signs of earlier activity beneath both barrows. Under the Hazleton North cairn there was a Mesolithic flint scatter. This may suggest continuity of use by hunter-gatherers who 'converted' to the Neolithic. However, the excavator, himself a Mesolithic specialist, believes the time period between the flint scatter and the barrow was substantial. There were also traces of early (pre-barrow) Neolithic activity – hearth structures and a midden deposit containing cereals and cereal-processing debris – so the barrow was probably constructed within a cleared area in the woodland landscape, one in which cereals had been grown in small plots for several decades before the cairn was built. Ascott has a similar background and biography. Farming first, monument building later. Hazleton is particularly important because it produced this rare evidence of the first phase of Neolithic occupation about 3900 BC beneath the burial mound. The cairn itself may have overlapped or been slightly later than timber longhouses such as White Horse Stone in Kent and Yarnton, nearby in the upper Thames Valley, Oxfordshire.

These two barrows were relatively intact so it is possible to estimate the number of people buried there, bearing in mind that when the Neolithic burial detail inserted new bodies, they tended to shift the earlier bones, creating a massive skeletal jigsaw puzzle. At Hazleton they moved the bones of individuals deeper into the chamber as new burials took place; some of the disturbed bones were put in discrete piles and the skulls placed by the chamber walls. However, the shortage of skulls suggests that some were removed and included in rites elsewhere. In some barrows, attempts were made to reconstruct disturbed skeletons – though not always with great anatomical precision. The Hazleton dead totalled thirty-three: twenty-one adults, with a majority of men. Ascott held twenty people (including a cremation), sixteen adults, six identified as men and three as women.

As mentioned earlier, it is a commonplace that Neolithic bodies were exposed and defleshed prior to burial, then the bones gathered together. In long barrows, the evidence for this is limited though it certainly did happen. At Raunds in Northamptonshire a timber structure stood on the edge of the River Nene; around it were human and cattle bones.[21] This was possibly a place where corpses were exposed, and the remains may have been placed in the river.

For generations, archaeologists have speculated about how many people were buried in long barrows and whether these were a limited proportion of the community. If only special people were elected for barrow burial, were they the elite of society or perhaps the kin group who first laid claim to the land? In simple societies where status is not inherited, some individuals achieve status in their lifetimes – as warriors, negotiators, spiritual guides or accumulators of wealth. The mixed age and genders of barrow occupants seem not to indicate such status in death, but if the purpose was to build the barrow as a mark of the communities' rights and abilities – a display for the neighbours and visitors – then the inhabitants served to symbolize their community.

We can be reasonably sure that not everyone was buried in a long barrow or other impressive types of tomb. Some people were cremated, or exposed so that their bones could be collected and deposited elsewhere. Some were probably placed in pits, the river or specialized mortuary enclosures. It is not unusual for human remains to be scarce in the archaeological record. Later, in the Iron Age (the first millennium BC), archaeologists find few burials. The disposal of bodies was done in such a way that they are not found. Anyone who has seen the funeral pyres at Varanasi alongside the River Ganges will understand the problem of the disappearing dead.

Compared with the earlier Mesolithic, we have a sizeable sample of human remains from Neolithic tombs in Britain. Analysing them is not straightforward because of the way they were treated within their own communities and more recently. For example, long barrows in general usually contain human bones representing fifteen to forty or fifty individuals buried over four or five generations (occasionally less). Reading the bones is not like reading a modern census. The tomb at Ty Isaf, Powys, illustrates the difficulty of calculating precise numbers. The bones indicated a minimum number of thirty-three individuals interred in the tomb, yet there were only three complete long bones (all humeri). There were also only seven skulls, with twenty-two mandibles. Clearly, skulls and long bones were going elsewhere. It took a great deal of painstaking forensic analysis to estimate the minimum number of individuals at Ty Isaf. Obviously, in a society that moved and used the bones of the dead, there could have been more individuals buried there originally. Some age groups are also under-represented: in tombs and elsewhere, neonatal and young children simply do not occur often enough.

To put it bluntly, there may be a thousand or so early Neolithic burial monuments in the British Isles but we cannot calculate the local or wider populations from them. In the 1970s the well-known human bone specialist Don Brothwell estimated the Neolithic population of the British Isles as about 10,000–40,000.[22] In view of the rapid discovery of monuments since then it seems reasonable to multiply that number by ten, but this is still no more than the crudest estimate to provide some sense of the relative scale of population.

We can be more specific about statistics at the individual level. In West Kennet the adult males varied from 1.57–1.80 m (5 ft 2 in.–5 ft 11 in.) in height. The women were smaller, at 1.47–1.60 m (4 ft 10 in.–5 ft 3 in.). At Ascott, the males averaged 1.65 m (5 ft 5 in.) with the tallest 1.78 m (5 ft 10 in.). The women averaged 1.57 m (5 ft 2 in.). These people were relatively gracile, though well muscled. Light-boned women had well-developed musculature, indicating that they did hard, physical work. However, pots found in the River Thames were decorated with finger impressions – from slim fingers with long nails: perhaps specialist women potters cared for their nails so that they could make decorative marks in soft clay.[23]

Many causes of death, particularly infectious diseases, leave little or no trace on the skeleton. Obviously, causes of death abounded – many Neolithic people died in their early thirties and few lived much beyond fifty. An almost universal problem, after the mid twenties, was arthritis, particularly in the hands. It has been suggested that this was the result of repetitive stress syndrome, caused by the frequent wielding of stone axes – heavy blows impacted upon human wrists as well as on tree trunks.

One of the first people to be buried in the Ascott-under-Wychwood tomb was a juvenile. He or she suffered with a nasty abscess on one side of the face, which must have been very painful and disfiguring. Blood poisoning could have killed the child. Such injuries are relatively common, and there is frequent tooth loss, though caries is relatively much less common than in societies with an addiction to sugar.[24] Nevertheless, early farmers were not strong on oral hygiene.

Neolithic people attempted to treat their physical problems and a number of plants suitable for herbal remedies appear in settlements. More spectacular and alarming is the evidence for trepanning – cutting a hole in the skull with a flint knife, possibly to relieve headaches, head injuries or evil spirits (mental illness?). The cure may look worse than the cause, yet two men buried in the Fussell's Lodge long barrow in Wiltshire survived the operation (there was regrowth of bone before death).

Increasingly, we can see that while there are similarities in the style of long barrows, the details of their biographies vary considerably. This is also true of how the monuments were 'closed'. At Fussell's Lodge, the guardians shut down the tomb in monumental style. At Ascott-under-Wychwood they walled it up. And at Hazleton, the intact body of an adult male was laid in the northern passageway. When he was excavated the archaeologists called him 'the flintknapper' because he was buried with a stone hammer and a flint core. These are not fancy grave goods. They are everyday, utilitarian objects and a reminder that all the bones in the tombs belong to individual human beings.

## Embracing the community

Today we take certain types of places for granted, such as dramatic arenas that emphasize performance: of gladiators, bulls, tennis players, baseball teams or footballers, musicians or religious charismatics, even public executioners in some god-forsaken countries. Such enclosures are designed to make people focus, develop a crowd mentality, intensify their emotions and respond with the precision of flocking birds. There are other types of enclosures that corral cattle, fold sheep or enfold the dead. In the village where I live, there are two walled cemeteries, divided by a road. In life these people lived alongside each other, spoke the same language, worked together. Yet Protestants and Catholics await their maker in separate enclosures, defining themselves for eternity by their religious differences. Some enclosures protect us from external threats, define 'us' and 'them' with walls, stockades, ditches, ramparts, towers and gateways. From these we look outwards, scanning the hostile barbarian world from relative safety. There are also enclosures that control and direct movement – of pilgrims and processions, marching groups, flocks and herds. These provide a sense of direction and ultimate destination.

If enclosures seem normal and routine today, it was not always so. Hunter-gatherers controlled the flight of animals to some extent, but formal enclosure, made by hacking out the earth to create ditches and banks strengthened with timber palisades or stone walls, became routine only in the British Neolithic. In Europe, arguably the earliest ditched enclosures were those created by the first farmers of the Tavoliere in southeast Italy and across the Adriatic in Dalmatia, from around 6000 BC (see Chapter 7). These new places acted as focal points for farming communities, hubs that promoted the concepts of settling down and community identity. Spaces became places, domesticated and separate from the wild. Huts appeared inside, cultural material was placed in the ditches alongside human remains, emphasizing and celebrating the boundary. Processing debris indicates that crops – cereals, peas and lentils – were harvested from surrounding plots; animals grazed on the land outside and wild resources – plants, molluscs, fish and deer – were still exploited.[25]

These ditched enclosures were associated with the domestic, as were the ditches around the longhouse communities of the *Linearbandkeramik* (LBK) and subsequent cultures in central and northwest Europe. By the later fifth millennium BC there were different types of enclosure with short lengths of interrupted ditches and causeways. These places existed in a world of more scattered settlement, with an increasing emphasis on herding cattle and social interaction on a larger scale than implied by the size and distribution of long barrows. By about 4500–4200 BC, enclosures of varying type and function were widespread from the Paris Basin into Germany – for example, the Aldenhovener Plateau (see page 140). Causewayed enclosures appeared in the Pas-de-Calais between 4300 and 4100 BC, and one of them, Mont d'Hubert, was actually on the Channel coast, just west of Calais and facing across the water to Britain.[26] The *Gathering Time* project concluded 'it is inconceivable from this perspective that causewayed enclosures in southern Britain could have been an innovation completely independent of that Continental background'.[27]

The continental causewayed enclosures of the later fifth millennium BC vary considerably in size, layout, construction and length of use. They do, however, have common characteristics: they bound the space in similar ways with segmented ditches, place what seem to be discrete ritual deposits of pottery, stone tools, animal bones and human remains within the ditches and in pits, and were not systematically used as settlements.

These enclosures did not appear in Britain immediately with the first farmers. As we have seen, the earliest monumental tombs, such as Coldrum in Kent and Ascott-under-Wychwood in Oxfordshire, were in use between about 3900 BC and 3700 BC. At about this later date causewayed enclosures began to appear in Britain, first in southern areas close to the coast in the Thames estuary and Sussex, then spreading into Wessex and the Cotswolds, the middle and upper Thames Valley, and into Wales probably towards the end of the 37th century BC.

Causewayed enclosures had a long history on the Continent. They may have taken on a mythical status and, it has been suggested, even been associated with a cult. After all, the massive 12th-century programme of church-building in Europe combined the power of religion, myth and active history (the expansion of the Normans and the creation of new elites). It is possible that causewayed enclosures represent the arrival of a new wave of immigrants into Britain, but there is no other material evidence to support this. The most likely scenario is that in the process of Britain becoming Neolithic it took a couple of centuries before local groups possessed the numbers, motivation and organization for this gear shift upwards in the business of creating places and communities. Some causewayed enclosures were on a scale that dwarfed wooden buildings and long barrows. In a competitive world, someone had just upped the ante; the group that cohered around large enclosures impressed rival communities, even members of its own, with this awe-inspiring novelty. The necessary ritual knowledge, as well as the engineering ambition, may have passed along those webs woven in order to exchange exotic axe heads; the idea may have been brought by charismatic travellers. People influential in the community must then have roused the rest to take part in the new joint enterprise.

The causewayed enclosures had implications for the communities that built them – some were projects on an unprecedented scale that needed a large labour force.[28] For some, such as Maiden Castle and Hambledon Hill in Dorset and Haddenham in Cambridgeshire, a great clearing had to be cut in the forest. The butt of a Langdale axe lay in one of Haddenham's ditches, although the Langdale axes are not the first to appear in southern Britain. Axe heads from Cornwall probably arrived earlier, in the early 37th century BC. One was found in the Hambledon enclosure and with it were pots made of gabbroic clay that originated on the Lizard Peninsula in Cornwall. A particularly evocative piece of evidence was some carbonized plant fragments found on the site. These were identified as an unusual heather (*Erica vagans*), which today only grows in Northern Ireland – and the Lizard Peninsula. Are we seeing some of the first packing material, used to transport the Cornish pots? It seems that the Cornish axes and pots were arriving in southern Britain within one or two generations of the start of manufacture; the Langdale axes appear in the south slightly later, about 3705–3540 BC.[29]

The enclosures rapidly multiplied on the Sussex downland, in the upper Thames Valley and the lower Welland and Nene valleys. The heyday of construction spanned about 150 years, in the 37th century BC and the first half of the 36th century BC. Neolithic communities were devoting serious time and labour to the construction of ditched enclosures, as the efforts put into monumental tombs declined. The *Gathering Time* project estimates that about 80% of the effort of building these enclosures was expended between about 3700 BC and 3500 BC, with some works continuing over a further two centuries.

Unlike megalithic tombs, causewayed enclosures are not usually impressive to the modern observer. At best one sees a low, oval earthwork. The infilled ditches are now slight, the banks denuded, the palisades long gone. These are enigmatic monuments, which have often been neglected by archaeologists.[30] This is surprising because the best-preserved causewayed enclosure at Windmill Hill, Wiltshire, above the great Avebury complex, was excavated in the 1920s and became the type site for the early Neolithic. This is hardly appropriate. We now know that these monuments did not appear at the beginning of the Neolithic and were not built everywhere in Britain. Nevertheless, Windmill Hill dominated the textbooks, almost as much as Star Carr did for the Mesolithic, in spite of the fact that the excavations were not fully published.

Unfortunately, human foibles can get in the way of scientific enterprise. Alexander Keiller, heir to the famous Dundee-based marmalade company whose jars sat on many British breakfast tables, wanted to excavate Windmill Hill in the 1920s. The rather snooty Wiltshire archaeological establishment more or less forced the wealthy but inexperienced outsider to employ Harold St George Gray to oversee the excavation. The two did not hit it off.

Keiller was hands-on and innovative, not hidebound by gentlemanly assumptions. He wrote in a letter of 9 August 1925: 'he is the one arch[aeologist] that I have met that I wholeheartedly despise'. So excavations of causewayed camps did not get off to a good start. The young Stuart Piggott admired Keiller's attempts to introduce rigour and discipline into excavation. He described how he copied Keiller, himself laying out precise, regular trenches on his dig in 1930, at The Trundle, Sussex. The top brass from the British Museum paid a visit: 'bowler hat, pince-nez glasses, dark suit with a rose in button-hole – and sizing up the situation, commented briefly "very marmaladish"'.[31]

The 1930 survey of British causewayed enclosures identified sixteen possible sites (in fact, four were incorrectly identified). Most survived as earthworks on the Wessex and Sussex downland with the exception of Abingdon, which is on a gravel terrace of the Thames. In more recent decades the number has risen to sixty-nine certain or probable sites thanks to the discoveries of aerial survey. There are particular concentrations in the middle and upper Thames and in the river valleys of eastern England. Causewayed enclosures do not appear in northern England, though stone enclosures in the Lake District, such as Green How and Carrock Fell, may be local variations, as are the stone tor enclosures of the South West, notably Carn Brea in Cornwall. There appear to be outliers also in Anglesey (Bryn Celli Wen), the Isle of Man (Billown) and Ireland (Donegore Hill).[32]

In spite of eighty years of research the purposes of causewayed enclosures remain enigmatic. They vary enormously in size from about 100 m (330 ft) to 600 m (2,000 ft) across, and the sub-circular spaces are defined by one or more circuits of interrupted ditches and banks. Originally, they were assumed to be nucleated villages (with people living in the ditches), then Isobel Smith, who drew together the unpublished Windmill Hill data, called them 'causewayed camps' because she saw no evidence of permanent occupation. This name went out of fashion among archaeologists but actually there is something to be said for it. Many of them may well be 'camps' where people came together for short periods, for ceremonies and seasonal gatherings. The obvious rituals seem to be associated with death, but, as in modern churches, new life and new partnerships could also be celebrated.

As we have already seen in Chapter 12, on the shores of the Swiss Lakes, anaerobic, wet conditions can be a boon to archaeologists. So the causewayed enclosure or camp at Etton in Cambridgeshire, excavated by Francis Pryor, is especially important.[33] It sat on a slight island, low-lying in the valley of the River Welland. The site could only be used at certain times of year because it flooded in winter. As a result, alluvium spread over the Neolithic ground surface protecting it from the plough, and in the enclosure ditches, waterlogging preserved organic material, particularly wood, as well as pollen and insects, which provide a vivid picture of the Neolithic environment. For example, the presence of scarab dung beetles (*Onthophagus nutans* – now extinct in Britain) is clear evidence for the corralling of stock. On the other hand, the insect assemblage suggests humans were not present for long periods. It seems that the enclosure sat within a grazed area, with a background of woodland. Excavations of ditches and banks in dry conditions give an impression of rather bare and stark sites. Etton tells a different story. Within the interrupted ditches there were fragments of waterlogged wood, much of which had been cut from coppiced stools that grew around the circuit of the camp. Some were alder but much was bird cherry (*Prunus avium*). In other words, we should imagine the enclosure not as a bare and austere place but flush with blossom in the spring, when visitors arrived after the winter floods had receded. Later in the year the cherries were crammed with fruit and thronged with noisy, greedy birds.

Maisie Taylor examined the trimmed wood fragments and found that useful rods had been cut from new growth and then removed from the site. The coppiced stools and their rapidly sprouting growth would also have screened the circuit and even made it impenetrable. The visitors to the enclosure made wooden bowls from the burr wood of the alder. The markings on alder burrs show that the stone axe was the tool of choice – an axe handle was split longitudinally, probably when it became embedded and stuck in the hard wood. There were parts of twenty-four stone axe heads left around the site – some from Cornwall, but predominantly from North Wales, and, of course, Cumbria/Langdale – and had clearly been used as tools. But there was more to it than that. Some seemed to have been deliberately burnt and broken, then placed carefully in what the excavators took to be ritual deposits.

The Etton enclosure held animals for part of the year and it was also a theatre for the performance of rituals. Francis Pryor suggests that the ditch hollows acted as a place where offerings were made and displayed – animal remains, human bones, pots and axes. No complete human skeletons were found – mostly the remains were single long bones, often with evidence of wear and tear, abraded and gnawed by dogs. The excavators believe that bodies were brought to the enclosure for excarnation – exposure so that the flesh would disappear, leaving clean, hard bone. People then selected some long bones to be placed in the outer circuit ditch. In contrast, the animal bones – mainly cattle, with pigs and some sheep – were fresh and had not been gnawed. These are probably the debris from feasting.

Inside the Etton enclosure there were no signs of solid, well-built houses. The people probably camped in slight, temporary structures. What they also did a great deal was dig pits – and in them placed more varied groups of material that commemorated individuals. In spite of the large number of pits none of them intercut each other – as if their locations were marked and respected. A complete Langdale axe sat in the top of one pit; another had a 'polissoir' (a tool for finishing or sharpening stone axes) made of a fine-grained quartzite pebble. Polissoirs are rare, although they have also been found at Abingdon and The Trundle. At West Kennet, one of the sarsen uprights was repeatedly used as a polissoir, as if sharpening the axe was part of the ceremonies. Near Avebury, in a field of sarsen stones, one stone was selected and constantly used as a polissoir: perhaps an indication of its particular power.

There were many animal bones at Etton, including wild aurochs and deer antler. Particularly fascinating is the evidence for the presence of a horse. Wild horses became extinct in Britain after the Ice Age in the early Mesolithic, although they survived on the Continent. Their bones are vanishingly rare in the British Neolithic (Yarnton in Oxfordshire may also have them). The Etton evidence does not point clearly to a domestic horse – could this be a tamed animal, sent from the Continent as a prestige gift? To possess a horse in the early fourth millennium BC would certainly set the owner apart.

At Windmill Hill, the things that were placed in the ditches varied from the inner to the outer circuit.[34] In the outer ring were human remains, notably infants. In the next ring there was evidence of butchery and animal joints, along with craft activities. The innermost ring seemed to have more everyday, domestic material, although the pots were types more suitable for drinking, such as small bowls, rather than storage. Windmill Hill also seems to have been a place for feasting, animal sacrifice and depositing parts of the dead.

The well-excavated enclosure at Hambledon Hill has a similar repertoire of material in its ditches and pits: flint tools were manufactured, animals butchered, cereals processed, material placed in ritual deposits, and human remains defleshed, taken apart and buried. The remains of cattle, which dominated the bones, suggest several were slaughtered and cooked at once. Several hundred people may have gathered for this great, beefy feast.

Much of the time the site was left empty – silent in the woods, except perhaps for scavenging foxes, the jays, the buzzards and the gathering crows.[35]

The discovery of exotic materials, such as polished axe heads from Cornwall and Langdale, led to the suggestion that causewayed enclosures were places created primarily as centres for trade and exchange. However, as the axes are mostly worn and were left at the site this seems illogical. Interestingly, however, the tor enclosure of Carn Brea lies close to an axe-head production centre, and the two possible Neolithic enclosures at Green How and Carrock Fell are not only on routes to the north and east, within 30 km (18 miles) of the Langdale factories, but also adjacent to a recently discovered axe quarry at White Crag.[36] These particular sites may have played a role in the redistribution of axe heads.

The flood of new dating information indicates that major innovations took place in the span of a lifetime. For example, Windmill Hill's successive ditches were dug possibly over twenty to fifty-five years; the four circuits at Whitehawk Camp on Whitehawk Hill, East Sussex, took about half a century to a century – both projects perhaps within a single lifetime. Some enclosures took longer, such as Hambledon Hill, but this complex site may have evolved into something other than a conventional causewayed enclosure.

Reconstruction drawing of Whitehawk Camp, East Sussex, a causewayed camp or interrupted ditch enclosure, showing the multiple entrances and concentric earthwork enclosures.

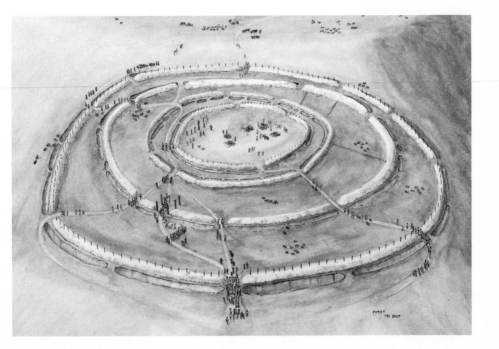

Other enclosures were in use for a surprisingly brief period, such as Abingdon, although the quantity of material such as pottery and animal bone deposited in pits and ditches indicates that large numbers of people must have congregated there during its heyday. At Hambledon Hill, the prolific number of butchered cattle bones suggests gatherings of many hundreds. When Don Benson and I mapped the upper Thames Valley we noted that several causewayed enclosures were sited relatively close together. These have not been excavated or dated. However, if, like Abingdon, they were short-lived, this may explain their frequency in the region. While individual sites could be short-lived, lasting less than a human lifetime, some, such as Windmill Hill, Etton and Hambledon, were probably in use for more than two centuries, and the currency of this monumental tradition as a whole lasted approximately 450 years.

At this stage of the Neolithic, from about 3700 BC, the admittedly low population had grown and dispersed into the countryside. Big houses were no longer the place for family or community gatherings in southern Britain. Long barrows were associated with small clans. A greater diversity of pottery styles suggests that communities were fragmenting, but contacts were widening, as shown by the spread of axes. There is, however, evidence for small-scale violence – individuals and small groups killed with axes and shot with arrows.[37] There was a need to develop ways to bring people together: to form alliances between clans, arrange marriages, settle disputes, and even exchange animals to ensure the viability of the herds and flocks. Communities wanted to establish their primacy in the Neolithic pecking order. Did the importance of clan tombs decline as causewayed enclosures helped to generate wider links?

The adoption of farming in a new country must have thrown up problems requiring new solutions. Some could be borrowed from the Continent – for example, we saw earlier the possibility that Neolithic raids were organized to steal women. This is an activity rare among hunter-gatherers, though frequently seen in small-scale farming communities. Farmers are easy to locate and have vulnerable stores and herds; they are worth attacking. Men who attack other humans, rather than animals, become warriors and gain status. They defend their community from their own kind, not because they are stronger than women, but because men are dispensable (especially in small, scattered communities). One bull goes a long way in the herd! Ironically, the male warrior role served to put women in an inferior position, socially vulnerable under male protection and landed with the most tedious, least prestigious and least gratifying jobs. When infanticide was practised, and it often was, then girls were most frequently the victims (and remain so today).

For farmers, warfare threatens production. Societies respond by either seeking peace through alliances or by creating alliances that give them regional dominance. Perhaps causewayed enclosures were places where people came together to form such alliances, at the personal and wider level: to expand the community, control reproduction and achieve a precarious equilibrium. Sacrifices, feasting, offerings and gift exchange would be part of the process. These enclosures do not seem to have been 'central places', but lie between areas of Neolithic settlement. Some, like Haddenham, are sited in woodland clearings. In the upper Thames Valley the enclosures are very obviously sited away from the monumental tombs earlier located on the Cotswold slopes and plateaus. This makes sense. As at the original Olympic Games, potential enemies and would-be allies should meet on neutral ground. The urban theorist Richard Sennett, looking at locations for urban markets and fairs, suggests placing them between communities to attract people from all sides; do not place them in the heartland of one community, which excludes the rest.

But did this work for Neolithic groups? The answer is 'yes' and 'no'. Relatively few enclosures have been excavated but at several, mostly in the West Country, there is very clear evidence that they were attacked with storms of arrows. Crickley Hill in Gloucestershire and Hambledon Hill in Dorset are two especially prominent enclosures, dominating the landscape from high ground. Both changed their character, becoming strongholds, defended with timber breastworks and gateways. In about 3450 BC a body of warriors armed with bows attacked Crickley Hill. Clouds of arrows descended on the defenders, clattering against the ramparts, where the flint arrowheads were found by the excavators. The attackers were successful and burnt down the enclosure.[38]

Hambledon Hill was built around 3690–3640 BC. At first, the pattern of ritual depositions and feasting was as normal. Then after fifty years or so the site was strengthened. This seems to have been done quickly. The hilltop defences included an earthwork over 1.25 km (¾ mile) long, ramparts and a reinforced gateway. Although there is not such clear evidence of a major attack as at Crickley Hill, nevertheless, there are traces of burning, and about 3400 BC an arrow pierced and killed a man carrying a child. The burning rampart collapsed on both their bodies.[39]

The excavator of Hambledon Hill, Roger Mercer, also investigated the tor enclosure at Carn Brea in western Cornwall.[40] Here a 2-m (6-ft) thick wall of granite enclosed the hilltop, with blocks weighing several tonnes closing the gaps between natural stone outcrops. Unusually, there was evidence for wooden buildings and these had been burnt. Across the site there were about eight hundred leaf-shaped arrowheads (these are distinctly Neolithic and some commentators say that they are ideal for warfare rather than hunting). The arrows were concentrated around the entrance and many were burnt in the conflagration.

If causewayed enclosures began by celebrating the dead and promoting alliances among the living it may be that their success led to some groups becoming dominant and aggressive. The increasingly defensive (or offensive?) nature of places like Crickley Hill suggests that either they themselves posed a threat to their neighbours, or the occupants were planning to resist the aggression of others. The result was pre-emptive attack or outright aggression from more powerful groups. It is possible that many causewayed enclosures saw out their lives peaceably and their occupants did not turn places of assembly, commemoration, feasting and alliance into fortifications. However, not for the first, and certainly not for the last, time, colonizing a new land was proving to be a bloody business, a matter of life and death. The battle of Crickley Hill marks the end of the early Neolithic.

CHAPTER FIFTEEN
# Sacred landscapes: Pilgrims and pathways

## Starting at Stonehenge

Readers who have a general knowledge of prehistory may well be asking themselves: Where does Stonehenge come into all this? In Chapter 10, I described Mesolithic activity in the Stonehenge area that showed that hunter-gatherers inhabited this landscape and even erected several enigmatic large posts in it. When farmers arrived, they constructed seven earthen long barrows – none of which has been scientifically excavated, although most of them have been prodded, poked and pillaged by antiquarians. Today the most visible of them squats dolefully at the eponymous Longbarrow Crossroads by the main A303 road to London, its long deep silence now rattled by passing traffic.

There are also a dozen or more oval barrows in the Stonehenge landscape – burial mounds belonging to the fourth millennium BC. So far there are no obvious early houses or settlements, although the Neolithic inhabitants of the area did leave one unusual feature: a large pit, which archaeologists named the Coneybury Anomaly, filled with the debris of a gargantuan feast. The leftovers included bones from ten domestic cattle, pigs and roe and red deer. The bones represent both an orgy of meat-eating and a Neolithic calling card. Interestingly, however, the farmers were supplementing their domestic animals with the call of the wild. Many of the bones were from young animals – fawns and calves born in the spring – which suggests the great feast took place in the summer. Some of the debris, including forty small pottery bowls and a large cooking vessel, were collected up and buried in this pit on Coneybury Hill. The 'Anomaly' is not well dated (a single radiocarbon date), although the style of the pottery indicates that the feast and the pit are about the earliest evidence we have of Neolithic activity in the vicinity of Stonehenge.

Rather more obvious in its impact on this landscape is Robin Hood's Ball, a causewayed enclosure that was listed by Curwen in 1930 and then carefully mapped by Stuart Piggott. Piggott distinguished two oval concentric circuits of ditches on high ground overlooking Stonehenge Bottom, a tributary valley of the River Avon. Small-scale excavation in 1956 recovered, among the locally made pottery, vessels of gabbroic clay from the Lizard Peninsula in Cornwall, 270 km (168 miles) to the west. Clearly, contacts with the far west went back a long way in the Stonehenge area. The local community exerted itself even more dramatically with the construction of the so-called Lesser Cursus and the more impressive Stonehenge Cursus, built in the mid to later fourth millennium BC. An antler pick from the bottom of the ditch provided a date of 3660–3370 BC. This was an escalation in the human determination to make marks on the land.

Early visitors to Stonehenge were not always impressed with what they saw. Samuel Pepys, the great diarist, commented after seeing the stones on 11 June 1668, 'God knows what their use was.' Several decades later, William Stukeley was determined to find out. It was Stukeley who firmly planted the idea of Druids at Stonehenge in the public imagination. Born in 1687, Stukeley studied law and medicine. A friend of Isaac Newton, he was a man of his time, part rationalist and a keen observer, but also still attracted to the irrational and the magical. And, of course, he had no concept of deep time. Nevertheless, for five seasons 'he walked and rode, measured and pondered'[1] the landscapes of Stonehenge and Avebury, at a time when the modern plough had not scoured and planed away many of the traces of prehistoric earthworks.

In August 1723, Stukeley recognized an enormous, long, straight avenue running east–west to the north of Stonehenge. This was formed by chalk-cut ditches 2.9 km (1¾ miles) long and up to 150 m (490 ft) apart. This oddly symmetrical construction reminded Stukeley of a racecourse, 'a fine design for the purpose of running' – a hippodrome for the 'games, feasts, exercises and sports of the ancient holy days'. So he named it the 'Cursus', from the Latin for a racecourse, and in so doing established a new class of Neolithic monument. Stukeley was prescient. He was at pains, he wrote, to 'perpetuate the vestiges of this celebrated wonder and of the barrows, avenues, cursus etc for I foresee that it will in a few years be universally plowd over and consequently defaced'.[2]

How right he was. Slight traces of the cursus remain but its line is now maintained and visible as a mown path in the grass with a gap cut in the plantation of trees at its western end to mark the line of its passage. In 2013, English Heritage published a very fine map entitled *Exploring the World Heritage Site: Stonehenge and Avebury* (at a 1:10,000 scale). This illustrates how boldly the cursus cuts, almost precisely east–west, across what was to evolve into Stonehenge's sacred landscape. Cursus monuments, according to the *Gathering Time* project, are 'notoriously difficult to date due to the paucity of associated material of any kind'.[3] It seems probable, however, that this type of monument began to appear in the 36th century BC and had a relatively long lifespan. Their appearance represents a radical new way of altering the earth and probably a means of participating in innovative rituals within monuments, some of which were built on a stunning scale.

It is easy to underestimate the scale of this undertaking because the cursus now appears so slight. In fact, its construction involved the removal of more than 7,000 cubic m (247,200 cubic ft) of chalk and about 40,000 person-hours of labour – say 20 people for 250 days in total.[4] This great avenue terminates in the east on a long barrow, Amesbury 42, unfortunately now scarcely visible. Nevertheless, the presence of the already venerable barrow must have influenced the siting of the cursus itself. There were other barrows in the area, but perhaps this one was particularly significant – or it fitted into the solar alignment.

The Stonehenge Cursus stops on the Amesbury 42 long barrow, but if its line is projected, it runs through the Cuckoo Stone – a natural slab of sarsen once elevated as a small megalith. The projected line then continues to Woodhenge, a monument of concentric timbers within a circular ditch, which sits just above the River Avon. We will return to this area later. However, already we can see the increasing complexity of the Stonehenge ceremonial landscape: a place where the past was curated and linked by sight lines and pathways, where over a period of two thousand years or more people constantly manipulated old monuments and created new ones in a shifting theatre of ritual actions.

Inevitably, the focus of most visitors at Stonehenge is on the circle of massive stones. These were late arrivals in the evolving cycles of stone shifting and earth moving. However, since 2003, the Stonehenge Riverside Project led by Mike Parker Pearson of University College, London, has dramatically transformed our understanding of Stonehenge and its wider landscape (see Chapter 17). In fact, the stone circles we see today were late arrivals in the evolving cycles of earth moving and stone shifting. The first project on the Stonehenge site itself, about 3000 BC, was the construction of an enclosure formed of disconnected pits similar to those in a causewayed camp. This earthwork consisted of an outer bank, the segmented ditch and an inner bank. Inside this there was a circle of pits, now known as the Aubrey Holes, from John Aubrey, the 17th-century antiquarian and gossipy author of *Brief Lives*, who first recorded them. It now seems these pits may have originally held bluestone uprights brought from the Preseli Hills of Pembrokeshire.

Cremation burials were also placed around the site and in the Aubrey Holes – probably gathered in bags closed fast with bone pins.

Stonehenge has had a chequered history of investigation. There is no doubt that excavations and recording in the past left much to be desired. Recent analysis and small-scale investigation of older excavations show that some of the cremations were primary burials from around 2950 BC, the others inserted after the bluestones had been removed from the pits. Mike Parker Pearson guesstimates that there could have been as many as 150 burials in total in the early phase of Stonehenge – that is to say, its first five hundred years – but with most of them being buried towards the end of that time, around 2500–2300 BC.[5] In other words, a small kin group or family initiated the use of the cemetery, then as the clan grew in numbers more and more people were eligible for burial as members of this prestigious lineage.

Outside the circle there was a line of standing stones, the most distant of which was aligned on the midsummer solstice sunrise for someone standing in the centre of the circle. This view was possible because by 3000 BC many of the trees in the landscape were gone and grass downland now predominated, grazed by cattle.

So by 3000 BC, Stonehenge was a special place, one which echoed the past, evoked distant places and predicted the future cosmological cycle. It was also a place that was constantly changing and to which we will return. For the next fifteen hundred years there would be a choreography of stones unlike anywhere else in Britain.

## The view from the air

Inevitably, we are drawn to Stonehenge. Aside from the spectacular stones themselves and the encircling burial mounds, it was here that cursus monuments were first recognized. But Neolithic Britain and Ireland are rich in unique Neolithic places, even though many of them have only reappeared recently thanks to aerial photography.[6]

The potential of aerial photography was recognized during World War I, although the military brass were slow to take advantage of it. One person who did appreciate the possibilities was O. G. S. Crawford. He had originally applied to join the Royal Flying Corps but was turned down because he could not ride a horse! Instead, in the summer of 1915 he was on the Somme in a unit responsible for map-making: plotting the up-to-date positions of enemy lines. To facilitate this, Crawford would climb ruined church towers and chimney tops in order to photograph the battleground from on high. He then discovered aerial photographs taken of the Front by the Royal Flying Corps and successfully applied to join the RFC as an observer. Unfortunately, on his first flight, German Fockers attacked his plane and a bullet smashed through his foot.

In spite of his experiences in the Great War, Crawford remained an optimist, a devotee of H. G. Wells, with a belief in the future and the value of studying the past. While convalescing he began to write a book that was published in 1921 as *Man and His Past*. 'The archaeologist's work may seem tedious', he wrote, but 'he travels through time upon the magic carpet of imagination'. In 1927 Crawford started his own journal, *Antiquity*, helped by a loan from Alexander Keiller, the upstart marmalade millionaire. This was an exciting time for archaeology. Spectacular discoveries – Tutankhamun's tomb, Leonard Woolley's excavations at Ur and Arthur Evans's revelations of Minoan Crete – excited the public imagination. Stuart Piggott, Gordon Childe and Grahame Clark, the 'young Turks' of the 1920s, were all regular contributors to *Antiquity*.

Crawford was not himself an excavator; aerial photography provided him with a wider view of the landscape. He hit the news by revealing the line of the Stonehenge Avenue, and in 1928 he published *Wessex from the Air*, showcasing the revelatory and beautiful images that he captured thanks to Keiller's support. Keiller was also a pilot and he put up the money to hire a plane equipped with a fine camera that had been captured from the Germans. They then photographed southern England – from Berkshire to Dorset – checked their discoveries on the ground and mapped them. This was pioneering work that transformed the focus of archaeology from individual sites to extensive landscapes. Crawford called his photographs 'heralds of innumerable queer resurrections'. Kitty Hauser writes: 'The aerial archaeologist has to be in the right place at the right time; he is a geomancer in collusion with the sun, the weather and the crops in the field'.[7]

One of the most successful geomancers, inspired by Crawford, was Major George Allen. He was the wealthy head of an engineering firm based in Cowley, near Oxford, who owned his own plane, which he parked nearby so that he could take to the air as soon as the conditions were right. Allen depended upon no one else: he flew the plane, navigated and took the photographs. The Thames Valley was on his doorstep – this was relatively flat, fertile ground that had been ploughed for centuries. On the chalk downland, Crawford and others discovered the power of shadows. In low winter sun the slight earthworks of causewayed enclosures, such as Windmill Hill, were exaggerated by the slanting light. They stood out even better if there was a light dusting of snow. On the arable lands of the upper Thames, Allen relied on a different phenomenon. There were very few upstanding earthworks thanks to the scouring impact of the plough. However, beneath the ground lay the lines of infilled ditches. These provided a richer and often damper mulch for the penetrating roots of barley and wheat than the surrounding shallow, well-drained soils. The result was that, over ancient sites, cropmarks appeared – lines where the cereals grew taller and ripened slowly. Green lines in the crop announced the presence of previously invisible ancient sites, Crawford's 'queer resurrection'.

Allen had discovered an unexplored ancient world. He wrote in 1933: 'I have been overwhelmed with air work. The whole of the Thames Valley and its tributaries have come out in a violent rash, circles and marks everywhere.' Among his discoveries were ritual prehistoric landscapes at Stanton Harcourt and Dorchester-on-Thames. Stonehenge and Avebury were not alone. Neolithic and later prehistoric people had marked and transformed almost the entire British landscape.

I diverted to the subject of aerial photography in order to explore further the locations and distribution of cursuses. The Stonehenge cursuses were the first to be recognized, but they are not the only examples of the phenomenon, nor the earliest to be built.

### The Dorchester-on-Thames ritual complex

In the 1930s, Major Allen photographed a remarkable collection of Neolithic and Bronze Age monuments around Dorchester-on-Thames. The most striking feature was a huge henge monument, given the name 'the Big Rings'. Henge monuments are a class of archaeological site named after Stonehenge, but the name is confusing. Stonehenge is literally 'the hanging stones' because of its five enormous trilithons (pairs of upright stones with horizontal stone lintels joining them across the top). These are unique in Britain. Most henges, in fact, consist of a ditch forming an oval or circular enclosure, with an external (so non-defensive) bank. There are many very small henges, and a few very large ones, such as the largest of all at Avebury. Some, like Avebury, contain circles of standing stones but only Stonehenge has the 'hanging stones'.

PREVIOUS PAGE ABOVE  The facade of the passage grave of Newgrange, County Meath. The roof box above the entrance allows the sun's rays to reach the interior at midwinter. Blocking the entrance is a great stone carved with spirals and lozenge decoration.

PREVIOUS PAGE BELOW  Deep in the interior of the Newgrange tomb, the midwinter sunlight reflects on the spiral decoration carved into an upright stone.

OPPOSITE Excavation of the Ness of Brodgar, Orkney, with its well-preserved Neolithic stone structures on the peninsula between the Loch of Harray and the Loch of Stenness.

ABOVE The Stones of Stenness, Orkney. Part of the ritual landscape which includes the Ring of Brodgar and the Maeshowe chambered tomb. The stones demonstrate the clean, angular shapes typical of Orkney's Old Red Sandstone.

OPPOSITE ABOVE  The Neolithic
long barrow of Wayland's Smithy,
Oxfordshire. Beneath this great
barrow lay an earlier burial
chamber containing victims of a
raid. The entrace facade of sarsen
stones is similar to that at West
Kennet (see page 273).

OPPOSITE BELOW  The Neolithic
cairn of Hazleton North,
Gloucestershire, under excavation.
The burial passages and chambers
are midway along the long axis.

BELOW  Aerial view of the three great
henges at Thornborough, Yorkshire.
The most northerly, in the distance,
lies in the circle of trees.

LEFT  The gold cup from Rillaton, Cornwall. This distinctive Bronze Age handled cup reveals a maritime Channel network of exchange and communication along the south coast of Britain and into the Continent.

BELOW LEFT  Similar in fashion to the Rillaton Cup, the Ringlemere Cup was found in 2001 by a metal detectorist at the opposite end of the maritime network, in Kent.

OPPOSITE ABOVE
Stonehenge under a dusting of snow which highlights the earthwork enclosure surrounding the great stones. Beyond the stones the parallel lines of the Avenue are visible, running northeast before curving southeast toward the River Avon.

OPPOSITE BELOW  The timber circle of Holme-next-the-Sea, Norfolk, popularly known as Seahenge. The outer ring forms a continuous wall of oak, with an inverted oak bole in the centre. Beyond there are dark traces of the peat which once blanketed and preserved the monument before the sea encroached upon it.

Silbury Hill, Wiltshire, prehistoric
Europe's largest mound, rises above the
water which fills the quarry from which
much of the mound was dug.

Access into henges was usually controlled through one or two entrances so it is assumed that the rituals that took place on the inside were screened from the outside. The larger ones are also often sited so that the landscape beyond is invisible from the inside. Participants may have felt that they were enclosed within their own cosmology: a universe defined by the great circular banks and the sky above.

Around the Big Rings, Allen photographed a rash of smaller, mostly mortuary monuments. The most 'queer resurrection' was an almost straight pair of parallel lines that passed close by the Big Rings, on its east side, running northwest–southeast for about 1,700 m (1,800 yd), parallel to the River Thames and towards its confluence with the Thame. We now know that Dorchester-on-Thames was a virtual 'cursus central', with at least five of these monuments relatively close together, and nine near the River Thames between Lechlade and Goring.

The Stanwell/Heathrow cursus, which lay beneath Heathrow airport – rather like a prehistoric runway – was investigated in 1998–99.[8] Its parallel ditches have been traced from the River Poyle, across the River Colne, for 3.6 km (2¼ miles) before disappearing under modern Stanwell. The Stanwell/Heathrow ditches were only 20 m (65 ft) apart and in the central zone contained an earthen bank. For this reason it is sometimes classed as a 'bank barrow' rather than a cursus. The two classes of monument shade into each other. The bank-barrow construction provided an elevated internal platform, perhaps for display. Observers standing near to the River Colne would see those processing along the raised bank silhouetted against the horizon in the east.

Richard Bradley has suggested that we should look to Scotland for the origins of this innovation – where the land was first marked with elongated extensions of either the house or long-barrow forms.[9] At Douglasmuir, Angus, for example, a rectangular enclosure 65 × 20 m (213 × 65 ft) was formed of massive timbers up to 1 m (3 ft) in diameter. At Holywood North and Holywood South, two cursuses (400 m/1,300 ft and 285 m/935 ft long respectively) ran between the River Nith and a tributary. As well as banks and ditches these monuments were defined by lines of timber posts – destroyed by fire like so many early Neolithic structures in Scotland. There is, however, a problem with dating these sites – most of their radiocarbon dates come from old wood samples. (Big oak timbers can be a century or more old when they are incorporated into a monument and so will provide older dates than the actual time of construction).[10]

As a class of monuments, cursuses are not well dated throughout Britain. However, in several cases such as at Etton (see Chapter 14), they cut across earlier causewayed enclosures and we are probably not far off in putting their origins a little before 3500 BC; the Stonehenge and Drayton cursuses are perhaps as early as 3550 BC. It seems that in the mid fourth millennium BC the ceremonial focus shifted from causewayed enclosures to these dramatic, long processional ways.

Up to now, the Continent had provided the inspiration for the British Neolithic – its animals and plants, houses and halls, tombs and causewayed enclosures. With the cursus, for the first time, the British had produced a creation of their own, a genuinely insular monument. But why build elongated ditched enclosures, some with no obvious entrance, some a couple of hundred metres long, others up to 4 km (2½ miles), and the largest of all, the Dorset Cursus, 10 km (6 miles) long? Stukeley gave these things a name, in Latin admittedly, but the problem remains, what was the cursus for? The Dutch travel writer Cees Nooteboom said of churches: 'The silent and usually cold building starts to bombard you with messages. That's the symbolic side, which was as clear as crystal to medieval man.'[11] The meaning of the cursus must have been obvious to Neolithic people, but five thousand years of silence is a difficult gap to bridge. However, while the causewayed enclosure evidence suggests many groups indulged in their own feasts, sacrifices and ceremonies in a somewhat anarchic way, the cursuses indicate control and direction, and a more ordered ceremonial setting.

Julian Thomas pointed out that the Dorchester Cursus 'represents an unusually large investment of effort, joining two separate groups of (earlier) monuments together and imposing a spatial ordering upon them all' and 'a massive manifestation of corporate labour'.[12] Is this what they are about? A way of emphasizing the ancestral collective by drawing a line around ancient monuments already sitting in the landscape? Some archaeologists have suggested that the cursus formalized an existing pathway. Others have speculated that it was the work that mattered – the ongoing collective effort of ditch digging – to bind people together and to their past.

The linearity of cursuses also suggests processions – controlled walking across the landscape – often between and past earlier tombs. However, a construction wider than a modern motorway or airport runway is no mere path. Were these lines for the living or did they connect the souls of the dead? The Dorchester-on-Thames sacred complex continued to attract its adherents.

Around 160 cremations were buried in the earlier third millennium BC, several centuries after the construction of the cursus and the deliberate burning of a timber circle within it, then perhaps in the mid third millennium (the dating is imprecise) the Big Rings henge monument was built alongside the cursus to the west. Like Stonehenge, Dorchester was an ongoing project. Across the country there were many others, from Maxey in East Anglia to Catholme on the rivers Trent and Thame (Staffordshire), to Blackhouse Burn in the upper Clyde valley.

Also like Stonehenge, Dorchester-on-Thames was a major focus of ritual activity where, over many centuries, burial sites and monuments were built, destroyed and manipulated on a flat stretch of gravel terrace by the confluence of the Thames and the Thame. The remarkable cluster of cursuses in the area may be explained by the presence and attraction of the Dorchester complex itself. However, I suspect that the Neolithic ritual landscape was very much bigger. It has all the features of a sanctuary that draws people from afar. These elements occur from Delphi in ancient Greece to Mecca in the present day. The type of place that Mircea Eliade has termed 'hierophanies' – a location where the other world of gods and ancestors communicate with the living.[13]


## Watching the pilgrims

Universally, mythology is anchored in geography. Pausanias acts as a guide to ancient Greece, describing how shrines at Delphi, Dodona and Olympia were conduits to the gods, who spoke through the oracles, the rustling of trees and the entrails of sacrificed animals. From modest beginnings these places became famous throughout the Greek world and retain their magnetism today, even if the motivations and expectations of visitors have changed. Across the world, monuments do not exist in isolation, in the middle of nowhere, they are places that are linked by social practices and by pathways. Once they exist, they attract people, rituals, objects and continued building projects.

One Sunday morning, I sat for several hours in a plaza in front of a miraculous stone wedding cake. Many Spanish churches are austere, harsh and tough. Yet, when they set their minds to it, Spanish stonemasons can make stone seem to melt. The Cathedral of Santiago de Compostela reaches heavenward like peaks of icing sugar and draws people from afar.

For the pilgrim, the journey is as important as the arrival. The point about Santiago de Compostela is that it does not stand alone – it is the hub of a network of churches, monasteries and shrines linked by a network of paths known as the Camino de Santiago. From the Pyrenees, these paths radiate across France, like the image of a hand, the fingers leading through scores of other important religious sites. The pilgrim is not starved of spiritual sustenance and stimulation on the long trek – there are oases in the form of magnificent Romanesque churches, such as Vézelay in Burgundy and Saint-Guilhem-Le-Désert and Saint-Gilles in Languedoc. Some shrines, such as Mont Saint-Michel and Le Puy, stand atop spectacular natural phenomena. These are places of local pilgrimage and worship in their own right, but they are also links in the pathways on which pilgrims have flowed incessantly across Europe for centuries.

Today, probably the most impressive and complex sacred geography survives in India, where the remarkable mythosphere of interconnected shrines, tombs, caves, hilltops and rivers can be traced back at least two thousand years. However, the concept of the land as the fragmented body of the goddess is far older, pervasive and accepted by many creeds. Some of the most ancient sites of Indian pilgrimage mark fords or river crossings, and many sacred sites are on rivers at confluences. These are also places of spiritual crossing, where the gods are close.[14]

Does this help to make sense of the sacred geography of Neolithic Britain? If we look at Dorchester-on-Thames, the burial monuments, cursuses and henges – large and small – are clearly associated with the rivers, at a crossing point. The ford was first made archaeologically visible when the Romans built a fort there and their road (the main road to Silchester/Calleva Atrebatum) across the Thames, alongside a distinctive pair of hills, the twin mounds of Wittenham Clumps, which dominate the Thames Valley and are visible for miles.

What is remarkable is the sheer quantity of Neolithic sacred monuments in the area. If Dorchester was the focus and principal theatre of religious activity, then there were many lesser places close by, satellite cursuses both up and down the river that reflect the river's direction of flow. For Neolithic people, water and the rivers were not just arteries of communication, but sacred beings, bringers of life and channels in which to place the dead. The cursuses around Dorchester-on-Thames provide avenues alongside the river that then lead to the ceremonial focal points. Like the Stonehenge cursuses, they embrace or focus on older monuments and attract new ones.

These cursuses imply that there had been a major effort of tree clearance in the Thames Valley. Excavations at the Drayton Cursus, which is actually two monuments facing each other across a stream, revealed large numbers of tree-throw holes. It is uncertain whether the clearance had already taken place or was part of the construction project. At any rate, fragments of polished flint and greenstone axes were found in and around the Drayton Cursus.[15]

As we move north and west, up the river from Dorchester-on-Thames, there are a series of great ceremonial complexes, usually where tributaries join the main river. At Abingdon/Radley, alongside the causewayed enclosure, there was a Neolithic burial ground, Barrow Hills. An oval barrow containing two flexed bodies and its grave goods had a distinctly Yorkshire connection, such as a belt slider made of Whitby jet. The avenue of large barrows aligned on the Neolithic enclosure belonged to the Bronze Age, showing that, like so many of these places, Barrow Hills retained its significance for centuries, even millennia.

Further up the Thames, at the confluence of the River Windrush, was Devil's Quoits, Stanton Harcourt, the burial place of our polished axe. This large henge monument sat in grassland and was also eventually surrounded by Bronze Age barrows (these were the circles observed so prolifically by Major Allen). The area around the henge was not impinged upon by later prehistoric farmers, who continued to respect the site, until the Middle Ages when Christian farmers, who judging from the name they gave to the monument certainly did not respect the place, began to knock over the ring of megaliths and bury the stones in the furrows of their new strip fields. The process was continued by the Ministry of Defence during World War II – the remaining stones were bulldozed in order to lay out an aerodrome. Following excavation, Oxford Archaeology and the owners of the gravel quarry that operated the site reinstated the surviving stones and reconstructed the surrounding bank and ditch. So the Thames Valley now has a 'new' henge monument (see page 13).[16]

As we continue up the Thames, beyond Stanton Harcourt, there is yet another ceremonial site at Lechlade where a pair of cursuses face each other across the river, again attracting clusters of barrows. Anyone familiar with the geography of the upper Thames Valley might well ask, 'What about the Cherwell confluence?' This is the site of the city of Oxford so not easily accessible to prehistorians. Nevertheless, in 1976, England experienced a '*canicule*' – a heatwave – which parched the normally lush lawns of Oxford. In the University Parks distinct large circles appeared. For the first time, the traces of a major Bronze Age barrow cemetery could be seen. Since then, excavations beneath the Ashmolean's Sackler Library have found another barrow and the ditch of a henge monument near Keble College, just across the road from the University Parks. So Oxford is, in fact, built on top of a major Neolithic/ Bronze Age ceremonial complex.

We have just followed the Thames upstream. It is possible that each of these cursus/henge/barrow complexes marks the territory of a distinct group of prehistoric people, like parish churches in the landscape today, but perhaps they also mark lines of communication along the river – people moving with animals or as pilgrims along a sacred routeway. It is worth noting that there is another possible route along the Thames that diverts up the valley of the River Kennet. That route would take us to Avebury – Stonehenge's rival or companion in sheer scale. If instead, we continue northwards into the interior of Britain we find similar ceremonial or sacred complexes along other rivers such as the Nene, the Ouse and the Trent.[17] These rivers were major lines of communication. At Etton-Maxey, where we observed the well-preserved causewayed enclosure (see Chapter 14), a cursus 2 km (1¼ miles) long ran between two rivers. The cursus, long enclosures and late long barrows represent segments of these routes. As in the Thames Valley, the cursuses here seem to formalize what may have been existing pathways and processionary lines along the river and across confluences and fording points.[18]

The sanctity of the River Thames and others is reflected in the many ritual deposits – stone axes, Neolithic pots, human remains and later metal weapons – that were routinely placed in the water. I do not wish to give the impression that the Neolithic had some fixed ritual guidebook. There do, however, seem to be common ideas at work, interpreted with great variety and subtlety by different communities in different landscapes. The sacred complexes, sited on a network of trackways, must have helped in the mediation of inter-community issues, of alliances, exchange and conflict. If causewayed camps operated at the local and even regional level, these later complexes of cursuses and then henges seem to indicate an even wider network of contacts. It would be surprising if the later Neolithic in Britain became a peaceable place, yet there are fewer cases of violence apparent in the archaeological record.

## Beyond Stonehenge

Archaeologists have often chosen to focus on the prehistory of Wessex, but these sacred landscapes take us much further afield. For example, the Walton Basin lies on the borders of Powys and Herefordshire. Here there are two cursuses, Hindwell and Walton, about 1.6 km (1 mile) apart and separated by two streams. A stone circle close to the Hindwell Cursus probably dates to the third millennium BC. A massive oval palisaded enclosure (the Hindwell enclosure), 800 m (2,600 ft) across, was built in the late Neolithic about 2800–2500 BC. Another impressive enclosure between the two streams is demarcated by huge post pits. There is a similar complex in the valley bottom at West Kennet, on the edge of the Avebury complex. Little is known about the purpose of these impressive sites, but in the later Neolithic the Walton Basin, in what has previously been regarded a backwater, rivals Wessex in the scale of its monuments.

Further north in Yorkshire there is another impressive complex of sites. Once I gained the disapproval of some of my southern colleagues by claiming at a conference that the Thornborough Henges (see page 301) were as important as Stonehenge. At the time, these henges were threatened by gravel extraction, which should be inconceivable in a civilized society. So a certain amount of hyperbole was, I think, forgivable. In Yorkshire, God's own county, my claim was regarded, of course, as just plain common sense.

The Thornborough monuments are seriously impressive and would have been even more so five thousand years ago. They sit in a broad valley, north of York, which separates the Yorkshire Dales in the west from the North Yorkshire Moors in the east and the Yorkshire Wolds in the southeast. The valley is formed principally by the River Swale and the River Ure, which both curve to the west and form natural routeways. They take us into the Lake District and the Cumbrian sources of greenstone axes.

Along a 12-km (7½-mile) section of the valley there are no fewer than six large henge monuments – three at Thornborough and others at Nunwick, Hutton Moor and Cana Barn – their double entrances aligned along the axis of the valley. The three at Thornborough are almost identical, evenly spaced in a straight line aligned northwest–southeast. One cursus runs adjacent to the Northern Henge on the same axis; a second runs beneath and so predates the Central Henge, at right angles to the River Ure. By the Southern Henge there is an avenue of pits. As usual, there is a collection of barrows – or rather ring-ditches, as they have been ploughed flat. Recent excavation shows that the three henges were constructed together, as a single concept, about 2800 BC.[19]

Jan Harding, the excavator, has emphasized the importance of this routeway, particularly in relation to the distribution of Cumbrian axes into Yorkshire. Following the Ure southwards towards the confluence with the Swale there are several further henges and, nearby, the massive alignment of megaliths known as the Devil's Arrows. Moving northwards upriver, the Swale turns to the west at Catterick where there is another henge monument, and a massive timber enclosure dated to 2580–2480 BC, discovered in 2007.[20] On the north bank of the Swale is yet another (the Scorton) cursus.

Even further west along the Swale is a small henge known as Maiden Castle, which takes us close to the watershed with the River Eden and what may have been an important Neolithic routeway across the Pennines and into Cumbria, though the valley of the River Ure, Wensleydale, also provides a direct more southerly route into the core area of Langdale axe production. If we pursue the route back to the source of the axes, in the Eden Valley, there are further significant places – the stone circles of Grey Croft and Castlerigg and the henge monument at Mayburgh. It is at places like this where the Cumbrian axes may have first changed hands in their journey around Britain.[21]

This string of monumental centres provides us with some of the most compelling evidence for long-distance Neolithic routeways in Britain (a distance of about 70 km/45 miles from Maiden Castle, via Catterick and Thornborough to the Devil's Arrows). This route would explain the quantity of Cumbrian axes that have been found in Yorkshire, particularly on the chalk uplands, the Wolds, where the farming population was relatively high.[22]

Engraving, 1725, showing the megaliths known as the Devil's Arrows in Yorkshire.

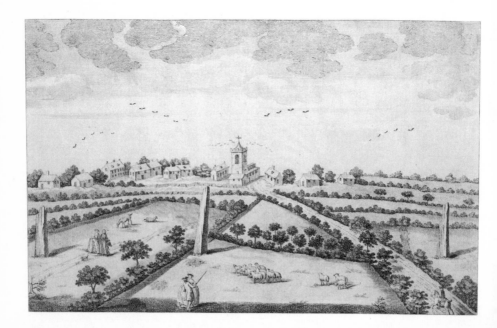

It is interesting to consider why the Thornborough cult centre developed in this area. The most obvious functional reason is that it lies on a band of Magnesian Limestone, which runs from Nottinghamshire in the English Midlands to the River Tees in the northeast and provides a natural routeway that avoids the fragmented uplands of the Pennines to the west and the forested floodplain to the east. From this north–south route there are branches to the east coast along the Humber and into the well-populated Yorkshire Wolds along the Vale of Pickering to the North Sea. It is from this area (80 km/50 miles away) that most of the Thornborough flint tools arrived. This was the 'Northern Wessex' that attracted antiquarian barrow diggers. It has a spectacular collection of long barrows, mortuary enclosures and early round barrows, and the largest cursus complex in the north at Rudston. The Wolds have a plentiful supply of flint, yet people here valued the greenstone, and perhaps the social, political and religious connections it brought them both with Cumbria and communities further south.

If we continue on this routeway to the south we reach what Aubrey Burl described as 'one of the most astonishing megalithic settings in Western Europe'[23] – the four (possibly five) giant standing stones at Devil's Arrows, Boroughbridge. Beyond this, near to the rivers Wharfe and Aire, lie two more large henges: Newton Kyme and Ferrybridge. This is an incredible sequence of monuments, along what could be called the Neolithic 'great north route'.

Similar sequences can be traced along long-distance routes in Scotland. The Dunragit complex in Dumfries and Galloway, which includes the Droughduil Mound (comparable to Silbury Hill), timber circles and a timber avenue, lies by the side of a Roman road, a medieval droveway, the railway and the modern A75 road. Important historical routeways pass through Meldon Bridge, North Mains and Forteviot. Scotland's recent motorways also seem to be remarkably attracted to Neolithic henges.

But surely the Thornborough Henges – an enormous and spectacular physical undertaking – were more than the prehistoric equivalent of a motorway service station. I prefer to see them as great cult centres, places of pilgrimage and religious worship. People are often initially attracted to places that are naturally numinous, awe-inspiring and mysterious – to mountains, caves, springs, rock outcrops or groves of trees where the spirit world penetrates the mundane. Today, visitors would be hard-pressed to see the mystery in the Thornborough landscape with its modern roads, quarries, intensive agriculture and well-drained fields. Five thousand years ago the place was very different. The routeway ran between mires and peatbogs. In the Celtic language, the name of the River Ure means 'the holy one' and three Cumbrian axes placed in the edge of the marsh were probably gifts to the gods, offerings which reflect the spiritual importance of water.

There is another natural feature that may have both attracted and alarmed Neolithic people. The Thornborough complex lies alongside a geological band of gypsum (calcium sulphate) 3 km (2 miles) wide, a soft Permian rock that runs from Catterick in the north to Doncaster in the south. The gypsum has two particular qualities. The first is that it dissolves and creates dramatic sinkholes that can suddenly appear as the ground collapses. Even today sinkholes can swallow up trees or small buildings. The Thornborough Henges sit in the area most prone to this phenomenon.[24] It would be surprising if Neolithic people were not impressed by the appearance of these gateways into the underworld.

The other important characteristic of gypsum is its sheer whiteness. The henge builders used it to coat their earthworks. The glaring banks must have been spectacular when they were first built, just as in the south of England many of the chalk-covered burial mounds and henge banks also stood out as gleaming white statements in the green landscape. Gypsum is also found with burials and may have symbolized bones, death or perhaps regeneration. At any rate, white was a powerful colour as were black and red, judging from the deliberate use of stone of these colours in other monuments.

In the mid fourth millennium BC, Neolithic farmers created the first, founder monument at Thornborough – a triple-ditched round barrow into which the possibly defleshed remains of two adults and a child were placed. Over the next few centuries Thornborough became one of the great cult centres of northern Britain. As with a number of major ceremonial sites, the sky was as important as the underworld. From the Central Henge the midwinter solstice sunrise appeared in the centre of the entrance. As a site of pilgrimage on a major trail across Neolithic Britain, this was a hub for people to meet, form alliances and exchange or acquire objects such as Langdale axes.

This seems to be a time when there was an unprecedented level of communication and interaction across the British Isles and Ireland. The links were fewer with continental Europe. Instead, Britain was establishing regional networks and even its own insular identity. From Orkney to Wessex, from Yorkshire and Cumbria to the Isle of Man and Ireland, new pathways arranged around pilgrim routes and sacred complexes led to the exchange of ideas, material culture and genes.

CHAPTER SIXTEEN
# If you build it they will come

### The tale of the Boyne: the choreography of the cosmos

The Boyne is a small river with a big reputation. It is a holy river, steeped in mythology. St Patrick lit a fire on a nearby hill to announce the arrival of Christianity; Ireland's Protestants make toasts in 'Boyne water'. Its patron saint is William of Orange, a Dutchman mounted on a white horse like St Iago or St George, favoured by God to suppress Catholics and King James. The Battle of the Boyne, fought on 1 July 1690, was a small affair that looms large in Irish history. The Boyne seems to attract attention.

Five thousand years ago people gathered here and built one of the outstanding groups of megalithic tombs in Europe.[1] Ireland has its fair share of megaliths, thanks to a good supply of natural stone. There are almost fifteen hundred known Neolithic tombs in total. They come in various shapes and sizes: court tombs cluster in the north; wedge tombs in the west. The passage tombs are the most impressive. A belt of large cemeteries, such as Carrowmore, Carrowkeel and Loughcrew, run from County Sligo in the northwest to County Meath in the east, marking the northern edge of Ireland's central lowlands. Such tombs are familiar all along Europe's Atlantic seaboard, from Iberia to Brittany and Orkney. Aside from demonstrating a dexterity with massive stones, the builders also carved abstract designs and symbols on the tombs and orientated them towards significant astronomic alignments. These farming societies may still have been relatively egalitarian, but increasingly we see the signs of an emerging elite, powerful figures who through esoteric knowledge controlled fundamental issues of life, death and fertility; performed seasonal rituals; and encouraged the gatherings of large congregations who came not only from the local area, but also from far afield.

In its short course to the Irish Sea, the Boyne is forced by a ridge of hard rock to loop to the south. Along this ridge, overlooking the Bend of the Boyne, lie the great tombs of Knowth, Newgrange and Dowth, built around 3000 BC.[2] The Irish name for the Bend, Brú na Bóinne, means 'the mansion of Bóinne'. This place reeks of seriously competitive tomb building and perhaps more than anywhere else provides an opportunity to reconstruct Neolithic ritual or liturgy. The stones themselves tell of both near and distant connections. The so-called greywacke was probably quarried a few kilometres to the north; granite and siltstones originated further afield on the coast, 50 km (30 miles) to the north. The most distinctive material is the sparkling, white quartz brought from the Wicklow Mountains, 60 km (35 miles) to the south or from an offshore source. Other tombs, as far away as Loughcrew 40 km (25 miles) distant, are aligned on the centre of Brú na Bóinne and form a network of sacred places linked across the landscape.

The Boyne tombs are massive. Knowth's diameter is 88 m (290 ft) with a mound 10 m (33 ft) high and passages 30 m (100 ft) long. Newgrange and Dowth are similar in size. Small circular tombs spawn around Knowth, a community of the dead huddling together for companionship. Others spread along the ridge to the east between Newgrange and Dowth.

Knowth, the westernmost tomb, has two internal passages. These are precisely aligned so that the rising and setting sun, at the spring and autumn equinoxes, illuminates them. Around the outside of the tomb there are 127 large kerbstones, most of them decorated with carved abstract images. Brú na Bóinne has the largest collection of megalithic carvings in Europe – spirals, zigzag lines, triangles and sinuous curving lines. Around the world

One of the decorated stone basins in the Knowth tomb, County Meath, probably used as a surface on which to grind human bones.

similar patterns tell many stories and deliver different messages: they warn of dangers, bring good luck, promote fertility and ward off evil. The repetitive iconography both here and at other megalithic sites must have conveyed a clear meaning to the Neolithic devotees, like the stained glass windows of medieval churches. At Knowth the pilgrims gathered at the equinoxes to greet the dawn. Access into the tombs was limited, so probably the initiates inside witnessed and announced the good news of the sun's arrival. The congregation then processed clockwise, with the sun's movement, around the tomb and the illustrated frieze of symbols.

Newgrange is aligned with the rising sun at the midwinter solstice, the shortest day. The tomb was skilfully designed so that the midwinter sunrise shone down a roof-box built over the entrance passage (see page 297). This is arguably Neolithic Europe's most dramatic choreography of light. The performance would have lasted for fifteen minutes as a slim shaft of sunlight penetrated the roof-box and then the tomb passage behind. As the sun's rays expanded and illuminated the passage floor, the light arced across and reflected off the passage walls into the high corbelled roof of the inner chamber. In a far recess, the light finally struck the image of a triple spiral, carved into an upright stone. The spiral may have represented the vortex connecting the three tiered worlds of Neolithic cosmology: the passage between the realms of the earth, the underworld and the heavens.[3] Who knows? However, any modern theatre designer would be proud to have pulled off this feat of solar drama.

For the sun to gain entry to the Newgrange tomb those choreographing the ritual had to slide back stone slabs covering the mouth of the roof-box. They then clambered over the massive kerbstone, carved with spirals and sinuous lines, to reach into the passage. While the congregation waited expectantly outside, the privileged or initiates must have entered the tomb so that they could witness the sun's rays strike and vitalize the spiral. Solstices and equinoxes mark the end and the start of seasons – the promise of renewed light and fertility, of rebirth, regeneration and growth. Such events must have loomed large in the annual cycle of early farmers, as they did in later agricultural communities.

To the east of Newgrange the third great tomb of Dowth has been less systematically investigated by archaeologists. Here, on the same day as Newgrange's great morning ceremony, the setting sun illuminated the southernmost of the two passage tombs. The pilgrims gathered there for the final evening ritual. Experiments with sound have found that deep voices reverberate within the tombs. Chanting by the priests could create trance states, and the abstract designs, it has been argued, are the entoptic images generated in the human brain while people are in a state of trance or influenced by psychotropic drugs. Such images are common around the world but are actively interpreted on the basis of specific cultures. The chanting vibrations from the tomb's echo chamber must have also generated a powerful experience for the congregation outside. I once witnessed a Russian Orthodox choir performing Mass in the basement of the cathedral in Odessa. The deep bass voices seemed to make the stones vibrate and ecstatic members of the congregation threw themselves on the stone floor, prostrate and spreadeagled before the altar.

As the Boyne pilgrims progressed around the large site there were a number of places where they stopped to watch and listen. Opposite the western entrance to the Knowth tomb there is a standing stone that is aligned on the axis of the passage. In front of the kerbstone there is a layer of white quartz and black pebbles supporting a stone platform – the ideal place for a celebrant to stand, directly on the line of the equinox sunrise. Adjacent to the tomb entrance there was a scoop in which lay a remarkable object: a conical stone 'sceptre', 25 cm (10 in.) long, carefully carved and remarkably like a phallus. Another similar shaft was placed by the Newgrange tomb entrance. Were these priestly props held aloft as the sun's rays struck? The standing stones would have also cast a long shadow into the passage. The tombs, perhaps representing the earth mother, were penetrated by the shafts of solar light.

The congregation must have been ecstatic, perhaps fuelled by excitement, alcohol, mind-altering drugs and drumming. Pilgrims do not come just from a sense of duty – they usually hope to have a memorable time. Some also hope for cures, or for fertility and good fortune. At Brú na Bóinne devotees may have brought the bones and ashes of the dead for incorporation into the sites of the ancestors.

Some of the most impressive objects in any of the tombs are massive stone basins. There are three of them at Knowth, placed in the eastern and western tombs, four at Newgrange and one at Dowth. One that was found in the small passage tomb, Newgrange Z, contained human remains. The most spectacular example was found by the distinguished Irish archaeologist, George Eogan, when he excavated the tomb recess at the end of Knowth's eastern passage (see page 316). This massive basin is rather like a baptismal font but, more probably, performed as a mortar where human bones and ashes could be ground to powder. David Lewis-Williams and David Pearce suggest that the designs on the basin represent the tiers of the cosmos linked by the vortex of the concentric circles that provided a routeway between the levels of under-world, earth and sky – so the basins were vehicles that allowed the dead to move to a new level of the cosmos.[4]

The art and architecture of the tombs promoted religious experiences, beliefs and practice, which at the same time brought clans and groups together in communal festivals orchestrated around the movement of the sun and the annual drama of life and death, dark and light, resurrection and growth.

From Knowth, there is a mace head that is a masterpiece of flint carving, with spirals, lozenges and an abstract human face. There are remarkably similar objects found in megalithic tombs in Portugal and in Orkney's great ceremonial centre. This mace, which seems to be a symbol of status similar to the famous Bush Barrow mace buried near Stonehenge, was concealed under a layer of shale in front of the stone basin in the eastern chamber at Knowth. George Eogan believes that the burial of the mace head may have been part of a dedicatory ceremony for the great tomb. So did the mace head represent political power? The spiral carved onto it is a much-repeated religious symbol. It is possible that for the first time we are seeing the emergence of priest-kings. As Lewis-Williams and Pearce have said, 'Politics and religion went hand in hand'. This would not be the last time in Europe that the powerful buttressed their authority with rituals, dogmas and the trappings of religion.

To return to polished axe heads: one of their symbolic roles was as guardian of the underworld and protector of thresholds. At the tombs of Creevykeel, County Sligo, and Ballymacaldrack, County Antrim, polished stone axes were placed in positions in the entrance passage and in the final blocking of the entrance. At a third tomb at Ballyalton, County Down, two stone axes were laid as offerings at the base of a stone in the forecourt of a court tomb. It seems that in Ireland, as in the earlier Gavr'Inis tomb in Brittany, stone axes retained their symbolic significance. In fact, the most prodigious find of axes in Ireland emphasizes the importance of river fords as ritual entrances or thresholds. At a crossing of Ireland's longest river, the River Shannon, at Killaloe, County Clare, pilgrims deposited more than eight hundred stone axes at what must have been a place of great ritual importance.

Like most sacred complexes, Brú na Bóinne continued to change and evolve with the building of new ceremonial foci. In the mid third millennium BC, three henges of various sizes appeared. The largest was a stone circle surround-ing the Newgrange mound. These new monuments may indicate a change in belief and liturgy, but at the same time there was clearly continuity of respect for the ancient sites. For example, the great stone circle was designed to interact with the older mounds – the shadows of its stones fell across the entrance of the Newgrange tomb at the midwinter solstice and the equinox sunrise. There were seventeen hearths around the front of the mound, the remains of many smashed pottery vessels and the bones of as many as a hundred slaughtered pigs. Fasting is often associated with ritual observance, but so is sacrifice to the gods, followed by feasting at major festivals. This was an opportunity for the powerful to demonstrate their largesse: for the assembled community to consume meat in large quantities.

The great burial mounds of Brú na Bóinne are sophisticated structures by any standards. Both technically and symbolically complex, they play on the fears and hopes of the participants, engaging them physically and mentally, bringing the ceremonies to a series of dramatic conclusions. After a thousand years, starting on the Atlantic seaboard and Brittany, megalithic architecture reached a peak in Ireland. As with medieval cathedrals, however, there are rivals for the prize. A short distance across the Irish Sea to the east, in Anglesey, there are the very fine tombs of Bryn Celli Ddu and Barclodiad-y-Gawres. In southwest Scotland, particularly Arran and Argyll, there are the so-called Clyde cairns, which have prominent forecourts.[5] But perhaps the most sophisticated achievement of this great architectural flowering around 3000 BC lies much further north.

### Heading north

Some years ago we were excavating the site of the medieval abbey at Eynsham, near Oxford, and a distinguished clergyman came to visit: the Bishop of Sodor and Man. His scattered maritime diocese consisted of the Isles of Man and the Hebrides – 'Sodor' derives from the Norse word meaning the 'southern isles'. His title inverts British geography. Most people live in the south and see the far north as remote, but a thousand years ago the Vikings or Norsemen visualized their world the other way around. The dramatic *Orkneyinga Saga* sees the earls of Orkney and their homicidal rivals constantly criss-crossing the seas between Scandinavia, Caithness, Orkney and Ireland. To the Norse, the Hebrides were the southern islands.

Judging from the distribution of megalithic tombs (and of stone axes) the western seaways of Britain were a frequented routeway in the fourth and third millennia BC. The islands off the west coast of Britain provided stepping stones to the north and vice versa. From their obvious familiarity with the heavens, built into so many of their monuments, Neolithic people probably had greater practical awareness of the position of the sun, the moon and the stars than most of us do today. They certainly would have had, routinely, a better view of the night skies, undimmed by modern pollution. This detailed knowledge of the skies must have contributed to their ability to undertake sea voyages. These were the Argonauts of the western seas. The tombs and their symbols and prestige objects provide evidence of common beliefs and practices along Europe's western seaways in the later fourth and third millennia BC.[6]

There are other links. The Brú na Bóinne 'penis' shafts have parallels in Portugal; there are also distinctive bone pins with mushroom heads from Irish tombs and Iberia. My favourite link along the European seaways is a living one – the Orkney vole (*Microtus arvalis orcadensis*). The genetics of this little fellow show that he, and obviously she, stowed away on a Neolithic craft from western France, or further north along the coast, and disembarked in Orkney, probably around 3000 BC. And this is where we find, arguably, the finest of all megalithic passage tombs, at Maeshowe.

Sailing across the often choppy and stomach-churning Pentland Firth from Thurso to Stromness, on Orkney's largest island, Mainland, the most prominent feature, off to starboard, is a natural monolith. This great red sandstone stack, known as the Old Man of Hoy, rises 137 m (450 ft) directly from the sea.[7] With its narrow shelves of stone, the Old Man forms a natural apartment block for seabirds. I once crossed back to Thurso with a bunch of rock climbers who had been scaling the Old Man live on television. They complained that the worst thing about the project was that the fulmars regularly dive-bombed them as they inched their way upwards, each time launching a stomachful of evil-smelling fish goo onto the intruders.

Orkney is a land that feels like it is being eaten by the waves. All around the coast there are stone stacks and rocky outcrops, broughs gnawed by the sea, the wind and rain, and geos and sinkholes where the sea sucks and grinds from below. Austere Celtic monks chose isolated rocks as places to retreat from the world, to perch like birds on the liminal northern edge of Europe, lashed by the winds and scourged by the sea, enduring the darkness of winter and the almost permanent daylight of summer. It hardly seems surprising that this landscape should have inspired the most evocative stone circles in

Europe, such as the Stones of Stenness and the Ring of Brodgar, which face each other across the narrow strip of water (see pages 298 and 299).

The nearby Maeshowe tomb faces southwest, aligned on the midwinter sunset like Newgrange. Certainly, tombs in Orkney show similarities with those in Ireland – common decorative motifs are carved into their stones, apparently branding these megalithic monuments with symbols of a mutual set of beliefs and rituals. Alison Sheridan suggests that, on both sides of the Irish Sea, communities in Ireland and Scotland were actively competing in the construction of impressive burial monuments, resulting in a kind of megalithic risk-taking and inflation.[8] Brú na Bóinne and Maeshowe were the ultimate achievements.

Today, Orkney has one of the finest surviving collections of henges, notably on the two peninsulas that almost meet each other between the Loch of Harray and the Loch of Stenness. The Ring of Bookan lies about 1.8 km (1 mile) northwest of the Ring of Brodgar, with a line of standing stones and a string of barrows between them. Across the narrow straits are the Stones of Stenness, and Maeshowe stands out in the landscape just over a kilometre to the north-west of Stenness, seeming to imitate the outline of the island of Hoy, in the distance. These places are some of the most atmospheric in Britain because of the way in which they seem to be suspended between sea and sky. In the early part of the third millennium BC these monuments were constructed in an open grassland environment grazed by cattle and sheep, with perhaps a few small plots of cereals. Orkney is also blessed with superb building stone – its Old Red Sandstone cleaves into clean shapes that make it possible to create slim, almost artificial-looking slabs. Orkney's elegant forms could substitute for the wisdom-imparting monolith that appears and reappears in Stanley Kubrick's film *2001: A Space Odyssey*, supposedly to inspire humankind, but the inspiration in Orkney and southern Britain was probably the same – natural rocks imbued with numinous power.

The stones that make up the rings of Stenness and Brodgar and other monuments in the area derive from varying sources on the island. It is possible that the great rings were not initially conceived as a designed entity, to be built as a single project and then utilized.[9] Instead, different, even competitive, groups dragged stones from their own locale to contribute to the evolving monuments. Yellow flagstones originated at Houton, on the south coast of Mainland. A fine-grained blonde sandstone from Staneyhill, the high ground to the east of the Ring of Brodgar, was also used in the central chamber of the

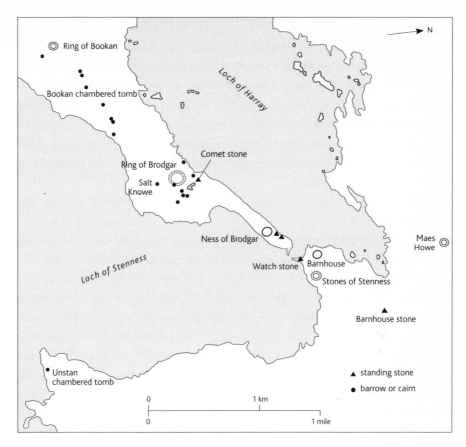

The Late Neolithic sites in the sacred landscape of Stenness and Brodgar, Orkney.

Maeshowe passage grave. Orkney people clearly had a detailed knowledge of local stone, its colour and material properties. Another quarry has been identified at Vestra Fiold, just north of the famous Neolithic village of Skara Brae. Investigations here in 2002 and 2003 located monoliths abandoned when the work went wrong. Slabs of Old Red Sandstone about 5 m (16 ft) in length and weighing up to 10 tonnes were levered from the bedrock, breaking with a distinctive angular top. These could be slid onto wooden cradles and then over rollers and transported the 9 km (5½ miles) to Brodgar and Stenness. The stones were then erected with the neat angular break, like a folded handkerchief, pointing skywards. The culmination of such communal effort – the quarrying, transportation and stone raising – was, as so often seen, feasting and celebration. Perhaps the title of this chapter should be 'They will come in order to build it'.

The existence of a chambered cairn at the Vestra Field quarry, marked by its own monolith, suggests that these stones were associated with the dead. The builders of the cairn placed a polished stone axe beneath the outer revetment wall of the cairn. This was made of Orkney siltstone, a soft material of little practical use. Not surprisingly, the axe was in good condition with no evidence of wear, so presumably it had been made specifically to be deposited as an offering. As we saw at earlier flint mines in Sussex (see Chapter 13), the act of quarrying was probably regarded as a sacred activity – the earth releasing its ancestral materials.

Colin Richards, from Manchester University and excavator of several important sites in Orkney, suggests that different communities brought stone representing their own ancestors, so that the stone circles were both a 'geography of stone' and a genealogy of the clans. The circles need not be complete to function; in fact, Stenness was never completed. Instead, they were a work in progress. Archaeologists have differed in their speculations. Did the stone circles represent cooperation and unity, or a risky form of inter-clan competition and status seeking?[10] We could ask the same question about the Olympic Games or the Football World Cup. In the weeks before the London 2012 Olympics there was a palpable sense of anxiety – would we make a mess of it? – followed by a huge sense of relief when the organization of the Games, the British athletic achievement and even the opening ceremony were seen to be successful. Ethnographic observations of megalithic movements have revealed a similar sense of risk and fear of failure. Because of its superbly built and well preserved monuments, Orkney has attracted the attention of archaeologists since at least the mid nineteenth century.[11] There has been a floruit of activity in recent decades. New work sometimes answers old questions; in Orkney it also raises new ones.

## Locating the living

Across Britain in the later fourth and third millennia BC, ritual monuments are often spectacular while the evidence of where people actually lived is scarce. Orkney seems to be an exception because of the remarkable settlements built in stone, such as Skara Brae and Rinyo. A great storm, blasting away the sand dunes, revealed the remains of Skara Brae in 1850. The site was taken into guardianship in 1924 and as a result of a destructive winter gale the authorities constructed a protective sea wall around the site.

Anxious to recover their costs and encourage visitors, the Office of Works set labourers to work to clear more of the stone ruins without much regard for detailed recording. Belatedly, our old friend Gordon Childe was asked to supervise the work. Childe had marvellous virtues as a prehistorian, but disciplined excavation was not among them. In fact, what he was able to undertake was little more than what today we would call a 'watching brief': retrieving snatches of information in the face of the bulldozer, or in his case the fearsome Orkney shovel-wielders. Sometimes he paid the occasional visit, no doubt with the inevitable question 'Have you found anything recently?'. For much of the time, the labourers followed the stone walls, removing associated floor levels and traces of earlier, slighter buildings.

The only building that was at all adequately investigated was House 7. This now-famous structure is an oval shape with massive stone walls and a sub-rectangular interior room approached through a narrow passageway from the outside, unlike other buildings. It was the oldest standing building in the village, and the only one not to have been abandoned and dismantled. Opposite the entrance there was a stone 'dresser' partly inserted into the

The best-preserved Late Neolithic house at Skara Brae, Orkney. A central square hearth, stone bed settings and shelves, or niches, built into the stone walls are all clearly visible.

back wall, a square stone-lined hearth in the centre, a bed recess to the left and a larger one to the right.[12] Remarkably, this basic arrangement appears in every Skara Brae house for more than five hundred years. Childe suggested that stone was used for furniture such as beds and dressers that would elsewhere, perhaps, have been made in timber, from wooden planks, so that these Neolithic modules could easily be transferred to other environments with different resources. Childe's view was proved to be prophetic. We will see these familiar plans again, in wood, at Durrington Walls and Marden near Stonehenge.

In its better-known later phases, Skara Brae was a highly integrated hamlet, its well-insulated houses clustered together, well provided with drains and linked by covered passages. I was taken to task by Alexandra Shepherd, the co-author of the upcoming Skara Brae report, for describing the inhabitants as 'hobbits' and the houses as buried in midden material.[13] She emphasizes that in their lifetime the houses were free-standing and well adapted to the local environment. There is certainly no doubt that in the early third millennium BC, Orkney was a remarkable and innovative place.

Childe wrongly believed that Skara Brae had been abandoned following a sandstorm and that the occupants of House 7 left in a hurry. He wrote: 'The observations made during its excavation accordingly afford a graphic and reliable picture of a stone age "interior". The first impression produced was one of indescribable filth and disorder. Scraps of bone and shells were lying promiscuously all over the floor, sometimes masked by broken slates laid down like stepping stones over the morass (filth). Even the beds were no cleaner; the complete skull of a calf lay on the left hand bed.' This is an interesting case of how archaeological perceptions change. Did Childe imagine that Neolithic people slept with cattle skulls? Had some Neolithic Godfather made someone an offer they couldn't refuse? In fact, much of what he observed, we now realize, resembles the ritual activity in tombs – the placing of animal skulls and deposits of bone and pottery covered by slate slabs or fragments. There was even a grave containing the bodies of two adult females under the bed on the right-hand side of the room. It is not unusual for houses, when finally abandoned, to be ritually closed with the placement of symbolic objects.

Since Childe's work in the 1920s other settlements have emerged and been more carefully investigated. The tiny island of Wyre lies between Mainland and Rousay. Here, since 2007, archaeologists have investigated a settlement at Ha'Breck that dates to the later fourth millennium (3300–3000 BC) and predates Skara Brae. This, along with the Knap of Howar site on Papa Westray, is one of Orkney's oldest farming communities. The building, House 3, had thick stone walls probably about 1.5 m (5 ft) high originally and central posts that supported the pitched roof. The interior space, about 8 × 4 m (26 × 13 ft), was divided into two by stone walls. In the northern half there were thick layers of charred material, which included tens of thousands of barley grains. The fire might have been deliberate as there were signs that extra wood had been thrown into it to intensify the blaze. After the fire, the burnt layer was deliberately covered with a clay floor into which a quern rubber was set, along with a polished stone axe head (one of fifteen from the site). This does look like a ceremonial closing deposit.

Adjoining the granary to the south was a second building, House 5, with an interconnecting doorway. It was also sub-rectangular and divided into one large room and one very small chamber. The entrance to the 'granary' was blocked with clay and then quantities of midden debris were used to level up the ground outside the building. Underneath the spread midden soil there was a surprise for the excavators – another building – but this one was made out of timber. It is a commonplace to say that Orkney was cleared of its somewhat stunted tree cover early in the Neolithic and stone substituted as the regular building material. So a timber building was unexpected, as was the second (there are also possible timber buildings at Wideford, excavated by Colin Richards). Environmental studies on Orkney (and in areas like the Cairngorms) suggest that the paucity of woodland in the Neolithic far north may have been exaggerated, but the impact of farmers in clearing the landscape is evident around Brodgar and Stenness.

So where were the farmers on the tiny island of Wyre buried? There are no known tombs on Wyre, but Rousay lies only about a kilometre away, northwards across narrow straits, and here at least fifteen tombs crowd onto this small island (10 km/6 miles across). The excavators suggest that Rousay was the isle of the dead.[14]

About 3000 BC, Orkney witnessed major changes. Nucleated settlements, such as Skara Brae, emerge with cellular structures clustered together, either linked by passageways or built around central courtyards, where craft activities such as pottery and leatherworking took place. Again, the tomb architecture was modified to reflect that of the domestic houses.

## Living among the monuments

The most remarkable discoveries have been two settlements actually within the great Brodgar/Stenness ceremonial complex. The Barnhouse Settlement, excavated by Colin Richards in the 1980s, lies on the end of the southern peninsula, just north of the Stones of Stenness. Like Skara Brae, the oval houses, built of drystone walling, contain central hearths, dressers, beds and a drainage system. There are also two massive buildings that dwarf the normal domestic structures. So-called House 2 was divided down the middle, with a hearth in each side with angular, buttressed corners creating three niches in each half – a layout that resembles the interior space of the Maeshowe tomb. Entry, as at Maeshowe, was through a passageway, which crosses over a cist burial. It was necessary to pass over this burial to enter the building.

House 2, in the words of the excavator, 'eclipsed' the other dwellings.[15] It stood prominently on the western edge of the village, and from outside this large rectangular building with rounded corners – twice the size of its neighbours and built of fine-quality masonry – would have dominated the settlement. Inside, the masonry was also of exceptional quality, rivalling Maeshowe, and the layout, with recesses, similarly reflected that of passage graves.

When Gordon Childe discussed late Neolithic society in Orkney he used the apparent uniformity of houses to argue for a relatively egalitarian society. In contrast, Colin Renfrew saw the appearance of large henges here, and in southern Britain, as reflecting the emergence of more complex social structures, the growth of inequality, and of hierarches in communities dominated by chiefdoms – to put it crudely, big projects needed dominant leaders. More recently, this idea has been challenged by those arguing that such projects can be communal efforts, though often influenced or promoted by charismatic individuals seeking personal (as opposed to inherited) status.

Colin Richards proposes that House 2 was a cult or ceremonial house, rather than the dwelling of a chieftain or community leader – a place where rituals took place and purity or cleanliness were carefully observed. A polished chisel blade was buried in the floor of the east recess. Access into the building was through a low and narrow passageway and once inside the architecture of the building controlled movement around the space. Cooking, the processing of cereals and meat, took place around the eastern, much-used hearth. A mace-head fragment was one of four such highly polished objects made of distinctive stone (ten in total have been found in the area). These volcanic or metamorphic rocks ranged from a particular black-and-white material to banded red-and-black stone. Clearly, these were beautiful and striking objects reminiscent of the Irish maces. The excavators suggest that they may have been polished within House 2 and originally kept there.

Perhaps one function of House 2 was to store ritual paraphernalia. The impression is of a building with restricted access, where rituals were carried out away from the public gaze and where, afterwards, the space was fastidiously cleaned. There are obvious similarities with the passage graves and the seasonal ceremonies that were held there. Perhaps House 2 was restricted to the use of initiates.

The interpretation of the Barnhouse complex was further complicated by the discovery of a massive building, Structure 8, which resembled an inflated version of a Skara Brae house. It is unlike anything else discovered in late Neolithic Orkney, though sizeable areas of Barnhouse remain unexcavated. As Structure 8 was built late in the settlement sequence it is possible that it represents a fundamental change in house style.

Across the narrow water to the north we now know that there is another remarkable site. The Ness of Brodgar is an extensive mound, the size of five football pitches – the nearest thing Neolithic Britain gets to a Middle Eastern tell – and it was only discovered in 2002. I can modestly claim that I walked across it several times without noticing it. Since geophysical surveys located the site, excavations have revealed part of a remarkable complex. Building 1 is 15 m (50 ft) long and 10 m (33 ft) wide with walls surviving to a height of 1 m (3 ft). Inside, it has six regular recesses like Barnhouse but with two opposing entrances rather than the single tunnel-like entrance. While it was built as a free-standing structure, midden material was dumped around the building as if attempting to hide it.

On the high point of the Ness of Brodgar mound lies the largest building so far discovered in Neolithic Orkney, revealed in 2008/9. This is Structure 10, 25 m (82 ft) long and almost 20 m (65 ft) wide, squarish with rounded corners, superb masonry and walls 5 m (16 ft) thick. The central chamber had walls built of non-local sandstone that is red and yellow – similar to that used in Orkney's great cathedral of St Magnus in Kirkwall. This chamber is cruciform in shape, like the interior of Maeshowe, on which Structure 10 is aligned. It is possible that it post-dates all other buildings on the Ness of Brodgar mound so that it would have stood in 'splendid isolation' (to quote the site director, Nick Card), dominating the spit of land opposite the Standing Stones of Stenness.

Across the water, Card suggests that Barnhouse was dominated by Structure 8 at this time. Geophysical survey has, however, revealed the presence of several other large buildings. It will require many years of excavation and more accurate modelling of radiocarbon dates before we understand the full complexity of this marvellous site. There is, however, one other important feature that has emerged – an enormous curtain wall up to 4 m (13 ft) wide, and in parts widened to 6 m (20 ft) (thicker than Hadrian's Wall), possibly enclosing an area 125 × 75 m (400 × 250 ft).[16]

So what on earth is this place, with its Great Wall of Orkney, and its neighbouring settlement at Barnhouse? I have visited the Brodgar and Stenness circles several times and found it natural to regard these henge monuments as the focal points of Neolithic activity, along with Maeshowe, but now the spectacular buildings of Barnhouse and Ness of Brodgar appear themselves as important cult centres. Pilgrims would have entered through the portal of the Ring of Brodgar in the northwest or the Stones of Stenness in the southeast. These may have been built across an existing path or corridor (rather like the Thornborough Henges – although the entrances of the Ring of Brodgar are remarkably narrow), which then ran along the Ness past the two cult centres marked by standing stones, while mounds, such as Maeshowe, mirrored the distant forms in the Orkney landscape. This was the heart of the north – Orkney's great ritual centre. Or were the two settlements at the Ness of Brodgar and Barnhouse a microcosm of Orkney society – places with 'big houses' where the islands' clan groups gathered and perhaps drew people from afar, like the later cult centres of the classical world such as Delphi or Epidauros, where the faithful processed and gathered, trying to grasp hold of sense and security in an uncertain world, while competing for status? Perhaps oracles and miracle workers could be found in Orkney. In 1977, Evan MacKie suggested that Orkney was home to astronomer-priests.[17] At the time, such ideas were unfashionable in British archaeology – they smacked of Stukeley and Druids – but now MacKie's view seems prescient.

## Pots for the henges

One thing that certainly can be found in Orkney is a distinctive new type of pottery known as Grooved Ware. These are handmade pots (the potter's wheel would not arrive in Britain for more than two millennia) with flat bases and incised or applied decoration – hence the name. Some of them resemble woven baskets but are made in clay. Grooved Ware is eventually found across much of Britain, notably in the henge monuments of the south, and is associated with feasting. There are large, bucket-shaped pots in which food may have been cooked, and smaller ones into which the food was served. Because of its association with henge monuments, it has been suggested that Grooved Ware is a form of elite ceramics, used by the privileged on ritual occasions. This may be an assumption too far as relatively few non-ritual sites of the third millennium BC have been excavated. Grooved Ware does also turn up in what seem to be isolated pits (usually found while excavating sites of other periods). At present, limited radiocarbon dates place Grooved Ware in Orkney and northern Scotland before anywhere else in Britain. Could the ceramics be closely associated with a social and religious revolution in the north that spread south along the seaways into Ireland and southern Britain? This is a large claim based on an uncertain chronology; the period desperately needs a *Gathering Time*-style project.

Grooved Ware sherds from Barnhouse were found to be consistently impregnated with lipids or fatty acids. The vessels held foodstuffs such as beef (only found in the cult building), possibly cow's milk and barley. Another contained traces of a cow's stomach. Some had been sealed with tree pitch or resins, probably to make them less porous. Interestingly, given the location, there was no evidence that Orkney people cooked fish or the flesh of sea mammals.

It seems, however, that people came to the great Orkney cult centre from far and wide to take part in ceremonies and feasting. The types of Grooved Ware found within the complex are stylistically and technically varied, suggesting that they were brought by pilgrims, probably along with the

Grooved Ware, the ceramic which characterizes the era of the henges in Britain. This pot is incised with distinctive decoration and has a flat base.

animals to be sacrificed and foodstuffs to be consumed. If this seems alien behaviour it is worth remembering that in the Classical world it was a ubiquitous feature of cult centres, where congregations came together to hold picnics in sacred orchards or banquets in special rooms at sacred centres where cooking facilities were provided. St Paul tells of Christians in Corinth joining in pagan sacrificial feasts in temple grounds (1 Corinthians 8:10). St Paul may have disapproved, but, of course, Christianity itself was to absorb the 'Last Supper' and the ritual consumption of bread and wine, the Eucharist, into its own most important ritual. Early Christian funerary meals were also notoriously drunken affairs – though Christians were probably indulging in a long tradition.[18] The spread of monuments and ceramics suggests strongly that a common belief system and set of rituals had taken hold in Britain and Ireland in the third millennium BC.

British (or at least English) archaeology has tended to be biased towards the south, especially Wessex. In the case of these important late Neolithic cultural changes, the ideas and innovations as represented by the material culture can arguably be seen as flowing from the west and the north. In Scotland there are sacred complexes, such as Balfarg in Fife, which also produced early Grooved Ware and evidence of ritual feasting. Stuart Piggott directed the first systematic excavation of a Scottish henge at Cairnpapple Hill, West Lothian. This site has a long and complex history comparable with Balfarg and sites to the south such as Avebury – which, like Cairnpapple Hill, has a cave-like setting of stones. Scotland also has other spectacular late Neolithic monuments, comparable with the largest in the south, such as the huge concentric rings of oak posts, with a stone bank between them, at Blackhouse Burn. This enclosure is 300 m (985 ft) across. Unusually, it occupies an upland basin above the upper Clyde valley, and, more typically, is adjacent to a major north–south routeway (a Roman road and the A72 run nearby).

Grooved Ware appears in the south and became one of the most distinctive elements in the material culture of the big henges. Sherds of pottery are not usually among the more exciting finds on archaeological excavations, but there were two exceptions when my colleagues at the Oxford Archaeological Unit were digging at Barrow Hills, Radley, adjacent to the Abingdon causewayed enclosure.[19] This was a long-lived ritual complex with a different trajectory to some of the other sites we have considered. Alongside the causewayed enclosure there were two oval Neolithic barrows. The place continued as a site for burial and eventually there was a great avenue of Bronze Age barrows aligned on the old enclosure. Excavators tend to concentrate on spectacular monuments, but there can be interesting evidence lying between the individual monuments.

Among the most distinctive and common features of third millennium Neolithic archaeology are simple pits dug into the ground and often including Grooved Ware. The motivation for pit digging may not, itself, have been simple. Often they contain carefully structured material deposits full of symbolic meaning. Pit 3196 at Barrow Hills was unusually large. Placed within it were four flint scrapers; ash deposits containing the charcoal of hazel, hawthorn, blackthorn, oak and buckthorn; charred apple pips and hazelnut shells; the bones of butchered pigs, cattle, sheep, dogs and red deer; and an awl made from the ulna of a white-tailed eagle (*Haliaeetus albicilla*). In itself this was an interesting collection of the domestic and the wild; a reminder that around 2500 BC the Thames Valley landscape had not yet been completely domesticated by human beings.

The broken remains of several Grooved Ware pots also found in the pit generated excitement. One vessel was exceptionally finely made, decorated with a lattice pattern of applied clay strips, which formed neat lozenges. There were also seventy-four sherds in the pit from a large, thick-walled vessel decorated with parallel grooved lines and opposing grooved spirals. Remarkably, the decorations on these two pots from Oxfordshire almost perfectly match those carved on the superb flint mace head buried in the Boyne tomb at Knowth (see page 319). These symbols of megalithic arts, so prolific at Brú na Bóinne, were in the mid third millennium BC applied to ceramics and presumably other media such as wood, textiles, basketry and perhaps even the skin, as tattoos.

The gravel terraces of the Thames Valley are a long way from the megalithic shrines of the Boyne and Orkney, but the communities in these places had symbols and probably beliefs in common. The pathways along the River Thames to Dorchester-on-Thames and beyond eventually reach the River Kennet. About two days on foot or canoe would bring pilgrims to the greatest ceremonial complexes of all: Avebury, Silbury Hill and Stonehenge.

CHAPTER SEVENTEEN
# Arise Stonehenge

## The sacred landscapes of Wiltshire

From about 3800 BC, farming – a radically new way of life – spread rapidly across Britain. While there were local and regional differences, what is remarkable is the uniformity of ideas and practices represented by monuments, burials, the use of pottery and demand for exotic polished stone axes. Communities were competitive and at times aggressive. While these groups were unlikely to have developed formal, inherited hierarchies, as we see with later chiefdoms, aristocracies and kingship, community leaders no doubt emerged – so-called 'great men' and 'big men' – people who successfully controlled the ceremonial exchange of objects of desire or were seen as ritual experts. Others were successful in warfare, and perhaps particularly at raiding cattle or the seizure of female captives. Through alliances, gifts and feasting, such people (and they were probably most often men) could have built their reputations and promoted the construction of monuments, the voluntary coming together of labour forces to implement the innovations that created the varied tomb types, enclosures and linear monuments.

Such alliances were probably unstable and short-lived, however: 'big men' make enemies, attract competitors and grow old. Alternatively, perhaps, greater stability was maintained through descent groups or clans, resulting in causewayed enclosures, some of which were used for as many as twelve generations and attracted more widely spread communities. Other places had their spectacular but brief appearances in the limelight, such as the Abingdon causewayed enclosure. Unlike some enclosures that rapidly disappeared from folk memory, Abingdon became the focus for a long-lasting and spectacular burial tradition in the adjacent area known as Barrow Hills. Cursuses and henges were also often built in landscapes already marked by ancestral constructions. In contrast, there is little visible evidence of the economic activity of Neolithic farmers such as hedges, fences or drainage ditches (with the exception of western Ireland). Instead, the Neolithic landscape was structured and memorialized for the gods and the ancestors.

Outside of Orkney and Brú na Bóinne, the evolving and emerging prehistoric landscape of monuments is most prominent today in the World Heritage complex of Avebury and Stonehenge. The North Wessex Downs, with the River Kennet providing a routeway to the Thames, were first marked by long barrows and megalithic tombs such as West Kennet. Within a largely wooded landscape the causewayed enclosure of Windmill Hill was sited prominently on a high point. The great henge of Avebury – with its massive circular earthen ramparts, 400 m (1,300 ft) across, and Britain's largest stone circle – was linked by its stone-lined avenues to other ritual foci. The West Kennet Avenue runs 2.5 km (1½ miles) southeast towards the river and the Sanctuary on Overton Hill, an impressive structure of four concentric rings of timber and two circles of stone. The Beckhampton Avenue runs from Avebury's western entrance towards the huge sarsen known as the Longstones, the Longstones enclosure and the South Street long barrow.

The impression gained is of processional routes joining nodes of ritual activity, which accumulated over a timespan of a thousand years or more. Fieldwork, aerial photography and geophysical survey continue to add detail to this amazing complex – for example, two huge timber palisaded enclosures straddled the River Kennet to the south of the henge. These were only discovered by aerial photography in the late 1980s. Limited excavation uncovered large quantities of pig bone and Grooved Ware pottery, suggesting that feasts took place at these spectacular constructions. Dating at this point is imprecise but they were probably in use in the second half of the third millennium BC, around the time of the construction of the Avebury stone circle and the Beckhampton Avenue.

In the earlier third millennium BC, possibly for several centuries, the Avebury area was a hive of activity. Hundreds of workers must have come together to cut timber, dig ditches, drag stones and erect the largest prehistoric mound in Europe, Silbury Hill. Sitting on low ground close to the river and its source, Silbury Hill eventually rose to a height of 31 m (102 ft) and was 145 m (475 ft) across the base. It is estimated that there are 239,000 cubic m (8.4 million cubic ft) of chalk in the mound, quarried from a surrounding pit that when filled with water forms a mirror pool around the mound.

Silbury Hill grew as a result of regular communal gatherings. The mound started modestly: initially, a small gravel tump was constructed in a landscape of grassland and some trees, then basketloads of topsoil, clay-with-flints, chalk and gravel, with some boulders of sarsen, were dumped on the mound until it stood about 6 m (20 ft) high and 35 m (115 ft) across. The excavators believe this was not a random dump but consisted of soils and rock deliberately brought from different parts of the landscape. It is reminiscent of Orkney, where varied sandstones were quarried and brought together. At Silbury, communities were literally combining their homeland soils.

Next, a circular enclosure ditch was excavated in segments around the mound, resembling other contemporary enclosures. In fact, the ditch was backfilled and recut several times on expanding perimeters, as if the builders became increasingly ambitious in their efforts. The chalk was not merely dumped on the mound. Instead, it was laid in flat layers and revetted with chalk blocks to provide stability. It was the tinkering of antiquarians, archaeologists and Welsh miners working for the BBC that undermined this fine piece of Neolithic engineering and generated emergency works in the early 2000s, when English Heritage began a complex restoration and recording project following the collapse of a vertical shaft originally dug into the hill in 1776.[1]

For many years, archaeologists believed Silbury Hill was an eccentric one-off – a symbolic, surreal mountain emerging from its artificial lake; a place for processions around the slope and perhaps sky rituals on the small flat summit. Now there is evidence that Silbury was not alone. In this part of Wessex, around 2400 BC or later, there was competitive mound building going on, as local communities sought to be the biggest and the best in demonstrating their muscular paganism. Downstream from Silbury, the Marlborough Mound lies in the grounds of Marlborough College. Capped by trees, it was thought for a long time to be simply a feature of 18th-century garden landscaping. Radiocarbon dating now confirms that it is Silbury's smaller twin (half as high at 18 m/60 ft) also built around the mid third millennium BC.[2]

Another mound of similar size, the Hatfield Barrow, no longer exists – it was undermined by antiquarians and collapsed. It stood within the huge henge monument of Marden. This important site, one of the five big Wessex henges,[3] lies north of Stonehenge along the River Avon on the routeway to Avebury. In spite of its size it is scarcely known to the general public, as it is not today a major feature of the landscape. Excavations in the early 1970s located a timber circle associated with Grooved Ware, and radiocarbon dates put the construction of the great ditch in the period 2570–2290 BC. This is the time when the large sarsen stones forming trilithons were erected at Stonehenge. These sarsen stones may have been hauled from the Marlborough Downs via the Marden henge.

## Dragging the sarsen stones

Mike Parker Pearson, whose achievements we will discuss later, has examined the possible routes from the Marlborough Downs to Stonehenge. Until recently, one of William Stukeley's drawings lay quietly unregarded in Oxford's Bodleian Library, then Mike noticed that it depicts two be-hatted gentlemen and a third mounted on a horse by a crossroads at Clatford, a crossing point of the River Kennet east of Avebury in 1723. Lying around them are eleven large sarsen blocks – not in appearance like natural, irregular grey wethers, but remarkably 'Stonehenge' shaped. Mike speculates that this might have been a marshalling yard for the Stonehenge sarsens.[4] From Clatford the line of least resistance southwards would pass through the Marden henge, halfway along the route.

Excavations at Marden by English Heritage have found traces of a rectangular building with a chalk-plaster floor and a gravel roadway heading towards the River Avon. Was this the crossing point of the Avon for the Stonehenge sarsens? If so, Parker Pearson proposes that this, along with the Kennet crossing at Clatford, would be the place to look for causeways revetted with timbers across the boggy ground. The dream scenario would be to find preserved timbers with tree rings, holding the answer to the question: what year were the sarsens dragged to Stonehenge? Sweet dreams are made of this. Mike's proposal is not so far-fetched. We followed exactly the same logic to locate and precisely date the construction of Roman roads in the Thames Valley.

It is this kind of imaginative approach based on detailed research, careful fieldwork and intelligent questioning that has thrown so much new light on Stonehenge – combined with an awareness, as we have seen in Yorkshire, Ireland and Orkney, that Neolithic communities were neither parochial nor isolated.

## Making sense of Stonehenge

It is an unfortunate fact that in Britain we know relatively little about some of our best-known, and consequently least understood, monuments. This is in part because such sites are protected by law, and some have been for over a century. When protected sites, notably Stonehenge, were investigated in the past, the work was not always of the highest quality and sometimes remained unpublished. As a result, caution and conservation have often taken precedence over investigation and the spirit of enquiry. To put it bluntly, archaeologists have been discouraged from digging 'famous' sites.

It was in part to achieve a more balanced approach, and to allow access for focused investigations and new scientific techniques, that English Heritage brought researchers and curators together in the early 2000s to contribute to a Stonehenge research framework.[5] At the same time, English Heritage, the National Trust and other groups responsible for the land management of Stonehenge attempted to take much of the land out of damaging arable farming to put an end to the erosion of the past, as predicted by Stukeley.

There was also a considerable quantity of unpublished data, recorded in earlier 20th-century excavations, which was analysed with forensic thoroughness by Ros Cleal and a team of specialists. This provided the basis for a systematic programme of radiocarbon dating.[6] The result is that in the new millennium there has been a stream of new light shed on the old stones. More than that, Stonehenge can now be seen in the context of its wider landscape. We are beginning to see why and when this became such a special place to people in Britain in the third millennium BC.

The sarsen trilithons of Stonehenge; these features give the famous monument its name. To the right, Stone 56 lacks its lintel (fallen on the ground), but on the top the tenon is visible, and the large stone has clearly been shaped.

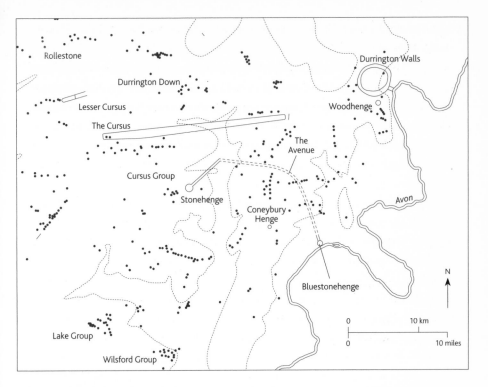

Map of the Stonehenge sacred landscape. The earlier Cursus cuts across the area
north of Stonehenge. Durrington Walls is joined to the River Avon by a short avenue.
Bronze Age barrows, mostly on higher ground, surround the Stonehenge bowl.

We last saw Stonehenge, in Chapter 15, around 3000–2900 BC. The surrounding landscape already contained old long barrows, enclosures and cursuses. It
should be emphasized that Stonehenge is an extremely complex monument
where people in the past constantly rearranged the furniture – they dug pits
and ditches, buried the dead, erected and removed timber structures and
constructed circles and arcs of stone, then dismantled, reorganized and rebuilt
them – so we cannot say with certainty or precision exactly how and when
all the shifting elements in Stonehenge took shape. That does not mean, of
course, that archaeologists have failed to bend their minds, or risked their
sanity, in trying to unravel this greatest of prehistory puzzles.

For most of my career, Stonehenge's chronology was based on the sequence
proposed in 1979 by Professor Richard Atkinson. At the time, he had a grand
total of five radiocarbon dates to work with (plus four from the Avenue).
In 1995, Ros Cleal and her colleagues, as part of the English Heritage

Stonehenge Project, revised the dating scheme based on fifty-two useable radiocarbon dates. In spite of more sophisticated Bayesian modelling, there still remains the critical problem of interpreting the stratigraphical data of earlier excavations. Following 21st-century excavations and further radiocarbon dating, the specialists involved came together to propose a new sequence and chronology based on the most up-to-date information. They do not claim that this is definitive, but it is the best we have at the moment – a model for Stonehenge that proposes eight stages of construction between about 3000 BC and 1900–1600 BC.[7]

Stonehenge Stage 1 begins with the digging of the enclosure ditch and an internal bank – hence it is not a classic henge (with an external bank) but what is termed a 'formative henge'. This activity is dated to about 2955–2830 BC. Neolithic people did some strange things – in this case, they placed cattle and deer bones, which were between 110 and 360 years old at the time, in the bottom of the ditch. Presumably, these had been curated as objects of ritual significance in another shrine, then placed in the enclosure to provide a significant charge to the new cult centre. Within the enclosure was a circle of pits known as the Aubrey Holes (see also page 293), which arguably contained fifty-six bluestones from Preseli, into which human cremations were inserted – creating the largest burial ground known at this time. There were probably some stones – sarsens and perhaps bluestones – on the site from the beginning. Around 2900–2600 BC, Stage 2, the bluestones were rearranged. At this time, a Neolithic visitor would not have found Stonehenge particularly impressive.

The significance of the place expanded enormously in Stage 3 (dated about 2500 BC). In the words of the researchers, the site was transformed from a 'fairly commonplace' monument to a structure 'quite unique in the ancient world'. It was at this stage that Stonehenge took on its familiar form with a circle of massive sarsen stones and the horseshoe shape of trilithons which give Stonehenge – the 'hanging stones' – its name. They were erected on what became Stonehenge's principal axis, the solstitial alignment, marked by the rising midsummer sun in the northeast and in the southwest by the setting midwinter sun.[8] Nowadays, people gather in their thousands at Stonehenge to shiver and, if the cloud allows, experience the midsummer sunrise. Four and a half thousand years ago the even more inhospitable midwinter solstice was probably the principal focus of attention. This was not only the most solemn occasion, the turn of the dying year, but also the quiet period in the farming calendar, when people had time to spare for ritual and festive occasions. Today, only the most dedicated gather for the midwinter solstice.

During Stage 3 the builders erected a double bluestone circle outside the trilithon horseshoe, possibly using stones taken from the Aubrey Holes. In the later Stage 4, the bluestones were reorganized yet again into an oval setting and an outer circle. The bluestones are some of the most mobile elements at Stonehenge, probably because they were smaller and easier to shift than the massive sarsens. Three of the bluestones have tenon projections and two have mortice holes showing that, like the great sarsen trilithons, bluestones were also, at some stage, incorporated into a monument with lintels, imitating a carpentry construction in wood. Two bluestones also have tongue and grooved jointing, which suggests that the double bluestone circle had a framed entrance before it was reorganized in Stage 4. It is striking how the beautifully prepared bluestones resemble, on a much larger scale, polished stone axes.

## A message from Madagascar

Back in 1998 Mike Parker Pearson, then an archaeologist at Sheffield University, visited Stonehenge with a colleague from Madagascar named Ramilisonina. Mike had been working in Madagascar, where there was a long tradition of creating standing stones and megalithic funerary monuments – a way of life and death that flourished into the 19th century and the arrival of Christian missionaries. On the basis of his own experience of Madagascan traditions, Ramilisonina suggested that Stonehenge, a place of hard, durable material, represented the dead as an active presence and influence in the world. The living lived in houses made of wood, but inhabited a landscape that included the realm of the dead. Standing stones were a powerful means of communicating with them; the stones enticed the spirits back, became a place of encounter and a means of linking the past and the present, of invoking memory in a world without written history.[9]

In the Madagascan world view the living, especially the young, were seen as soft, fluid, transient and associated with organic materials. Wood, like the human body, decomposes. In contrast, bone and stone are hard, indestructible and everlasting and represent the permanence of the dead; the dead were also seen as composed of ash. Parker Pearson and Ramilisonina published their ideas in a controversial paper in *Antiquity,* suggesting that the Stonehenge landscape could be separated into a realm of the living and a realm of the dead.[10] Stonehenge itself commemorated the ancestors, the immortal dead, who could continue to advise, chastise and provoke action in the world of the living.

The direct use of ethnological analogy is controversial in archaeology, especially as it usually involves comparing behaviour and ideas in societies often thousands of miles and many centuries apart. Critics see the British and European Neolithic as unique and doubt that recent ethnography provides a key. Archaeologists clearly need to keep their own specific evidence clearly in focus.[11] However, as one commentator sensibly noted: 'neither anthropological nor archaeological theories based on ethnographic data will correspond to a particular prehistoric society, but they might give a fruitful approach to interpretations that may corroborate with archaeological material'.[12]

## The Stonehenge Riverside Project

If the Madagascan analogy had simply remained a matter of theoretical debate then it would have been of limited value. However, it helped to stimulate research – the Stonehenge Riverside Project – which from 2003 put boots on the ground and generated fieldwork to test specific questions. The project proved to be one of the most exciting and productive in Britain in many decades, in spite of being judged 'too speculative' by one major grant-giving body.[13]

The team asked the question: if Stonehenge was the domain of the dead, where were the living? They set their sights on the Durrington Walls henge monument, the great circular earthwork that lies about 3 km (2 miles) north-east of Stonehenge, close to the west bank of the River Avon. Stonehenge and Durrington Walls were believed to be contemporary. The world-famous site was made, substantially, of stone and included burials; its less well-known neighbour contained timber structures (found during excavations in advance of road widening in the 1960s) and no human remains. Were these the contrasting realms of the living and the dead symbolized in timber and stone? Mike Parker Pearson reasoned that the two sites should be connected, possibly by the river itself. After all, in many mythologies the dead are transported over water.

I mentioned earlier, in relation to Neolithic timber buildings, that archaeologists sometimes focus too much on the obvious. The answers to some questions lie outside the most prominent archaeological features. The Riverside team appreciated this and first began to excavate between

Durrington Walls's southwest entrance and the River Avon; in 2005 and 2006 they found an avenue running directly from the Durrington Walls entrance to the river. It consisted of a flint road surface, 15 m (50 ft) wide, with a chalk bank on either side. What's more, the avenue was orientated to the west, virtually on the midsummer solstice sunset. Excavations in 1967 had revealed the so-called Southern Circle, a great structure of concentric timber posts, just inside the southeastern entrance of the henge. This was orientated on the sunrise at the midwinter solstice. It seems that the avenue was more precisely aligned with the setting sun in midsummer. This loomed largest in the minds of the builders, who were aware of exactly where the sun disappeared behind the horizon of the relatively steep valley.

Another major discovery supported the 'realm of the living' theory. On either side of the avenue were traces of seven houses of a regular pattern: squarish, about 5 × 5 m (16 × 16 ft), with a central hearth, chalk-plaster floors and stake holes indicating the position of wattle and daub walls. These remains were very clear, but slight and fragile. They were protected by a build-up of soil outside the henge bank. On a more exposed site with thin topsoil, ploughing would have rapidly scoured them away, which partly explains the rarity of such Neolithic buildings in southern Britain.

At Durrington, before the construction of this great earthwork, there existed a massive settlement of 17 hectares (42 acres), probably filled with small houses with two impressive timber circles at the centre. The Durrington houses bear surprising similarities to the well-known Skara Brae structures in Orkney. In fact, House 7 at Skara Brae is exactly the same size and layout as the largest at Durrington. Some surprisingly intimate details survived: by one of the Durrington fireplaces there were knee-prints where someone had cooked in Grooved Ware pots and kept the fire burning. The floors were kept clean except for the odd flint arrowhead or bone pin that lurked behind the furniture when the house was swept. The large number of arrowheads from the site, sizeable fragments of pots and animal bones did not resemble the assemblage of finds from a typical farming settlement. These certainly indicated the presence of the living; possibly several thousand of them gathered together for a special project – to build what we now call Stonehenge Phase 2.

Mike Parker Pearson suggests that huge gatherings of people took place seasonally at the Durrington Walls site – prior to the construction of its great henge bank and ditch. The settlement was laid out in four quarters with possibly as many as a thousand houses and an open area in the middle.

We could be looking at a temporary settlement of four thousand people. In addition to the two timber-post circles mentioned above, there was another set of concentric rings known as Woodhenge just to the south. Bayesian modelling of radiocarbon dates places the occupations of the settlement at about 2480–2440 BC. The great henge ditch was dug across the site shortly afterwards, so the Durrington seasonal gathering probably occurred over forty years, during which Stonehenge 3 was built.[14]

If these gatherings were seasonal, when did they occur? The answer comes from unexpected sources: the age at slaughter of the animals that were consumed and the lipids from milk products found in pots. These pieces of evidence indicate people were present in both summer and winter. Given the importance of the midsummer sunset and midwinter solstice in local orientations it seems that, as at Brú na Bóinne, this was when the congregation came together from across southern England, and possibly as far away as Wales and Scotland. By about 2800 BC, Grooved Ware pottery had spread across the country, possibly originating in Orkney along with the house types. At Brodgar, around 3000 BC, we saw a remarkable complex of henges, tombs, settlements and standing stones. Did these represent some form of cult that spread across Britain?

The animal bones at Durrington Walls tell a fascinating story. Many belonged to domesticated pigs, killed at nine months. Some had been shot with arrows, but not from close range. It looks as if Neolithic archers demonstrated their skill by targeting the ill-fated animals needed for the feast. Clearly, this was about as sporting as British pheasant-shooting today. The burnt bone ends show that the pigs ended up on the barbecue. The limited age distribution of the pigs is evidence that they were not being reared around Durrington Walls. That animals were brought from elsewhere, especially for the feast, is confirmed by isotopic analysis of the teeth of cattle from the site. These also were not raised on the chalk downland that surrounds Durrington Walls. Some originated in the far west: Devon, Cornwall or even west Wales; others came from lowlands beyond Wessex, either to the east or west. Even the pigs, not the easiest animals to herd, had walked at least 32 km (20 miles) to meet their fate. Some serious logistics were required to organize the Durrington gathering, provide it with food, fuel, timber for the local monuments and houses, tools and latrines. Environmental studies estimate that trees of sufficient size for the building project must have come from at least 16 km (10 miles) away.

The Stonehenge Riverside Project has produced strong evidence to link the great Durrington Walls gathering of the living with the Stonehenge memorial to the ancestors. The newly discovered Durrington Avenue leads down to the bank of the River Avon. The river flows south in a series of large loops to approach Stonehenge; the Riverside team noted that following this course is quite disorientating. If the dead were carried this way on their final journey the effect may be deliberate. It is not unusual in mortuary rituals to attempt to 'confuse' the deceased so that they cannot return to the land of the living.

If funerary parties passed along the River Avon in vessels carrying the dead, where did they disembark to reach Stonehenge itself? An obvious routeway from the river would have been along the Stonehenge Avenue, the parallel banks and ditches that run for 2.8 km (1¾ miles) from the River Avon to the great stone circle. The avenue heads northeast from near the river, curves west at King Barrow Ridge and then, in low-lying ground, turns southwest to run 600 m (650 yd) in a dead straight line on rising ground towards the stones. This is the most dramatic way to approach Stonehenge: as one processes up the avenue the stones appear above the horizon, themselves rising like the sun in a masterpiece of theatrical choreography.

Returning to the river, the problem for the Stonehenge Riverside Project was that no one had ever proved that the avenue actually reached the riverbank. Some argued that it stopped on higher ground, north of the village of West Amesbury. The project team needed support for their idea that the river was fundamental to the link between the realm of the living and the dead so they undertook a battery of geophysical surveys in the field by the river in an attempt to locate the avenue. Unfortunately, in the Middle Ages, West Amesbury village extended down to the river and the remains complicated the picture. So the team settled for the archaeologists' last resort – and starting digging. In appalling conditions at the very end of the field season they found a section of enigmatic curving ditch, and a pit containing an antler pick that was radiocarbon-dated to 2466–2190 BC – about the same date as the Stonehenge Avenue.

A year later, in 2009, the team returned and extended the excavation. At last, beneath the medieval village, they found traces of the avenue close to the river. What was more unexpected – the curving ditch found the previous year proved to be part of a small henge monument. Within it (but predating it) there had been an arc of standing stones. Nine stone holes were found within the trench, but if extended beyond to form a circle, there would have been twenty-five monoliths, probably bluestones judging from the pillar-like imprints found in the base of the postholes. So the team named the new monument Bluestonehenge. It looked like they had found the entrance to the realm of the dead, and possibly the place where bodies were cremated, though this remains to be proven.

Mike Parker Pearson suggests that these bluestones were eventually removed, to be added to those from the Aubrey Holes in the phase of Stonehenge reorganization when a bluestone configuration was erected inside the circle of larger sarsen stones (now designated Stage 3). Once the stones had been removed about 2469–2286 BC, the site was demarcated by the curving ditch, which forms a classic small henge about 35 m (115 ft) across. It is obvious that the avenue does not follow the most direct route from the river to Stonehenge. Mike Parker Pearson suggests that it might have been constructed following the dismantling of Bluestonehenge to mark the route taken by those who dragged the bluestones to Stonehenge.

The project team decided to excavate the area where the avenue approaches Stonehenge's northeast entrance. They made a remarkable discovery: the avenue was actually sited over natural periglacial ridged features that, by coincidence, aligned on the midsummer/midwinter axes of the solstice. The Stonehenge builders were clearly aware of this natural phenomenon because they positioned Stonehenge's northeast entrance at the end of it and then enhanced the natural lines with the avenue's banks and ditches. Mike Parker Pearson suggests that this natural feature was an axis mundi, where heaven and earth came together. As at the Thornborough Henges, the Brú na Bóinne or Orkney, it was the natural landscape that first inspired the imaginations of Neolithic monument builders.

There may have been wider issues of geographical and political importance. Stonehenge lies on a natural routeway – today the main road from London to the West Country, the A303, passes right by the site (and has caused endless problems as vehicle numbers have multiplied over the past fifty years). There are river routes to the north linking the River Kennet and the Thames, which flow east; to the Severn Estuary and Wales in the west; also to the south and the Channel coast. It is possible that this route, along several rivers known by the same name 'Avon' (derived from the British word 'abonā', meaning 'the river'), provided a means for navigators along the Channel coast or the Severn estuary to divert inland and cut off the long, difficult maritime route round the Cornish peninsula. In recent years archaeologists have emphasized

Stonehenge's links to the west, obviously because the source of the bluestones lies there in Pembrokeshire's Preseli Hills. Less geological analysis has been undertaken on the great sarsen stones that, as we have already seen, probably derived from near Avebury. However, it is worth remembering that the first use of sarsens by Neolithic people was not in Wessex but in Kent. If Stonehenge is the great pilgrimage centre in the south, it may also have had ancestral links with the Thames estuary.

## The bluestone question

Much of this book has considered the human obsession with the material character and qualities of stone, and particularly its movement in the Neolithic over long distances, either as axes from the Alps, Langdale and other British quarries, or as a building material for inclusion in great monuments. The bluestones represent the most spectacular physical achievement of stone transportation in prehistoric Britain. The energy required was not merely muscular, however; it was also generated from the human mind, powered by common beliefs and made possible by cooperative efforts.

For decades there have been arguments about the sources of bluestones. One theory proposed that they were glacial erratics, rocks dumped during the Ice Age in the Salisbury Plain area. This idea is now generally regarded as disproven. Bluestone is the popular name for a variety of igneous rocks, notably rhyolites, dolerites and tuff, that occur in outcrops in the Preseli Hills of west Pembrokeshire, 225 km (140 miles) west-northwest of Stonehenge. In spite of its name, the rock is dark green in colour, not unlike Langdale tuff, and there is also a distinctive spotted dolerite that contains quartz crystals. Neolithic builders, ever aware of the qualities of stone, seem to have been fond of quartz, for its pure white colour and ability to reflect light. I can see why from the window where I sit to write – I overlook a canyon carved through igneous rock and on a moonlit night the quartz and feldspar in the rocks in the river actually sparkle.

It was as early as the 1920s that Herbert Thomas proposed an origin in the Preseli Hills for Stonehenge's spotted dolerite megaliths. Since then more detailed analysis has pinned down the sources to an area around Carn Goedog on the northern slopes of the Preseli Hills. Rob Ixer and Richard Bevins of the National Museum of Wales have, in recent years, also attempted to unravel the geological complexity of the bluestones and locate the possible sources of the material that was quarried and transported to Stonehenge.[15] In the spring of 2014, I decided to follow in their footsteps and see how the possible bluestone sources compared with the jadeitite magic mountain, Monte Viso, and the Langdale axe source.

Of course, the Preselis cannot compete in sheer height with Monte Viso. They are nevertheless impressive; they feel high. On previous visits I had come up from the south and been confronted with rocky outcrops, monoliths like stark fingers emerging from the summit. Sometimes it is spooky in the mist, but when the sky is clear you can feel you are on top of the world, at the edge of Britain. Was this Britain's magic mountain? I had always assumed the Stonehenge rocks came from near the Preseli Hills crest and were dragged southwards to the sea near Milford Haven for transportation along the south coast of Wales. Ixer and Bevins have rather muddied the waters of Milford Haven, however, identifying another important outcrop of bluestone in the valley of the River Nevern, behind the northern slopes of the Preselis, at Craig Rhos-y-Felin.

I approached this place from the north, having spent the night in a comfortable pub in the village of Newport, where the River Nevern reaches the sea. I followed the course of the Nevern inland, then as it turned eastwards, followed its tributary. The road took me onto high ground, but according to Ixer and Bevin's plan, counter-intuitively, I needed to be in the deep wooded valley below. I plunged downwards and found a ford; the dogs plunged into the water. The river curved around the edge of a small meadow, the banks lined with daffodils and primroses. It was almost a shock to see an outcrop of bluestone monoliths rearing out of the valley floor. These are supposed to be up on the bare mountains, penetrating the sky, not here in this dark, soggy Celtic bottomland. It might not be what I expected, but Craig Rhos-y-Felin still had tremendous atmosphere, even if the rather damp white horse that sheltered morosely at the foot of the rocks did not look impressed.

These rocks, geologically, look like strong candidates for Stonehenge rhyolites. The Stonehenge Riverside Project team had also been here and their excavation (from 2011 to 2015) found evidence for prehistoric quarrying: hammerstones, a 4-tonne monolith 4 m (13 ft) long and stone 'rails' from the quarry to where it had been left, ready to be placed on a cradle. The large monolith was quarried about 2000 BC, possibly a millennium after the first bluestones reached Stonehenge. However, there was evidence of earlier quarrying in the mid to late fourth millennium BC when rhyolite fingers of rocks were extracted

Outcrops of 'bluestone' rock in Pembrokeshire's Preseli Hills. The Stonehenge bluestones came from a variety of sources (and possibly existing monuments) in this area.

from the outcrop, probably by hammering in timber wedges. The re-estimate of the weight of bluestones for Stonehenge now suggests that they were lighter than originally thought, at about 2 tonnes.[16]

Detailed fieldwork by Tim Darvill and Geoff Wainwright on the higher ground has thrown a great deal of light on activity there, but there is a problem with quarrying and mining – one generation usually removes the traces of its predecessors.[17] Dating early workings can be problematic, if they can even be located. On present evidence, it seems that Bronze Age quarry-workers also extracted bluestones from this higher ground, but several centuries after the material from the northern flanks had been transported to Stonehenge, and possibly for local use.

The rock sources in the valley on the north side of the Preselis give rise to another question. How did they get from there to Stonehenge? Mike Parker Pearson proposes an alternative to the usual 'sea-route-by-raft' theory. He suggests an overland route – the eighty or so rocks bound for Stonehenge placed in cradles and hauled on rollers on a low route designed to avoid major Welsh river crossings, but fording the River Severn at Longford, north of Gloucester. The bluestone haulers may then have followed a route through the pass near to the Crickley Hill causewayed enclosure and south to Salisbury Plain – a distance of about 350 km (220 miles). Traditional rock haulers necessarily avoid water and boggy ground as much as possible, and also take pride in recruiting great numbers of helpers. The bluestones for Stonehenge would have required a team of almost sixty people for each stone. Rock hauling was an occasion, a communal festival, an opportunity for singing shanties and work songs, an excuse for a party. In Britain nearly five thousand years ago, were the bluestones passed, like an Olympic torch relay, from one community to another across South Wales? One other possibility should also be considered: that the bluestones were second-hand. Originally quarried in the Preseli Hills to make a local stone circle, perhaps they were then dismantled and transported across Wales and into Wessex. This part of Pembrokeshire is one of the finest areas in Britain for megalithic monuments, such as the nearby dolmen of Pentre Ifan (see page 268).

If the bluestones travelled overland there was probably already an established route, like the Ridgeway originally established by migrating herds. To the west, near St David's with its magnificent cathedral, there is a so-far unlocated source of rhyolite used to make polished stone axes (known as Group VIII in axe studies jargon). These axes are distributed across South Wales, but are mostly found inland and not on the coast.[18] This distribution suggests the existence of a centuries-old route avoiding the estuaries and rivers near the coast.

Why bring the bluestones such a distance? Clearly there were powerful forces at work. Monte Viso and Langdale may have been places of spiritual power releasing their spectacular stones, close to the gods like Mount Olympus. Tim Darvill and Geoff Wainwright suggest that the bluestones were seen as having healing powers – partly because of such claims for Stonehenge's stones by Geoffrey of Monmouth in his 12th-century *Historia Regum Britanniae*. I find it difficult to believe that this lurid storyteller and mythmaker had any special information about attitudes three thousand years before his time. Perhaps archaeologically more relevant is the question: if these were healing stones, why were they not more widely distributed than just Stonehenge? In Ghana I climbed up to rock outcrops that were said to have spiritual and healing powers. The slumbering spirits could be woken with a shotgun. Fragments of such powerful rocks were transported around Ghana, to Accra and even New York for 'shrine franchising' – creating shrines charged with the power of the original site. Those rocks went to many different destinations.[19]

In contrast, Parker Pearson looks to the idea of political alliances harnessed to the power of ancestors to explain the long-distance movement of the bluestones. Pembrokeshire is a hotspot for megalithic builders.[20] If Stonehenge, as the acknowledged axis mundi of Britain where sun, moon and earth coincided, was acknowledged as the centre of ritual unity in Britain in the third millennium BC, did a powerful western clan now cement their alliance by contributing their most valuable stones to Britain's omphalos? If we could also source some of the sarsens to the land of the earliest Neolithic colonists in Kent, this hypothesis would begin to look seriously strong. Gordon Childe was impressed by the 'fantastic feat' of transporting the bluestones from Wales, which he concluded 'must illustrate a degree of political unification or a sacred peace'.[21]

An alternative theory is that people from southwest Wales moved to the Salisbury Plain area, possibly earlier in the fourth millennium BC, and brought bluestones from their ancestral territory to incorporate them in the facades of long barrows such as Boles Barrow (20 km/12 miles west of Stonehenge). Then, with the establishment of the initial mortuary monument at Stonehenge about 3000 BC, they gathered together the ancestral bluestones from sites around Salisbury Plain. It is worth remembering that some of the animal bones deposited at this time were carefully curated antiques. There is a tantalizing fragment of evidence for migration from the west of Britain. Strontium and oxygen isotope results obtained from a male burial of about 3630–3360 BC beneath Winterbourne Stoke long barrow, 2.4 km (1½ miles) from Stonehenge, indicate that he grew up in a region of high rainfall and Silurian/Devonian geology characteristic of the west; but one individual does not a clan migration make. Future samples on a larger scale may help to refine our ideas about the movement of people in the Neolithic period.

Once established at Stonehenge the bluestones continued to be moved and modified. Stonehenge is the only megalithic site in Britain where the stones are chipped and hammered to form elegant shapes. When the bluestones were first set up, they were rough and ready. It was only later, when the great sarsen stones were shaped and erected, that the bluestones were also shaped like giant axes, to bring out their colour and material qualities, and perhaps to emphasize their place of origin – the ancestral mountains of the west.

The Neolithic is identified with the first farmers, yet the fourth and third millennia BC in Britain are a time when people devoted huge efforts to creating monuments, celebrating ancestors and choreographing seasonal rituals connected to the cosmology of the sun and the moon. These places became increasingly complex, relating new and larger ritual structures to older ones that retained memories and myths of communal origin. Across Britain and Ireland there developed a common religion. Originally having close continental contacts, Britain became more insular, with a greater sense of its own identity. The religious gatherings and pilgrimages may have promoted at least some element of unity, perhaps coordinated by an elite with arcane and religious knowledge. There is also a decline in the archaeological evidence for inter-communal violence.

As a devoted cynic I hesitate to suggest this was a 'golden age', but with the henges we seem to see a period of cooperation and inter-communal contacts across the British Isles. If Neolithic Britain had found a degree of stability, identity and cultural cohesion based on the religious glue represented by its henges, this was not to last. The northwest peninsula of the Eurasian land mass was always liable to be rocked by the shock waves of change radiating from the Continent – and these were on their way.

CHAPTER EIGHTEEN
# New ages: New landscapes

## From ancestors to heroes

'Stonehenge presents an appearance of massive continuity, but it does so against a background of drastic change' wrote Richard Bradley, capturing the essence of the great monument.[1] Prehistoric monuments, like Christian churches, can reflect major transformations in society: changes in belief, practice and power, even in the economy. Sometimes the transformations are subtle, or on a different timescale to events in the wider world. After the construction of the sarsen trilithons, there were further modifications at Stonehenge, notably new settings for the bluestones. In the last two stages (7 and 8) holes were dug near the standing stones. By about 1600 BC, after almost fifteen hundred years of shifting the scenery, activity ceased at Stonehenge.

In its later stages, Stonehenge witnessed dramatic technological, economic and social changes. Most obviously, there was the appearance of new substances that human beings had never experienced before. Metals such as copper, gold, silver, tin and bronze generated a technological revolution; stimulated exploration, travel and trade; and affected how people dressed, expressed their status and accumulated wealth. Metallurgy encouraged craftsmanship and an interest in the enchanting and the exotic; it promoted the development of new tools and weapons. Human societies would become more hierarchical, greedy for materials and status. Warrior elites emerged, ready to defend their status and aggressively extend it. Farming would have to increase productivity to feed more people with greater demands. The days of our polished stone axe, as a tool and a weapon, were numbered, though it would not entirely lose its symbolic attraction. The Bronze Age world was harsher than the later Neolithic, and in many ways more familiar to us.

Colin Renfrew eloquently encapsulated the changing identities: 'The economic basis of the European Neolithic permitted the formation of *group-oriented societies* whose religious and ideological aspirations found expression in and were given shape by monuments. The shift towards *individual prestige* was accompanied by the specifically European combination of bronze, weapons and masculinity, reinforced later by the horse and chariot and then by cavalry.'²

It took about four thousand years for the Neolithic Revolution – or at least some elements of it, such as domesticated plants and animals, pottery and stone axes – to spread from the Near East across Europe to the British Isles. During that time the core areas – in Mesopotamia, the Levant and Anatolia – did not remain static. They continued to develop, creating hierarchical societies, cities or proto-states dominated by theocratic kings, and massive ritual complexes, driven by more intensive, irrigated agriculture. Power was harvested through the wheel, the plough and draught animals. The ass and donkeys pulled carts with solid wheels in the mid third millennium BC. By 1900 BC, rulers commanded horse-drawn chariots with spoked wheels. Kings portrayed themselves as conquerors, seated on thrones, weapons and booty piled around them, the defeated prostrate at their feet. In these developing states there was enormous demand for prestige goods, and rare and exotic materials.

City states required bureaucracies to keep tally of their agricultural produce, textile production and slaves. Cylinder seals and early systems of writing for book-keeping appeared about 3000 BC. Soon rival dynasties in Egypt, Babylon and Anatolia (the Hittites) were communicating by diplomatic letters. About 1755 BC, Hammurabi, ruler of a large territory based on Babylon, had his famous 'Law Code' inscribed on a stele, portraying himself alongside the sun god 'Shamash'. For the first time in human history we can know the names of kings and gods, of cities and people.

The American archaeologist Timothy Earle, in describing 'Bronze Age economics', emphasized the relationship between the developments in metallurgy and the rise of states and chiefdoms, and the 'Bronze Age warrior idea'. Europe's earliest and perhaps greatest work of literature, *The Iliad*, is devoted to the Bronze Age hero, the joy of carnage, the brevity of life and the fickleness of the gods. The warrior, such as Achilles – mad, bad and dangerous to know – was the hero, wielding the sword, spear and the bow to deadly effect. These themes were sung by generations of bards, whose illiteracy probably promoted prodigious feats of memory: the ability to remember thousands of lines of verse.³ Their works would eventually be written down in Greece, and then in many other societies – for example, the *Táin Bó Cúailnge* (*The Cattle Raid of Cooley*) in medieval Ireland. Early England admired the deeds of Beowulf and Arthur. France had Roland, and the north its Norse Sagas. The epics praised the warrior hero; meanwhile, an army of peasants toiled to pay into their protection racket.

## The transformation of stone: rocks to metal

So how did metal first appear and then spread around the Middle East and Europe? The Three Age System prioritizes it: after the Stone Age come the ages of bronze and then of iron. In Western Asia and much of Europe it is also customary to add another 'age' – the Chalcolithic, reflecting the use of copper, before the appearance of bronze, which is an alloy of copper and tin. In fact, the use of copper appears remarkably early; copper even predates pottery in the Neolithic of Anatolia. The geological prospectors of the Neolithic were drawn to mountains by the lure of exotic materials that could be polished to form axes of distinctive colour. The volcanic mountains of Anatolia were the source of the finest obsidian – the gleaming, glassy material from which razor-sharp blades and arrowheads could be made. Such complex geologies are a rich source of many minerals. By 8300 BC, near the obsidian source of Göllü Dağ, pre-pottery Neolithic craftspeople had spotted the attraction of another type of stone. Cold-hammered it could be made to form distinctive, reddish shapes of a material like no other they had ever seen. They had found copper.

Aşikli Höyük was a settlement of tightly packed houses, huddled together for protection against the harsh Anatolian winter. Here, people produced the earliest copper objects in the world. Metallurgy is not an instant invention any more than is farming. It requires generations of practice, experimentation, trial and error, luck and interchange of ideas. Someone realized that heat-treating made copper easier to work and by 7000 BC heat was applied to lead-rich galena ores. Fairly quickly early metalworkers made open and then two-piece moulds in which they could cast larger, more complex objects.

This knowledge spread to, or was independently invented in, southeast Europe. By the early fifth millennium BC there were copper mines in Bulgaria and Serbia. At Belovode, near Belgrade, some of the first smelting was carried out to extract copper from its ore. At about the same time prospectors spotted specks of native gold in streams and began panning. In the Varna Cemetery we see for the first time, about 4500 BC, the conspicuous display of gold: a new way of enhancing the status of the individual, of displaying prestige that retains its power even today. While gold ingots are hidden in dark vaults as a support for national currencies, in other societies gold retains greater magic – incorruptible, glowing with the power of the sun.

In Anatolia and the Levant early metal objects circulated along the obsidian routes that had also carried early plant materials (see page 97). Knowledge of metallurgical processes was probably closely guarded and spread slowly. Certainly, for a long time stone axes continued to vastly out-number copper ones. But it could not last; demand, especially from the Levant and Mesopotamian power centres, was too great.

The site of Tel Tsaf in the central Jordan Valley around 5200–4600 BC provides remarkable evidence for the development of the sort of hierarchi-cal society where families and individuals could accumulate wealth and gain access to valued materials. Here there were large courtyard structures with above-ground silos for storing grain. Grain silos were well known around this time and often had a capacity of a few hundred kilograms. Two or three silos would feed a family for a year. At Tel Tsaf, however, some of the silos were huge, capable of holding anything from twelve to twenty-four times the requirements of a normal family. It seems that here we have clear evidence that certain elite families had gained control of the means of production. With their accumulated wealth they could afford exotic luxuries such as fine Ubaid pottery from Mesopotamia, Egyptian ostrich shells, obsidian and copper artefacts. In addition, there were large numbers of animal bones, which pointed to a privileged diet. The excavator sums up: 'It can be safely concluded that already the Middle Chalcolithic Period witnessed the creation of elite groups that bequeathed their power to the next generation.'[4]

By the mid fifth millennium BC, copper axes and shaft-hole axes – power-ful weapons cast in a two-piece mould – became the 'must-have' objects in the east, as the jadeitite axes were in western Europe. Someone, somewhere between Anatolia, the Black Sea shores and the Balkans, had a bright idea. They made the first dagger – a two-edged, special purpose fighting weapon – 'with no stone precedent and a great future ahead of it'.[5]

A cave in modern Israel, at Nahal Mishmar, demonstrates the continued advances in the Middle East, about 4000–3500 BC, as farming was first taking hold in Britain. In 1961, while searching for Dead Sea scrolls hidden in inacces-sible caves in sheer cliffs, a group of archaeologists came upon an unexpected discovery. This included 140 kg (310 lb) of copper objects of very distinctive, if odd, shapes. These were probably cult objects from a nearby shrine, perhaps at Ein Gedi. The metallurgists showed remarkable virtuosity and sophistication, making complex fluted and knobbed 'standards' and 'crowns' capped with ibex figures of arsenical copper, and used the *cire perdue* (lost wax) process. The desired object was first made in wax, then a close mould was shaped around it. Molten copper was poured in, melting the wax object and forming the desired shape as it solidified in the mould.

Nahal Mishmar's superb preservation in the dry desert illustrates other important trends in the Chalcolithic Middle East: the growing demand for craftsmanship, and the increasing significance of woollen and linen textiles. Agriculture also continued to develop. In the cave, pomegranates, nuts and, most importantly, olives were stored. No pioneer farmer begins with olives – they take ten years to become productive (so they say; I'm still waiting for mine) and then only fruit productively every other year. So olives were a secondary development of mature farming. Yet with vines, olives would become iconic of Mediterranean agriculture, a vital element in long-distance trade and the basis, with cereals and sheep, for Mediterranean civilization.

In Europe, metallurgy emerged first in the Balkans. Colin Renfrew suggested nearly five decades ago that Iberia, like the Balkans, could be a centre for autonomous development. Subsequent discoveries have proved him right. In 1994 rescue excavations at Cerro Virtud in Almeria, southeast Spain, uncovered a Neolithic settlement dating to the first half of the fifth millennium BC.[6] Here, people were smelting copper in a distinct, if slightly archaic way. They used so-called vase ovens, unique to Iberia, to reduce ore with charcoal; they did not possess the crucibles or clay tuyeres that were found further east. Centuries before farming reached Britain, communities in Bulgaria and Spain were manufacturing copper. In spite of thriving in several centres, however, metalworking was slow to spread across Europe. There is evidence that Neolithic elites were aware of copper products,[7] but perhaps they did not possess the wealth or incentive to acquire them.

North of the Alps, men preferred polished stone axes as their symbols of power. Someone who stood, and died, on this technological frontier was the now-famous ice mummy, commonly called Ötzi, who was found in 1991 on the edge of the Ötztal Alpine glacier (just inside the Italian border with Austria). Ötzi has been subjected to a barrage of forensic analysis – he is the ultimate cold case. The detail is unparalleled and a stark reminder of how little survives in a 'normal' archaeological context. The revelation is how well equipped he was for his environment, and the importance to him of organic materials. He wore a coat, leggings and a loincloth of goat hide. His cap and the soles of his shoes were bearskin; the uppers were deer hide. He had a belt and pouch of calfskin, containers of birchbark, a yew bow, a leather quiver and arrows. He had a flint knife – and a copper axe. At this time in the later fourth millennium BC, northern Italian communities had recently developed metallurgy as a result of contacts with the Balkans. It was old technology that killed Ötzi, however: someone, near the Alpine peaks, shot him with an arrow tipped with flint. In the age of metal, he would not be the only person to die violently.

## The Beaker phenomenon

About seven hundred years later, in the 24th century BC, another man from the Alpine area died. He had travelled across northern Europe and ended his days near Stonehenge. Archaeologists from Wessex Archaeology found him in 2002 on Boscombe Down (5 km/3 miles east of Stonehenge) when they were exploring land where a school and houses were about to be built. The Wessex chalk is soft but it does not preserve like the chill of ice. Nevertheless, the grave was remarkably rich: the body of an adult male, in his later thirties or forties, lay in a timber chamber with an exceptionally large number of burial offerings that were iconic of a new phenomenon in Britain – the Bell Beaker package. In fact, this is the largest burial assemblage of its kind to be found in northern Europe and the man in the grave became almost as well known as Ötzi. He was named the Amesbury Archer. The *Daily Mail* asked in its headline: 'Was this the King of Stonehenge?' I very much doubt it. He was, however, part of a cultural phenomenon sweeping across western Europe and beyond in the mid to late third millennium BC, which takes its name from the distinctive drinking vessels found in his grave.[8]

Exceptionally, he was buried – almost packed around – with five Bell Beakers and many other artefacts associated with the Bell Beaker package: copper knives and a tanged dagger; a large cache of flint arrowheads (the organic remains of the shafts were gone, as was the bow that probably lay alongside him) and two stone wrist guards; a circular shale belt ring; a cushion stone, probably for working copper or gold; a boar's tusk (possibly a metalworker's tool); and arguably the earliest gold objects in Britain – a pair of basket-shaped earrings or hair ornaments.

However, it was not his impressive Beaker kit that elevated the Amesbury Archer to the ranks of archaeological superstar. Rather, it was the isotopes that were fixed in his tooth enamel as a child. His oxygen isotopes derived

ABOVE Plan of the Amesbury Archer burial. Britain's richest Beaker burial, found 5 km (3 miles) east of Stonehenge, included five beakers, gold objects, copper daggers and (RIGHT) a fine set of flint arrowheads.

mainly from drinking water; the strontium isotopes came from food that reflected the geology of the area where it was produced. The Amesbury Archer was clearly not a native of Britain. His origins more likely lay in the Alpine area of southern Germany. His grave goods identified him as a high status warrior-archer and metalsmith, or at least someone connected with the trade in metalwork. He had another characteristic. Like the smiths of mythology – the Greek Hephaestus, and the Germanic Wayland – he was lame. He had no left patella (kneecap) and his left femur and tibia were atrophied. He must have walked with a limp and lived with considerable pain.

The Amesbury Archer lay close to another, younger man, who died aged 20–25 years, now known as 'the Companion'. His grave goods were less prolific but he also had a boar's tusk and a pair of gold basket earrings or hair ornaments. His isotopic signature indicates that he spent his early childhood on the chalklands of southern England, and may, in his teens, have visited the continental homeland of the older man who, from distinctive skeletal traits, appears to have been related, probably his father or perhaps brother.[9]

In April 2003, while watching the digging of a trench for a water pipe about 600 m (650 yd) to the north of the Amesbury Archer, the archaeologists found another early Bell Beaker grave. This burial group was complex and partly disturbed, but it included a collective grave for four adult men buried around 2300 BC with Beaker paraphernalia: eight beakers, a boar's tusk, an antler pendant (possibly a miniature bow, used to decorate a quiver), flint arrowheads, scrapers and strike-a-lights. This group of men were labelled 'the Boscombe Bowmen'. Isotopic analysis indicated that they, too, were not local to Stonehenge.

At first it was suggested that they originated in western Britain – and inevitably, the source of the Preseli bluestones came to mind. Were they the Welsh contingent who had contributed to Stonehenge? Probably not: the artefacts and style of burial have no parallels in west Wales. The isotopic signature was not precise – the 'Bowmen' could have come from the valley where I have written this book, a granite area in the French Massif Central where there are megaliths on the horizon and I am surrounded by old copper mines. I can even pan gold in the river below my window. The specialists, in their report, did in fact include this area in their list of possible places of origin. The international-style pottery, antler pendant and the communal cist in which they were successively buried suggest a continental origin: Brittany would be an alternative homeland for them.

The Beaker package may have had its origin among the metal-rich communities of Iberia. By 2700 BC there were Bell beakers in Iberia, which evolved from the drinking vessels of the metal-producing elite of the Tagus estuary. These were people with a strongly developed sense of hierarchy and identity, living in fortified settlements and controlling their territories, yet with well-developed links into Europe.

This was also a period of agricultural intensification and demographic expansion. The influence of these Beaker-using people, along with explorer-travellers, spread northwards into France and beyond to meet up with other powerful cultural influences emerging from the East. From the East came dramatic new engines for change as the horse-riding cattle and sheep herders of the steppes moved westwards. These were not backward barbarians but metal users with generations of contact into the sophisticated world of Mesopotamian cities such as Uruk. For these people, the mounted warrior, the cattle raider, personified their mythic hero.[10] Cattle represented wealth and the object of sacrifice to the gods. Their arrival in eastern Europe from the steppes beyond the Black Sea brought new threats, but also new weapons, technologies and attitudes. The horse, the covered wagon and animal traction delivered speed and power into Europe's agricultural communities.

At this time people were moving about, criss-crossing Europe and spreading new ideas and technology. This is supported by strontium isotope studies of Beaker-period burials in the Upper Danube Valley, which showed that about 60% of the sampled population had grown up elsewhere. We cannot be sure what caused people to move, but at this time individuals and even populations were surprisingly mobile. There were now different views as to how people should live in the world, reflected by the innovative fashion for conspicuous display – prestige items that announce the arrival of the metalworker, the archer/warrior, the traveller hero. The Amesbury Archer is important not only for his wealth of artefacts, but also because he represents this new phase of pan-European contact and ideological change.

The Beaker phenomenon has been discussed endlessly by archaeologists. When 'invasion' still dominated archaeological explanation, Bell beakers were seen to represent newcomers – the aggressive Beaker people (also known as the Beaker folk) who swept across Europe and into Britain wielding metal weapons and casting aside the megalithic farmers. In the 1940s, Grahame Clark wrote about 'fresh waves of invaders...with beaker-shaped pots...spreading from Brittany...into the heart of Wessex'.[11] As 'invasion' hypotheses were rejected, first by Clark himself, new explanations were sought. Parallels were drawn with the spread of cults, such as the Peyote Cult in 19th-century America which took a distinctive package of artefacts from Mexico as far north as Canada. I remember in the 1960s there were quite a few references to Coca-Cola bottles and the spread of American ideology and lifestyles – not necessarily by invasion or mass movement of peoples.

Thanks to isotopic analysis and the more precise identification of artefacts, there is now a more nuanced view. Humans have been transporting and exchanging desirable and enchanting materials for millennia – notably, polished stone axes. We can now see that individuals, like the Amesbury Archer, travelled long distances; studies of Beaker communities in Europe show that he was not an exception. Mary Helm's idea of the heroic traveller seems appropriate. Detailed analysis of French Beaker burials distinguishes a small male elite of long-distance travellers, whose knowledge and exotic origins added to their status.[12] Like Ulysses, they had seen the world and its wonders.

The Amesbury Archer is probably such a person, arriving at the famous northern cult centre of Stonehenge, his status and arcane knowledge announced by the copper daggers that were ostentatiously displayed on his chest and upper arms, the gold ornaments dangling by his face, his archery equipment (a characteristic weapon of metallurgist and smith burials in Europe) and the stone 'bracer' (wrist guard) on his arm.[13] He represents the first phase of the Beaker phenomenon in Britain when, to judge by the distribution of burials, it still represented a minority among the Grooved Ware-using British communities.

Perhaps we are seeing evidence of the arrival of a family group from the Continent, skilled and practised in the new technologies. Judging from the varied styles of beakers found, some settled in the south, while others headed further north. The initial Beaker burials may indicate a relatively small number of migrants crossing the Channel from northern France up to the Rhine Delta in the Netherlands. Their presence, however, coincides with some of Britain's *grands projets*, such as the construction of the timber palisaded enclosures in the West Kennet Valley, Silbury Hill and ongoing developments at Stonehenge.

Eventually, from the 23rd century BC, local men and women would adopt Beaker symbols of authority in Britain, aspiring to the ideology of the new elite. These later Beaker pots and other artefacts copied continental prototypes, but were, like their owners, made in Britain. The beakers were more varied and some show traits familiar from the Low Countries. In spite of the presence of metal, a new prestige item appears: the stone battle-axe perforated to take a haft.

## Britain meets the metal age: the end of the stone axe

As the demand for metal increased so did the efforts of prospectors. The discovery that harder, shinier bronze could be made by alloying copper with tin must have renewed their efforts. Compared with copper ores, tin sources are rare. Those who controlled the access to valued materials could increase their power and authority. The changes in European society would be profound.

In Britain and Ireland it was continental incomers who brought the arcane knowledge of metalworking and sought out the earliest sources of metal ore. At Ross Island, County Kerry, copper mining began in the 25th century BC. The prospectors probably came from France, most likely Brittany.[14] Beaker elements in Ireland also reflect influences from central Europe. Local people probably thought that exotic newcomers, arriving from different parts of Europe, had something to offer: access to new wealth from the ground; new lifestyles; and trading, political and social contacts and alliances. Despite this, Ireland did not adopt the Beaker package to the same extent as Britain – for example, it retained a more traditional burial style with the court cairn.

The period of copper use in Britain lasted from the 25th to the 22nd century BC. Nevertheless, some British archaeologists are reluctant to admit a Chalcolithic period into the conventional Three Age System,[15] principally because copper production and the supply of artefacts seem to have remained relatively small scale. However, Ross Island copper certainly reached as far as northeastern Scotland and into southern Britain. Axes were the main products of Irish smiths – was this a deliberate attempt to compete with the major networks in Ireland and Brittany that distributed polished stone axes? The association of the old and new can be seen at the Ballyrisode copper mine in County Cork, where there was a cache of polished stone axes. Copper axes were also deployed in similar ways to stone ones: rarely placed with the dead, they were often deposited as offerings in wet places, first in bogs and then, more frequently, in rivers. But what about their practical use?

In 1999, I found myself involved in one of British archaeology's most remarkable recent discoveries. An oval enclosure of fifty-five oak posts, standing tightly together, appeared on a beach in North Norfolk, at Holme-next-the-Sea.

The sea was rapidly eroding this coastline and, as a protective layer of peat disappeared, the posts emerged (see page 303). This unusual structure turned out to be a prehistoric monument and its most distinctive feature was the bole of an oak tree, weighing 2.5 tonnes, inside the timber enclosure. It had been cut and placed upside down in a deep pit, its roots in the air. While the Norfolk Archaeological Trust with Francis Pryor and Maisie Taylor did the interesting fieldwork, I went to lots of meetings, faced the massed ranks of angry local people in the village hall (to explain why we were removing their potential tourist attraction) and attended the High Court to take out an injunction to stop neo-pagans from occupying the site (in order to protect it from archaeologists, they claimed). 'Seahenge', as it was dubbed, became a *cause célèbre*.[16]

As with Ötzi, the ice mummy, organic survival at Seahenge opened new windows on the past. Firstly, there was the existence of the 'tree monument'. Oak uprights were placed close together with the bark retained on the outside. There was only a small hole for access to the interior. Inside, surrounded by a wall of raw wood, was the inverted oak bole. In Indo-European mythology and shamanism, inverted trees play an important role as portals between the sky, the earth and the underworld. Those who entered Seahenge must have felt that they were literally inside a tree, enclosed by wood and wrapped in its scent. The second major breakthrough here was the dating. Thanks again to Alex Bayliss's Bayesian modelling we know that the large oak was cut down in 2050 BC and the outer timbers in 2049 BC.

There was a third revelation, particularly relevant to our question about the practical use of the metal axe. When Maisie Taylor examined the deeply buried and best-preserved timbers, she was able to calculate that the Seahenge woodworkers used at least fifty metal axes. These tools were relatively state of the art. It is interesting that a small community on the North Sea coast was so well equipped. There was not a sign of a stone axe. For me, Seahenge represents the death of the stone axe as a serious tool. It also provides us with the earliest evidence for timbers worked by metal axes in Britain. In Ireland, their use can be pushed back slightly earlier at Corlea, County Longford, where builders cut the timbers for a trackway across a bog about 2268–2250 BC.

So it seems that copper and bronze axes caught on quickly. Mike Parker Pearson has made an interesting observation. At Durrington Walls, his team excavated vast numbers of artefacts, again with a notable lack of polished axes. The Durrington builders were cutting increasingly large timbers and in the chalk base of the henge ditch there were cut marks that resemble those made by metal axes. Could it be that as early as 2300 BC metal axes were in use, replacing the old technology of stone?

## Britain's early Bronze Age

Bronze was a material awaiting its time. It was known in ore-rich Afghanistan in the fourth millennium BC but in Europe it did not seriously emerge until the 22nd century BC – and it happened in Britain and Ireland. Suddenly, bronze became *the* metal for tools, weapons and ornaments.[17] The reason for this transformation was Cornish (and Devon) tin – the largest source in Europe. There was another in the Erzgebirge (Ore Mountains) of central Europe, but supplies from there were drawn into the wealthy, sophisticated orbit of the Aegean and the Near East. It may have been Erzgebirge prospectors who first came to Britain and informed the natives that this was their lucky day.

As a result, Britain's first industrial revolution led to the opening of not only tin mines but also more copper mines. After five hundred years, Ross Island production came to an end. Its persistent flooding was a problem beyond the available technology. However, other mines more than filled the production gap: in Ireland at Mount Gabriel, County Cork, and, earlier in Wales, at Copa Hill near Aberystwyth, where from 2100 BC there was an open-cast copper mine with wooden drains to carry water away. The most prolific source lay deeper in the ground at Great Orme, the headland above the present-day North Wales seaside resort of Llandudno. The copper ore was exposed in the cliffs so, from about 2100 BC and for the next six centuries, Welsh miners pursued the ore down complex galleries, hewing and hacking out one of the biggest copper mines in prehistoric Europe.

As well as the Bronze revolution, Ireland had a gold rush, probably starting a little earlier. Prospectors, crawling all over western Britain, discovered gold in the Wicklow Mountains and also in the streams flowing off the Mourne Mountains. The new elites had to have it: the most lustrous, sun-infused material of all. Irish gold workers introduced extravagant new products such as lunulae, great crescent-shaped sheets of gold, which were worn around the neck and across the chest, a blatant statement of power and authority. Most of the lunulae stayed in Ireland (eighty-five of them); the piece from Blessington, County Wicklow, is among the finest, but others have been found in Scotland, Wales and Cornwall, and even more in northern and western France – perhaps the home of Ireland's original prospectors. These gold sheets were beautifully decorated with geometric patterns, like rays that reflect the light. In Mold, North Wales, an elite man or woman wore a cape of gold, decorated to look like strings of beads.

Craftsmanship flourished across Britain and Ireland, Beakers were copied locally and new materials, such as jet from Whitby on North Yorkshire's coast, were used for buttons and prestige jewelry – a spectacular multi-stringed bead necklace with flat space-plates found at East Kinwhirrie, Angus, was an elite piece worn by a woman. The distribution of jet artefacts is especially pronounced along the east coast of Scotland into Orkney, suggesting that the east coast sea route was active in the Bronze Age. The discovery of wooden boats for the first time at Ferriby in the Humber estuary, Yorkshire, provides us with tantalizing evidence of boatbuilding, albeit a vessel that may have been more at home in the river and the sheltered estuary.

Ironically, as bronze became the material of choice, the age-old craft of flint working rose to the challenge. In a number of Beaker graves there are beautifully flaked flint daggers, imitations of the metal ones trying to compete with the glamorous new material. Craftspeople were also innovating: blue faience, arguably made in Britain from about 1900 BC, was the first glass, probably a by-product of the pyrotechnics involved in tin and copper smelting.[18] The material must have been a new wonder of the world for those who first saw it in the form of iridescent blue beads, circular, segmented and star-shaped, sometimes strung together with amber. Both amber and faience were probably imbued with amuletic powers. Like tin, faience had been transformed from the mundane to the magical. By stringing faience together with amber and jet, such necklaces provided protection as well as prestige for the wearers, and a sense of awe in the lesser mortals who observed them.

The most impressive collection of early Bronze Age grave goods comes from the barrows that increasingly encircled the ancient site of Stonehenge. On the chalk ridges the barrow mounds, initially capped in startlingly white chalk, would have stood out against the sky. In the earlier prehistoric ritual landscape long barrows were used for communal burial and causewayed enclosures had relatively open access. Increasingly, it seems, monuments became places where access was limited to the privileged or the initiated. Few people would qualify for entry into the Stonehenge inner sanctum or the platform at the top of Silbury Hill.

As the monuments developed so did the elites who organized the rituals.[19] With the arrival of a new ethos from the Continent along the Beaker pathways, the Wessex elite began to emphasize their identity as individuals, reflecting their personal status in clothing, artefacts and possibly even their hairstyles or tattoos – and presumably in their behaviour. Now powerful people merited their own burial, first in Beaker flat graves, but later under large mounds or barrows. Between about 2000 BC and 1500 BC 'Wessex' graves were outstanding for their wealth and exotic finery.

The rise of the Wessex Bronze Age aristocracy has been put down to their role as middlemen in the tin and copper network. At the focal point of Neolithic pilgrim routes by land and sea, they were ideally situated within Britain and for links to the Continent through cross-channel harbours such as Poole and Chichester. Beyond the Channel, in Brittany, there were also elite graves at this time belonging to another group of powerful people with access to tin and to rare, high-status objects such as silver beads. For oligarchs the world over, symbols of power matter. The fact that the 'Wessex' graves orbit Stonehenge, like planets round the sun, is a reminder of the continuing religious authority imbued in the stone circle and its satellites, as well as the other great Wessex henges: Avebury, Marden and Mount Pleasant. Many of the prestige items probably had cosmological significance, to buttress the power of the wearer.[20]

The earlier group of graves (they are chronologically divided by different dagger types) includes the most spectacular burial, at Bush Barrow, south of Stonehenge. This massive mound was laid over the corpse of a man enhanced by some remarkable objects. These can now be properly appreciated in the new displays at the Wiltshire Museum. The Bush Barrow objects are exceptional for the quality of their craftsmanship, notably a dagger whose hilt is studded with tiny pins of gold. Another dagger was probably made in Brittany. There is also a stone mace head with bone fittings on its wooden staff, which could be a 'princely' or 'priestly' symbol. Grave goods were placed by the mourners or the funeral organizers, but if these objects were regalia worn or carried in life then the Bush Barrow man could not have failed to make an impact, especially with the large lozenges of sheet gold and a gold plaque on his chest.

Wessex women also had style. One buried at Upton Lovell had a necklace of five strands of amber beads, the strands held apart with spacer plates (similar to the jet necklaces in Scotland). She also had a gold plaque, gold studs and beads, a cone of Kimmeridge shale (the southern alternative to Whitby jet) covered in gold sheet, a bronze knife, a pottery urn and a distinctive little grape cup, decorated with clay bobbles, thought to be an incense burner. There is a distinctly 'priestess'-like quality to this woman's grave goods. What struck me when I saw these burial assemblages 'en masse' for the first time at Devizes was how many objects resembled the paraphernalia of shamans, well known from material collected in the 19th century from communities close to the Arctic Circle. In particular, shamans often wore objects that clashed, jangled and sparkled when they danced and entered a trance state. Shamans do not always have political power, but the Wessex elite may have combined religious and secular authority with diplomatic and trade connections.

Social and economic changes were not confined to Wessex. Elite objects were valued across Britain, notably the Mold cape found in North Wales (now dated between 1900 BC and 1600 BC). Irish gold lunulae and Yorkshire jet were in demand in Wales and Scotland, and Scotland was home to some of the most skilled metalworkers. Large barrow cemeteries appeared across southern and eastern England, often closely associated with older henges, as at Devil's Quoits, Stanton Harcourt, in Oxfordshire. The evolution of such a 'Wessex'-type cemetery, culminating in an avenue of barrows, can be best seen at Barrow Hills, Radley, in Oxfordshire where Oxford Archaeology excavated not only the barrow sites, but also the areas between, which contained a mind-boggling variety of flat graves.[21]

From the early Bronze Age, while barrows dominate the landscape of Wessex and the English river valleys, the remains of houses are insubstantial. These people were probably relatively mobile, following herds of cattle, which represented wealth and status. A Beaker burial at Irthlingborough in Northamptonshire provides evidence of a spectacular funerary feast: the burial pit was capped with a stone cairn and the remains of more than a hundred cattle. The bones of the beasts were left piled on the mound, in honour of the gods and as a memorial to a carnivorous orgy.

## The Channel highway

Amber is a particularly fascinating material of enormous cosmological significance. Wessex craftspeople made amber bead necklaces with distinctive spacer plates using material probably transported from the Baltic. The beads have been found as far north as Orkney, and even in the shaft graves of Mycenae. Were these powerful religious amulets that travelled with consignments of Cornish tin to Greece, or were they worn by a diplomatic bride helping to cement trans-European connections? The Mycenaeans may not have designed Stonehenge – as used to be suggested in those not-so-far-off days before radiocarbon dating – but they may have heard rumours of the Hyperborean temple of the remote north!

The expanse of trading networks in the second millennium BC emerges most clearly from recent discoveries along the Channel coast of Britain and France. Stuart Needham, formerly of the British Museum, has drawn attention to maritime zones of interaction stimulated by the need to exchange metals and other materials such as amber. This, of course, implies the existence of seaworthy vessels. In 1992 the most spectacular Bronze Age vessel found so far turned up, appropriately, in Dover. It is one of the most significant artefacts to survive from the European Bronze Age. The boatbuilders constructed this craft, 13 m (42 ft) long, from precisely carved oak planks cut with bronze axes and adzes about 1550 BC. The planks were sewn together and waterproofed with moss, beeswax and animal fat. To modern eyes it is a strange way to build a boat, yet it was capable of crossing the Channel – although its crew would have been wise to keep a weather eye out and avoid rough water. A fragment of Dorset shale dropped in the boat suggests the crew had voyaged along the south coast of Britain.[22] Cornish pottery, known as Trevisker ware, is also a telltale marker of such voyages as it reaches Kent and the Pas-de-Calais. Divers made another discovery just outside Dover Harbour in Langdon Bay. On the seabed they located a collection of more than four hundred French bronze artefacts of unusual types not normally found in Britain. This must be the cargo of a French vessel that sank close to the British shore.

There is another link in this maritime Channel network that takes the form of spectacular-handled gold cups (see page 302). The best known is the Rillaton Cup, unearthed in Cornwall (and said to have resided in Buckingham Palace for a number of years, used as a royal shaving mug). In fact, there are sixteen of these cups known, some made of silver or shale and found on both sides of the Channel. In 2001 a metal detectorist dug up a superb example at Ringlemere Farm, just inland from Sandwich in Kent. Like the Rillaton Cup its body was finely corrugated, designed to sparkle and reflect the light. The detectorist reported his discovery and provided a great opportunity to examine the context of the cup's burial. Subsequent archaeological excavation then showed that the cup had been placed in the top of a barrow mound (not in a grave), which lay within a ritual complex that had a long history back into the Neolithic.[23]

These spectacular cups were designed to be held – elevated like a chalice, not placed on a flat surface – because when full of liquid they would topple over. It is likely, then, that the cups were ritual vessels used for libations among initiates, perhaps by heroic sea travellers. These people were directly connected with the Channel maritime exchange nexus, transporting precious metals from the west, together with prestige Wessex valuables and amber from across the North Sea. The distribution of Ringlemere–Rillaton cups is distinctly coastal from Cornwall to Kent. Some were taken to the Continent, where they are found in Brittany; others were transported down the Rhine. The cups emphasize that the movement of materials at this time was not part of some large-scale mercantile activity so much as the long-distance exchange of objects of ritual and symbolic power in the tradition of the jadeitite axes.[24]

## An *entente cordiale*

Since the 1990s, French archaeologists working across the Channel, close to the coast of La Manche, have also been able to take advantage of developer-funded (rescue) archaeology – what in French translates as 'preventative archaeology'. There is increasing evidence in northern France of a British connection, particularly from about 1750 BC: 'It becomes more and more obvious that both areas are part of the same economic network and share the same cultural connections,' said French archaeologists working in the area.[25] Burials, metalwork, pottery and settlements are remarkably similar on both sides of the Channel.

One of the most intriguing sites (found during motorway construction) is 'Mont Bagarre' at Étaples. By around 1800 BC there was a large settlement on a promontory overlooking the sheltered estuary of La Canche, Pas-de-Calais. Its houses and pottery would be at home in Bronze Age England. The location is ideal for cross-Channel contact; was this the destination of a fine-weather Dover ferry or even the base for a British colony? At the very least, it was a hub for the 'transmanche' network – a predecessor for the great sixth-century AD Merovingian emporium of Quentovic, which lies on the opposite bank of the river. By 1300 BC, 'Mont Bagarre' was abandoned. The Bronze Age network in which Britain was so closely attached to the Continent fragmented and the peoples on either side of La Manche turned their backs on each other.

## A Bronze Age farming revolution

Gordon Childe's idea of the Neolithic Revolution was driven by the change of humankind's mode of production: from hunter-gathering to farming, to the domestication and cultivation of certain plants and animals. Farmers arrived in Britain from the Continent bringing cereals, sheep, cattle and pigs, but in reviewing how these people made an impact on the British landscape and their way of life, we have mainly considered their monuments, graves, rituals and technology.

Two archaeologists who specialize in the study of plants, Chris Stevens and Dorian Fuller, have asked an interesting question in relation to Britain: 'Did Neolithic farming fail?'[26] There is no doubt that the first farmers brought the Neolithic 'package': the domestic animals, cultigens, pottery and stone axes. Early farmers cultivated cereals, particularly emmer wheat, free-threshing wheat (*Triticum* sp.) and six-rowed hulled barley. As the *Gathering Time* project showed, these cereals rapidly spread across the British Isles. We know this from the presence on sites of charred cereal remains.[27] Yet on the same sites there is often considerable evidence for the exploitation of wild plants, particularly hazelnuts (the staple of the Mesolithic hunter-gatherers, see page 185). Occasionally, archaeologists find considerable quantities of preserved cereals, as at Balbridie, where the free-threshing club wheat was identified, charred among the remains of a timber building consumed by fire. Usually, however, the amounts recovered on Neolithic sites are very small. It is worth remembering that on the 'prehistoric' experimental farm at Butser Hill, Hampshire, a plot of land only 10 × 10 m (33 × 33 ft) could produce over 100,000 grains of wheat.

The impression is that Neolithic farmers were growing small quantities of cereals, but is this simply the bias of the archaeological record? To be preserved in normal conditions cereal remains need to be carbonized. In the Iron Age, below-ground storage pits for grain are routine on many settlements. These were often burnt to clean them and as a result vast quantities of grain debris in the pits were carbonized and survived. In the Neolithic in Britain such large underground silos were not yet in use. Grain, as at Balbridie and in continental Lake Villages, may have been stored in pots or baskets in the house and, for the most part, failed to enter the archaeological record.

When we excavated the early Neolithic midden at Dorney, the site of the Olympic and Eton College rowing course, we recovered ninety-seven cereal grains and fifty-three hazelnut shell fragments – minute quantities of cereals compared with those found on later Iron Age settlements nearby in the Thames

Valley. Grain is, nevertheless, present, and as far north as Shetland, at the Scord of Brouster site, hardy farmers were growing naked barley (*Hordeum vulgare L.* var. *nudum*). There is no sign of the hardier spelt wheat until the Bronze Age.

There is no doubt that cereals were grown and consumed in the British Neolithic. The questions are: how easy were they to cultivate and did they contribute significantly to the food supply compared with wild plants and domestic animals? The detailed analysis of cereal remains, reliably radiocarbon-dated, indicates their arrival in Britain about 4000 BC, a rapid adoption of the Neolithic package, and that they were widely present in settlements between 3800 and 3000 BC. There is then a significant reduction in their presence both in Britain and Ireland. One explanation for the decline is that cereals in Britain initially had a 'honeymoon' period: they were grown in small plots in a wooded landscape, in rich soils, with few pests and optimal climatic conditions, then yields may have tailed off. Alternatively, there could have been social and economic factors that discouraged cultivation.

Stevens and Fuller have analysed more than seven hundred radiocarbon dates specifically taken from cultigens and wild food from British and Irish sites. Initially, cereals spread along with farmers and the increasing human population,[28] but in the middle and late Neolithic the number of dates drops off drastically because there is so little cereal material available. The consumption of hazelnuts declined from 3200 BC to 2500 BC. After that, their contribution to the Bronze Age diet was negligible.

The initial decline in cereals conforms to the first construction of causewayed enclosures. Are we seeing mixed farmers, with their longhouses, moving towards a more mobile, and more pastorally based, economy? Many prehistorians have emphasized the decline in evidence for cereal and arable farming, the apparent local regeneration of woodland and the lack of settlement evidence. The most recent study puts this shift, across a broad area of Britain, at about 3350 BC. This would represent a drastic collapse in cereal production for the best part of a thousand years, with the exception of many of Britain's offshore islands where some cultivation continued.

There is a tendency to assume that agriculture, once established, represents a ladder of inevitable upward progress. This need not be the case. There are many examples of agricultural decline or changes to more sustainable systems based on pastoralism and wild resources. As in the Swiss and German Lake communities (see Chapter 12), climatic deterioration could cause population reduction and an increasing dependence on wild foodstuffs. And there are other cases as far afield as Japan, India and Mongolia. Societies do not march ever onwards and upwards and mixed arable farming is not always the optimum strategy. One possible scenario is that a series of poor harvests around 3300 BC, linked to climate deterioration, led to a shift towards domestic livestock and also back to wild plants and animals, which were available in the still extensive forests (especially on the margins) and the marshes.

There is some evidence for the localized reintroduction of cereals in the early Beaker period, for example in the Thames Valley, then production surged from about 1500 BC. Mixed farming was back in a big way. Stevens and Fuller sum it up this way: 'Rather than the Neolithic it is perhaps the middle Bronze Age that represents the real agricultural revolution in the British Isles.' They plead for a 'need to escape the tyranny of the "Neolithic" label and its assumption of unchanging village farmers'.

As I hope I have shown, 'unchanging village farmers' is hardly an appropriate label for the British from 4000 BC to 2000 BC. Increasingly, however, evidence from fieldwork supports the concept of a middle Bronze Age agricultural revolution – an idea that in itself is not new. Gordon Childe referred to it in his book *Prehistoric Communities of the British Isles* in 1940. In the middle of the second millennium BC in Britain and Ireland communities shifted their efforts from building monuments to taking a grip on the land to increase agricultural productivity. Boundaries, fields and farmsteads spread across the countryside.

## The view from the motorway

Anyone driving along the M4 motorway just south of Reading and west of London can see where my colleagues from Oxford Archaeology and I first discovered our personal Bronze Age agricultural revolution. By the late 1980s we had spent almost two decades flying over the Thames Valley analysing thousands of aerial photographs and excavating hundreds of hectares of land in advance of new housing development and gravel pits. We had investigated many Neolithic and early Bronze Age ritual sites – henges, cursuses, burials and barrows. We also had a pretty good idea what was going on in the Iron Age – the first millennium BC – with its dozens of settlements, some seasonal and pastoral, but most semi-permanent mixed arable farms with dozens of below-ground storage pits.

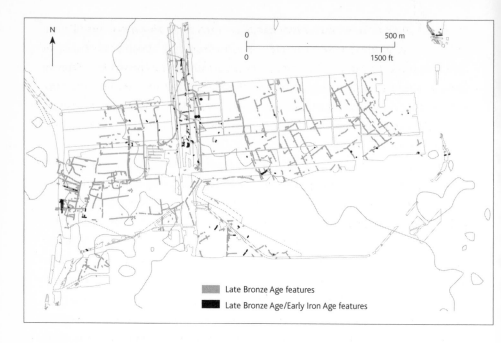

Plan of the Late Bronze Age ditched fields excavated at Heathrow Airport in advance of the construction of Terminal 5.

We had found very little evidence relating to the middle to late Bronze Age. Then, in 1986, we were asked to evaluate a huge block of land south of Reading, Berkshire, in advance of the construction of a business park. This low-lying land was extensively covered by alluvial flood deposits from the Kennet/Thames. There was little evidence on the surface or on aerial photographs for any archaeological remains, but all that changed when we began to dig a chequerboard of evaluation trenches with a machine. Beneath the alluvium we found a series of low, dry gravel islands, and every one of them contained a middle to late Bronze Age settlement. Eventually, many hectares of land were stripped of the alluvium blanket, exposing the middle to late Bronze Age land surface. It was a revelation. Here was a fully-fledged farming landscape: dozens of substantial round houses, ditches, enclosures and fields, many elevated four-post storage buildings, waterholes and pits, and midden deposits.[29]

From about 1500 BC an agricultural complex emerged in the valley – farms and hamlets of the sort we can recognize today. Admittedly, the highly standardized thatched houses were circular – rather like those in some African villages – but otherwise with its trackways, fields, storage facilities and places to water animals it was agriculture as we know it, and a transformation from the ritual landscape of the Neolithic. Because of the number of pits and waterlogged deposits, the environmental and economic evidence was prolific. This was a community that kept animals and grew cereals – a fully organized agricultural establishment with plenty of storage facilities for grain and fodder. The land was divided into manageable units (otherwise known as fields), bounded by droveways, banks, ditches and, probably, hedges. We take fields for granted – but here are the first to be found in the region.

After the discovery of the Reading Business Park complex, the floodgates opened. Thanks to new planning regulations (Planning Policy Guidance Note 16 in the jargon in England) developers were required to assess proposed development sites for archaeology. This has resulted in a revolutionary expansion of knowledge for many periods.[30] Proposed developments were very rarely stopped because of archaeology. Usually, any sites discovered were excavated, recorded and published. It is fair to say that our understanding of the middle to late Bronze Age was transformed. Across the middle and lower Thames Valley and into Essex and East Anglia huge areas of settlements and fields appeared. On the chalk downlands linear ditches defined large blocks of land that resemble present-day parish boundaries.

Not everywhere was the same, however – activity was less intense in the upper Thames Valley. It seems that by 1500 BC the early ritual complexes there had lost their significance. The focus had shifted to the middle and lower Thames Valley and the Thames estuary, which became a major part of the Bronze Age nexus with the Continent. Religious rituals still played a major role but now they were much more focused on the river and wet places. Valuable metal objects were placed in the water as offerings, probably along with human remains. There was a Bronze Age arms race, with new swords, spears, daggers and shields, and even armour and cavalry equipment.

From the early 1980s, Francis Pryor and his team excavated a superbly preserved late Bronze Age complex, dating to about 1300–900 BC, on the fen edge at Flag Fen, near Peterborough. The occupants drove tens of thousands of timbers into the marsh to form causeways and platforms. Most remarkable were the ritual deposits of metalwork, such as rapiers, swords, daggers and spearheads, as well as other objects such as quernstones, an axe haft and Britain's earliest-known wheel (dating to the 13th century BC).

The religious emphasis seems to have shifted from monuments associated with the heavens. Eyes now turned downwards into the murky water of the rivers and fens. The timber structures and objects offered to the gods of the mire and water are spectacular survivals, but even more important is the sheer extent of Bronze Age field systems, droveways and settlements across the surrounding landscape. Fengate also reveals structured farming on a massive scale.[31]

Power may have shifted from Stonehenge and Wessex to the southeast as the 'ritual' transport of metal objects shifted to a more mercantile arrangement. New elites had new priorities. Perhaps they were less mystical, and less concerned with ancestors and trances. They needed weapons, scrap metal from the Continent as British sources dried up and agricultural produce to pay for them. Judging from the appearance of spindle whorls and clay loom weights, textile production may have become economically important in the lower Thames Valley. Around the region large defended enclosures appeared – perhaps the strongholds of this warrior aristocracy. The community no longer dug to build henges, Silbury Hills or barrows. Now the effort went into digging ditches around fields and intensifying agricultural production to pay for foreign imports of bronze as British mines ceased production. These elites still had a taste for power and needed new ways to enhance it. Peasant agriculture supported warrior chieftains and their retinues. By the end of the Bronze Age, hillforts were beginning to dominate many of the high places of Britain. If the Neolithic henges marked a time of relative peace, the hillforts symbolized rivalry and discord.

The move to increased agricultural production can be seen elsewhere in Britain. On Dartmoor, for example, extensive field systems (reeves), covering as much as 10,000 hectares (24,700 acres), appeared. The land was divided into large blocks subdivided by drystone walls, like medieval parishes. The blocks included varied resources from lowland areas with watercourses to upland grazing. Cultivation and grazing pushed into the uplands. Pollen diagrams show that serious inroads were being made into the surviving forests. On Dartmoor and the Pennines, as well as the middle and lower Thames Valley, East Anglia and Wessex, agriculture was at its most extensive.

The climate, however, would play its hand. In the later second millennium BC there was a shift to cooler and wetter weather. In the uplands, on the 'Wuthering Heights', blanket bog expanded and farming retreated. The moorlands evoked by writers such as the Brontës, Arthur Conan Doyle and Ted Hughes are essentially Bronze Age creations – an example of what happens when optimistic farmers confront climatic deterioration. Similarly, the brecklands and heathlands of southern Britain probably developed around this time.

The deterioration of agricultural land was not necessarily disastrous. The population had grown, probably stimulated by increased food supply and the need for labour, so in many lowland areas, farming intensified further. In the middle and lower Thames Valley much of the best land and the most extensive settlements were on the floodplain. Faced with rising water tables and flooding, the people retreated and the land turned to grazing. In the upper Thames Valley, with its extensive elevated gravel terraces and limestone slopes, the population increased and many new farms appeared.

In contrast, Ireland may have been more seriously affected by the cooler, wetter conditions. There are signs there that woodland regenerated and the population may have declined. Nevertheless, the emergence of new, powerful hierarchies, probably controlling land and backed by retinues of warriors, is reflected in the appearance of strongholds dominating the landscape in high places, surrounded by concentric rings of earthworks and ramparts. Sites such as Rathgall in County Wicklow and Haughey's Fort in County Armagh flourished between about 1200 BC and 900 BC.

In eastern Britain, farmsteads growing cereals and rearing cattle and sheep were scattered across the increasingly enclosed countryside. Clay loom weights suggest textile manufacture was a growing specialization here, too. New, high-status ring forts also appear, the impressive eyries of the elite, bounded by striking banks, ditches and palisades. At Thwing in East Yorkshire, the enclosure, surrounded by double ditches, was over 100 m (330 ft) across with a large timber house at the centre. In the circular fort at Springfield Lyons in Essex, bronze-mould fragments lay in the terminals of the ditches at the eastern and western entrances: bronzesmiths were at work, and they were making swords. From the 13th century BC, long bronze slashing swords entered Britain from the Continent, along with other warrior equipment, such as spears and shields. The spear was popular in Britain; its use was demonstrated at Queensford Mill, near Dorchester-on-Thames: the tip of one was snapped off in the pelvis of a young man.

By the later Bronze Age a productive peasantry cultivated the land, intensively reared animals and manufactured by-products, particularly textiles. A well-armed warrior elite was in control, however, at least until more powerful rivals turned up.

## The age of iron

The middle and lower Thames Valley may eventually have been buffeted by other, economic changes. Not far away, on the north side of the Kennet Valley, is the site of Hartshill Copse at Upper Bucklebury, West Berkshire. Recent excavations revealed the earliest ironworking site in Britain, dating to the tenth century BC.[32] Here there was a round house, seemingly residential, next to another circular building that was used as a workshop. Large quantities of hammerscale and other debris connected with ironworking lay scattered around the workshop.

It is surprising to find this activity so early. In Britain, the transition from tools and weapons in bronze to those in iron occurred between the ninth and seventh centuries BC. The implications are considerable. The great advantage of iron over bronze is that the iron ores are common. The consumers of bronze in the Thames Valley had to look to the Continent for supply , like the sunken cargo found off Dover, which failed to arrive. However, iron ore was all around them, though not necessarily of a high quality. High temperatures are needed to smelt it, so iron involves an escalation in all kinds of activities. For example, to produce 1 kg (2 ¼ lb) of finished iron takes 20 kg (44 lb) of ore, 90 kg (198 lb) of wood for fuel and 40 kg (88 lb) of clay. The process includes ore roasting, smelting, bloom smithing and blacksmithing. This can involve a number of specialists based in different places. Smithing, in particular, is usually locally based.

Iron production has a big impact on the environment, but it provides harder, sharper swords and axes – and more of them. Iron production, operating locally and regionally, undermined the international trade links of the Bronze Age. Bronze still had a place – some magnificent drinking vessels, mirrors and cauldrons were displayed at the feasts of the aristocracy and their horses wore bronze. The riders, however, were men of iron.

The days of the polished stone axe were long gone. The polished stone axe felled the first trees, established a fondness for the exotic, created pathways to the magic mountains of the Alps, West Wales and Langdale, and drew pilgrims to the sacred sites. The axe was the symbol of authority carried by the community's most influential men. It guarded liminal places like fords and the entrances to tombs. From this society emerged others obsessed with rank and hereditary status, with new materials that both expressed their roles in society and served to elevate them further. They organized labour to increase agricultural production. In the fields the peasant tilled, sowed and reaped in a never-ending cycle of hard work. The wild retreated: forests shrank and marshes dried, but soils eroded, flooding increased and animals went extinct. Britain's green and pleasant land, with its tamed landscape and domesticated people, would become a target for empire builders and tax collectors. In Rome, and later in Normandy, greedy eyes saw the possibilities of a productive land prepared and tended by generations of farmers.

# Ploughing on regardless?

### Was farming a mistake?

Arguably, the Neolithic Revolution was inevitable – once such a large-brained, curious species as *Homo sapiens* appeared and rapidly colonized the Earth and the climate veered from the last glacial to the relatively stable Holocene. The Natufians in Western Asia experimented with and consumed about 150 different wild plants – among those plants was the ancestor of wheat, whose genetic plasticity caused it to develop into one of the great providers of calories for human beings. It was probably the stress of climatic change in the Younger Dryas that stimulated the increased population of human plant experts to experiment with the techniques of reproduction that led to domestication. In other parts of the world, at about the same time, humans explored the potential of different plants, animals and environments.

Thirteen thousand years ago hunter-gatherers around the Yangtze River ate wild rice (*Oryza rufipogon*). After the shock of the Younger Dryas they, too, had learnt how to cultivate what would become another great staple food of humanity. In northern India rice was probably independently domesticated at the same time, and in more northerly parts of China millet appeared as the staple crop. Soybeans, pigs and chickens would eventually enliven the diet, though a dubious future awaited all of them – thanks to humans. In highland New Guinea there were garden plots at least seven thousand years ago in which taro and yams grew.

America was the last continent (except for Antarctica) to be settled by humans, and by 10,000 BC people had reached its southern extremity. This New World with its megafauna, innocent of the new deadly predator, must have provided rich pickings for the hunter-foragers. Nevertheless, domestication and plant food production appears in the early Holocene and by 6,500 years ago domesticated peanuts, manioc and chile peppers had spread well beyond their original homelands. In Central and South America, tomatoes, beans, squashes, arrowroot, avocadoes, pineapples, chocolate, potatoes and pumpkin contributed to a diet rich in plants, but few wild animal species were suitable for domestication (although the camelids – llama, vicuña and alpaca – were domesticated in the Andes by about five thousand years ago).

The most remarkable American plant must be maize (*Zea mays*), a plant transformed out of all recognition by the genetic changes that led to its adoption by humans on a massive scale. Maize evolved several thousand years ago as a result of a rapid series of mutations in an undistinguished grass known as teosinte (Nahuatl for 'mother of corn'). Instead of a few small seeds on a rachis, like most grasses, maize underwent a massive sexual transformation. Its female organs moved from the top of the plant to a huge sheathed ear in the middle of the stalk and became irresistibly attractive to humans with its package of bulging seeds, which is just as well – without humans to strip away the husk this mutation could not reproduce itself and would go extinct. Instead, maize evolved into a marvellous foodstuff. By about two thousand years ago it was cultivated in the region that would become New York. Native American farmers, seven hundred years ago, ate about 500 g (1 lb) of maize each day – approximately half their diet.

Traditionally, agriculture has been seen as a step upwards on the ladder of inevitable human progress towards civilization. This may be naive, and recently attitudes have shifted to the opposite extreme. The super-surfers of human history, historians with a grand view who encapsulate a conclusion in a nutshell, are not fond of the Neolithic. It is fashionable to decry the switch from hunter-foraging to farming. For many recent commentators the development of farming was not so much a giant step for humankind, as a turn in the wrong direction. For example, Yuval Noah Harari, in his bestseller *Sapiens*, declares: 'The Agricultural Revolution was history's biggest fraud.' And who was the perpetrator? Why, wheat of course, along with those other devious grasses, rice and corn. 'We did not domesticate wheat. It domesticated us,' says Harari. What's more 'The Agricultural Revolution was a trap....Nobody agreed to this deal.'[1] Poor old humankind – conned again by nasty nature and its infinite rattle-bag of evolutionary tricks.

I feel uncomfortable with this attitude. There is no doubt that wheat, rice and maize, and for that matter sheep, pigs, cattle and chickens, have expanded across the world and rocketed in terms of numbers, thanks to their starring role in the Neolithic drama. In a later phase of the agricultural revolution, large numbers of black West African people were transported like livestock across the Atlantic to plantations in Brazil, the West Indies and North America. As a result, West African genes have colonized the Americas, but I have never heard any black American thank slave traders for their evolutionary leg-up or apologize for entrapping the unsuspecting plantation owners.

There is no doubt that human beings are poor predictors of the future, often victims of unforeseen consequences. Nevertheless, Harari seems to suggest that we were barely active agents in the process of domestication. This lets us off the hook of responsibility. We are already too inclined to blame other species for the ills of the world, without portraying the agricultural revolution as a disaster imposed on us by wheat and sheep, driven by evolutionary forces. Not everything can be explained in evolutionary terms – sometimes humans have to consider their own ethical behaviour.

Jared Diamond is probably the most widely read of the pessimists.[2] For him agriculture was 'the worst mistake in the history of the human race'. He emphasizes the supposed decline in the quality of the Neolithic diet and the physical condition of farmers. This argument is based on relatively small samples from restricted areas and yet has been the basis for wildly pessimistic views of early farming life. In fact, across Eurasia it is often difficult to compare the physical condition of hunter-foragers and farmers because of the lack of evidence. These negative views also fail to take account of the varied lifestyles and continued exploitation of wild resources in differing environmental zones. Not all human beings in the Neolithic in Eurasia lived in crowded villages on a diet of cereals and chickpeas. The suppression of women and the rise of aristocracies is not an inevitable corollary of farming – some agricultural societies have consciously sought to remain relatively egalitarian. While Jared Diamond sees agriculture as 'a catastrophe from which we never recovered' (and humans as helpless pawns?), many traditional societies have shown incredible ingenuity at harvesting water supplies, conserving soils, breeding crops appropriate to their environment and managing well-balanced diets. If the Neolithic was a mistake, then so was the evolution of a big brain, the development of language and cooking. Life would be simpler without them, but there would be no human consciousness.

Modern food faddists have extolled the 'Palaeolithic diet' – as if there was such a thing – blaming the supposed dramatic shift to the three great grasses, wheat, rice and maize, for such problems as skin disorders, multiple sclerosis, Parkinson's disease, schizophrenia and autism. The Ohalo evidence indicates that humans were eating these 'unnatural' foods – grass seeds – more than ten thousand years before the Neolithic. In evolutionary terms this is still a short time span; humans, however, have shown themselves capable of adapting to the consumption of new foodstuffs, such as milk from domestic animals, far more quickly.

The pessimistic view of agriculture overlooks the problems that beset hunter-foragers: food shortages, overhunting and species extinction; socially stratified societies and warfare were also not unknown in the pre-Neolithic Garden of Eden. When hunter-gatherer populations increased and wild food resources became depleted, food production became the only long-term survival strategy for human beings. There is a certain irony when academic commentators wish away agriculture – the system that made writing, universities and book publication possible. The fact is, domestication and farming did happen. What is important is to understand its consequences and where we go from here.

## In search of variety

Food security has always been the dominant priority for humans. Empires from Mesopotamia to Rome and Nazi Germany have been built on the drive to acquire land and its produce. Because of this quest, the agricultural revolution has rarely stopped. Once it started rolling, so did the search for new, better and more valuable plants and animals. The search for the exotic, and a reliable supply of staples, stimulated travel and trade, as well as imperial conquest. Egypt was Rome's breadbasket; North Africa its oilfields (producing olive oil). Only a fool would idealize the Roman Empire – its treatment of those who resisted its embrace was remorselessly harsh. Nevertheless, it is possible to argue that the *Pax Romana* also brought stability (at times), an improved standard of living for many and population increase.

During our archaeological exploration of the Thames Valley we witnessed a dramatic rise in the number of farming settlements after the Roman Conquest in the first century AD. There were technical improvements – for example, a far greater use of iron tools, including innovations such as the scythe for cutting hay. There were also new, more productive varieties of sheep and cattle, roads, trackways, hedges and irrigated enclosures, carefully constructed wells and more sophisticated houses and barns.

In one early Romano-British farmstead, Barton Court Farm near Abingdon in Oxfordshire, a new form of kitchen equipment was found – a large ceramic bowl, or mortarium, with grit impressed into the surface to allow spices and other foodstuffs to be ground with a pestle. There was a maker's stamp impressed into the rim of the mortarium – it said, in Latin, 'SOLLUS F.' (Sollus made [this]). Sollus was a potter who probably came from Gaul and set up his workshop alongside the road between Londinium (London) and Verulamium (St Albans). We only know his name and what he made, but Sollus is nevertheless one of the earliest people to be recorded in British history. More important, perhaps, is what he represents: northwest Europe's contact with the Mediterranean, and new equipment for new foodstuffs.

The expansion of Rome brought olive oil and wine to Britain. Within decades of the Conquest by the emperor Claudius, in AD 43, the farming families of the Thames Valley had new flavours – coriander, cumin, fennel and opium poppy seeds – to grind in their new mortaria. Almost two thousand years before Elizabeth David revived the jaded post-war British palate with the taste of the Mediterranean, the Romans provided Britons with a glimpse of the culinary good life. And yet this was not, of course, Italian cuisine as we know it today. Only with the Columbian Exchange of the late 15th and 16th centuries AD did Europe discover and slowly adopt American treasures such as the tomato – the *pomodoro* (golden apple), which now seems so quintessentially Italian – or the potato, which became the North European staple from Poland to Ireland.

As early as the 12th century the Venetians had established a foothold at Tyre, in the East Mediterranean, which provided a link to the ancient trade routes that crossed Asia to China and brought luxury goods such as silk, musk, incense, pearls and indigo into the Mediterranean world, as well as foodstuffs to titillate the European palate – lemons, oranges, figs, almonds, olives and sugar cane. Even the greatest delicacy of my own Yorkshire homeland – rhubarb – was first transported down the Volga into the conduits of trade controlled by the Muslims. The pragmatic and often unscrupulous Venetians, and their rivals in Genoa and Pisa, maintained a balancing act with the Muslims who controlled access to this Oriental cornucopia.

The Italian cities dreamt of their own monopoly access to the products of the Far East. The Genoese Christopher Columbus headed west in 1492 – with unforeseen consequences. Five years later Vasco da Gama succeeded in cutting out the Muslim middlemen by also sailing into the Atlantic but then around the Cape of Good Hope eastwards into the Indian Ocean. The result was eventually to stimulate the imperial adventures of the Dutch and the British, who encircled the world, and a new agricultural revolution. This revolution led to sugar and tobacco plantations driven by slavery (Columbus himself headed west in search of slaves) as well as new food staples in Europe and Asia: a vastly improved and varied diet for those who could afford it. Even for the poor, the calorific boost of new crops such as the potato led to dramatic population increases.

The pursuit of new foodstuffs continued into the Pacific. Captain Bligh is best known for provoking the mutiny on the *Bounty*. It is often forgotten why he was in Tahiti in 1789 – to collect breadfruit, accompanied by botanists from the Royal Botanic Gardens at Kew – in an attempt to establish it as a new crop in the West Indies to feed the slave population.

One of the largest transformations took place in North and South America, where Europeans introduced alien plants and animals, at the expense of indigenous populations. The Plains Indians themselves adopted the horse to pursue buffalo, while European immigrants wiped out the great herds with industrial indifference, almost to the point of extinction. The Native Americans were themselves more than decimated by the land-hungry immigrants and scythed like wheat by virulent diseases whose origins went back to the Eurasian Neolithic.

The transformation from hunter-foragers to agriculturalists of increasing complexity has clearly not come without enormous consequences – the destruction of wild animals and environments, the suffering of enslaved peoples, the spread of disease and starvation when crops fail. On the other hand, the great civilizations of the world – Mesopotamia and Egypt, China, Cambodia and Japan, the Inca and Maya of the Americas – were based on agriculture. In the Classical world of Greece and Rome about 90% of the population were peasant farmers or estate slaves. They made it possible for architects, philosophers, poets, dramatists, craftspeople, scientists and soldiers to thrive, although they themselves led lives of relentless drudgery.

## Go forth and multiply

It can be claimed, with a degree of truth, that hunter-foragers practised the most successful and persistent lifestyle in the career of our species. For 100,000 years humans lived off the bounty of nature. They made relatively little impact on the environment of the Earth (although they may have contributed to the extinction of late and post-glacial megafauna). Their numbers were few, until they spread out of Africa. Even then, hunters rarely averaged more than one person per 2.5 sq. km (1 sq. mile). With the onset of agriculture things changed.

As a strategy for supporting human life, agriculture has been largely successful for the past ten millennia. It kick-started amazing cultural, social and technical developments around the world. Northwest Eurasia and Britain are just a small part of the story. Its success is reflected in the growing human population. Although agriculture allowed the *Homo sapien* population to grow, it was only around AD 1800 that humans achieved the figure of one billion individuals. Since then the number has multiplied with frightening speed. It took another 130 years to reach two billion (1930), then a further thirty years to hit three billion (1960). During my adult life the world's population has leapt from four billion in 1973 to six billion in 1999. On Monday, 31 October 2011, the United Nations identified a Filipino baby girl, Danica May Camacho, as the (symbolic) seven billionth human being on Earth. No one noted whether any chimpanzees, our closest relatives, were born that day. If so the chimp baby would have been about number 150,000.

The human numbers sound alarming. In fact, population growth is slowing thanks to the education of women, job opportunities and access to birth control. Medical improvements, leading to lower child mortality rates, initially caused populations to rise. However, the overall effect, in most parts of the world, has been to reduce the size of families. Reproduction rates of about 2.2–2.3 children are required to keep the population steady. Now some twenty-five countries have fertility rates below 2: in Europe, Brazil, the Middle East and the industrialized democracies of East Asia. At 1.2, South Korea is the bottom of the fertility table. China's birth rate is low as a result of its intrusive and now-abandoned one-child-policy – though such a draconian measure was probably unnecessary in view of the trends in industrialized societies.

However, it is not just a problem of numbers. The Western lifestyle consumes a prodigious quantity of the Earth's energy and resources, and developing countries aspire to the same unsustainable standards. Increasingly, each of us stands heavily on the planet. Open democratic societies cannot plead ignorance nor demand exemption from the inevitable. Although there have been and are serious problems of food shortage and famine in specific areas, these have usually been caused in the past century by cruel, idiotic and even bizarre political policies (in the USSR, China and colonial Africa, for example), warfare, climatic fluctuations and bad communications, or the enforced export of foodstuffs, rather than a basic world shortage of food.

In the early modern world, the greatest wealth was generated by luxury crops – sugar, coffee and tobacco – which were unnecessary for subsistence

Peter Breughel the Elder's *The Harvester*, representing the month of August, is an unsentimental view of rural life in the 1560s. Agricultural labour is hard but it is communal and the countryside retains a patchwork of fields and woods.

and, we now know, harmful to consumers. Traders, masters of ships and plantation owners made vast fortunes at the expense of slaves, serfs, peasants and their customers. The American plantation system outdid all others in the extent of its cruelty and exploitation of human beings. By the late 18th to 19th centuries, however, the world's population was expanding rapidly thanks to the availability of the relatively new American crops now cultivated in Europe, Asia and Africa: prolific foodstuffs such as potatoes, maize and peanuts (groundnuts as they were called in Europe).

Climate still had a part to play as the Little Ice Age in the medieval period exacerbated crop failures and chronic food shortages. Against a background of increasing agricultural productivity and population growth there were also catastrophes such as the Irish potato famine. Thanks to a diet of potatoes, combined with milk from the family cow, the number of Ireland's small tenant farmers had shot up. In 1845, Ireland's population stood at eight million people. In 1845 and again in 1846 and 1848 a horrendous blight (*Phytopthora infestans*, brought from the United States) wiped out much of the crop. Neither Ireland nor its peasants held much in the way of reserves. About a million Irish people starved to death and twice as many emigrated across the Atlantic. In India and China far greater numbers died as a result of famines caused by monsoon failures in the late 1870s and early 20th century. These catastrophes could have been avoided by fairer and more far-sighted political systems. There was not a fundamental worldwide shortage of food.

## The Anthropocene

When our potter Sollus stamped his work (Sollus F.) he literally declared himself to be a 'manufacturer' – a maker by hand. By the mid 19th century in Britain, the United States and Germany the term meant something else – the mass production of materials in factories. James Lovelock, the author of the *Gaia* concept, draws our attention to a fundamental event.[3] In 1712, Thomas Newcomen installed a steam-powered pump in a coal mine near Dudley in the West Midlands that removed water from mines and made deep coal accessible. Since the first farmers arrived in Britain, generations had stripped away the forests. The supply of wood was inadequate for the incipient Industrial Revolution that demanded power; Newcomen tapped into a prodigious power bank. Lovelock believes that this was the biggest thing to happen to the planet in two billion years, an event, he argues, as momentous as the arrival of photo-synthetic plants that captured solar energy. By harnessing fossil fuel buried deep in the ground, Newcomen launched what geologists now refer to as the 'Anthropocene'.[4]

The Nobel laureate, Paul Crutzen, who researched the ozone hole, introduced the term 'Anthropocene' (the age of humans) because a single species – us – was having a significant impact on the planet. He identified the start as about AD 1800 when the machines of the Industrial Revolution began to spew out methane and carbon dioxide into the atmosphere and influence the Earth's climate. Bill Ruddiman, of the University of Virginia, has detected an earlier start by charting greenhouse gases trapped in the Antarctic and Greenland ice sheets. He observes a steady rise in methane from about eight thousand years ago and suggests that humans, rather than nature, now controlled (or perhaps we should say 'were responsible for') methane emissions.

At this period early agriculture provides the smoking gun, especially the spread of rice paddies in eastern Asia.

The Industrial Revolution was accompanied by major changes in agriculture: new equipment such as the sowing drill, more efficient hoes and ploughs that required less animal power, an emphasis on increased productivity by breeding new varieties of crops and animals, efficient rotation systems and reorganization of landholdings at the expense of the peasantry. Oliver Goldsmith in 1750 regretted the trend: '... a bold peasantry, their country's pride/When once destroyed can never be supplied.' The new factories demanded men, women and children: human beings tied to the clock and the machine. By 1900, only 5% of Britain's working population was employed in agriculture. In contrast, France was slower to change. In 1950, about a third of the French labour force still worked the land – hence the European Union's emphasis on farming.

The massive increases in populations in the late 18th century into the 20th century created an enormous demand for food. Traditional farmers gave way to the scientist, men like Carl Sprengel who in 1828 demonstrated that plants needed specific chemicals to grow properly, or Justus von Liebig the author in 1840 of *Organic Chemistry in its Application to Agriculture and Physiology*. The British Society for the Advancement of Science commissioned this work in an attempt to explain why crop yields were declining in exhausted soils. One temporary solution was to import guano – bird droppings from the islands off the coast of Peru – a British enterprise powered by Chinese labour working in horrendous conditions. In the longer term, Western agriculture shifted from organic fertilizers to industrially manufactured chemical fertilizers. From the 1920s synthetic fertilizers produced by energy-intensive systems such as the Haber-Bosch process have supported population growth. It is estimated that half the population of the world are fed as a result of synthetic nitrogen fertilizer use.[5] Synthetic fertilizers, however, have a serious downside. Run-off from fields, encouraged by irrigation, pollutes watercourses and, in the worst cases, creates dead zones in lakes and the sea where, for lack of oxygen, no life can exist. At the same time, present-day human hunters, operating industrial-scale trawlers, deplete the remaining fish resources.

Industrial agriculture also depends upon the use of pesticides. In 1962, Rachel Carson's book *Silent Spring* shocked the world with its exposure of the impact of DDT.[6] It then took a decade to ban the use of this poison in the USA, and another thirty years to take twelve of the worst Persistent Organic

Pollutants (POPs) out of circulation, even though some were implicated in the epidemic of type 2 diabetes. Arguments still rage about the powerful pesticide neonicotinoids that may be partly responsible for the collapse of bee populations. In Britain, the massive decrease in the number of insects has also caused a collapse in the populations of birds such as skylarks, wagtails, whitethroats, yellowhammers and starlings.

As the food market expanded exponentially the first agribusinesses appeared, controlling the supply of staples, such as grain, and industrialized food processes – the bastard children of technology, science and imperialism. As the British rejected the slave trade, their ships turned to carrying palm oil and cacao. Lever Brothers built Port Sunlight on the Mersey, made palm oil soap, dominated West African exports and became one of the largest food companies in the world.

The emphasis on highly productive, industrialized agriculture and industrialized food production has continued into the 21st century. At times, science gives cause for optimism. Between the 1950s and 1970s innovations in plant breeding, particularly rice and wheat, led to what is known as the Green Revolution. The new wheat grew prolifically on short, sturdy stems when combined with large doses of fertilizer and irrigation. Norman Borlaug, the scientist who is most associated with the initial success of the Green Revolution in Mexico, India and Pakistan, was awarded the Nobel Peace Prize in 1970. He believed that population growth was still the long-term problem. The Green Revolution looked like a win-win situation.

However, there were unforeseen consequences. Many Asian farmers could not afford the fertilizers. Large landlords, their eyes set on big profits, ejected tenants from their land and bought tractors to replace them. In the decade after the Green Revolution kicked off, Pakistan imported more than 100,000 tractors. Many villages were impoverished for lack of work while entrepreneurs grew rich. In India, farmer suicide rates have soared (over 17,600 in 2009) in the face of what the United Nations (in 1995) called 'ruin and a crisis of existence'. In Mexico a small number of wealthy landlords came to dominate the ownership of farms. In the United States and Britain the family farm, once numbered in millions, has gone into freefall. Financial companies controlling pension schemes, and in the USA the Mormon Church, are now among the largest owners of agricultural land. Rising population and demand continue to increase the prices of foodstuffs and make agriculture an attractive investment opportunity with the emphasis on growth, efficiency and productivity.

## Is there intelligent life in the universe?

Increasingly, we have to confront the downside. As a United Nations report stated: 'Anthropogenic climate change has recently become a well-established fact.' In 2015, Pope Francis circulated an encyclical emphasizing the effects of climate change, global inequality and the destruction of nature, problems that are 'real, urgent and must be tackled'.[7]

At the end of 2015, 196 countries attending the United Nations Climate Change Conference in Paris reached a global agreement accepting the need to reduce climate change, calling for zero net anthropogenic greenhouse gas emissions to be reached during the second half of the 21st century. The conference agreed 'to pursue efforts' to limit the world's temperature increase to 1.5°C, which it is estimated requires zero emissions by 2030–50. A pessimist could see this agreement as lacking teeth and a defined set of actions. At least, though, there is a global awareness of the problems and a widespread desire to tackle them.

The world faces a crisis – of rising temperatures and sea level, environmental destruction, species extinction, extreme weather events, fires, water shortage, soil deterioration and desertification. Industrial farming is a major contributor to these problems, producing food but with enormous energy costs and making no sustainable sense. The Haber-Bosch process now generates 100 million tonnes of artificial nitrogenous fertilizer per year. The largest producer by far is China, where 60% of production is currently based on coal, using small energy-inefficient plants (although the greatest contributors in the recent past have been the USA, Germany and Britain). Around the world much of the fertilizer helps to produce maize, the Central American wonder crop, but half of the maize is fed to animals instead of humans.

Livestock rearing is itself a major producer of the principal greenhouse gases – carbon dioxide, methane and nitrous oxide – which drive global warming.[8] It generates far more than motor vehicles. The long-term concern about food security focuses on that apocalyptic horseman – famine. However, the present direction of food production, encouraged by tax support, promotes meat and dairy consumption and processed foods rich in salt, sugar and fat. US farms receive billions of dollars of subsidy from Washington – an estimated half of their income. The largest subsidies, $77 billion between 1995 and 2010, go to the growers of maize, the principal ingredient of the US 'cheap' meat culture. There were also massive subsidies for the inefficient ethanol fuel industry, used by farmers until 2011. This tide of taxpayers' money went

A cattle feed-lot in Texas. Farming achieves its ultimate industralized horror.

mainly to support rich corporate farms. The EU also subsidizes rich farmers at the expense of the poor. The results of this bizarre alliance of industry and politics are bad for the environment, the consumer, for poor farmers in less 'developed' countries and for livestock.[9]

Food shortages and nutrient deficiencies are a major problem in poorer countries, but obesity, heart disease and diabetes are growing modern curses, not only in the industrialized West, but also increasingly in Southeast Asia, South America and North and South Africa. The globalization of the Western diet, driven by the massive consumption of energy from fossil fuels, is arguably one of the greatest threats to humankind's future.

If animals thought they were getting a good deal by hitching a ride with humans, they must now be regretting their evolutionary mistake. Food producers love to advertise their wares with bucolic images of happy cows called Daisy, idyllic flower-strewn meadows and farmyards where hens safely cluck. Few of the industrialized world's more than 17 billion poultry enjoy such a lifestyle, however, let alone the 933 million pigs. Most of them exist crammed in power-hungry concentration camps, pumped full of hormones and antibiotics and surrounded by polluting lakes of filth. The great American writer,

Annie Proulx, catches the flavour of the industrialized hog farm in her everyday story of Texas panhandle folk: 'a huge fetid stink like ten thousand rotten socks, like decaying flesh, like stale urine and swamp gas, like sour vomit and liquid manure, a ghastly palpable stench that made him retch'.[10] Television programmes about the countryside never go there. If they did we might wish to see such units closed down. We might even change our diet: consume more vegetables, fruit and cereals, with responsibly reared meat reserved for feast days, as in the Neolithic.

There are some causes for optimism. Humans are incredibly adaptable, energetic and inventive, and good at communication and cooperation once we have stopped turning a blind eye to inconvenient situations. At present, we engage in an orgy of soil destruction, degrading 12 million hectares (29.6 million acres) a year, yet it would be feasible to mount a major effort to reinstate what we have harmed, as encouraged by the International Year of Soils in 2015. Similarly, we can plant trees – even do it ourselves. The industrialized diet is bad for our health: we could support the world's small farmers, grow our own, buy in farmers' markets, cook fresh food and avoid food waste and sugar-saturated drinks.[11] We might learn to respect animals, consume them less frequently and not at all unless they have had a decent life. A tasteless, hormone-inflated chicken, selling at a ridiculously cheap price, is not good for us – for our diet or our ethics. And it is irresponsible to argue that this rubbish is the staple diet of the increasingly unhealthy urban poor. As individuals and citizens of states we can create habitats for small creatures or even promote reserves for larger ones.[12] We can also communicate with the big food retailers, who are increasingly everywhere. In response to consumer pressure, supermarkets can get chickens out of cages or cows onto grass far more quickly than dilatory politicians. We might even demand that they supply real choice in foodstuffs.[13] Most of all, we might stop ignoring the abuse of domestic animals, the lunatic overuse of antibiotics in feedlots and poultry farms, and the misuse of science in the food industry. However, all is not doom and gloom. With advances in genetics and the use of precision technologies in agriculture and horticulture (delivering water and fertilizer more efficiently and effectively) we have the potential to transform agricultural productivity in the future.

As an archaeologist, I try to understand the past. I have no qualifications to pronounce about the future.[14] In the past humans like ourselves have faced massive problems, yet survived and sometimes flourished. Challenges like the Younger Dryas led to the domestication of plants and animals. In the 18th and 19th centuries new ways of capturing energy led to massive increases in population. Yet it is the resulting profligate expenditure of fossil fuels, and the cavalier treatment of the environment and other species, which now places us in danger. The world can shrug us off in the short term and the second law of thermodynamics inevitably will.

In the meantime, we exist in a period between the beginning and the end of the universe. It's a marvellous opportunity, like life itself. I love to browse the NASA website to peer into the deep past of the universe. The Nobel Prize-winning physicist Steven Weinberg said: 'the more the universe seems comprehensible the more it seems pointless', but the universe should make us feel lucky. It puts things in perspective. It is up to us to decide our purpose. While the Kepler Mission searches for habitable planets – the ultimate 'needle in a haystack' task – we already inhabit the best world that we know in the universe. In the Neolithic, early farmers went to Brú na Bóinne, Orkney and Stonehenge to observe the stars, to appeal for help from the gods, to pray for growth and fertility. The stars are indifferent. It is human genius that took us from the stone axe to the Kepler Mission and that should allow us to care for this unique planet and its inhabitants. We try to understand our past while we make our own future.

# Appendix

**Distribution of progenitors of Eurasian domesticated crops and animals**

| Wild progenitor | Modern species | Distribution of progenitor |
|---|---|---|
| Wild einkorn (*Triticum boeoticum*) | Cultivated einkorn (*T. amonococcum*) | Most commonly found in Turkey and Zagros Mountains – though many other sources. |
| Wild barley (*Hordeum spontaneum*) | Cultivated barley (*H. vulgare*) | Widely distributed from the Levant to Iran and Afghanistan and beyond. |
| Wild emmer (*Triticum dicoccoides*) | Cultivated wheats, cultivated emmer (*Triticum dicoccum*) | Found mainly in southeast Turkey, Levant, Taurus and Zagros Mountains. |
| Legumes – peas and lentils | | Widely distributed from Levant to the Caspian Sea. |
| Wild mouflon sheep (*Ovis orientalis*) | Domestic sheep | Distributed across the Taurus/Zagros mountain ranges |
| Wild bezoar goat (*Capra aegagrus*) (probable ancestor) | Domestic goat (*Capra hircus*) | Found from Turkey, through the Zagros Mountains to West Pakistan (Baluchistan) and into Central Asia. |
| Wild cattle – aurochs (*Bos primigenius*) | European domestic cattle (*Bos Taurus*); Indian humped or zebu cow (*Bos indicus*) | Distributed across Eurasia from the Atlantic to the Pacific. |
| Wild pig (*Sus scrofa*) | Domestic pig | Distributed across Eurasia from the Atlantic to the Pacific. |

These are the assumed wild prototypes of the principal domesticates and their distribution. It needs to be emphasized that estimating the distribution of wild animals 12,000 to 10,000 years ago is, to a considerable extent, shooting in the dark. To make matters worse, several wild progenitors – of horse, cattle and camel – are now extinct and we have to resort to their bones for information. For an admirably clear discussion of animal domestication with references, see J. Clutton-Brock, *Animals as Domesticates: A World View Through History*, East Lansing: Michigan State University Press, 2012.

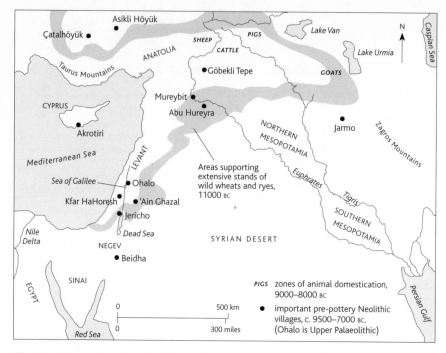

The Near Eastern homelands of the earliest domesticated plants and animals, showing sites mentioned in the text.

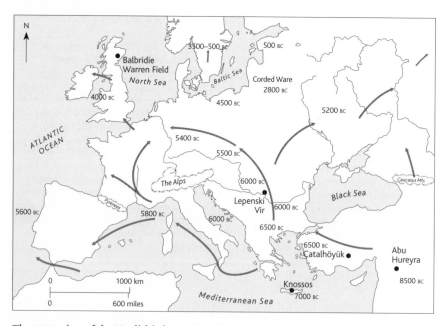

The expansion of the Neolithic in western Europe.

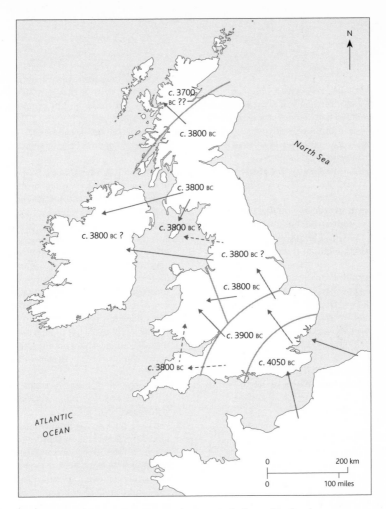

N

c. 3700 BC ??

c. 3800 BC

c. 3800 BC

North Sea

c. 3800 BC ?

c. 3800 BC ?

c. 3800 BC ?

c. 3800 BC

c. 3900 BC

c. 3800 BC

c. 4050 BC

ATLANTIC
OCEAN

| 0 | | 200 km |
| 0 | | 100 miles |

The spread of agriculture into and across Britain and Ireland
based on the latest modelling of radiocarbon dates.

# Notes

### Preface

1. M. de Voltaire, *An Essay on Universal History, the Manners, and Spirit of Nations: From the Reign of Charlemaign to the Age of Lewis XIV*, Edinburgh, 1777.
2. V. Gordon Childe, *Man Makes Himself*, London: Watts & Co., 1936, p. 4.
3. C. Renfrew, Prehistory: *The Making of the Human Mind*, London: Weidenfeld & Nicolson, 2007.
4. L. Murray, *Persistence in Folly*, Sydney: Angus & Robertson, 1984, p. 168.
5. W. G. Hoskins, *The Making of the English Landscape*, London: Hodder & Stoughton, 1955.
6. F. Fernández-Armesto, with D. Lord Smail, 'Food', in A. Shryock and D. Lord Smail, *Deep History: The Architecture of Past and Present*, Berkeley: University of California Press, 2011, pp. 131–59.

### Prologue

1. W. Greenwell, 'Notices of the examination of ancient grove-hills in the North Riding of Yorkshire', *Archaeological Journal*, 22, 1865, pp. 97–117.
2. G. Hey, 'The Devil's work', *British Archaeology*, Jul/Aug 2009, pp. 24–9.
3. N. Shepherd, *The Living Mountain*, Edinburgh: Canongate Books, 1977, pp. 2–3.
4. G. Parry, 'John Aubrey 1626–1697', in T. Murray (ed.), *Encyclopedia of Archaeology: The Great Archaeologists*, Santa Barbara: ABC-CLIO, 1999, p. 19.
5. B. G. Trigger, *A History of Archaeological Thought*, 2nd edn, Cambridge: Cambridge University Press, 2006, p. 97.
6. I. Hodder, *The Present Past: An Introduction to Anthropology for Archaeologists*, London: Batsford, 1982, p. 11.
7. There were more perceptive early commentators. Sir William Dugdale in his *History of Warwickshire* (1650) pronounced that stone objects were 'weapons used by the Britons before the art of making arms of brass or iron were known'. In 1685 polished stone axes were found at a megalithic tomb near Dreux in northern France. They were interpreted as tools, like those used by contemporary Native Americans.
8. Quoted in G. Daniel, *The Idea of Prehistory*, London: Pelican Books, 1964, p. 39.
9. Quoted in P. Rowley-Conwy, *From Genesis to Prehistory: The Archaeological Three Age System and its Contested Reception in Denmark, Britain and Ireland*, Oxford: Oxford University Press, 2007, p. 268.
10. S. Piggott, *The Neolithic Cultures of the British Isles: A Study of the Stone-using Agricultural Communities of Britain in the Second Millennium BC*, Cambridge: Cambridge University Press, 1954. Piggott was unlucky in his timing. Radiocarbon dates were only just beginning to appear and he could make use of only two: one from Stonehenge, and another from the henge complex at Dorchester-on-Thames, Oxfordshire.
11. C. Renfrew, Prehistory: *The Making of the Human Mind*, London: Weidenfeld & Nicolson, 2007, p. 44.
12. The work built on the mathematical modelling pioneered by Caitlin Buck (see C. E. Buck, W. G. Cavanagh and D. C. Litton, *Bayesian Approach to Interpreting Archaeological Data*, Chichester: Wiley, 1996) and Christopher Bronk Ramsay (see C. Bronk Ramsay, 'Bayesian analysis of radiocarbon dates', in *Radiocarbon*, 51, 2009, pp. 337–60). The impressive results appear in A. Whittle, F. Healey and A. Bayliss, *Gathering Time: Dating the Early Neolithic Enclosures of Southern Britain and Ireland* (2 vols), Oxford: Oxbow Books, 2011.
13. R. Bradley and M. Edmonds, *Interpreting the Axe Trade*, Cambridge: Cambridge University Press, 1993; M. Edmonds, *The Langdales: Landscape and Prehistory in a Lakeland Valley*, Stroud: Tempus, 2004.
14. M. Mauss, *Essai sur le Don*, Presses Universitaires de France, 1950, trans. W. D. Halls, *The Gift: Forms and Functions of Exchange in Archaic Societies*, London: Routledge, 1990.

## Chapter 1

1. T. Flannery, *Here on Earth: A New Beginning*, London: Allen Lane, 2010, p. 9.
2. As well as discovering 30 handaxes and flakes at Stanton Harcourt, Mr McRae also located 87 handaxes of flint and 24 of quartzite in the Berinsfield pits, north of Dorchester-on-Thames. He reckons he averaged a find for every 8 hours of searching.
3. See J. J. Wymer, *The Lower Palaeolithic Occupation of Britain*, Salisbury: Wessex Archaeology & English Heritage, 1999, pp. 54–5. For more spectacular finds at Stanton Harcourt, see K. Scott and C. Buckingham, 'A river runs through it: a decade of research at Stanton Harcourt', in S. Milliken and J. Cook (eds), *A Very Remote Period Indeed: Papers on the Palaeolithic Presented to Derek Roe*, Oxford: Oxbow Books, 2001, pp. 2, 7–13; P. Pettitt and M. White, *The British Palaeolithic: Hominin Societies at the Edge of the Pleistocene World*, Abingdon: Routledge, 2012, pp. 237–8.
4. M. Kohn and S. Mithen, 'Handaxes: products of sexual selection?', *Antiquity*, 73, 1999, pp. 518–26. For an alternative view, see D. Hodgson, 'Symmetry and humans: reply to Mithen's sexy handaxe theory', *Antiquity*, 83, 2009, pp. 195–8.
5. C. Gamble and R. Kruszynski, 'John Evans, Joseph Prestwich and the stone that shattered the time barrier', *Antiquity*, 83, 2009, pp. 461–75.
6. S. J. Gould, *Time's Arrow, Time's Cycle: Myth and Metaphor in the Discovery of Geological Time*, Cambridge, Mass.: Harvard University Press, 1987.
7. Clive Gamble and Robert Kruszynski had tracked down the handaxe photographed in 1859 to one in the Natural History Museum in London, where as catalogue number E5109, it lay with its fellows, cared for but its significance unappreciated. Gamble and Kruszynski, 'John Evans, Joseph Prestwich and the stone that shattered the time barrier', pp. 461–75.
8. A. Roberts and N. Barton, 'Reading the unwritten history: Evans and ancient stone implements', in A. Macgregor (ed.), *Sir John Evans 1823–1903: Antiquity, Commerce and Natural Science in the Age of Darwin*, Oxford: Ashmolean Museum, 2008, pp. 95–115.
9. R. Potts *et al.*, 'Small mid-Pleistocene hominin associated with East African Acheulean technology', *Science*, 305 (5680), 2004, pp. 75–8.
10. K. Oakley, *Man the Tool-Maker* (5th edn), London: Natural History Museum, 1967, p. 3.
11. K. D. Schick and N. Toth, *Making Silent Stones Speak: Human Evolution and the Dawn of Technology*, New York: Simon & Schuster, 1993.
12. M. Leakey, *Olduvai Gorge Vol 3: Excavation in Beds I & II 1960–1963*, Cambridge: Cambridge University Press, 1971.
13. B. Villmoore *et al.*, 'Early *Homo* at 2.8 mya from Ledi-Geraru, Afar, Ethiopia', *Science*, 347 (6228), 2015, pp. 1352–54.
14. It was the innovative archaeologist, the late Glynn Isaac, who first noted the geological skills of early hominins.
15. Colin Renfrew, one of the pioneers in this field, describes cognitive archaeology as 'the study, using the material record, of the development of human modes of thought'. C. Renfrew, *Prehistory: The Making of the Human Mind*, London: Weidenfeld & Nicolson, 2007, pp. 97–8, see also pp. 109–12.
16. Summarized in C. Gamble, J. Gowlett and R. Dunbar, *Thinking Big: How the Evolution of Social Life Shaped the Human Mind*, London and New York: Thames & Hudson, 2014.
17. *Ibid.*, p. 96.
18. R. Wrangham, *Catching Fire: How Cooking Made Us Human*, London: Profile Books, 2010.
19. For example, L. Aiello and P. Wheeler, 'The expensive-tissue hypothesis: the brain and the digestive system in humans and primate evolution', *Current Anthropology*, 36, 1995, pp. 199–221.
20. Gamble *et al.*, *Thinking Big*, pp. 129–38; R. Dunbar, *Human Evolution*, London: Pelican, 2014, pp. 154–66.
21. N. Alperson-Afil *et al.*, 'Spatial organisation of hominin activities at Gesher-Benot Ya'aqov, Israel', *Science*, 326, 2009, pp. 1677–80.
22. For example, the one-million-year-old

site at Chesowanja, Kenya, cited in
J. Gowlett *et al.*, 'Early archaeological
sites, hominid remains and traces of fire
from Chesowanja, Kenya', *Nature*, 294,
1981, pp. 125–9.
23. R. Dunbar, *Human Evolution*, pp. 147–9.

## Chapter 2

1. M. B. Roberts and S. A. Parfitt, *Boxgrove:
A Middle Pleistocene Hominid Site at
Eartham Quarry, Boxgrove, West Sussex*,
London: English Heritage, 1999, p. 329.
There is also a very readable account
of the project: M. Pitts and M. Roberts,
*Fairweather Eden*, London: Century
Books, 1997.
2. Not surprisingly, given the sparse
evidence, there is disagreement among
specialists. Some propose that the
earlier species *Homo habilis* was the
first to leave the home continent.
3. Cro-Magnons, Upper Palaeolithic
modern humans, were discovered in
France in 1868, twelve years after the
hominin remains in the Neander Valley
in Germany. See B. Fagan, *Cro-Magnon:
How the Ice Age Gave Birth to the First
Modern Humans*, New York: Bloomsbury
Press, 2010; for Piltdown Man, see
C. Stringer, *Homo Britannicus: The
Incredible Story of Human Life in Britain*,
London: Allen Lane, 2006, pp. 46–51.
4. R. Dunbar, *Human Evolution*, London:
Pelican, 2014, p. 183.
5. Svante Pääbo vividly explains the
problems of analysing genome diversity
and the difficulties of nomenclature and
taxonomy in his book *Neanderthal Man:
In Search of Lost Genomes*, New York:
Basic Books, 2014, pp. 227–50.
6. R. Dunbar, *Human Evolution*.
7. In discussing such axes, Lambros
Malafouris asks the question 'Where
does the knapper's mind end and the
stone tool begin?' For his sophisticated
discussion of archaeological metaphysics,
see L. Malafouris, *How Things Shape the
Mind: A Theory of Material Engagement*,
Cambridge, Mass.: MIT Press, 2013.
8. V. Papanek, 'Inuit Solutions', in S. Brown
and M. K. Mitchell (eds), *The Beauty of
Craft: A Resurgence Anthology*, Dartington
Totnes: Green Books, 2004, pp. 30–35.

9. Climate can be established from proxies
such as beetles. At Lynford, 224 beetle
taxa preserved in the waterlogged
deposits included types now extinct
in Britain and even Europe.
10. C. Gamble and Boismier, 'The Lynford
Neanderthals', in W. A. Bosmier,
C. Gamble and F. Coward, *Neanderthals
Among Mammoths: Excavations at Lynford
Quarry, Norfolk*, Swindon: English
Heritage, 2012, pp. 283–96.
11. I hope specialists will forgive this
simplification. The patchy evidence
provides a more complex picture: for
example, the skulls from Steinheim,
Germany; Swanscombe, England; and
Petralona, northern Greece. For a more
thorough discussion, see D. Papagianni
and M. A. Morse, *The Neanderthals
Rediscovered: How Modern Science is
Rewriting Their Story*, London and New
York: Thames & Hudson, 2013, pp. 59–64.
12. The comparison between brain and
body sizes gives us the 'encephalization
quotient' (EQ), which is 4.8 in
Neanderthals and 5.3 in *Homo sapiens*:
the largest figure of any hominin past
or present.
13. C. Gamble, J. Gowlett and R. Dunbar,
*Thinking Big: How the Evolution of Social
Life Shaped the Human Mind*, London
and New York: Thames & Hudson, 2014,
pp. 158–9.
14. R. Dunbar, *Human Evolution*, p. 205.
15. See Pääbo, *Neanderthal Man*.
16. G. M. Bowra, *Primitive Song*, London:
Weidenfeld & Nicolson, 1962.
17. S. Mithen, *The Singing Neanderthal: The
Origin of Music, Language, Mind and Body*,
London: Weidenfeld & Nicolson, 2005.

## Chapter 3

1. W. J. Burroughs, *Climate Change in
Prehistory: The End of the Reign of Chaos*,
Cambridge: Cambridge University Press,
2005.
2. A very clear guide to how and what we
know about the Ice Age is provided by
S. Buteaux, J. Chambers and B. Silva,
*Digging Up the Ice Age: Recognising,
Recording and Understanding Fossil and
Archaeological Remains Found in British
Quarries*, Oxford: Archaeopress, 2009.

See also B. Fagan (ed.), *The Complete Ice Age: How Climate Change Shaped the World*, London and New York: Thames & Hudson, 2009.

3. G. Walker, *Snowball Earth: The Story of the Great Global Catastrophe That Spawned Life As We Know It*, New York: Crown Publication, 2003.

4. T. Higham *et al.*, 'The timing and spatiotemporal patterning of Neanderthal disappearance', *Nature*, 512 (7514), 2014, pp. 306–9.

5. W. Davis, 'The Emergence of *Homo sapiens sapiens*', in B. Cunliffe, C. Gosden and R. A. Joyce (eds), *The Oxford Handbook of Archaeology*, Oxford: Oxford University Press, 2009, p. 296.

6. The development of lithic technology – in particular, the 'big deal about blades' – is discussed at length in C. Gamble, *Origins and Revolutions: Human Identity in Earliest Prehistory*, Cambridge: Cambridge University Press, 2007, see particularly ch. 7, pp. 157–204.

7. C. Gamble, J. Gowlett and R. Dunbar, *Thinking Big: How the Evolution of Social Life Shaped the Human Mind*, London and New York: Thames & Hudson, 2014. It may be easier to understand an example from life: Tony Blair *wondered* if the people *supposed* that he *intended* them to *think* that he *believed* in the existence of weapons of mass destruction in Iraq.

8. S. McBrearty and A. S. Brooks, 'The revolution that wasn't: a new interpretation of the origins of modern behaviour', *Journal of Human Evolution*, 39, 2000, pp. 453–563.

9. For the earliest-known rock art in Southeast Asia, see Tacon *et al.*, 'The global implications of the early surviving rock art of greater Southeast Asia', *Antiquity*, 88, 2014, pp. 1050–64.

10. S. Aldhouse-Green, *Paviland Cave and the Red Lady: A Definitive Report*, Bristol: Western Academic & Specialist Press, 2000.

11. S. E. Churchill *et al.*, 'The Upper Palaeolithic population of Europe in an evolutionary perspective', in W. Roebroeks *et al.* (eds), *Hunters of the Golden Age: The Mid Upper Palaeolithic of Eurasia 30,000–20,000 BP*, London: University of Leiden Press, 2000, pp. 31–51.

12. A. Sagona (ed.), *Bruising the Red Earth: Ochre Mining and Ritual in Aboriginal Tasmania*, Melbourne: Melbourne University Press, 1994.

13. T. Flannery, *Here on Earth: A New Beginning*, London: Allen Lane, 2010, p. 87. For the ecology of the steppe, see B. A. Yurtsev, 'The Pleistocene "tundra-steppe" and the productivity paradox: the landscape approach', *Quaternary Science Reviews*, 20, 2000, pp. 165–74.

14. For a vivid and more detailed account of Ice Age hunters, see B. Fagan, *Cro-Magnon: How the Ice Age Gave Birth to the First Modern Humans*, New York: Bloomsbury Press, 2010.

15. Vandiver *et al.*, 'The origins of ceramic technology at Dolni Vestonice, Czechoslovakia', *Science*, 246, 1989, pp. 1002–8.

16. P. Pettitt, review of Ezra Zubrow *et al.*, *The Magdalenian Household: Unraveling Domesticity*, New York: State University of New York, 2010, in *Antiquity*, 85, 329, 2011, pp. 1087–8.

17. For dog domestication, *see* J. Clutton-Brock, *Animals as Domesticates: A World View Through History*, East Lansing: Michigan State University Press, 2012, pp. 122–3.

18. P. Shipman, *The Invaders: How Humans and Their Dogs Drove Neanderthals to Extinction*, Cambridge, Mass.: Harvard University Press, 2015.

19. P. Pettitt, *The Palaeolithic Origins of Human Burial*, London: Routledge, 2011, pp. 201–7. As Pettitt points out, an alternative to the 'high status' interpretation is that everyone in the Sunghir community dressed in this elaborate way. The problem for archaeologists is that we do not have many cemeteries and burials to compare, unlike in later periods.

20. P. Pettitt and P. Bahn, 'An alternative chronology for the art of Chauvet Cave', *Antiquity*, 89, 2015, pp. 542–53. For the cave art, see J-M. Chauvet *et al.*, *Chauvet Cave: The Discovery of the World's Oldest Paintings*, London: Thames & Hudson, 1996; J. Clottes *et al.* (eds), *Return to*

*Chauvet Cave: Excavating the Birthplace of Art*, London: Thames & Hudson, 2003.

21. D. Lewis-Williams, *The Mind in the Cave: Consciousness and the Origins of Art*, London and New York: Thames & Hudson, 2002.

22. For the complexities and distortions, see R. Hutton, *Shamans: Siberian Spirituality and the Western Imagination*, London: Hambledon, 2001; for a different perspective, see C. Blacker, *The Catalpa Bow: A Study of Shamanistic Practices in Japan*, London: Routledge Curzon, 1999.

23. P. Bahn, *Prehistoric Rock Art: Polemics and Progress*, Cambridge: Cambridge University Press, 2010.

## Chapter 4

1. For Childe's career and ideas, see S. Green, *Prehistorian: A Biography of V. Gordon Childe*, Bradford on Avon: Moonraker Press, 1981; B. McNairn, *The Method and Theory of V. Gordon Childe*, Edinburgh: Edinburgh University Press, 1980; B. Trigger, *Gordon Childe: Revolutions in Archaeology*, London and New York: Thames & Hudson, 1980.

2. J. G. D. Clark, 'Russian archaeology: the other side of the picture', *Proceedings of the Prehistoric Society*, 2, 1936, pp. 248–9.

3. Biblical references to Lachish: Joshua 10.5; 2 Kings 14:19, 18:14, 17; 2 Chronicles 25:27; 32:9; Nehemiah 11:30; Isaiah 36:2; Jeremiah 34:7.

4. K. Kenyon, *Digging Up Jericho*, London: Ernest Benn Ltd, 1957.

5. G. J. Vermeij, *The Evolutionary World: How Adaptation Explains Everything from Seashells to Civilization*, New York: St Martin's Press, 2010, p. 126.

6. *Ibid.*, p. 143.

7. For details of the attine farming system, see B. Hölldobler and E. O. Wilson, *The Superorganism: The Beauty, Elegance, and Strangeness of Insect Societies*, New York: W. W. Norton & Co., 2009.

8. P. J. Richerson, R. Boyd and R. L. Bettinger, 'Was agriculture impossible during the Pleistocene but mandatory during the Holocene? A climate change hypothesis', *American Antiquity*, 66, 2001, pp. 387–411.

9. G. Crawford, 'East Asian plant domestication', in M. Stark (ed.), *Archaeology of Asia*, Oxford: Blackwell Publishing, 2006, pp. 73–95.

10. P. A. Colinvaux, *Why Big Fierce Animals Are Rare*, New Jersey: Princeton University Press, 1978.

11. J. Bocquet-Appel and P. Demars, 'Population kinetics in the Upper Palaeolithic in western Europe', *Journal of Archaeological Science*, 27, 2000, pp. 551–70; J. Bocquet-Appel and O. Bar-Yosef (eds), *The Neolithic Demographic Transition and its Consequences*, New York: Springer, 2008.

12. S. Mithen, *After the Ice: A Global Human History 20,000–5000 BC*, London: Weidenfeld & Nicolson, 2003.

13. This idea was suggested by Martin Jones of Cambridge University in his fascinating book *Feast: Why Humans Share Food,* Oxford: Oxford University Press, 2007. Martin starts each chapter with a short narrative, a word picture to describe the lives and particularly the eating habits of the people under discussion. This is the writer's equivalent of the reconstruction drawing or a museum diorama. For another example of the use of imagination and analogy to bring the past to life, see S. Mithen, *After the Ice: A Global Human History 20,000–5000 BC*, London: Weidenfeld & Nicolson, 2003.

14. Jones, *Feast*, p. 113.

15. D. Papagianni and M. A. Morse, *The Neanderthals Rediscovered: How Modern Science is Rewriting Their Story*, London and New York: Thames & Hudson, 2013, pp. 152–3.

16. This revolution was conceived by Kent Flannery. See K. Flannery, 'Origin and ecological effects of early domestication in Iran and the Near East', in Ucko and G. W. Dimbleby (eds), *The Domestication and Exploitation of Plants and Animals*, Chicago: Aldine, 1969, pp. 73–100.

17. Jones, *Feast*, p. 119.

18. The words of Cyprian Broodbank, in his magisterial opus, *The Making of the Middle Sea: A History of the Mediterranean from the Beginning to the Emergence of the Classical World*, London: Thames & Hudson, 2013.

19. K. Flannery and J. Marcus, *The Creation of Inequality: How Our Prehistoric Ancestors Set the Stage for Monarchy, Slavery, and Empire*, Cambridge, Mass.: Harvard University Press, 2012.
20. C. Broodbank, *The Making of the Middle Sea*, p. 146.
21. The role of humans in the extinction of the pygmy hippopotamus is contentious. But wiping out island fauna has become a habit for humans.

**Chapter 5**

1. V. Gordon Childe, *Man Makes Himself*, London: Watts & Co., 1936, p. 74.
2. C. Renfrew, *Prehistory: The Making of the Human Mind*, London: Weidenfeld & Nicolson, 2007, p. 202.
3. For the most comprehensive, up-to-date account of the subject on a worldwide basis, see G. Barker, *The Agricultural Revolution in Prehistory: Why did Foragers become Farmers?*, Oxford: Oxford University Press, 2006.
4. R. B. Lee and I. deVore (eds), *Man the Hunter*, Chicago: Aldine, 1968.
5. R. Dunbar, *Human Evolution*, London: Pelican, 2014.
6. J. Cauvin, *The Birth of the Gods and the Origins of Agriculture*, Cambridge: Cambridge University Press, 2000 (initially published in French in 1994).
7. C. Gamble, J. Gowlett and R. Dunbar, *Thinking Big: How the Evolution of Social Life Shaped the Human Mind*, London and New York: Thames & Hudson, 2014.
8. K. Schmidt, 'Göbekli Tepe', in M. Özdogan *et al.* (eds), *The Neolithic in Turkey Vol. 2*, Istanbul: Archaeology and Art Publications, 2011, pp. 41–83.
9. Only a small proportion of the site has been excavated. However, extensive geophysical survey shows that there are many more stone enclosures and megalithic pillars.
10. M. Heun *et al.*, 'Site of einkorn wheat domestication identified by DNA fingerprinting', *Science*, 278, 1997, pp. 1312–14.
11. G. Barker, *The Agricultural Revolution*, pp. 147–8, 410.
12. Y. Gorden, I. Segal and O. Bar-Yosef, 'Plaster artifacts and the interpretation of the Nahal Hemar Cave', *Journal of the Israel Prehistoric Society*, 25, 1993, pp. 120–31.
13. D. Q. Fuller, R. G. Allaby and C. Stevens, 'Domestication as innovation: the entanglement of techniques, technology and chance in the domestication of cereal crops', *World Archaeology*, 42, 2010, pp. 13–28.
14. D. Q. Fuller and M. Rowlands, 'Ingestion and food technology: maintaining differences over the long-term in West, South and Southeast Asia', in T. C. Wilkinson *et al.* (eds), *Interweaving Worlds: Systemic Interactions in Eurasia, 7th to the 1st Millennia BC*, Oxford: Oxbow Books, 2011, pp. 37–60.
15. G. Barker and M. Janowski, *Why Cultivate? Anthropological and Archaeological Approaches to Foraging-Farming Transitions in Southeast Asia*, Oxford, Oxbow Books, 2011, p. 2.
16. J. Bradshaw, *In Defence of Dogs: Why Dogs Need Our Understanding*, London: Allen Lane, 2011, p. 31.
17. M. Pollan, *The Omnivore's Dilemma: The Search for a Perfect Meal in a Fast-food World*, London: Bloomsbury, 2011.
18. G. Hillman and M. S. Davies, 'Measured domestication rates in wild wheat and barley', *Journal of World Prehistory*, 4, 1990, pp. 157–222.
19. P. L. Morrell and M. T. Clegg, 'Hordeum', in C. Kole (ed.), *Wild Crop Relatives: Genomic and Breeding Resources, Cereals*, Berlin: Springer-Verlag, 2011, pp. 309–19.
20. M. K. Jones *et al.*, 'Food globalization in prehistory', *World Archaeology*, 43, 2011, pp. 665–95.
21. N. Boivin, D. Q. Fuller and A. Crowther, 'Old World globalization and the Columbian Exchange: comparison and contrast', *World Archaeology*, 44, 2012, pp. 452–69; E. Lightfoot, L. Xinyu and M. K. Jones, 'Why move starchy cereals? A review of the isotope evidence for prehistoric consumptions across Eurasia', *World Archaeology*, 45, 2013, pp. 574–623. .
22. See Barker, *The Agricultural Revolution*, p. 137, for a fuller list of sites. See also P. Bellwood, *First Farmers: The Origins of Agricultural Societies*, Oxford: Blackwell Publishing, 2005, pp. 54–5.

# Chapter 6

1. G. Barker, *The Agricultural Revolution in Prehistory: Why did Foragers become Farmers?* Oxford: Oxford University Press, 2006, p. 146.

2. P. J. Richerson, R. Boyd and R. L. Bettinger, 'Was agriculture impossible during the Pleistocene but mandatory during the Holocene? A climate change hypothesis', *American Antiquity*, 66, 2001, pp. 387–411.

3. For some genetic results, see E. Weiss and D. Zohary, 'The Neolithic southwest Asian founder crops: their biology and archaeology', *Current Anthropology*, 52 (S4) S, 2011, pp. 237–54; M. Heun *et al.*, 'Site of einkorn domestication identified by DNA fingerprinting', *Science*, 278, 1997, pp. 1312–14; A. Badr *et al.*, 'On the origin and domestication of barley (*Hordeum vulgare*)', *Molecular Biology and Evolution*, 17, 2000, pp. 499–510; R. Bollongino and J. Burger, 'Neolithic cattle domestication as seen from ancient DNA', in A. Whittle and V. Cummings (eds), *Going Over: The Mesolithic-Neolithic Transition in North-West Europe,* Proceedings of the British Academy 144, Oxford: Oxford University Press, 2007, pp. 165–87; C. J. Edwards *et al.*, 'Mitochondrial DNA analysis shows a Near Eastern Neolithic origin for domestic cattle and no indication of domestication of European aurochs', *Proceedings of the Royal Society of London B: Biological Sciences*, 274, 2007, pp. 1377–85.

4. Quoted by the distinguished nature writer Richard Mabey, *Weeds*, London: Profile Books, 2010, pp. 40–41. I would take issue with Mabey's identification of Canaan (the land of Genesis's authors) as Mesopotamia – principally modern Iraq. Canaan was centred on modern Lebanon, Israel and western Jordan.

5. S. Wells, *Pandora's Seed: The Unforeseen Cost of Civilization*, London: Allen Lane, 2010. This is typical of the numerous moral histories that emphasize the problems set in motion by the Neolithic Revolution, see p. 210.

6. W. McNeill, *Plagues and Peoples*, New York: Norton, 1976.

7. C. S. Larsen, 'Life Conditions and Health in Early Farmers: A Global Perspective on Costs and Consequences of a Fundamental Transition', in A. Whittle and P. Bickle (eds), *Early Farmers: The View from Archaeology and Science*, Proceedings of the British Academy 198, Oxford: Oxford University Press, 2014, pp. 215–32.

8. In the Bible (Judges 13–16), Samson, eyeless in Gaza, is condemned by the Philistines to grind grain. Paintings and Cecil B. DeMille's lushly coloured 1949 film show the 'dumb hulk of muscle' (in *Variety*'s words) struggling with an anachronistic Roman donkey mill. It would be historically more accurate to show Samson humiliatingly, on his knees, pushing and pulling a rubbing stone on a saddle quern. It was constant work in this position that gave Neolithic women their stress injuries, which have also been observed in earlier Natufians who routinely ground wild cereals.

9. C. Broodbank, *The Making of the Middle Sea: A History of the Mediterranean from the Beginning to the Emergence of the Classical World*, London: Thames & Hudson, 2013, p. 166.

10. P. Bellwood, *First Farmers: The Origins of Agricultural Societies*, Oxford: Blackwell Publishing, 2005, p. 65.

11. For earlier Neolithic sites such as the clustered settlement at Aşikli Höyük, with its remarkable continuity of small buildings and the development of farming communities in eastern/central Turkey, see B. S. Düring, *The Prehistory of Asia Minor: From Complex Hunter-Gatherers to Early Urban Societies*, Cambridge: Cambridge University Press, 2011.

12. J. Mellaart, *Çatal Hüyük: A Neolithic Town in Anatolia,* London: Thames & Hudson, 1967.

13. R. Dunbar, *Human Evolution*, London: Pelican, 2014, p. 67.

14. C. Lévi-Strauss, *The Way of the Masks*, London: Jonathan Cape, 1973.

15. Burials of neonates and young children occur in the work areas, but never adults. It is common in many societies, for example in Roman settlements, for burial rules not to apply to the very young.

16. I. Hodder, *The Leopard's Tale: Revealing the Mysteries of Çatalhöyük*, London: Thames & Hudson, 2006, p. 146; plates 13 and 14; fig. 7.

17. H. G. K. Gebel, 'Walls. Loci of forces', in H. Gebel, B. Hermansen and C. Jensen (eds), *Magic Practices and Ritual in the Near Eastern Neolithic*, Berlin: Ex Oriente, 2002, pp. 119–32. Gebel argues that such deposits 'strengthen' the walls and protect against external spiritual or magical forces.

18. For details of pueblo organization and rituals, see J. Wilson, *The Earth Shall Weep: A History of Native Americans*, London: Picador, 1998, pp. 173–88. Wilson draws on A. Ortiz, *The Tewa World: Space, Time, Being, and Becoming in a Pueblo Society*, Chicago: Chicago University Press, 1969.

19. I. Hodder, *Entangled: An Archaeology of the Relationships between Humans and Things*, Chichester: Wiley-Blackwell, 2012.

20. Even in physics, the term is 'much misunderstood'. See A. Witze, '75 years of entanglement', *Science News*, 20 November 2010.

21. S. Atalay, 'Domesticating clay: the role of clay balls, mini balls and geometric objects in daily life at Çatalhöyük', in I. Hodder (ed.), *Changing Materialities at Çatalhöyük: Reports from the 1995–99 Seasons*, Cambridge: McDonald Institute for Archaeological Research/British Institute of Archaeology at Ankara Monograph, 2005, pp. 139–68.

22. J-F. Berger and J. Guilane, 'The 8200 cal BP abrupt environment change and theNeolithic transition', *Quaternary International*, 200, 2009, pp. 31–49.

**Chapter 7**

1. C. Broodbank, *The Making of the Middle Sea,* London: Thames & Hudson, 2013, pp. 155–6.

2. *Ibid.,* p. 214.

3. Domestic cats are all descended from wild cats (*Felis silvestris*). Genetically there are five lineages of wild cat: from China, Central Asia, South Africa, Europe and Western Asia. Our domestic pussycats all come from the last lineage. Presumably, wild cats were attracted to human settlements in Western Asia when, with piles of stored grain, these became mouse infested. Cats are, of course, quite unlike other domesticated animals, which tend to flock and follow a leader. The Neolithic was an opportunity for 'practical cats', borrowing T. S. Eliot's phrase. See J. Clutton-Brock, *Animals as Domesticates: A World View Through History*, East Lansing: Michigan State University Press, 2012, pp. 20–24.

4. For a vivid description of the varied Mediterranean, see P. Horden and N. Purcell, *The Corrupting Sea: A Study of Mediterranean History*, Oxford: Blackwell Publishing, 2000.

5. B. S. Düring, *The Prehistory of Asia Minor: From Complex Hunter-Gatherers to Early Urban Societies*, Cambridge: Cambridge University Press, 2010, pp. 125–6.

6. For a clear and well-referenced account, see J. Manco, *Ancestral Journeys: The Peopling of Europe from the First Venturers to the Vikings*, London and New York: Thames & Hudson, 2013, pp. 62–94. For a more technical, but still admirably understandable account of the genetic research into Neolithic demographics, see M. A. Jobling, M. Hurles and C. Tyler-Smith, *Human Evolutionary Genetics: Origins, Peoples and Disease*, Abingdon: Garland Science, 2004, pp. 309–24, especially p. 318, box 10.5, opinion: 'DNA and the Neolithic' by M. Richards.

7. L. L. Cavalli-Sforza, P. Menozzi and A. Piazza, *The History and Geography of Human Genes*, Princeton: Princeton University Press, 1994.

8. M. Richards *et al.*, 'Tracing European founder lineages in the Near Eastern mtDNA pool', *American Journal of Human Genetics*, 67, 2000, pp. 1251–76; P. Soares *et al.*, 'The archaeogenetics of Europe', *Current Biology*, 20, 2010, pp. R174–83.

9. M. Richards, 'Opinion: DNA and the Neolithic', in C. Jobling, M. Hurles and M. Tyler-Smith, *Human Evolutionary Genetics*, p. 318.

10. For a more detailed, yet admirably clear account of languages and genetics, see P. Bellwood, *First Migrants: Ancient Migration in Global Perspective*, Oxford: Wiley-Blackwell, 2013. See also

P. Balaresque et al., 'A predominantly Neolithic origin for European paternal lineages', PLOS Biology, 8 (1), 2010, p. 285. For the implications of the mitochondrial DNA studies on the demography of Europe, see Soares et al., 'The archaeogenetics of Europe', pp. R174–83.

11. C. R. Gignoux et al., 'Rapid, global demographic expansions after the origins of agriculture', Proceedings of the National Academy of Sciences (USA), 108, 2011, pp. 6044–9.

12. J. P. Mallory, In Search of the Indo-Europeans: Language, Archaeology and Myth, London: Thames & Hudson, 1989.

13. For an illuminating account of how languages and words change, see G. Deutscher, The Unfolding of Language: The Evolution of Mankind's Greatest Invention, London: Arrow Books, 2006.

14. C. Renfrew, Archaeology and Language: The Puzzle of Indo-European Origins, London: Jonathan Cape, 1987; P. Bellwood and C. Renfrew (eds), Examining the Farming/Language Dispersal Hypothesis, Cambridge: McDonald Institute for Archaeological Research, 2002.

15. D. W. Anthony, The Horse, the Wheel and Language: How Bronze-Age Riders from the Eurasian Steppes Shaped the Modern World, Princeton: Princeton University Press, 2007; J. P. Mallory, 'The homelands of the Indo-Europeans', in R. Blench and M. Spriggs (eds), Archaeology and Language I, London: Routledge, 1997, pp. 93–121.

16. A. Parpola, 'Proto-Indo-European speakers of the late Tripolye culture as the inventors of wheeled vehicles: linguistic and archaeological considerations of the PIE homeland problem', in K. Jones-Bley et al. (eds), Proceedings of the Nineteenth Annual UCLA Indo-European Conference, Journal of Indo-European Studies Monograph 54, Washington DC: Institute for the Study of Man, 2007, pp. 1–59; J. Clackson, 'Time depth in Indo-European', in C. Renfrew, A. McMahon and L. Trask (eds), Time Depth in Historical Linguistics, Cambridge: McDonald Institute for Archaeological Research, 2000, pp. 441–54.

17. For 'leapfrogging', see J. Zilhão, 'The spread of agro-pastoral economies across Mediterranean Europe: a view from the far west', Journal of Mediterranean Archaeology, 6 (1), 1993, pp. 5–63.

18. Horden and Purcell, The Corrupting Sea.

19. S. Forenbaher and P. T. Miracle, 'The spread of farming in the eastern Adriatic', Antiquity, 79, 2005, pp. 514–28.

20. P. Halstead, 'Sheep in the garden: the integration of crop and livestock husbandry in early farming regimes of Greece and southern Europe', in D. Serjeantson and D. Field (eds), Animals in the Neolithic of Britain and Europe, Oxford: Oxbow Books, 2006, pp. 42–55.

21. A. J. Legge and A. M. T. Moore, 'Clutching at straws: the Early Neolithic of Croatia and the dispersal of agriculture', in A. Hadjikoumis, E. Robinson and S. Viner (eds), Dynamics of Neolithisation in Europe, 2011, pp. 176–95.

22. S. Forenbaher and P. T. Miracle, 'The spread of farming in the eastern Adriatic', pp. 514–28. For greater detail, see also S. Forenbaher, A Connecting Sea: Maritime Interaction in Adriatic Prehistory, Oxford: Archaeopress, 2009.

23. P. Biagi, 'A Review of the Late Mesolithic in Italy and Its Implications for the Neolithic Transition', in A. J. Ammerman and P. Biagi (eds), The Widening Harvest. The Neolithic Transition in Europe: Looking Back, Looking Forward, Boston: Archaeological Institute of America, 2003.

24. Ibid.

25. K. Brown, 'Domestic settlement and the landscape during the Neolithic of the Tavoliere, south-east Italy', in P. Topping et al. (eds), Neolithic Landscapes: Neolithic Studies Group Seminar Papers 2, Oxbow Monograph 86, Oxford: Oxbow Books, 1997, pp. 125–37; R. Skeates, 'The social dynamics of enclosure in the Neolithic of the Tavoliere, south-east Italy', Journal of Mediterranean Archaeology, 13.2, 2000, pp. 155–88.

26. C. Broodbank, The Making of the Middle Sea, p. 192. The Tyrrhenian Sea is that part of the Mediterranean off the west coast of Italy and bounded by Sicily in the south and Corsica and Sardinia to the west.

27. C. Runnels, 'The origin of the Greek

Neolithic: a period view', in A. J. Ammerman and P. Biagi, *The Widening Harvest*, p. 126.

28. The Portuguese data is taken from J. Zilhão, 'The Neolithic transition in Portugal and the role of demic diffusion in the spread of agriculture across west Mediterranean Europe', in A. J. Ammerman and P. Biagi, (eds), *The Widening Harvest*, pp. 207–23.

29. B. Cunliffe, *Europe between the Oceans: 9000 BC–AD 1000*, New Haven: Yale University Press, 2008.

## Chapter 8

1. The chapter title is taken from Hemingway's novel of 1950. He borrowed it from the last words of the Confederate General Stonewall Jackson.

2. It is important to remember that as a result of generations of farming the landscape has changed; in particular, it has been levelled out by ploughing and blanketed in places by soil deposition.

3. J. Manco, *Ancestral Journeys: The Peopling of Europe from the First Venturers to the Vikings*, London and New York: Thames & Hudson, 2013, pp. 92–3.

4. C. Perlès, *The Early Neolithic in Greece*, Cambridge: Cambridge University Press, 2001, p. 15.

5. For a useful discussion of the development of Greek archaeology and on tell studies in particular, see K. Kotsakis, 'Across the border – unstable dwellings and fluid landscape in the earliest Neolithic of Greece', in D. Bailey, A. Whittle and V. Cummings (eds), *(Un) settling the Neolithic*, Oxford: Oxbow Books, 2005, pp. 8–15.

6. While house fires have been interpreted as acts of aggression, Ruth Tringham argues that ritual house burning created 'material of continuity'. See R. Tringham, 'Weaving house life and death into places: a blueprint for a hypermedia narrative', in D. Bailey, A. Whittle and V. Cummings (eds), *(Un)settling the Neolithic*, pp. 98–111.

7. P. Halstead, 'Resettling the Neolithic: faunal evidence for seasons of consumption and residence at Neolithic sites in Greece', in D. Bailey, A. Whittle and V. Cummings (eds), *(Un)settling

*the Neolithic*, pp. 38–50; P. Halstead, 'Farming, material culture and ideology: repackaging the Neolithic of Greece (and Europe)', in A. Hadjikoumis, E. Robinson and S. Viner (eds), *Dynamics of Neolithisation in Europe*, Oxford: Oxbow Books, 2011, pp. 131–51.

8. I. Hodder, *The Domestication of Europe*, Oxford: Blackwell, 1990.

9. P. Halstead, 'Land use in postglacial Greece: cultural causes and environmental effects', in P. Halstead and C. Frederick (eds), *Landscape and Land Use in Postglacial Greece*, Sheffield: Sheffield Academic Press, 2000, pp. 110–28.

10. The most prolific farmers, in recorded history, produce about 10 or 11 infants, although many would not reach adulthood in societies where infant mortality was high. Nevertheless, farmers routinely outbred foragers.

11. M. Pappa and M. Besios, 'The Makriyalos project: rescue excavations at the Neolithic site of Makriyalos, Pieria, northern Greece', in P. Halstead (ed.), *Neolithic Society in Greece*, Sheffield: Sheffield Academic Press, 1999, pp. 108–120.

12. Sling-bullets are discussed in Perlès, *The Early Neolithic in Greece*, pp. 228–31.

13. C. Sugaya, quoted in Perlès, *The Early Neolithic in Greece*, p. 231.

14. J. Chapman, 'Enchantment and enchainment in later Balkan prehistory: towards an aesthetic of precision and geometric order', in A. Hadjikoumis, E. Robinson and S. Viner (eds), *Dynamics of Neolithisation in Europe*, pp. 152–75.

15. M. W. Helms, *Ulysses' Sail: An Ethnographic Odyssey of Power, Knowledge, and Geographical Distance*, Princeton: Princeton University Press, 1988.

16. W. Schier, 'Uivar: a late Neolithic–early Eneolithic fortified tell site in western Romania', in D. Bailey, A. Whittle and D. Hofmann (eds), *Living Well Together? Settlement and Materiality in the Neolithic of South-East and Central Europe*, Oxford: Oxbow Books, 2008. pp. 54–67.

17. D. Srejović, *Europe's First Monumental Sculpture: New Discoveries at Lepenski Vir*, London: Thames & Hudson, 1972. See

also A. Whittle, *Europe in the Neolithic: The Creation of New Worlds*, Cambridge: Cambridge University Press, 1996, pp. 24–9, 144–6.

18. I. Hodder, *The Domestication of Europe*, pp. 21–31.

19. P. Bogucki, 'Neolithic dispersals in riverine interior central Europe', in A. J. Ammerman and P. Biagi (eds), *The Widening Harvest. The Neolithic Transition in Europe: Looking Back, Looking Forward*, Boston: Archaeological Institute of America, 2003, p. 262.

20. P. Bellwood, *First Migrants: Ancient Migration in Global Perspective*, Oxford: Wiley-Blackwell, 2013, p. 167; G. Larson *et al.*, 'Ancient DNA, pig domestication and the spread of the Neolithic into Europe', *Proceedings of the National Academy of Sciences* (USA), 107, 2007, pp. 7686–91; W. Haak *et al.*, 'Ancient DNA from European early Neolithic farmers reveals the Near Eastern affinities', *PLOS Biology*, 8 (11), 2010, e1000536.

21. Much archaeology is nationally based, and at worst nationalist. Childe always looked at the big picture, but in Germany, France, the Netherlands, Britain and Hungary etc., archaeologists developed their own 'national' culture names. Most of these remain imprecisely dated so a synthesis of European-wide development is not without its problems.

22. For a summary, see A. Whittle, 'The people who lived in longhouses: what's the big idea?', in D. Hofmann and P. Bickle (eds), *Creating Communities: New Advances in Central European Neolithic Research*, Oxford: Oxbow Books, 2009, pp. 249–63.

23. J. Manco, *Ancestral Journeys*; see also P. Foster and C. Renfrew, 'Europe and the Mediterranean: DNA', in C. Renfrew and P. Bahn, *The Cambridge World Prehistory Vol. 3*, Cambridge: Cambridge University Press, 2014, pp. 1747–52.

24. E. Lenneis, 'Perspectives on the beginnings of the earliest LBK in east-central Europe', in D. Bailey, A. Whittle and D. Hofmann (eds), *Living Well Together?*, pp. 164–77.

25. For this section on LBK crops I have relied on the broad-ranging article by

S. Colledge, J. Conolly and S. Shennan: 'The evolution of Neolithic farming from SW Asian origins to NW European limits', *European Journal of Archaeology*, 8, 2005, pp. 137–56.

26. J. Burger *et al.*, 'Absence of the lactase-persistence-associated allele in early Neolithic Europeans', *Proceedings of the National Academy of Sciences* (USA), 10, 2007, pp. 3736–41.

27. E. Classen, 'Settlement history, land use and social networks of early Neolithic communities in western Germany', in D. Hofmann and P. Bickle (eds), *Creating Communities*, pp. 95–120.

28. There is a problem with these so-called 'borrow pits'. Some of them are dug into subsoils, such as gravel, which are unsuitable for plastering walls. Richard Bradley suggested (pers. comm.) that they may have been dug out after the longhouse had been abandoned in order to bury the remains. This would have serious implications for the chronology of LBK houses, which are often dated by the contents of these pits.

29. W. Startin, 'Linear Pottery Culture houses: reconstruction and manpower', *Proceedings of the Prehistoric Society*, 44, 1978, pp. 143–59.

30. O. Rück, 'New aspects and models for Bandkeramic settlement research', in D. Hofmann and P. Bickle (eds), *Creating Communities*, pp. 159–85.

31. The presence of the pond turtle (*Emys orbicularis*) in central and north Europe supports the interpretation of high water levels and warm summers.

32. W. Pryce, *Architecture in Wood: A World History*, London and New York: Thames & Hudson, 2005, pp. 242–3.

33. R. Bradley, 'Orientation and origins: a symbolic dimension to the longhouses in Neolithic Europe', *Antiquity*, 75, 2001, pp. 50–56.

34. P. Bickle *et al.*, 'Roots of diversity in a *Linearbandkeramik* community: isotope evidence at Aiterhofen (Bavaria, Germany)', *Antiquity*, 85, 2011, pp. 1243–58.

35. D. Bailey, A. Whittle and D. Hofmann, *Living Well Together?*

36. M. Hobart, 'As I lay laughing: encountering global knowledge in

Bali', in R. Fardon (ed.), *Counterworks: Managing the Diversity of Knowledge*, London: Routledge, 1995.

37. For ethnographic examples, see J. Overing and A. Passes, *The Anthropology of Love and Anger: The Aesthetics of Conviviality in Native Amazonia*, London: Routledge, 2000.

38. For details of LBK mass graves, see Christian Meyer *et al.*, 'Mass Graves of the LBK', in A. Whittle and P. Bickle, *Early Farmers: The View from Archaeology and Science*, Proceedings of the British Academy 198, Oxford: Oxford University Press, 2014, pp. 307–25.

39. A. Zeeb-Lanz *et al.*, 'The LBK settlement with pit enclosure at Herxheim, near Landau (Palatinate) – first results', in D. Hofmann and P. Bickle (eds), *Creating Communities*, pp. 202–19; B. Boulestin *et al.*, 'Mass cannibalism in the Linear Pottery Culture at Herxheim (Palatinate, Germany)', in *Antiquity*, 83, 2009, pp. 968–82; J. Orschiedt and M. Haidle, 'Violence against the living, violence against the dead on the human remains from Herxheim, Germany: evidence of a crisis and mass cannibalism?', in R. Schulting and L. Fibiger (eds), *Sticks, Stones and Broken Bones: Neolithic Violence in a European Perspective*, Oxford: Oxford University Press, 2012, pp. 121–37.

## Chapter 9

1. S. Toucanne *et al.*, 'Timing of massive "Fleuve Manche" discharges over the last 350 kyr: insights into the European ice-sheet oscillations and the European drainage network from MIS 10 to 12', *Quaternary Science Reviews*, 2009, pp. 1238–56.

2. V. Gaffney, K. Thomson and S. Fitch, *Mapping Doggerland: The Mesolithic Landscapes of the Southern North Sea*, Oxford: Archaeopress, 2007. For an excellent, less technical account, see V. Gaffney, S. Fitch and D. Smith, *Europe's Lost World: The Rediscovery of Doggerland*, CBA Research Report 160, York: Council for British Archaeology, 2009. Professor Bryony Coles of Exeter University resurrected interest in the submerged North Sea basin and provided the memorable name, referring to the shallow water of the Dogger Bank where many artefacts and bones had been found: B. Coles, 'Doggerland: a speculative survey', *Proceedings of the Prehistoric Society*, 64, 1998, pp. 45–81.

3. C. Reid, *Submerged Forests*, Cambridge: Cambridge University Press, 1913.

4. J. Glimmerveen *et al.*, 'The North Sea Project: the first palaeontological, palynological, and archaeological results', in N. C. Flemming (ed.), *Submarine Prehistoric Archaeology of the North Sea*, CBA Research Report 141, York: Council for British Archaeology, 2004, pp. 43–52.

5. I. Oxley, 'Constructive conservation in England's waters', in N. C. Flemming (ed.), *Submarine Prehistoric Archaeology*, pp. 95–8.

6. For a fuller account, see A. Firth, 'Submerged prehistory in the North Sea', in A. Catsambis, B. Ford and D. Hamilton (eds), *The Oxford Handbook of Maritime Archaeology*, New York: Oxford University Press, 2011, pp. 786–808.

7. For horse carvings in mammoth ivory and antler, see J. Cook, *Ice Age Art: Arrival of the Modern Mind*, London: The British Museum Press, 2013, pp. 214–16, 263. 'Megalith-still' is a quote from Ted Hughes's poem 'The Horses', 1957.

8. P. Bahn and P. Pettitt, *Britain's Oldest Art: The Ice Age Cave Art of Creswell Crags*, Swindon: English Heritage, 2009.

9. Fifty-six engraved figures were eventually recorded in Church Hole Cave, and single figures in Robin Hood Cave and Mother Grundy's Parlour. Creswell Crags has a superb visitor centre and is well presented to the public.

10. There is no associated animal bone evidence at Howburn, but evidence for the presence of horses and reindeer at this time has been found in cave deposits in the far northwest of Scotland. For details, see T. B. Ballin *et al.*, 'An Upper Palaeolithic flint and chert assemblage from Howburn farm, South Lanarkshire, Scotland: first results', *Oxford Journal of Archaeology*, 29, 2010, pp. 323–60.

11. S. Mithen and K. Wicks, 'The voyagers of Rubha Port an t-Seilich: the discovery of late glacial hunters on Islay',

British Archaeology, 145, Nov/Dec 2015, pp. 24–29; S. Mithen et al., 'A Lateglacial archaeological site in the far north-west of Europe at Rubha Port an t-Seilich, Isle of Islay, western Scotland', Journal of Quaternary Science, 30, 2015, pp. 396–416.

12. Other nearby sites include Church Lammas, near Staines, and Three Ways Wharf, Uxbridge. For details, see D. Schreve et al., 'The terminal Pleistocene-early Holocene transition (MIS2-1)', in G. Hey et al., Thames Through Time: The Archaeology of the Gravel Terraces of the Upper and Middle Thames, Early Prehistory to 1500 BC, Thames Valley Landscapes Monograph 32, Oxford: Oxford Archaeology, 2011, pp. 143–9.

13. F. W. M. Vera, Grazing Ecology and Forest History, Oxford: CABI Publishing, 2000.

14. B. J. Coles, Beavers in Britain's Past, WARP Occasional Paper 19, Oxford: Oxbow Books, 2006.

15. S. Heaney, 'Churning Day', in Selected Poems 1965–1975, London: Faber & Faber, 1980, pp. 16.

16. The detailed reconstruction of sea levels and land limits in the Irish Sea is still a work in progress. Certainly, the gap between Scotland, England, Wales, islands such as the Isle of Man and Ireland would have been much narrower than today. For a more detailed discussion, see J. P. Mallory, The Origins of the Irish, London and New York: Thames & Hudson, 2013, pp. 30–36. It is possible that humans settled or, at least, visited Ireland before 8000 BC. There is no conclusive evidence at present.

17. C. J. Edwards and D. Bradley, 'Human colonisation routes and the origins of Irish mammals', in S. McCartan et al. (eds), Mesolithic Horizons, Oxford: Oxbow Books, 2009, pp. 217–24.

Chapter 10

1. P. Spikins, 'Mesolithic Europe: glimpses of another world', in G. Bailey and P. Spikins (eds), Mesolithic Europe, Cambridge: Cambridge University Press, 2008, p. 2.

2. R. Bradley, The Social Foundations of Prehistoric Britain, London: Longmans, 1984, p. 11.

3. G. Clark, Mesolithic Prelude: The Palaeolithic-Neolithic Transition in Old World Prehistory, Edinburgh: Edinburgh University Press, 1980.

4. Ibid. He was referring to his book, The Mesolithic Age in Britain, Cambridge: Cambridge University Press, 1932.

5. G. Bailey and P. Spikins (eds), Mesolithic Europe, Cambridge: Cambridge University Press, 2008.

6. P. H. Barrett and R. B. Freeman (eds), The Works of Charles Darwin, Volume 2: Journal of Researches, Part One, London: William Pickering, 1986.

7. R. J. Braidwood, Prehistoric Men, Chicago Natural History Museum Popular Series, Anthropology 37 (3rd edn), Chicago: Chicago Natural History Museum Press, 1957, p. 22.

8. M. Sahlins, Stone Age Economics, London: Tavistock Publications, 1972.

9. K. Flannery and J. Marcus, The Creation of Inequality: How Our Prehistoric Ancestors Set the Stage for Monarchy, Slavery, and Empire, Cambridge, Mass.: Harvard University Press, 2012, p. 58

10. G. Warren, Mesolithic Lives in Scotland, Stroud: Tempus, 2005, pp. 119–21.

11. For examples of axe depositions, see C. Conneller and G. Warren (eds), Mesolithic Britain and Ireland: New Approaches, Stroud: Tempus, 2006, pp. 27, 111; for axes deposited in water and caches, see pp. 109–12; T. Collins and F. Coyne, 'Fire and water...Early Mesolithic cremations at Castleconnell, Co Limerick', Archaeology Ireland, 64, 2003, pp. 24–7.

12. R. Bradley, The Passage of Arms: An Archaeological Analysis of Prehistoric Hoards and Votive Deposits, Cambridge: Cambridge University Press, 1990.

13. For Leach's work, see M. Bell, Prehistoric Coastal Communities: The Mesolithic in Western Britain, CBA Research Report 149, York: Council for British Archaeology, 2007, pp. 12.

14. N. A. Chagnon, Yanomamö: The Fierce People (2nd edn), New York: Holt, 1977.

15. In fact, it has become a fairly major topic. See L. Keeley, Warfare before Civilization: The Myth of the Peaceful Savage, Oxford: Oxford University Press, 1996; G. Azar,

*War in Human Civilization*, Oxford: Oxford University Press, 2006; the bestseller, S. Pinker, *The Better Angels of Our Nature: A History of Violence and Humanity*, London: Penguin, 2012; J. Chapman, 'The origins of warfare in the prehistory of central and western Europe', in J. Carman and A. Harding (eds), *Ancient Warfare: Archaeological Perspectives*, Stroud: Sutton, 1999, pp. 101–42; R. Schulting and L. Fibiger (eds), *Sticks, Stones and Broken Bones: Neolithic Violence in a European Perspective*, Oxford: Oxford University Press, 2012.

16. For a more nuanced view of what can be seen as ambiguous evidence, see D. Hofmann, 'The emotional Mesolithic: past and present ambiguities of Ofnet Cave', in N. Milner and P. Woodman, *Mesolithic Studies at the Beginning of the 21st Century*, Oxford: Oxbow Books, 2005, pp. 94–211; for other evidence of violence and decapitation in the later Mesolithic, see M. A. Jochim, 'The Mesolithic of the Upper Danube and Upper Rhine', in Bailey and Spikins (eds), *Mesolithic Europe*, 2010, pp. 203–20.

17. B. Boulestin, *Approche taphonomique des restes humains. Le cas des Mésolithiques de la grotte des Perrats et le problème du cannibalisme en préhistore récente européenne*, British Archaeological Reports International Series 776, Oxford: Archaeopress, 1999.

18. For fun in war and 'joyful slaughter', see J. Bourke, *An Intimate History of Killing: Face-to-Face Killing in Twentieth-Century Warfare*, London: Granta, 2000, pp. 30–33, 140–41.

19. D. E. Smith, 'The Storegga disaster', *Current Archaeology*, 179, 2002, pp. 468–71.

20. J. G. D. Clark, *Excavations at Star Carr*, Cambridge: Cambridge University Press, 1954; A. J. Legge and P. A. Rowley-Conwy, *Star Carr Revisited*, London: Birkbeck College, 1988.

21. N. Milner *et al.*, *Star Carr: Life in Britain after the Ice Age*, York: Council for British Archaeology, 2013.

22. C. Waddington (ed.), *Mesolithic Settlement in the North Sea Basin: A Case Study from Howick, North-East England*, Oxford: Oxbow Books, 2007.

23. A. Saville, 'The material culture of Mesolithic Scotland', in A. Saville (ed.), *Mesolithic Scotland and Its Neighbours*, Edinburgh: Society of Antiquaries of Scotland, 2004, pp. 185–220.

24. S. Mithen, *After the Ice: A Global Human History, 20,000–5000 BC*, London: Weidenfeld & Nicolson, 2003, pp. 202–3.

25. P. Mellars, *Excavations on Oronsay*, Edinburgh: Edinburgh University Press, 1987; P. Mellars and M. Wilkinson, 'Fish otoliths as indicators of seasonality in prehistoric shell middens: the evidence from Oronsay (Inner Hebrides)', *Proceedings of the Prehistoric Society*, 46, 1980, pp. 19–44.

26. S. Mithen and K. Wicks, 'The voyagers of Rubha Port an t-Seilich: the discovery of late glacial hunters on Islay', *British Archaeology*, 145, Nov/Dec 2015, pp. 24–9.

27. P. C. Woodman, *Excavations at Mount Sandel, 1973–77*, Belfast: HMSO, 1985.

28. J. P. Mallory, *The Origins of the Irish*, London and New York: Thames & Hudson, 2013, p. 46; see also F. McCormick, 'Hunting wild pig in the late Mesolithic', in H. Roche *et al.*, *From Megaliths to Metal: Essays in Honour of George Eogan*, Oxford: Oxbow Books, 2004.

29. R. Phillips, *Wild Food: A Complete Guide for Foragers*, London: Macmillan, 2014, p. 188.

30. M. Bell, *Prehistoric Coastal Communities*, pp. 4–5, 18.

31. S. Aldhouse-Green *et al.*, 'Prehistoric Human Footprints from the Severn Estuary at Uskmouth and Magor Pill, Gwent, Wales', in *Archaeologia Cambriensis* CXLI, 1992, pp. 14–55.

32. M. Bell, *Prehistoric Coastal Communities*.

33. F. Healey, M. Heaton and S. J. Lobb, 'Excavations of a Mesolithic site at Thatcham, Berkshire', *Proceedings of the Prehistoric Society*, 58, 1992, pp. 41–76.

34. D. Jacques, T. Phillips and T. Lyons, 'Return to Blick Mead: exploring the Mesolithic origins of Stonehenge's ritual landscape', *Current Archaeology*, 293, 2014, pp. 24–9.

35. G. Momber *et al.*, *Mesolithic Occupation at Bouldnor Cliff and the Submerged Prehistoric Landscapes of the Solent*, CBA Research Report 164, York: Council for British Archaeology, 2011.

36. M. Taylor, 'Waterlogged wood', in Momber *et al.*, *Mesolithic Occupation at Bouldnor Cliff*, pp. 84–9.

37. C. Evans and I. Hodder, *A Woodland Archaeology: Neolithic Sites at Haddenham*, Cambridge: McDonald Institute for Archaeological Research, 2006, pp. 185–7.

38. R. Scales, 'Footprint: tracks of people and animals', in M. Bell, *Prehistoric Coastal Communities*, pp. 139–59.

39. C. Smith, *Late Stone Age Hunters of the British Isles*, London: Routledge, 1992, pp. 137, 171.

40. C. Christensen, A. Fischer and D. R. Mathiassen, 'A great sea rise in the Storebælt', in L. Pedersen, A. Fischer and B. Aaby (eds), *The Danish Storebælt since the Ice Age*, Copenhagen: Storebælt Publications, 1997, pp. 45–54.

41. C. R. Wickham-Jones, 'Summer walkers? – Mobility and the Mesolithic', in Milner and Woodman (eds), *Mesolithic Studies at the Beginning of the 21st Century*, pp. 30–41.

42. The uses and misuses of the word are discussed in R. Hutton, *Shamans: Siberian Spirituality and the Western Imagination*, London: Hambledon, 2001. For the rituals and regalia of north shamans, see P. R Anawalt, *Shamanic Regalia in the Far North*, London and New York: Thames & Hudson, 2014. Caroline Humphrey emphasizes the variety of shamanic belief and practice: 'shamanism is not one thing but many'. See N. Thomas and C. Humphrey (eds), *Shamanism, History and the State*, Ann Arbor: University of Michigan Press, 1994, pp. 208. For a well-illustrated account of the variety of shamanic practice and belief, see P. Vitebsky, *The Shaman: Voyages of the Soul, Trance, Ecstasy and Healing from Siberia to the Amazon*, London: Macmillan, 1995.

43. L. N. Grosman, D. Munro and A. Belfer-Cohen, 'A 12,000-year-old Shaman burial from the southern Levant (Israel)', *Proceedings of the National Academy of Sciences* (USA), 105, 2008, pp. 17665–69; illustrated in C. Broodbank, *The Making of the Middle Sea: A History of the Mediterranean from the Beginning to the Emergence of the Classical World,* London: Thames & Hudson, 2013, p. 147.

44. R. Bradley, *The Significance of Monuments: On the Shaping of Human Experience in Neolithic and Bronze Age Europe*, London: Routledge, 1998, pp. 20–35.

45. N. Bird-David, 'The giving environment: another perspective on the economic system of gatherer-hunters', *Current Anthropology*, 31, 1990, pp. 183–96.

## Chapter 11

1. It did occasionally happen. In Sweden, close to the possible limit of agriculture, communities adopted farming and then returned to hunter-gathering for about a thousand years, then they permanently flipped back to farming.

2. T. Ingold, *The Perception of the Environment: Essays in Livelihood, Dwelling and Skill*, London: Routledge, 2000, p. 72.

3. D. Naveh and N. Bird-David, 'How persons became things: economic and epistemological changes among Nayaka hunter-gatherers', *Journal of the Royal Anthropological Institute*, 20, 2014, pp. 74–92.

4. For example, C. Bonsall, 'The Mesolithic of the Iron Gates', in G. Bailey and P. Spikins (eds), *Mesolithic Europe*, Cambridge: Cambridge University Press, 2008, pp. 238, 279.

5. Figures and references quoted in D. E. Lieberman, *The Story of the Human Body: Evolution, Health and Disease*, New York: Vintage Books, 2014, p. 198, fig. 18.

6. C. Smith, *Late Stone Age Hunters of the British Isles*, London: Routledge, 1992; C. Smith, 'The population of Late Upper Palaeolithic and Mesolithic Britain', *Proceedings of the Prehistoric Society*, 58, 1992, pp. 37–40.

7. *The Times*, 'How early Europeans came north and grew out of their dark skin', 8 April 2015.

8. M. Edmonds, C. Evans and D. Gibson, 'Assembly and collection – lithic complexes in the Cambridgeshire Fenlands', *Proceedings of the Prehistoric Society*, 65, 1999, pp. 47–82.

9. L. Verhardt, 'New developments in the study of the Mesolithic of the Low Countries', in G. Bailey and P. Spikins (eds), *Mesolithic Europe*, pp. 158–81.

10. C. French *et al.*, *Prehistoric Landscape*

*Development and Human Impact in the Upper Allen Valley, Cranborne Chase, Dorset*, Cambridge: McDonald Institute for Archaeological Research, 2007.

11. D. A. Henderson *et al.*, 'Regional variations in the European Neolithic dispersal: the role of the coastlines', *Antiquity*, 88, 2014, pp. 1291–1302; J. P. Bocquet-Appel *et al.*, 'Understanding the rates of expansion of the farming system in Europe', *Journal of Archaeological Science*, 39, 2012, pp. 531–46; N. Isern and J. Fort, 'Modelling the effect of Mesolithic populations on the slowdown of the Neolithic transition', *Journal of Archaeological Science*, 39, 2012, pp. 3671–6.

12. For valuable attempts to improve European Neolithic chronologies, *see* K. Manning *et al.*, 'The chronology of culture: a comparative assessment of European Neolithic dating approaches', *Antiquity*, 88, 2014, pp. 1065–80.

13. For example, the formation of the European Research Council (www.erc. europa.eu) in 2007 allowed the financing of research on a grand scale, not confined by national boundaries. There has been a huge proliferation of archaeological data in most European countries in recent decades, particularly from developer-funded archaeology, and also of sampling for dating, environmental and other scientific data. The problem is to make sense of it.

14. H. P. Blankholm, 'Southern Scandinavia', in G. Bailey and P. Spikins (eds), *Mesolithic Europe*, pp. 107–31.

15. P. Rowley-Conwy, 'Westward Ho! The spread of agriculture from central Europe to the Atlantic', *Current Anthropology*, 52, 2011, pp. S432–51.

16. There is some evidence that farmers attempted to develop land further north, but were foiled by the constraints of climate.

17. Ecclesiastes 3:2.

18. L. Bedault, 'First reflections on the exploitation of animals in Villeneuve-Saint-Germain society at the end of the early Neolithic in the Paris Basin (France)', in D. Hofmann and P. Bickle (eds), *Creating Communities: New Advances in Central European Neolithic Research*, Oxford: Oxbow Books, 2009, pp. 111–31.

19. J. P. Bocquet-Appel and J. Dubouloz, 'Traces paléoanthropologiques et archéologiques d'une transition démographique néolithique en Europe', *Bulletin de la Société Préhistorique Française*, 100, 2003, pp. 699–714. Having worked and lived in France for much of the past two decades I find that standards and approaches to archaeological investigation are very varied, especially between regions, which makes the comparison of data difficult or impossible; for example, the relative importance of different foodstuffs.

20. C. Scarre, 'Changing places: monuments and the Neolithic transition in western France', in A. Whittle and V. Cummings (eds), *Going Over: The Mesolithic-Neolithic Transition in North-West Europe*, Proceedings of the British Academy 144, Oxford: Oxford University Press, 2007, pp. 243–61.

21. Excavations directed by the French archaeologist Serge Cassen, have revealed the complexity and sequence of the complex of monuments at Locmariaquer. S. Cassen (ed.), *Autour de la Table: Explorations Archéologiques et Discours savants sur des Architectures Néolithiques à Locmariaquer, Morbihan (Table des Marchands et Grand Menhir)*, Nantes: Laboratoire de Recherches Archéologiques, CNRS and Université de Nantes, 2009.

22. K. Flannery and J. Marcus, *The Creation of Inequality: How Our Prehistoric Ancestors Set the Stage for Monarchy, Slavery and Empire*, Cambridge, Mass.: Harvard University Press, 2012.

23. D. Garrow and F. Sturt, 'Grey waters bright with Neolithic Argonauts? Maritime connections and the Mesolithic–Neolithic transition within the 'western seaways' of Britain, *c.* 5000–3500 BC', *Antiquity*, 85, 2011, p. 59–72.

24. The Channel Islands were attached to mainland France 12,000 years ago, then as the waters rose Guernsey became an island about 11,000 years ago, Alderney 2,000 years later. Jersey was still attached in 5000 BC when the Neolithic had

already arrived in northern France. The Scillies are much closer to Cornwall, on the British mainland.

25. A. Whittle, F. Healey and A. Bayliss, *Gathering Time: Dating the Early Neolithic Enclosures of Southern Britain and Ireland*, vol. 2, Oxford: Oxbow Books, 2011, p. 632.

26. Ferriter's Cove produced seven cattle bones in a Mesolithic context. There are other possible domesticated animal imports into Ireland but the evidence is less secure. See J. Thomas, *The Birth of Neolithic Britain: An Interpretive Account*, Oxford: Oxford University Press, 2013, pp. 266–7.

## Chapter 12

1. For a more detailed discussion and French and German references, see D. Hofmann, 'Living by the lake: domestic architecture in the Alpine foreland', in D. Hofmann and J. Smyth (eds), *Tracking the Neolithic House in Europe: Sedentism, Architecture and Practice*, New York: Springer, 2013, pp. 197–227.

2. R-M. Arbogast *et al.*, 'The significance of climate fluctuations for lake level changes and shifts in subsistence economy during the late Neolithic (4300–2400 BC) in central Europe', *Vegetation History and Archaeobotany*, 15 (4), 2006, pp. 403–18.

3. U. Maier, 'Agricultural activities and land use in a Neolithic village around 3900 BC: Hornstaad Hörnle IA, Lake Constance, Germany', *Vegetation History and Archaeobotany*, 8 (1), 1999, pp. 87–94.

4. P. Bogucki, 'Hunters, fishers and farmers of northern Europe, 9000–3000 BCE', in C. Renfrew and P. Bahn, (eds), *The Cambridge World Prehistory Vol. 3*, Cambridge: Cambridge University Press, 2014, pp. 1835–59.

5. The detailed discussion of the origins of the Neolithic in Britain (see J. Thomas, *The Birth of Neolithic Britain: An Interpretive Account*, Oxford: Oxford University Press, 2013, pp. 189–204) has virtually nothing to say about the Mesolithic of Britain in the fifth millennium BC, the key centuries prior to the adoption of farming.

6. P. Booth *et al.*, *On Track: The Archaeology of the High Speed 1 Section 1 in Kent*, Oxford: Oxford-Wessex Archaeology, 2011; for a very thorough account of the building in its Neolithic context, see P. Garwood, 'Early prehistory', ch. 3, pp. 67–91.

7. The beginning of the Neolithic in Britain coincides with a period of rapid change across the Channel and the North Sea: in France, this period is known as the Chasséen culture; in northeastern France and West Germany, the Michelsberg culture; and in northern Germany and southern Scandinavia, the TRB culture.

8. J. Last, 'The end of the longhouse', in Hofmann and Smyth (eds), *Tracking the Neolithic House in Europe*, pp. 261–82.

9. A. Whittle, F. Healey and A. Bayliss, *Gathering Time: Dating the Early Neolithic Enclosures of Southern Britain and Ireland*, Oxford: Oxbow Books, 2011.

10. This is based on fifteen 'likelihoods' from nine sites, so there is room for future refinements. See Whittle *et al.*, *Gathering Time*, vol. 2, pp. 731, 898.

11. *Ibid.*, p. 668.

12. J. S. Thomas, 'The Mesolithic-Neolithic transition in Britain', in J. Pollard (ed.), *Prehistoric Britain*, Oxford: Blackwell, 2008, pp. 58–89.

13. A. Sheridan, 'The Neolithization of Britain and Ireland: the big picture', in B. Finlayson and G. Warren (eds), *Landscapes in Transition*, Oxford: Oxbow Books, 2010, pp. 89–105.

14. J. N. G. Ritchie, 'Excavation of the chambered cairn at Achnacreebeag', *Proceedings of the Society of Antiquaries of Scotland*, 102, 1970, pp. 31–55.

15. Whittle *et al.*, *Gathering Time*, vol. 2, p. 869.

16. Thomas, *The Birth of Neolithic Britain*, p. 377.

17. L. P. Louwe Kooijmans, 'Hunters before farmers: early Neolithic B and middle Neolithic A', in L. P. Louwe Kooijmans *et al.* (eds), *The Prehistory of the Netherlands Vol. 1*, Amsterdam: Amsterdam University Press, 2005, pp. 249–71.

18. The Lough Gur house was first assumed to be medieval, then stone axes and Neolithic pottery turned up.

19. K. Molloy and M. O'Connell, 'Palaeoecological investigations towards the reconstruction of woodland and

land-use history at Lough Sheeauns, Connemara, Western Ireland', *Review of Palaeobotany and Palynology*, 67, 1991, pp. 203–20.

20. S. Caulfield, 'Neolithic fields: the Irish evidence', in H. C. Bowen and P. J. Fowler (eds), *Early Land Allotment in the British Isles*, Oxford: British Archaeological Reports, 1978, pp. 137–43.

21. G. Cooney, *Landscapes of Neolithic Ireland*, London: Routledge, 2000.

22. For an excellent catalogue and discussion of attitudes and implications, see J. Smyth, *Settlement in the Irish Neolithic: New Discoveries at the Edge of Europe*, Prehistoric Society Research Paper 6, Oxford: Oxbow Books, 2014.

23. A. Whittle *et al.*, *Gathering Time*, vol. 2, p. 833. For an overview of early Neolithic structures, see A. Sheridan, 'Early Neolithic habitation structures in Britain and Ireland: a matter of circumstance and context', in D. Hofmann and J. Smyth (eds), *Tracking the Neolithic House in Europe*, 2015, pp. 283–300.

24. C. Evans and I. Hodder, *A Woodland Archaeology: Neolithic Sites at Haddenham*, Cambridge: McDonald Institute for Archaeological Research, 2006.

25. R. Bradley, *The Prehistory of Britain and Ireland*, Cambridge: Cambridge University Press, 2007, p. 59.

26. M. W. Helms, 'House life', in R. A. Beck, *The Durable House: House Society Models in Archaeology*, Carbondale: Center for Archaeological Investigation, Southern Illinois University, 2007, pp. 487–504.

27. Thomas, *The Birth of Neolithic Britain*, pp. 290–313.

28. G. Noble, *Neolithic Scotland: Timber, Stone, Earth and Fire*, Edinburgh: Edinburgh University Press, 2006; see ch. 3 on burning. See also H. Murray and C. Murray, 'Discussion of the structure', in H. Murray, C. Murray and S. Fraser (eds), *A Tale of the Unknown Unknowns: A Mesolithic Pit Alignment and a Neolithic Timber Hall at Warren Field, Crathes, Aberdeenshire*, Oxford: Oxbow Books, 2009.

29. For other early Neolithic buildings in England and Wales, such as Lismore Fields, Derbyshire, and smaller structures, such as Harton, Middlesex, see J. Last, 'The end of the longhouse', in D. Hofmann and J. Smyth (eds), *Tracking the Neolithic House in Europe*, pp. 274–7.

30. For an excellent synthesis of the early prehistory of the Thames Valley where there has been a prodigious amount of archaeological fieldwork in advance of development, see G. Hey *et al.*, *Thames Through Time: The Archaeology of the Gravel Terraces of the Upper and Middle Thames, Early Prehistory to 1500 BC*, Thames Valley Landscapes Monograph 32, Oxford: Oxford Archaeology, 2011.

31. A. Brown, 'Dating the onset of cereal cultivation in Britain and Ireland: the evidence from charred cereal grains', *Antiquity*, 81, 2007, pp. 1042–52.

32. M. P. Richards *et al.*, 'Sharp shift in diet at onset of the Neolithic', *Nature*, 425, 2003, p. 366.

33. R. J. Schulting, 'An Irish sea change: some implications for the Mesolithic-Neolithic transition', in V. Cummings and C. Fowler, *The Neolithic of the Irish Sea: Materiality and Traditions of Practice*, Oxford: Oxbow Books, 2004, pp. 22–8.

34. J. Hamilton, R. J. M. Hedges and M. Robinson, 'Rooting for pigfruit: pig feeding in Neolithic and Iron Age Britain compared', *Antiquity*, 83, 2009, pp. 998–1011.

## Chapter 13

1. The stones are often referred to in general terms as jade or jadeitite. Technically, the most spectacular Monte Viso material is jadeitite.

2. For an account of the research and detailed bibliography, see P. Petréquin *et al.*, 'Eclogite or jadeitite: the two colours involved in the transfer of alpine axeheads in Western Europe', in V. Davis and M. Edmonds (eds), *Stone Axe Studies III*, Oxford: Oxbow, 2011, pp. 55–97.

3. A large collection of Kanak cultural material now resides in the Quai Branly Museum in Paris, which is where I acquired the information about the Kanak and their relationship with jade axes.

4. The practice and theory of 'giving', 'exchange' or 'prestation' among

tribal people has generated a huge anthropological literature, since Malinowski described the Kula system in *Argonauts of the Western Pacific* (London: Routledge, 1922) and Marcel Mauss's *Essai sur le Don* was published in 1950 (in English, *The Gift*, 1954).

5. M. W. Helms, *Ulysses' Sail: An Ethnographic Odyssey of Power, Knowledge, and Geographical Distance*, Princeton: Princeton University Press, 1988. Even today, the competitive super-rich indulge in their own form of Kula cycle, an annual circumnavigation of the globe. See Robert Frank, 'Life is more than a beach for the super-rich', *International New York Times*, 22 Jun 2015.

6. The Copper Age cemetery was found in 1972 and excavated by Ivan Ivanov of the Varna Museum. Like many other Western archaeologists I learnt of it thanks to Colin Renfrew's writing. See C. Renfrew, *Problems in European Prehistory*, Edinburgh: Edinburgh University Press, 1979, pp. 377–88; 'Varna and the social context of early metallurgy', *Antiquity*, 52, 1978, pp. 199–203.

7. S. Potter and L. Sargent, *Pedigree: Words from Nature*, The New Naturalist Series, vol. 56, London: Collins, 1973; A. Meaney, *Anglo-Saxon Amulets and Curing Stones*, Oxford: British Archaeological Reports British Series 9, 1981; for the 'Scottish' axe, see A. Sheridan *et al.*, 2011, fig. 8, pp. 918–19.

8. Quoted in M. Barber and C. Dyer, 'Scouting for shafts: aerial reconnaissance and the Neolithic flint mine at Stoke Down, West Sussex', in P. Topping and M. Lynott (eds), *The Cultural Landscape of Prehistoric Mines*, Oxford: Oxbow Books, 2005, pp. 30–50. See also D. Field, 'The landscape of extraction: aspects of the procurement of raw material in the Neolithic', in P. Topping *et al.* (eds), *Neolithic Landscapes: Neolithic Studies Group Seminar Papers 2*, Oxbow Monograph 86, Oxford: Oxbow Books, 1997.

9. Gender and age roles are contentious. In most ethnographic studies miners are restricted to men. However, some female bodies were found in the Sussex mines,

although how and why they got there is not clear. And some shafts were only accessible to very small people.

10. P. Topping, 'Shaft 27 revisited: an ethnography of Neolithic flint extraction', in Topping and Lynott (eds), *The Cultural Landscape of Prehistoric Mines*, pp. 63–93.

11. P. Petréquin and A-M. Petréquin, 'The twentieth-century polished stone axeheads of New Guinea: why study them?', in V. David and M. Edmonds (eds), *Stone Axe Studies III*, p. 340.

12. For the importance of trees in the life, crafts and industry of the Lake District, see M. Edmonds, *The Langdales: Landscape and Prehistory in a Lakeland Valley*, Stroud: Tempus, 2004.

13. W. F. Grimes, 'The history of implement petrology in Britain', in T. H. McK. Clough and W. A. Cummins (eds), *Stone Axe Studies*, CBA Research Report 23, London: Council for British Archaeology, 1979, pp. 1–4. There are also major non-flint axe-producing centres in Cornwall, North Wales, Graig Lwyd and Mynydd Rhiw, Pembrokeshire, Northern Ireland, Brockley and Tievebulliagh (porcellanite) as well as a number of minor quarries. Several of the quarries are dramatically sited on peaks or headland, notably Mynydd Rhiw; others are on islands, which may also have been regarded as places of spiritual importance – for example, Rathlin Island, Co. Antrim, a source of porcellanite. The Langdale axes were also copied in Ireland. Clearly, there was toing and froing across the Irish Sea in the Neolithic.

14. R. Bradley and M. Edmonds, *Interpreting the Axe Trade*, Cambridge: Cambridge University Press, 1993.

15. V. Davis and M. Edmonds, 'A time and place for the Belmont Hoard', in V. Davis and M. Edmonds (eds), *Stone Axe Studies III*, pp. 167–86; A. Whittle, F. Healey and A. Bayliss, *Gathering Time: Dating the Early Neolithic Enclosures of Southern Britain and Ireland*, vol. 2, Oxford: Oxbow Books, 2011, p. 791, fig. 14.131 p. 793.

16. Petréquin *et al.*, 'Eclogite or jadeitite', in V. Davis and M. Edmonds (eds), *Stone Axe Studies III*, p. 59.

17. Y. Maigrot, 'Neolithic polished stone axes

and hafting systems: technical use and social function at the Neolithic lakeside settlements of Chalain and Clairvaux', in V. Davis and M. Edmonds (eds), *Stone Axe Studies III*, pp. 281–94.

## Chapter 14

1. S. Schama, *Landscape and Memory*, New York: Random House, 1995, pp. 6–7.
2. K. Basso, 'Speaking with Names: Language and Landscape among the Western Apache', *Cultural Anthropology*, 3 (2), 1988, pp. 99–130.
3. T. Ingold, *Being Alive: Essays on Movement, Knowledge and Description*, London: Routledge, 2011, pp. 145–55.
4. J. F. Weiner, *Tree Leaf Talk: A Heideggerian Anthropology*, Oxford and New York: Berg, 2001, p. 30.
5. D. L. Eck, *India: A Sacred Geography*, New York: Harmony Books, 2012, p. 48.
6. Richard Bradley took the phrase 'altering the earth' from Raymond Williams's *People of the Black Mountains: The Beginning vol. 1* (London: Chatto & Windus, 1989, pp. 149–50). He used it as the title for the 1992 Rhind Lectures, published as *Altering the Earth*, Society of Antiquaries of Scotland Monograph 8, Edinburgh: Society of Antiquaries of Scotland, 1993.
7. A. Whittle, F. Healey and A. Bayliss, *Gathering Time: Dating the Early Neolithic Enclosures of Southern Britain and Ireland*, vol. 1, Oxford: Oxbow Books, 2011, pp. 380–1, figs 7.27, 7.28.
8. R. M. Cleal, 'The dating and diversity of the earliest ceramics of Wessex and south-west England', in R. Cleal and J. Pollard (eds), *Monuments and Material Culture: Papers in Honour of an Avebury Archaeologist: Isobel Smith*, East Knoyle: Hobnob Press, 2004, pp. 166–92.
9. A. Whittle, *The Archaeology of People: Dimensions of Neolithic Life*, London: Routledge, 2003, p. 120.
10. J. Last, 'The end of the longhouse', in D. Hofmann and J. Smyth (eds), *Tracking the Neolithic House in Europe: Sedentism, Architecture and Practice,* New York: Springer, 2013, p. 268.
11. For a beautifully presented account of Welsh megaliths and how to build them, see S. Burrow, *The Tomb Builders in Wales 4000–3000 BC*, Cardiff: National Museum of Wales, 2006.
12. A. Saville, *Hazleton North, Gloucestershire, 1979–82: The Excavation of a Neolithic Long Cairn of the Cotswold-Severn Group*, London: English Heritage, 1990. Paul Ashbee's calculations for the construction of the Fussell's Lodge barrow is about the same. See P. Ashbee, 'The Fussell's Lodge long barrow excavations 1957', *Archaeologia*, 100, 1966, pp. 1–80. Bill Starting calculated the construction of Fussell's Lodge at 6,900 person-hours and the biggest megalithic tombs at almost 16,000 person-hours. This contrasts with 2,200–3,200 person-hours for the large timber longhouses of the LBK.
13. G. Cooney, *Landscapes of Neolithic Ireland*, London: Routledge, 2000, p. 232.
14. The *Gathering Time* volumes dealt principally with the dating of causewayed enclosures. Prior to that, Alex Bayliss, Alasdair Whittle and colleagues tackled the development and dating of five long barrows in southern Britain. See A. Bayliss and A. Whittle, 'Histories of the dead: building chronologies for five southern British long barrows', *Cambridge Archaeological Journal*, 17, no. 1 (supplement), 2007.
15. A. Whittle, 'Wayland's Smithy, Oxfordshire: excavations at the Neolithic Tomb in 1962–3 by RJC Atkinson and S Piggott', *Proceedings of the Prehistoric Society*, 57 (2), 1991, pp. 61–101.
16. J. Whitley, 'Too many ancestors', *Antiquity* 76, 2002, pp. 119–26.
17. R. Bradley, *The Social Foundations of Prehistoric Britain: Themes and Variations in the Archaeology of Power*, London: Longman, 1984, p. 16.
18. Whittle *et al.*, *Gathering Time*, vol. 2, p. 896.
19. D. Benson and A. Whittle, *Building Memories: The Neolithic Cotswold Long Barrow of Ascott-under-Wychwood, Oxfordshire*, Oxford: Oxbow Books, 2007.
20. Saville, *Hazleton North, Gloucestershire, 1979–82*,1990.
21. H. Harding and F. Healy (eds), *The Raunds Area Project: A Neolithic and Bronze Age Landscape in Northamptonshire*, London: English Heritage, 2007, p. 10.

22. D. Brothwell, 'Palaeodemography and early British populations', *World Archaeology*, 4, 1972–3, pp. 75–87; for the Irish population, see J. P. Mallory, *The Origins of the Irish*, London and New York: Thames & Hudson, 2013, p. 96.

23. J. Cotton with R. Johnson, 'Two decorated Peterborough bowls from the Thames at Mortlake, and their London context', in J. Cotton and D. Field (eds), *Towards a New Stone Age: Aspects of the Neolithic in South-east England*, CBA Research Report 137, York: Council for British Archaeology, 2004, pp. 128–47.

24. C. Roberts and M. Cox, *Health and Disease in Britain: From Prehistory to the Present Day*, Stroud: Sutton Publishing, 2003, pp. 55–74.

25. R. Skeates, 'The Neolithic enclosure of the Tavoliere, south-east Italy', in G. Varndell and P. Topping (eds), *Enclosures in Neolithic Europe*, Oxford: Oxbow Books, 2002, pp. 51–8.

26. J. Thomas, *The Birth of Neolithic Britain: An Interpretive Account*, Oxford: Oxford University Press, 2013, p. 78.

27. Whittle *et al.*, *Gathering Time*, vol. 2, p. 878.

28. In 1973, Colin Renfrew suggested that constructing a causewayed enclosure was, on average, ten times the effort of a long barrow. However, there are also smaller enclosures like Etton, and a series of small (unexcavated) enclosures in the upper Thames Valley. See C. Renfrew, 'Monuments, mobilization and social organizations in Neolithic Wessex', in C. Renfrew (ed.), *The Explanation of Culture Change*, London: Duckworth, 1973, pp. 539–58.

29. For the dating and location of axe heads, see Whittle *et al.*, *Gathering Time*, vol. 2, pp. 789–94; for Hambledon Hill, see R. Mercer and F. Healey, *Hambledon Hill, Dorset, England: Excavation and Survey of a Neolithic Monument Complex and Its Surrounding Landscape*, Swindon: English Heritage, 2008.

30. Cecil Curwen published his pioneering 1930 study 'Neolithic camps' in *Antiquity* (4, pp. 22–54) and excavated the visible earthworks at Whitehawk Camp, Sussex, in the early 1930s. The next major synthesis was the English Heritage survey: A. Oswald, C. Dyer and M. Barber, *The Creation of Monuments: Neolithic Causewayed Enclosures in the British Isles*, London: English Heritage, 2001.

31. Keiller's opinion of St George Gray and the Piggott anecdote are recorded in Oswald *et al.*, *The Creation of Monuments*, pp. 18–21.

32. Oswald *et al.*, *The Creation of Monuments*, fig 1.1; P. D. Horne, D. MacLeod and A. Oswald, 'The seventieth causewayed enclosure in the British Isles?', in G. Varndell and P. Topping, *Enclosures in Neolithic Europe*, pp. 115–20.

33. F. Pryor, *Etton: Excavations at a Neolithic Causewayed Enclosure near Maxey, Cambridgeshire, 1982–7*, London: English Heritage, 1998. This volume includes reports on the preserved wood by Maisie Taylor, insects by Mark Robinson and stone axes by Mark Edmonds, plus other important specialist reports.

34. The *Gathering Time* project showed that Windmill Hill was not designed as a unitary project. First, the builders dug the inner enclosure, then the outer and finally the middle one. The nearby West Kennet barrow was probably built (by the same people or a rival group?) in the interval between Windmill Hill's outer and middle circuits. So were the roles of the different monuments complementary at this stage? See Whittle *et al.*, *Gathering Time*, vol. 2, p. 892; p. 104, fig. 3.28.

35. F. Healy, 'Cows in the Wood', in M. J. Allen, N. Sharples and T. O'Connor (eds), *Land and People: Papers in Memory of John G Evans*, Oxford: Oxbow Books, 2009, pp. 104–11.

36. T. Pearson and P. Topping, 'Re-thinking the Carrock Fell Enclosure', in G. Varndell and P. Topping (eds), *Enclosures in Neolithic Europe*, pp. 121–7.

37. R. J. Schulting and L. Fibiger, 'Violence in Neolithic North-West Europe: A Population Perspective', in A. Whittle and P. Bickle (eds), *Early Farmers: The View from Archaeology and Science*, Proceedings of the British Academy 198, Oxford: Oxford University Press, 2014, pp. 281–306. See also J. Heath, *Warfare in Prehistoric Britain*, Stroud: Amberley, 2009; M. Smith and M. Brickley, *People of*

the Long Barrow: Life, Death and Burial in the Earlier Neolithic, Stroud: The History Press, 2009.

38. P. Dixon, 'The Neolithic settlements on Crickley Hill', in C. Burgess et al. (eds), Enclosures and Defences in the Neolithic of Western Europe, Oxford: British Archaeological Report International Series 403, 1988, pp. 75–88.

39. Mercer and Healey, Hambledon Hill, Dorset, England.

40. R. Mercer, 'Excavations at Carn Brea, Illogan, Cornwall 1970–73', Cornish Archaeology, 20, 1981, pp. 1–204.

**Chapter 15**

1. Quoted from R. Hill, Stonehenge, London: Profile Books, 2008.

2. Quoted in S. Piggott, Ancient Britons and the Antiquarian Imagination: Ideas from the Renaissance to the Regency, London: Thames & Hudson, 1989, p. 127.

3. A. Whittle, F. Healey and A. Bayliss, Gathering Time: Dating the Early Neolithic Enclosures of Southern Britain and Ireland, vol. 2, Oxford: Oxbow Books, 2011, pp. 724, 907.

4. A. Burl, The Stonehenge People, London: Dent, 1987, p. 44.

5. M. Parker Pearson, Stonehenge: Exploring the Greatest Stone Age Mystery, London: Simon & Schuster, 2012.

6. Stonehenge was the first archaeological site to be photographed from the air in 1906, from a balloon.

7. The account of Crawford's career is taken from a fascinating and beautifully written book: K. Hauser, Bloody Old Britain: O. G. S. Crawford and the Archaeology of Modern Life, London: Granta Books, 2008.

8. When we excavated this monument, I did suggest to the British Airport Authority that they mark the line of the monument ditches on the floor of the new airport Terminal 5 building. They agreed, but unfortunately the idea fell foul of the accountants.

9. R. Bradley, The Prehistory of Britain and Ireland, Cambridge: Cambridge University Press, 2007.

10. G. Noble, Neolithic Scotland: Timber, Stone, Earth and Fire, Edinburgh: Edinburgh University Press, 2006, pp. 49, 52, 157–61;

A. Whittle, F. Healey and A. Bayliss, Gathering Time: Dating the Early Neolithic Enclosures of Southern Britain and Ireland, vol. 2, Oxford: Oxbow Books, 2011, pp. 907–9.

11. C. Nooteboom, Roads to Santiago, London: Harvill Press, 1998, pp. 173–4.

12. J. Thomas, Understanding the Neolithic, Abingdon: Routledge, 1999, pp. 194–5.

13. R. Loveday, Inscribed Across the Landscape: The Cursus Enigma, Stroud: Tempus, 2006.

14. D. L. Eck, India: A Sacred Geography, New York: Harmony Books, 2012, p. 11.

15. For the Drayton Cursus, see A. Barclay et al., Lines in the Landscape: Cursus Monuments in the Upper Thames Valley, Thames Valley Landscapes Monograph 15, Oxford: Oxford Archaeology, 2003.

16. G. H. Lambrick and T. G. Allen, Gravelly Guy, Stanton Harcourt Oxfordshire: The Development of a Prehistoric and Romano-British Community, Thames Valley Landscapes Monograph 21, Oxford: Oxford Archaeology, 2004; A. J. Barclay, M. Gray and G. Lambrick, Excavations at the Devil's Quoits, Stanton Harcourt, Oxfordshire 1972–3 and 1988, Thames Valley Landscapes Monograph 3, Oxford: Oxford Archaeology, 1995; for the reconstruction of the Devil's Quoits henge, see G. Hey, 'The Devil's work', British Archaeology, Jul/Aug 2009, pp. 24–9.

17. J. Last, 'Out of the blue: cursuses and monument typology in eastern England', in A. Barclay and J. Harding (eds), Pathways and Ceremonies: The Cursus Monuments of Britain and Ireland, Neolithic Studies Group Seminar Papers 4, Oxford: Oxbow Books, 1999, pp. 86–97.

18. For a discussion of processions and cursuses, albeit speculative, see R. Johnston, 'An empty path? Processions, memories and the Dorset Cursus', in A. Barclay and J. Harding (eds), Pathways and Ceremonies, pp. 39–48.

19. J. Harding, Cult, Religion, and Pilgrimage: Archaeological Investigations at the Neolithic and Bronze Age Monument Complex of Thornborough, North Yorkshire, York: CBA Research Report 174, Council for British Archaeology, 2013.

20. D. Hale and A. Platell, 'A grandstand view', Current Archaeology, 209, 2007, pp. 43–7.

21. R. Bradley and M. Edmonds, *Interpreting the Axe Trade: Production and Exchange in Neolithic Britain*, Cambridge: Cambridge University Press, 2005, pp. 152–3.

22. T. Manby, 'Typology, material and distribution of flint and stone axes in Yorkshire', in T. H. McK. Clough and W. A. Cummins (eds), *Stone Axe Studies*, CBA Research Report 23, London: Council for British Archaeology, 1979, pp. 65–81.

23. A. Burl, 'The Devil's Arrows, Boroughbridge, North Yorkshire: the archaeology of a stone row', *Yorkshire Archaeological Journal*, 63, 1991, pp. 1–24.

24. In the Mendips, Somerset, solution holes, or 'swallets', also suddenly appear. The Neolithic Priddy Circles, another third millennium BC alignment of henges, occupy this area. The 'cenotes', or sinkholes, of the Yucatán Peninsula, most obvious near the Mayan city of Chichén Itzá, are probably the best-known examples of the phenomena. Sinkholes also swallow modern houses in Florida.

**Chapter 16**

1. For a well-illustrated and vivid account of the Boyne tombs and Irish megalithic tombs in general, see C. Jones, *Temples of Stone: Exploring the Megalithic Tombs of Ireland*, Cork: The Collins Press, 2007.

2. The Irish tombs are less well dated than some of the southern English examples. The earliest Irish tombs probably began about 3550 BC, the largest of the Boyne tombs half a millennium later. See A. Sheridan, 'Megaliths and megalomania: an account, and interpretation, of the development of passage tombs in Ireland', *The Journal of Irish Archaeology*, 3, 1986, pp. 17–30; A. Sheridan, 'Ireland's earliest 'passage' tombs: a French connection?', in G. Burenhult (ed.), *Stones and Bones*, Oxford: British Archaeological Reports 1201, 2003, pp. 9–26.

3. For a more detailed interpretation of Brú na Bóinne, see D. Lewis-Williams and D. Pearce, *Inside the Neolithic Mind*, London and New York: Thames & Hudson, 2005, pp. 198–249.

4. D. Lewis-Williams and D. Pearce, *Inside the Neolithic Mind*, pp. 221–5.

5. For the regional patterns of Scottish megalithic tombs, see G. Noble, *Neolithic Scotland: Timber, Stone, Earth and Fire*, Edinburgh: Edinburgh University Press, 2006.

6. For the development of this theme in European prehistory and early history, see B. Cunliffe, *Europe between the Oceans: 9000 BC–AD 1000*, Newhaven and London: Yale University Press, 2008.

7. P. Friend, *Scotland: Looking at the Natural Landscape*, Collins New Naturalist Library, London: Harper Collins, 2012.

8. A. Sheridan, 'Megaliths and megalomania', pp. 17–30; A. Sheridan, 'Ireland's earliest 'passage' tombs: a French connection?', in G. Burenhult (ed.), *Stones and Bones*, pp. 9–26.

9. For a detailed discussion about the construction and social meaning of the stone rings, see C. Richards (ed.), *Dwelling among the Monuments: The Neolithic Village of Barnhouse, Maeshowe Passage Grave and Surrounding Monuments at Stenness, Orkney*, Cambridge: McDonald Institute for Archaeological Research, 2005; C. Richards *et al.*, 'Monumental risk: megalithic quarrying at Staneyhill and Vestra Fiold, Mainland, Orkney', in C. Richards (ed.), *Building the Great Stone Circles of the North*, Oxford: Windgather Press, 2013, pp. 119–48; J. Downes *et al.*, 'Investigating the great Ring of Brodgar, Orkney', in Richards (ed.), *Building the Great Stone Circles of the North*, pp. 90–118.

10. Colin Renfrew suggested that stone circles represented a harmonious joint effort; Colin Richards emphasizes competition and focuses on the varied sources of stone. So who organized the digging of the massive ditch at Brodgar, which Renfrew estimates would have taken about 80,000 person-hours – or 100 people for 100 days? Stenness is about half the size. See C. Renfrew, *Investigations in Orkney*, London: Thames & Hudson, 1979, p. 213.

11. The preservation of the landscape is due, in part, 'to the persistence in Orkney until recent years of traditional and non-destructive farming methods'. See C. Renfrew, *Investigations in Orkney*, p. 3.

12. I am grateful to Dr David Clarke of the National Museums of Scotland for the account of the Skara Brae excavations: see D. V. Clarke, 'Once upon a time Skara Brae was unique', in I. Armit *et al.* (eds), *Neolithic Settlement in Ireland and Western Britain*, Oxford: Oxbow Books, 2003, pp. 84–92.

13. A. Shepherd, 'Breaking hobbit habits', *Current Archaeology*, 298, 2015, p. 4. I am grateful to Alexandra Shepherd for detailed accounts of the stratigraphy.

14. D. Lee and A. Thomas, 'Orkney's First Farmers: Early Neolithic Settlement on Wyre', *Current Archaeology*, 268, 2012, pp. 12–19.

15. C. Richards (ed.), *Dwelling among the Monuments*, p. 129.

16. N. Card, 'Neolithic temples of the Northern Isles: stunning new discoveries in Orkney', *Current Archaeology*, 241, 2010, pp. 12–19.

17. E. W. MacKie, *Science and Society in Prehistoric Britain*, London: Paul Elek, 1977.

18. R. MacMullen, *Paganism in the Roman Empire*, New Haven: Yale University Press, 1981, pp. 36–7.

19. G. Hey *et al.*, *Thames Through Time: The Archaeology of the Gravel Terraces of the Upper and Middle Thames, Early Prehistory to 1500 BC*, Thames Valley Landscapes Monograph 32, Oxford: Oxford Archaeology, 2011, pp. 364–6, 374–5; A. Barclay and C. Halpin, *Excavations at Barrow Hills, Radley, Oxfordshire, Vol 1: The Neolithic and Bronze Age Monument Complex*, Thames Valley Landscapes Monograph 11, Oxford: Oxford Archaeology, 1999.

**Chapter 17**

1. There is an excellent account of past and recent work on Silbury Hill in J. Leary and D. Field, *The Story of Silbury Hill*, Swindon: English Heritage, 2010. For a more personal but brilliantly evocative account of Silbury Hill, see A. Thorpe, *On Silbury Hill*, Dorchester: Little Toller Books, 2014.

2. J. Leary *et al.*, 'The Marlborough Mound, Wiltshire: a further Neolithic Monumental Mound by the River Kennet', *Proceedings of the Prehistoric Society*, 79, 2013.

3. The other henges are Stonehenge, Avebury, Durrington Walls and Mount Pleasant.

4. M. Parker Pearson, *Stonehenge: Exploring the Greatest Stone Age Mystery*, London: Simon & Schuster, 2012, pp. 294–9.

5. T. C. Darvill, *Stonehenge World Heritage Site: An Archaeological Research Framework*, London and Bournemouth: English Heritage and Bournemouth University, 2005.

6. R. Cleal, K. E. Walker and R. Montague, *Stonehenge in its Landscape: Twentieth Century Excavations*, London: English Heritage, 1995.

7. T. Darvill *et al.*, 'Stonehenge remodelled', *Antiquity*, 86, 2012, pp. 1021–40.

8. The trilithon setting is dated by a single antler pick in the socket of stones 53/54, which provides a radiocarbon calibration of 2585–2400 BC.

9. For a more detailed discussion of the complex meanings of stones, see Z. Crossland, *Ancestral Encounters in Highland Madagascar: Material Signs and Traces of the Dead*, Cambridge: Cambridge University Press, 2014; T. Cole, 'Malagasy and Western conceptions of memory: implications for post-colonial politics and the study of memory', *Ethos*, 34 (2), 2006, pp. 211–43.

10. M. Parker Pearson and Ramilisonina, 'Stonehenge for the ancestors: the stones pass on the message', *Antiquity*, 72, 1998, pp. 308–26.

11. R. Bradley, *An Archaeology of Natural Places*, London: Routledge, 1991, p. 30.

12. T. Oestigaard, *The Deceased's Life Cycle Rituals in Nepal*, Oxford: British Archaeological Reports, 2000, p. 3, quoted in T. Insoll, *Archaeology, Ritual, Religion*, London: Routledge, 2004, p. 115.

13. For the Stonehenge Riverside Project, see M. Parker Pearson, *Stonehenge: Exploring the Greatest Stone Age Mystery*, London: Simon & Schuster, 2012, quoted text p. 62. For recent analysis of lipids in pots indicating milk consumption and feasting see O. E. Craig *et al.*, 'Feeding Stonehenge: cuisine and consumption at the late Neolithic site of Durrington Walls', *Antiquity*, 89, 2015, pp. 1096–1109.

14. Stop Press. While putting the finishing

touches to this book, Vince Gaffney (who explored Doggerland) and an international team of geophysical prospectors revealed a startling discovery. Their new Ground Penetrating Radar survey indicates that as many as two hundred megaliths stood in a curving row, arcing around the Durrington Walls settlement. The team suggest that the stones were toppled in order to build the Durrington Walls earthworks. If this interpretation of the GPR survey is correct it would certainly undermine the timber/stone–living/dead theory of the organization of the Neolithic landscape. However, the survey, at the time of writing, has not been ground-truthed. In other words, someone should quickly excavate to see if the anomalies really do indicate toppled stones rather than another timber monument. For an account of the geophysical survey at Durrington Walls, see 'Stone row near Stonehenge gets even bigger', *British Archaeology*, Nov/Dec 2015, p. 10.

15. R. A. Ixer and R. E. Bevins, 'The detailed petrography of six orthostats from the bluestone circle, Stonehenge', *Wiltshire Archaeological and Natural History Magazine*, 99, 2011, pp. 1–9. The arguments are summarized in M. Parker Pearson, *Stonehenge*, pp. 263–6.
16. M. Parker Pearson *et al.*, 'Craig Rhos-y-felin: A Welsh bluestone megalithic quarry for Stonehenge', *Antiquity*, 89, 2015, pp. 1331–52.
17. T. Darvill and G. Wainwright, 'Beyond Stonehenge: Carn Menyn Quarry and the origin and date of bluestone extraction in the Preseli Hills of south-west Wales', *Antiquity*, 88, 2014, pp. 1099–1114.
18. W. A. Cummins, 'Neolithic stone axes: distribution and trade in England and Wales', in T. H. McK. Clough and W. A. Cummins (eds), *Stone Axe Studies*, CBA Research Report 23, London: Council for British Archaeology, 1979, pp. 5–12.
19. See T. Insoll, 'Shrine franchising and the Neolithic in the British Isles: some observations based upon the Tallensi, northern Ghana', *Cambridge Archaeological Journal*, 16 (2), 2006, pp. 223–38.
20. A. Sheridan, 'The Neolithization of Britain and Ireland: the big picture', in B. Finlayson and G. Warren (eds), *Landscapes in Transition*, Oxford: Oxbow Books, 2010, pp. 89–105.
21. V. Gordon Childe, *The Dawn of European Civilization*, London: Routledge & Kegan Paul, 1925, p. 331.

**Chapter 18**

1. R. Bradley, *The Significance of Monuments: On the Shaping of Human Experience in Neolithic and Bronze Age Europe*, London: Routledge, 1998, p. 99.
2. C. Renfrew, *Prehistory: The Making of the Human Mind*, London: Weidenfeld & Nicolson, 2007, p. 169.
3. For the achievements of contemporary bards (*bhopas*) in Rajasthan, see 'The Singer of Epics' in W. Dalrymple, *Nine Lives: In Search of the Sacred in Modern India*, London: Bloomsbury, 2009, pp. 78–111.
4. Y. Garfinkel, 'The Levant in the Pottery Neolithic and Chalcolithic Periods', in C. Renfrew and P. Bahn (eds), *The Cambridge World Prehistory Vol. 3*, Cambridge: Cambridge University Press, 2014, pp. 1439–61; *see also* Y. Garfinkel *et al.*, 'Large-scale storage of grain surplus in the sixth millennium BC: the silos of Tel Tsaf', *Antiquity*, 83, 2009, pp. 309–25.
5. C. Broodbank, *The Making of the Middle Sea: A History of the Mediterranean from the Beginning to the Emergence of the Classical World*, London: Thames & Hudson, 2013, p. 246. Cyprian Broodbank suggests that growing demand in the Ubaid city states of Mesopotamia stimulated trade and innovation.
6. A. Ruiz-Taboada and I. Montero-Ruiz, 'The oldest metallurgy in western Europe', *Antiquity*, 73, 1999, pp. 897–903.
7. A. Sheridan, 'Post-Neolithic Western Europe', in C. Renfrew and P. Bahn (eds), *The Cambridge World Prehistory Vol 3*, pp.1885–1911. The so-called 'Sépulture de Chef' at Pauilhac, Gers, in southwestern France, contained gold sheet ornaments similar to material from the Varna Cemetery.
8. Bell beakers are often assumed to have contained alcohol. In this grave, the only lipid evidence pointed to milk.

9. For the published report of the Amesbury Archer and associated burials (plus specialist reports by 31 other contributors), see A. P. Fitzpatrick, *The Amesbury Archer and the Boscombe Bowmen*, Wessex Archaeology Report 27, Salisbury: Wessex Archaeology, 2011.

10. D. W. Anthony, *The Horse, the Wheel and Language: How Bronze-Age Riders from the Eurasian Steppes Shaped the Modern World*, Princeton: Princeton University Press, 2007. For the myth of the cattle-raiding hero see pp. 134–5.

11. G. Clark, *Prehistoric England*, London: Batsford, 1944, p. 8.

12. The study by Laure Salanova is quoted by A. Sheridan, 'Post-Neolithic Western Europe', in C. Renfrew and P. Bahn (eds), *The Cambridge World Prehistory Vol 3*, p. 1890.

13. For a discussion of wrist guards, see A. Woodward and J. Hunter, *An Examination of Prehistoric Stone Bracers from Britain*, Oxford: Oxbow Books, 2011.

14. W. O'Brien, *Ross Island: Mining, Metal and Society in Early Ireland*, Bronze Age Studies 6, Galway: National University of Ireland, 2004.

15. For the contrasting attitudes in the papers published, *see* M. J. Allen, J. Gardiner and A. Sheridan, *Is there a British Chalcolithic? People, Place and Polity in the Late 3rd Millennium*, Prehistoric Society Research Paper 4, Oxford: Oxbow Books, 2012.

16. I explained this complex case in D. Miles, 'Ramsar designation and the case of Seahenge', in B. Coles and A. Olivier (eds), *The Heritage Management of Wetlands in Europe*, Brussels: EAC Occasional Paper 1 and WARP Occasional Paper 6, 2001, pp. 157–64. For details of the excavation, see M. Brennand and M. Taylor, 'The survey and excavation of a Bronze Age timber circle at Holme-next-the-Sea, Norfolk, 1998–9', *Proceedings of the Prehistoric Society*, 69, 2003, pp. 1–84; F. Pryor, *Seahenge*, London: Harper Collins, 2001.

17. C. F. E. Pare (ed.), *Metals Make the World Go Round: The Supply and Circulation in Bronze Age Europe*, Oxford: Oxbow Books, 2000.

18. A. Sheridan and A. Shortland, '"... beads which have given rise to so much dogmatism, controversy and rash speculation": faience in Early Bronze Age Britain and Ireland', in I. A. G. Shepherd and G. J. Barclay (eds), *Scotland in Ancient Europe: The Neolithic and Early Bronze Age of Scotland in Their European Context*, Edinburgh: Society of Antiquaries of Scotland, 2004.

19. J. C. Barrett, *Fragments from Antiquity: An Archaeology of Social Life in Britain, 2900–1200 BC*, Oxford: Blackwell, 1994, pp. 9–32.

20. S. Needham, 'Power pulses across a cultural divide: cosmologically driven acquisition between Armorica and Wessex', *Proceedings of the Prehistoric Society*, 66, 2000, pp. 151–207.

21. A. Barclay and C. Halpin, *Excavations at Barrow Hills, Radley, Oxfordshire, Vol. 1: The Neolithic and Bronze Age Monument Complex*, Thames Valley Landscapes Monograph 11, Oxford: Oxford Archaeology, 1999.

22. P. Clark (ed.), *The Dover Bronze Age Boat*, Swindon: English Heritage, 2004.

23. S. Needham, K. Parfitt and G. Varndell (eds), *The Ringlemere Cup: Precious Cups and the Beginning of the Channel Bronze Age*, London: British Museum, 2006.

24. S. Needham, 'Encompassing the sea: "Maritories" and Bronze Age maritime interactions', in P. Clark, *Bronze Age Connections: Cultural Contact in Prehistoric Europe*, Oxford: Oxbow Books, 2009, pp. 12–37. See also B. Cunliffe, *Facing the Ocean: The Atlantic and its Peoples, 8000 BC–AD 1500*, Oxford: Oxford University Press, 2001. This is a major work that emphasizes the role of the sea and rivers in human communications, a theme also explored by R. Van de Noort in 'Argonauts of the North Sea – a social maritime archaeology for the 2nd millennium BC', *Proceedings of the Prehistoric Society*, 72, 2006, pp. 267–87.

25. J. Bourgeois and M. Talon, 'From Picardy to Flanders: Transmanche connections in the Bronze Age', in P. Clark (ed.), *Bronze Age Connections*, pp. 38–59.

26. C. J. Stevens and D. Q. Fuller, 'Did Neolithic farming fail? The case for a Bronze Age agricultural revolution in the British Isles', *Antiquity*, 86, 2012, pp. 707–22.

27. Pollen analysis is an important technique for understanding the make-up of plant communities in the area around the sample site(s). Unfortunately, it is difficult to separate cereal-type pollens. Consequently, to identify cereal production, carbonized grains are needed from secure, well-dated contexts.

28. A. Brown, 'Dating the onset of cereal cultivation in Britain and Ireland: the evidence from charred cereal grains', *Antiquity*, 81, 2007, pp. 1042–52.

29. J. Moore and D Jennings, *Reading Business Park: A Bronze Age Landscape*, Thames Valley Landscapes Monograph 1, Oxford: Oxford Archaeology, 1992.

30. Dave Yates of Reading University has, with great diligence, pulled together the evidence from hundreds of archaeological evaluations to reveal the extent of later Bronze Age field systems. See D. T. Yates, *Land, Power and Prestige: Bronze Age Field Systems in Southern England*, Oxford: Oxbow Books, 2007.

31. F. Pryor, *Flag Fen: Life and Death of a Prehistoric Landscape*, Stroud: The History Press, 2005; C. Evans with E. Beadsmore, M. Brudenell and G. Lucas, *Fengate Revisited: Further Fen-Edge Excavations, Bronze Age Fieldsystems and Settlement and the Wyman Abbott/Leeds Archives*, Oxford: Oxbow Books, 2009. Stop Press: The excavation in early in 2016 at Must Farm, near Peterborough, revealed a late Bronze Age piled roundhouse, marvellously preserved as it had caught fire and collapsed into waterlogged ground. Complete pots, foodstuffs, metalwork and a wheel demonstrate the sophistication of the farming family that once inhabited the house.

32. M. Collard, T. Darvill and M. Watts, 'Ironworking in the Bronze Age? Evidence from a 10th century BC settlement at Hartshill Copse, Upper Bucklebury, West Berkshire', *Proceeding of the Prehistoric Society*, 72, 2006, pp. 367–422.

### Epilogue

1. Y. N. Harari, *Sapiens: A Brief History of Humankind*, London: Harvill Secker, 2014.

2. J. Diamond, *Guns, Germs and Steel: The Fates of Human Societies*, New York: W. W. Norton, 1997.

3. J. Lovelock, *Gaia: A New Look at Life on Earth*, Oxford: Oxford University Press, 1979. See also J. Lovelock, *The Revenge of Gaia*, London: Allen Lane, 2006.

4. G. Vince, 'An epoch debate', *Science*, 333 (6052), 2011, pp. 32–7.

5. J. W. Erisman *et al.*, 'How a century of ammonia synthesis changed the world', *Nature Geoscience*, 1 (10), 2008, pp. 63–9.

6. R. Carson, *Silent Spring*, Boston: Houghton Mifflin, 1962.

7. Pope Francis, *Laudato Si': On Care for our Common Home*, 2015.

8. According to the United Nations, raising animals for food 'is one of the top two or three most significant contributions to the most serious environmental problems, at every scale from local to global...Livestock's contribution to environmental problems is on a massive scale'. For details and references of the impact of livestock production, see J. S. Foer, *Eating Animals,* London: Penguin Books, 2009; P. Lymbery and I. Oakeshott, *Farmageddon: The True Cost of Cheap Meat*, London: Bloomsbury, 2014.

9. See J. E. Stiglitz, *The Price of Inequality*, London: Penguin Books, 2013.

10. A. Proulx, *That Old Ace in the Hole*, New York: Scribner, 2002.

11. M. Pollan, *The Omnivore's Dilemma: The Search for a Perfect Meal in a Fast-food World*. London: Bloomsbury, 2011.

12. G. Monbiot, *Feral: Rewilding the Land, the Sea, and Human Life*, London: Penguin, 2014.

13. R. Patel, *Stuffed and Starved: From Farm to Fork. The Hidden Battle for the World Food System*, New York: Melville House, 2012.

14. For futurology, see N. Silver, *The Signal and the Noise: The Art and Science of Prediction*, New York: Penguin Group, 2012; for the possible future of agriculture (and its past history), see D. A. Cleveland, *Balancing on a Planet: The Future of Food and Agriculture*, Berkeley: University of California Press, 2014.

# Acknowledgments

My thanks and appreciation are due to a generation of dedicated archaeological surveyors, excavators, scientists and curators who have recently transformed our knowledge of the emergence of modern humans and farming around the world, and particularly in Western Asia and Europe. In Britain and Ireland I have been fortunate to be able to use the results of work by Stephen Aldhouse-Green, Graeme Barker, John Barrett, Martin Bell, Don Benson, Richard Bevins, Richard Bradley, Cyprian Broodbank, Ros Cleal, Bryony and John Coles, Gabriel Cooney, Barry Cunliffe, Tim Darvill, Mark Edmonds, George Eogan, Chris Evans, Andrew Fitzpatrick, Vince Gaffney, Clive Gamble, Jan Harding, Ian Hodder, Rob Ixer, Martin Jones, Frances Lynch, J. P. Mallory, Roger Mercer, Steve Mithen, Gary Monber, Stuart Needham, Mike Parker Pearson, Paul Pettitt, Mike Pitts, Josh Pollard, Francis Pryor, Colin Renfrew, Colin Richards, Peter Rowley-Conwy, Alan Saville, Rick Schulting, Alison Sheridan, Chris Stringer, Maisie Taylor, Julian Thomas, Geoff Wainwright, Francis Wenban-Smith, Alasdair Whittle, Dave Yates and many others.

I am particularly grateful to colleagues in Oxford and at Oxford Archaeology: Tim Allen, Alistair Barclay, Pippa Bradley, Anne Dodd, Paul Garwood, Frances Healy, Rob Hedges, Gill Hey, George Lambrick, John Moore, Simon Palmer and Mark Robinson.

And at English Heritage (now Historic England): Alex Bayliss, Martin Barber, Bob Bewley, Andrew David, Dave Field, Jonathan Last, Simon Mays, Dave McOmish, Sebastian Payne, Jane Sidell and Pete Topping and the ever-helpful staff at English Heritage's Library, the London Library and Library at the Society of Antiquaries of London.

At Thames & Hudson: firstly Colin Ridler, who collared me in the British Museum and invited me to write this book; big thanks for his patience and advice. Thanks too to the ever-diligent Jen Moore and the hawk-eyed Jo Murray; and to Louise Thomas, Rowena Alsey and Celia Falconer for their hand in the book's design. I am also grateful to Fiona Coward and Alasdair Whittle, who kindly read and commented on sections of the text, for their insights, corrections and improvements.

Special thanks to Richard Bradley and Alan Saville for their advice and friendship over many years, and to Keith Branigan and Peter Fowler, who between them got me started in the archaeology business.

Most of all my love and thanks to my wife, Gwyn Miles, who constantly prevented my descent into chaos when she would rather have been in the garden. This book is dedicated to her.

# Sources of illustrations

Images are listed by page number
a = above; b = below; l = left; r = right

**2** from William Stukeley, *Stonehenge, A Temple Restor'd to the British Druids*, 1740. **13** A.P.A. (UK)/Alamy. **22** Rock Art Research Institute, University of Witwatersrand, Johannesburg. **27** Bibliothèque d'Amiens Métropole. **28** Natural History Museum, London. **31** John Gowlett. **39** John Sibbick. **45** Alban Donohoe/REX Shutterstock. **55** Wellcome Library, London/ Wellcome Images. **58** Moravské Zemské Muzeum, Brno. **64** after J. Cauvin, *The Birth of the Gods and the Origins of Agriculture*, 2000, fig. 70. **67** Institute of Archaeology, London. **70** Bettmann/Corbis. **89** Israel Museum, Jerusalem. **91** Hemis.fr/SuperStock. **108** John Swogger. **122** Courtesy The Tavoliere-Gargano Prehistory Project, funded by the British Academy, the Institute of Archaeology, UCL and the National University of Ireland, Galway. **123** Museu Arqueològic Municipal Camil Moltó, Alcoy. **134** Národní Museum, Prague. **137** Photo Wolfgang Sauber. **143** after Association pour le Sauvetage Archéologique de la Vallée de l'anise (ASAVA). **158** after G. Eogan, *Knowth and the Passage Tombs of Ireland*, 1986, fig. 68. **163a** ML Design/Rowena Alsey, after B.J. Coles, *Proceedings of the Prehistoric Society* 64, 1998. **163b** Keith Morris/Alamy. **178** Wellcome Library, London/Wellcome Images. **185** Alan Sorrell. **198** National Geographic Image Collection/Alamy. **229** Image courtesy HS1 Ltd., the Oxford Wessex Archaeology Joint Venture (OWAJV). Photo from P. Booth, T. Champion, S. Foreman, P. Garwood, H. Glass, J. Munby and A. Reynolds, *On Track: the archaeology of High Speed 1 Section in Kent*, 2011, Oxford Wessex Archaeology Monograph 4. **237** Drazen Tomic, © Thames & Hudson Ltd., London. **255** Terry Ball/Reproduced by permission of English Heritage/SuperStock. **268** Photo Jack Hackett. **273** Photo © Thames & Hudson Ltd., London. **287** Courtesy Ian Dennis, Archaeology Department, Cardiff University. **309** from William Stukeley, *Itinerarium Curiosum*, 1776. **316** Commissioners of Public Works in Ireland. **323** Drazen Tomic, © Thames & Hudson Ltd., London. **325** Ministry of Public Buildings and Works, Edinburgh. **331** Salisbury Museum. **338** Victor Kiev/shutterstock.com. **339** Drazen Tomic, © Thames & Hudson Ltd., London. **349** Joan Gravell/Alamy. **359** Wessex Archaeology. Drawing by Elizabeth James. **359** Wessex Archaeology. **374** Drazen Tomic after BAA, Oxford Archaeology and Wessex Archaeology, © Thames & Hudson Ltd., London. **387** The Metropolitan Museum of Art, New York/Rogers Fund, 1919. **392** Richard Hamilton Smith/ Corbis. **396–397** Drazen Tomic, © Thames & Hudson Ltd., London.

## Colour plates
**145** Photo Aaron Hayden, © Thames & Hudson Ltd., London. **146** Deutsches Archäologisches Institut, Berlin. **147** after Mellaart (1966). **148a** Javier Trueba/MSF/Science Photo Library. **148b** Hofhauser/shutterstock.com. **149a, 149b** Alain Guilleux/age fotostock/SuperStock. **150a** Hemis/Alamy. **150b** Photo Myrabella. **151a** Photo Aleks. **151b** National Museums of Scotland. **152a** C. Vancoillie/shutterstock.com. **152b** after Czekaj-Zastawny, 2008. **297a** Photo Cary Bass-Deschenes. **297b** Dúchas, The Heritage Service, Dublin. **298** © Hugo Anderson Whymark. **299** John Brain/shutterstock.com. **300a** Robert Estall/Corbis. **300b** Alan Saville. **301** A.P.S. (UK)/Alamy. **302a, 302b** British Museum, London. **303a** Skyscan/Corbis. **303b** Photo © Thames & Hudson Ltd., London. **304** shutterstock.com.

# Index

Mesolithic 185–9; Neolithic 232, 235, 238–42, 247, 267, 313, 320
sea levels 49, 52, 54, 72, 82, 165, 175, 179, 195–6, 199–200, 230
Seahenge **303**, 364
seeds, exchange and distribution 97–8, 113
Sennett, Richard 289
Sesklo 126, 127–8, 129, 130
Severn Estuary 192–3, 195, 198, *198*, 200
shaft-hole axes 356
shamans 62, 89, 181, 201, 364
Shanidar 47
sheep 7, 36, 38, 69, 91, *91*, 93, 98, 100, 103, 104, 106, 112, 119, 129, 139, 244
shell 54, 123, 131, 153, 154, 176, 182, 186, 210, 219, 251
shellfish 124, 171, 175, 188, 200, 211, 213
Shepherd, Alexandra 326
Shepherd, Nan 14
Sheridan, Alison 235, 322
Shetland 187, 210, 372
Silbury Hill **304**, 335–6, 362, 366
Sixpenny Hadley 211
Skara Brae 324–7, *325*, 343
Skateholm 202
skulls: plastered 71, 89, 109; size and shape 46, 52, 272; 'skull cult' 109, 112; trepanned 280
Smith, Christopher 208, 209
Smith, Isobel 284
Sollus 384, 388
Somerset Levels 200, 240, 255–6
Sorrell, Alan 184
South Queensferry, Lothian 186
Spain 40, 47, 62, 124, 361
Spikins, Penny 174
*Spondylus* shells 153, 154
Sprengel, Carl 389
Springfield Lyons 377
Srejović, D. 134
Stanwell/Heathrow cursus 305
Staosnaig 185–6, 188
Star Carr 175, 183–5
Startin, Bill 142
Stellmoor 179
Stenness **299**, 322, *322*, 323, 330
Stevens, Chris 371, 372
Stonehenge 12, 19, 87, 195, 218, 245, 269, 291–6, **303**, 306, 319, 334–53, *338*, *339*, 362, 36–7; Riverside Project 342–8
Storakaig 189
Stukeley, William 292, 337
Sturt, Fraser 221
Sunghir 60–61
Swale, River 265, 311–12
Sweet Track 255
Switzerland 223–5

symbolism: attached to objects 7, 61, 63, 80, 107, 220, 319, 367, 378; symbolic thinking 6, 53, 56, 62, 86–7, 88, 106, 112

Table des Marchand 218, 236, 248
Talheim 155
Tavoliere 121–22, *122*, 281
Taylor, Maisie 197, 285, 364
Tel Tsaf 356
Tell Lachish 68
tell settlements 126–7, 131–2
Téviec 182, 216, 217
textiles 119, 357–8, 376, 377
Thames, River 160, 161, *163*, 169, 243; deposits 179, 260, 310
Thames Valley 93, 309–10, 347; aerial photography 12, 24, 238, 295–6, 373; Bronze Age 373, 374–5, 376, 377; cursuses 305, 308–9; enclosures 276, 282–4, 288, 289; Iron Age 371–2, 378; Neolithic 230, 232–6, 333; Roman 308, 337, 383–5
Thatcham 185, 194
Theocharis, Demetrios 126
Thessaly 121–2, 125–6, 127–8
Thomas, Herbert 347
Thomas, Julian 241, 306
Thomsen, Christian 17
Thomson, William 17
Thornborough **301**, 311–14
Thurnham, John 272
Thwing 377
tin 363, 365, 367
Tinkinswood 269
Tobias, Philip 32
Topping, Pete 257
Toraja people 143–4, **152**
Toth, Nick 32
Toumba I, Thessaly 125
trade and exchange 56, 80, 82, 97–8, 204, 212, 215, 267, 287, 314–15, 334, 369, 370, 378; axes 19, 235, 247–8, 259–60, 282; pottery 267, 292; *see also* gift-giving
Trajan 135
tranchet axes 178, *178*, 179, 196, 197
Transdanubia 135–8, 144
*Trichterbecherkultur* (TRB) 213
Trobriand Islands 251
Ty Isaf 279

Uivar 132
United Nations 390, 391
Upton, Derek 193
Upton Lovell 367–8
uranium-series dating 54

Varna burial 251–2, 273, 355
Vermeij, Geerat J. 72

Vestra Field 324
Vignely 'La Porte aux Bergers' 214–16
Villeneuve-Saint-Germain (VSG) cultural group 214–15
violence 16, 107, 155, 179–83, 267, 275, 288, 310, 352, 357
Vlasac 133–4

Waddington, Clive 185
Wainwright, Geoff 349, 350
Wales 49, 54–5, 178; Bronze Age 365, 366; Mesolithic 191, 193, 198–99; Neolithic 193, 267, 268, 269, 279, 284, 320
Warren Field 238–42
Waugh, Evelyn 37
Wayland's Smithy 271–6, **300**
Weinberg, Steven 394
Weiner, James F. 263
West Kennet 272–3, *273*, 275, 276, 279, 286, 311, 335, 362
wheat 119, 380, 381–2, 390; British Isles 239, 243, 244, 267, 371; domesticated 73, 91, 92, 93, 96, 99, 100, 106, 128, 138–9, 211, 214–15, 223, 380, 381–2; wild 69, 77, 78, 88
Wheeler, Mortimer and Tessa 69
White Crag 287
White Horse Stone 227–32, *229*, 264–5
Whitehawk Camp 287, *287*
Whittle, Alasdair 17, 154, 232, 276
Wicks, Karen 168, 189
Windmill Hill 283, 284, 286, 287, 288, 296, 335
Winterbourne Stoke 351
women 41, 59, 102, 129, 142, 205, 279, 288–9, 386; access to 105–6, 181–2, 213, 275; roles of 102–3, 129, 142, 190–1, 205
Woodhenge 293
woodlands 169–73, 177–8, 187, 193, 327
Woodman, Peter 190
woodworking 197–8, 260–61, 285, 364–5
Wordsworth, John 183
Wrangham, Richard 35–6, 37
Wyre 326–7

Yadin, Yigael 68
Yámana people 48, 176
Yanomamö of Venezuela 181–2
Yarnton 242, 243, 286
Younger Dryas 81–2, 86, 99, 167–8, 190, 380, 394
Yuchanyan Cave 111

Zagros Mountains 92, 97–8, 100
Zilhão, João 124